International Organizations and Legal Sanctions Against Governments

Dimitris Liakopoulos

Academica Press
Washington - London

Library of Congress Cataloging-in-Publication Data

Names: Liakopoulos, Dimitris, author. |
Title: International Organizations and Legal Sanctions Against Governments / Dimitris Liakopoulos
Description: Washington : Academica Press, 2020. | Includes references.
Identifiers: LCCN 2020944048 | ISBN 9781680531381 (hardcover)

Contents

CHAPTER 3

CHAPTER 1

Interpretative trends and standards of proof of fact for the attribution to the State of individual conduct in the recent jurisprudence of international courts

1.1. Introduction

In the last twenty years the theme of attribution of state responsibility for individual conduct has known one of the most compelling moments in its history. There are many challenges to legal operators in attributing conduct to the State, not only from the new types of offenses-think of cybernetic ones-but also from classic scenarios such as armed conflicts. Just think of the Israeli-Palestinian conflict, or the self-proclaimed Islamic State to understand that new challenges test the rules on attribution. If the subject was of different interpretations and clashes especially between the International Court of Justice (ICJ) and the International Criminal Courts, what Simma has defined as the dialogue des sourdes[1] has for some years been a new interlocutor in ECtHR. While working in the framework of ECHR, ECtHR has found itself growing in number with the need to analyze attribution profiles in interstate causes as much as in individual appeals. The present work aims to analyze the most recent interpretative tendencies of ECtHR starting from Sargsyan[2] and Chiragov[3] cases in the Nagorno-Karabakh region, in comparison with the last practice on the attribution of ICJ. Regarding the latter however, it will not be enough to refer to Croatia v. Serbia of 2015 case, or to Bosnia v. Serbia-Montenegro case of 2007, but we will have to return to Nicaragua

---

[1]B. SIMMA, Universality of international law from the perspective of a practitioner, in European Journal of International Law, 20, 2009, pp. 280ss.

[2]Sargsyan v. Azerbaijan of 16 June 2015. For further details see: A. VAN AAKEN, I. MOTOC, The ECHR and general international law, Oxford University Press, Oxford, 2018, pp. 194ss. T. RODENHÄUSER, Organizing rebellion: Non-state armed groups under international humanitarian law, human rights and international criminal law, Oxford University Press, Oxford, 2018.

[3]Chiragov and others v. Armenia of 16 June 2015.

v. USA sentence by ICJ on attribution matter. The point that will be supported is that ECtHR determines the imputability of the conduct without really trying it. The attribution is rather "deduced" starting from a generic finding on the exercise of jurisdiction. This method can be shared if one considers that the Court does not look so much at the attribution, but at the violation of the positive obligations placed on states parties by ECHR. However, if this position is adopted, the jurisdiction must be verified on the basis of concrete elements. In other words, the interpretative tendency of the Court is very pragmatic but can be appreciated if, from a legal point of view, it remains based on clear evidence and provided that ECtHR clarifies when it condemns a State for violation of its positive obligations. At the other extreme, ICJ runs the risk of consolidating its jurisprudence on the assignment of conduct for serious international wrongdoing on the basis of a mixed interpretation of typical standards of public and criminal law.

1.2. Attribution and international Courts, some definitions

Given the complexity of the theme, it is best to start with some references. For the attribution of conduct to the State we mean "the fact of ascribing the subject to international law(...)."[4] What are the implications for the judges? Conduct attribution involves a sometimes complex interpretive exercise. In the case of a de jure body, attribution is easier for the judge, although he must in any case verify the corresponding internal regulations. For the individual who is not an organ within the meaning of internal law, the judge must simultaneously interpret the facts and establish beyond what threshold the State was actually controlling the contested acts. The key to this exercise is therefore effectiveness. However, international courts often oscillate in identifying in what cases a state behaviour is actually decisive in guiding individual actions. This phenomenon has become more visible since other courts in addition to ICJ have dealt with attribution, because the criteria used by the Court of Hague have been reinterpreted or questioned. The consolidated method in international jurisprudence derives from the combined reading of articles Project[5] elaborated by the International Law Commission (ILC) in 2001 and ICJ

---

[4]J. SALMON, Dictionnaire du droit international public, ed. Bruylant, Bruxelles, 2001, pp. 587.

[5]Report of the International Law Commission to the General Assembly on the Work of its Fifty-Third Session, in Yearbook of International Law Commission, 2001, vol. 2, adopted from the General Assembly of 28 January 2002, GA/RES/58/63, UN Doc. A/587589.

jurisprudence,[6] with a focus on Nicaragua v. USA,[7] Bosnia v. Serbia-Montenegro[8] and Croatia v. Serbia[9] cases. In general, the beating heart of conduct attribution is in determining the link between State and individual's act regardless of whether these acts fit into the context of an international armed conflict or not. Articles Project highlights how the attribution rules revolve around two pillars:[10] Conduct attribution of a de jure organ ex art. 4[11] or acts attribution of an individual or a group pursuant to art. 8.[12] Articles Project with respect to art. 8 indicates three possibilities for attribution: 1) education; 2) direction and; 3) control. In the case of education, the attribution refers to the moment in which a decision is made, while the other two hypotheses are necessarily carried out with the execution of the act.[13] It is interesting to note that ILC refers to individuals "acting on instructions of, or under the direction or state control."[14] The focus of the law therefore seems to be not so much group act, but of state

---

[6]G. NOLTE, Treaties and subsequent practice, Oxford University Press, Oxford, 2013.
[7]ICJ, Case concerning military and paramilitary activities in and against Nicaragua (Nicaragua v. United States of America), sentence of 17 June 1986. R. KOLB, Theory of international law, op. cit., A. ZIMMERMANN, C.J. TAMS, K. OELLERS-FRAHAM, The Statute of the International Court of Justice. A commentary, op. cit.
[8]ICJ, Application of the Convention on the Prevention and Punishment of the Crime of Genocide (Bosnia and Herzegovina v. Serbia-Montenegro), sentence of 26 February 2007. R. KOLB, Theory of international law, op. cit., A. ZIMMERMANN, C.J. TAMS, K. OELLERS-FRAHAM, The Statute of the International Court of Justice. A commentary, op. cit.
[9]ICJ, Application of the Convention on the Prevention and Punishment of the Crime of Genocide, (Croatia v. Serbia), sentence of 15 February 2015. R. KOLB, Theory of international law, op. cit., A. ZIMMERMANN, C.J. TAMS, K. OELLERS-FRAHAM, The Statute of the International Court of Justice. A commentary, op. cit.
[10] This observation is valid with respect to the theme of this contribution. The authoritativeness of the Project is not only based on the determination of the de jure organ, but also, for example, on the definition of ultra vires behaviour by the organ or on responsibility for activities carried out by the insurrectional movements of ex. art. 10.
[11]Article, n. 4: "The conduct of any state organ shall be considered an act of the State under international law, whether that organ exercises legislative, executive, judicial or any other function, whatever position it holds in the organization of the State, and-whatever its character as an organ of the central government or of a territorial unit of the State. An organ includes any person or entity which has that status in accordance with the internal law of the State."
[12]Article n. 8: "The conduct of a person or group of persons shall be considered an act of a State under international law if the person or group of persons is in fact acting on instructions of, or under the direction or control of, that State carrying out the conduct."
[13]L. CAMERON, V. CHETAIL, Privatizing war: Private military and security companies under public international law, Oxford University Press, Oxford, 2013, 205-208. T.D. GILL, D. FLECK, The handbook of the international law of military operations, op. cit.
[14]G. NOLTE, Treaties and subsequent practice, op. cit.

forces to which the conduct must be attributed.[15] Precisely ICJ elaborating Nicaragua test[16] has consecrated state approach.

1.3. International Court of Justice to facts test

ICJ's approach to attribution issues can be summarized by a direct reference to Bosnia v. Serbia case.[17] It is in this dispute that ICJ introduces its current model of interpretation towards conduct attribution, being able to rely both on ILC draft articles adopted 6 years earlier and on its own jurisprudence in Nicaragua v. USA and Congo v. Uganda cases.[18] First ILC assesses whether the documents being judged were carried out by organs of the respondent State, i.e. bodies that are therefore the armed wing of the State. In the event that it is not shown that these are de jure organs, the Court checks whether the agents are individuals who acted under the instructions or the direct control of the third State.[19]

In particular, in Bosnia v. Serbia case ILC was to establish the relationship between Serbia and Bosnian Serb armed group of the Republic of Srprska. Bosnia argued that there was sufficient evidence of funding, coordination between military and statements by Serb officials that Belgrade controlled Bosnian Serb forces. According to ICJ, on the other hand, Republic of Srprska forces enjoyed a too high degree of autonomy, which could lead one to think they were not under the direction and effective control of Serbia.[20] In rejecting Bosnia's claims, the court

---

[15]A.J.J. DE HOOGH, Articles 4 and 8 of the 2001 ILC articles on State responsibility, in British Yearbook of International Law, 72, 2001, pp. 278ss. L. CAMERON, V. CHETAIL, Privatizing war: Private military and security companies under public international law, op. cit., pp. 162ss. Y. DINSTEIN, War, aggression and self-defense, Cambridge University Press, Cambridge, 2017. G. NOLTE, Treaties and subsequent practice, op. cit.

[16]Project of articles, op. cit., pp. 47-48.

[17]ICJ, Application of the Convention of the Prevention and Punishment of the Crime of Genocide (Bosnia- Herzegovina v. Serbia-Montenegro), sentence of 19 June 2007. A. ZIMMERMANN, C.J. TAMS, K. OELLERS-FRAHAM, The Statute of the International Court of Justice. A commentary, op. cit.

[18]ICJ, Case Concerning Armed Activities on the Territory of the Congo (Democratic Republic of the Congo v Uganda), sentence of 19 December 2005, para. 160. A. ZIMMERMANN, C.J. TAMS, K. OELLERS-FRAHAM, The Statute of the International Court of Justice. A commentary, op. cit..

[19]ICJ, Bosnia v. Serbia, op. cit, reaffirmed in the case: Nicaragua v. USA, para. 384, "it should be ascertained whether the acts in question were committed by persons who, while not organs of the respondent State, did nevertheless act on the instructions of, or under the direction or control of, the respondent (...)." A. ZIMMERMANN, C.J. TAMS, K. OELLERS-FRAHAM, The Statute of the International Court of Justice. A commentary, op. cit.

[20]ICJ, Bosnia v. Serbia, 471. A. ZIMMERMANN, C.J. TAMS, K. OELLERS-FRAHAM,

reiterated first of all that conduct attribution of non-organ individual to State must be considered exceptional. [21] In any case, the complete dependence on the State in question must be proven on the basis of Nicaragua test.[22]

1.4. Relationship between dependence and potential control in Nicaragua test

In Nicaragua v. USA sentence the issue of attribution to ICJ concerned the activities of contras paramilitary group and the alleged support provided to them by the United States in order to destabilize the regime in Nicaragua. The Nicaragua test consists of two parts, allowing ICJ to identify two categories of individuals to whom state acts can be imputed, if they are not de jure organs. The first group includes those agents that are totally dependent on the third State, i.e. paid, equipped and operating according to state directives. The second group, on the other, includes those who, despite the fact that there is evidence of cooperation or financing from the third State, still retain a certain degree of autonomy. This is the case with the paramilitary group of contras. In Nicaragua v. USA, ICJ establishes that the United States by training the contras have violated the customary prohibition of use of force, thereby incurring international responsibility. In paragraph 292, ICJ considers that the United States "by those acts of intervention referred to in subparagraph (3) here of [arming and training of the contras] which involve the use of force, has acted, against the Republic of Nicaragua, in breach of its obligation under customary international law not to use force against another State."[23] As argued in doctrine, the text suggests that ICJ acts attributes to the United States to prove its international responsibility are those made by the American officers in providing arms and training the contras.[24]

The Statute of the International Court of Justice. A commentary, op. cit.

[21] ICJ, Nicaragua v. USA, 390-392. A. ZIMMERMANN, C.J. TAMS, K. OELLERS-FRAHAM, The Statute of the International Court of Justice. A commentary, op. cit.

[22] ICJ, Bosnia v. Serbia, 471, "It has not been shown that the FRY army took part in the massacres, nor that the political leaders of the FRY had a hand in preparing, planning or in any way carrying out the massacres." A. ZIMMERMANN, C.J. TAMS, K. OELLERS-FRAHAM, The Statute of the International Court of Justice. A commentary, op. cit.

[23] A. ZIMMERMANN, C.J. TAMS, K. OELLERS-FRAHAM, The Statute of the International Court of Justice. A commentary, op. cit.

[24] The French version of par. 292 confirms this interpretation, placing the accent on the activity of US officials "(...) ainsi que par les actes d'intervention impliquant l'emploi de la force visés au sous-paragraphe (3) ci-dessus, ont, à l'encontre de la République du Nicaragua, violé l'obligation que leur impose le droit international coutumier de ne pas

Accepting this interpretation, however, conduct attribution to the State is uncertain. This is even more true given the clarity with which ICJ supports the non-attribution of acts for violations of international humanitarian law. Such violations committed by the contras are not attributable to the United States because for those specific acts there is not sufficient evidence to establish effective control. In other words, ICJ has no evidence that each of those violations was ordered by the United States, or that they forced the contras to complete them. The ratio decidendi of the Court seems to be guided by a specific cause-effect link: Dependence generates potential control. The greater the degree of dependence, the greater the control and responsibility. In other words, in the case of effective control, the heart of the decision is not to establish whether you are dealing with a de jure or de facto body, but whether the third State through its organs has guided and directed institution activities.

1.5. Effective control and test standard in Bosnia v. Serbia and Croatia v. Serbia

As already introduced, the authoritativeness of Nicaraguan test is confirmed by ICJ in Bosnia v. Serbia in 2007 and in Croatia v. Serbia in 2015. In both sentences, Nicaragua test is preferred over the approach adopted by Chambers Appeal of the International Criminal Tribunal for the Former Yugoslavia (ICTY) in Tadić.[25] The latter jurisdiction had in

recourir à la force contre un autre Etat (...)."

[25]ICTY, Chamber Appelas, Prosecutor v. Tadić, case n. IT-94-1-A, sentence of 15 July 1999. M.W. BADAR, The concept of mens rea in international criminal law. The case for a unified approach, Hart Publishing, oxford & Oregon, Portland, 2013. J. PEAY, Mental incapacity and criminal liability: Redrawing the fault lines?, in International Journal of Law and Psychiatry, 42, 2015, pp. 4ss. M.E. BADAR, The mental element in the Rome Statute of the International Criminal Court: A commentary from a comparative criminal law perspective, in Criminal Law Forum, 19 (3), 2008, pp. 477ss, "(...) a number of theories have emerged in criminal law to distinguish between dolus eventualis and advertent negligence, among others, the consent or approval (die Billigungs-oder Einwilligungtheorie), the indifference (die Gleichgültigkeitstheorie), the possibility (die Vorstellungs- oder Möglichkeitstheorie), the probability (die Wahrscheinlichkeitstheorie), the combination theory (Kombinationstheorien) etc. The non-exhaustive list of theories is illustrative of the plethora of approaches in the criminal law theory (...)." R.S. CLARK, The mental element in international criminal law: The Rome Statute of the International Criminal Court and the elements of offences, in Criminal Law Forum, 12, 2001, pp. 296ss. R. CRYER, H. FRIMAN, D. ROBINSON, E. WILMSHURST, An introduction to international criminal law and procedure, Cambridge University Press, Cambridge, 2010. A. ESER, Mental elements-Mistake of fact and mistake of law, in A. CASSESE, P. GAETA, G.R.W.D JONES (eds.), The Rome Statute of the International Criminal Court: A

fact considered that the acts of organized armed groups, such as the Bosnian Serbs, could be attributed to the State if it exercises an overall control over such groups. The overall control test was not meant to replace the effective control of ICJ, nor to be applied only in the verification of the international nature or not of an armed conflict.[26] This is particularly noticeable by the fact that the Chambers Appeal of ICTY refers to two different types of tests. On the one hand, (i) in the case of acts performed by individuals engaged by the State to perform specific violations, effective control is required for each action.[27] On the other, (ii) for actions carried out by military or paramilitary groups that have their own structure, according to Chamber it would be inappropriate to believe that each action can be directed by a third State.[28] This is where overall control comes into play. This is a standard that is satisfied in the presence of a general control, which still requires funding, training and coordination tests of military activity, but allows greater room for maneuver. The Chamber Appeals therefore does not dispute the ICJ method, rather it makes a distinction in the areas of application, on the one hand the effective control for the

---

Commentary, Oxford University Press, Oxford, 2002, pp. 890ss. A.G. GIL, Mens rea in co-perpetration and indirect perpetration according to article 30 of the Rome Statute. Arguments against punishment for excesses committed by the agent or the co-perpetrator, in International Criminal Law Review, 14, 2014, pp. 87ss. K.J. HELLER, The Rome Statute of the International Criminal Court, in K.J. HELLER, D. DUBBER (eds.), The handbook of comparative criminal law, Stanford Law Books, Stanford, 2011, pp. 597ss. S. PORRO, Risk and mental element: An analysis of national and international law on core crimes, ed. Nomos, Baden-Baden, 2014. K.M.F. KEITH, The mens rea of superior responsibility as developed by ICTY Jurisprudence, in Leiden Journal of International Law, 14, 2001, pp. 618ss. P.H. ROBINSON, J.A. GRALL, Element analysis in defining criminal liability. The model penal code and beyond, in Stanford Law Review, 35, 1983, pp. 685ss. D. FLECK, The law of non-international armed conflict, in D. FLECK (a cura di), The Handbook of International humanitarian law, Oxford University Press, Oxford, 2013, pp. 581-610. E. WILMSHURTS (a cura di), International law and the classification of conflicts, Oxford University Press, Oxford, 2012.

[26]In Tadić case, the juridical question that TPI Appeals Chamber for the former Yugoslavia finds itself resolving is primarily of jurisdiction. The Chamber of First Instance considered that Tadić was not responsible for serious violations of the four Geneva Conventions, ex art. 2 of the ICC Statute because this article was not applicable to internal conflicts such as the Bosnian Serb conflict. The Prosecutor appealing the decision had challenged the internal nature of the conflict. In this context, the rules of general international law concerning state responsibility were emphasized ad adiuvandum in interpreting when an armed movement belongs to a third State so as to make the nature of the international conflict as established in art. 4 (A) (2) of the III Geneva Convention. See in argument: A. CASSESE, The Nicaragua and Tadić test revisited in light of the ICJ judgment on genocide in Bosnia, in European Journal of International Law, 18 (4), 2007, pp. 649-668.

[27]ICTY, Prosecutoe v. Tadić, op. cit., par. 141.

[28]ICTY, Prosecutoe v. Tadić, op. cit., para. 131-137.

individual individuals, on the other the overall control for the armed groups.[29]

In the judgments of 2007 and 2015 we can see an increase in the standard used in Nicaragua v. US, stiffening the positions of the Court. Two elements are highlighted: 1) The restrictive interpretation of the Nicaragua test; 2) the use of typical criminal law standards to verify the subjective element of the state crime of genocide. On the first point, despite bearing the Nicaraguan test letter, ICJ refers only to groups or bodies that act in complete dependence on the third State.[30] In this sense, the method seen above-dependence generates potential control- is applied in an even more restrictive way. The Court in fact does not distinguish between the hypotheses of totally dependent agents and that retain a large degree of autonomy as it had in 1986.[31] The issue of attribution is dealt

---

[29]The test has also been applied in other international proceedings, in particular by the International Criminal Court (ICC) in the Lubanga case. See ICC, Pre-Trial Chamber I, Prosecutor v. Thomas Lubanga Dyilo, Decision on the Confirmation of Charges, case no. ICC-01/04-01/06, 2007, para. 208-211; CPI, Trial Chamber I, Prosecutor v. Thomas Lubanga Dyilo, causa n. ICC-01/04-01/06, Judgment Pursuant to Article 74 of the Statute, 2012, par. 551. For further details see: T.R. LIEFLÁNDER, The Lubanga judgment of the ICC: More than just the First Step?, in Cambridge Journal of International and Comparative Law, 2012, pp. 191–212. G.J. KNOOPS, Defences in contemporary international criminal law, Transnational Publishers, New York, 2001, pp. 97ss. J. GEERT, J. KNOOPS, Defenses in contemporary international law, The Martinus Nijhoff Publishers, The Hague, 2008, pp. 7ss. V. EPPS, L. GRAHAM, Examples and explanations for international law, Wolters Kluwer Law, Alphen aan den Rijn, 2014. E.R. FIDELL, E.L. HILLMAN, D.H. SULLIVAN, Military justice: Cases and materials, Lexis Nexis, New York, 2012. J.D. OHLIN, Targeting and the concept of intent, in Cornell Law Faculty Publications, paper 774, 2013, pp. 84ss. T. WEIGEND, Intent, mistake of law, and co-perpetration in the Lubanga Decision on the confirmation of charges, in Journal of International Criminal Justice, 8, 2008, pp. 476ss. G. WERLE, F. JESSBERGER, Principles of international criminal law, Oxford University Press, Oxford, 2014. G. WERLE, F. JESSBERGER, Unless otherwise provided: Article 30 of the ICC Statute and the mental element of crimes under international criminal law, in Journal of International Criminal Justice, 3, 2005, pp. 37ss. K. AMBOS, Der Allgemeine Teil des Völkerstrafrechts: Ansätze einer Dogmatisierung, Duncker and Humblot, Berlin, 2002. J. CROWE, K. WESTON-SCHEUBER, Principles of international humanitarian law, op. cit., pp. 149ss. P. WEBB, International judicial interpretation and fragmentation, Oxford University Press, Oxford, 2013, pp. 140ss. M. WELLER, The oxford handbook of the use of force in international law, op. cit., pp. 724ss. C. NYSTEN, S. CASEY-MASLEN, A. GOLDEN BERSAGEL, Nuclear weapons under international law, Cambridge University Press, Cambridge, 2014.

[30]ICJ, Bosnia v. Serbia, op. cit., para. 392, "(...) provided that in fact the persons, groups or entities act in "complete dependence" on State, of which they are ultimately merely the instrument (...)." A. ZIMMERMANN, C.J. TAMS, K. OELLERS-FRAHAM, The Statute of the International Court of Justice. A commentary, op. cit.

[31]S. TALMON, The responsibility of outside powers for acts of secessionist entities, in

with in a limited way in 2015. The Court does not consider it necessary to rule further on conduct attribution since the objective element of the genocide has not been verified.[32] The terms "Serbs" and "Serbian forces" are both used in the sentence without prejudice to the attribution of malicious behaviour to the State.[33] As regards the standard of proof, ICJ refers to "(...) fully conclusive evidence."[34] The level of certainty required is beyond reasonable doubt, typical terminology of criminal law. In particular, the Court uses this standard of criminal law typical of the verification of individual men's trial to determine the existence of offense. In Croatia v. Serbia the Court did not explicitly mention the standard, but this is deducible from its approach.[35] ICJ in fact believes that dolus

---

International and Comparative Law Quarterly, 58, 2009, pp. 498ss. S. NTUBE NGANG, The position of witnesses before the International Criminal Court, ed. Brill, The Hague, 2015.

[32] ICJ, Croazia v. Serbia, op. cit., parr. 441-442. A. ZIMMERMANN, C.J. TAMS, K. OELLERS-FRAHAM, The Statute of the International Court of Justice. A commentary, op. cit.

[33] ICJ, Croazia v. Serbia, op. cit., par. 104. A. ZIMMERMANN, C.J. TAMS, K. OELLERS-FRAHAM, The Statute of the International Court of Justice. A commentary, op. cit.

[34] ICJ, Bosnia v. Serbia, op. cit., para. 208, "claims against a State involving in charges of exceptional gravity and must be proved by evidence that is fully conclusive. The Court requires that it be fully convinced that allegations made in the proceedings (...) have been clearly established. The same standard applies to the proof of attribution for such acts (...)."

[35] S. SCHACKELFORD, Holding States accountable for the ultimate human rights abuses: A review of the ICJ's Bosnian genocide case, in Human Rights Brief, 2007. See art. 1 of Convention on the Prevention and Punishment of the Crime of Genocide, 9 December 1948, 78 UNTS, pag. 277. Y. BEIGBEDER, International Criminal Tribunals, ed. Palgrave, London, 2011. R.S. SÁNCHEZ REVERTE, Referencia al crimen de genocidio aproximation genocido crime, in Revista de Estudios Juridicos, 16, 2016. M.J. KELLY, The debate or genocide in Darfur, Sudan, in Davis Journal of International Law & Policy, 19 (1), 2012, pp. 208ss. C. LINGAAS, Imagined identities: Defining the racial group in the crime of genocide, in Genocide Studies and Prevention: An International Journal, 9 (1), 2016, pp. 80ss. R. MAISSON, Justice pènale internationale, ed. PUF, Paris, 2017. D.S. BETTWY, The genocide Convention and unprotected groups: Is the scope of protection expanding under customary international law?, in Notre Dame Journal of International and Comparative Law, 1 (1), 2011, pp. 102ss. H. BLAISE NGAMENI, La diffusion du droit international pènal dans les ordres juridiques africaines, ed. L'Harmattan, Paris, 2017. K. CALVO-GOLLER, La procèdure et la jurisprudence de la Cour pènale internationale, ed. Lextenso, Paris, 2012. M.A. DRUMBL, Rule of law amid lawlessness: Counseling the accused in Rwanda's domestic genocide trials, in Columbia Human Rights Law Review, 29, 1998. H. ALONSO, Current trends on modes of liability for genocide, crimes against humanity and war crimes, in C. STAHN, L. VAN DEN HERIK (eds.), Future perspectives on international criminal justice, T.M.C. Asser press, The Hague, 2010, pp. 522-524. S. MANACORDA, C. MELONI, Indirect perpetration versus Joint Criminal Enterprise: Concurring approaches in the practice of international criminal law?, in Journal of International Criminal Justice, 9 (1), 2011, pp. 165ss. A. CASSESE, The nexus requirement

specialis of the genocide is determined when the probative elements "could only point to the existence of such intent."[36] The standard of proof used is therefore a mixed standard, which refers to criminal law but which applies to state responsibility of an illicit fact.

By virtue of the genocidal act gravity, it is not surprising to adopt such a criterion. However, the use of criminal jurisdiction standard complicates the development of ICJ argumentation, because on the one hand it does not make it possible to distinguish between civil, public or state. On the other, it is almost impossible to prove the illicit genocide. Faced with this rigor, ECtHR seems to be completely different.

1.6. ECtHR between jurisdiction and attribution

The attribution to a State of para-state or separatist organizations conduct is not a new matter for the Court of Strasbourg. Since the late nineties of the last century with the creation of Northern Cyprus, ECtHR has indeed had to deal frequently with institutions such as Transnistria, South Ossetia and Nagorno-Karabakh. The presence of separatist bodies in the territory of a State Party to the Convention places the Court in addresses legal issues related both to the status of these entities and to their relationship with third States. Two judgments were made in June 2015 concerning the violation of property rights as protected by article 1 of the first Protocol[37] to ECHR in the Nagorno-Karabakh region.[38] Chiragov et

---

for war crimes, in Journal of International Criminal Justice, 10, 2012. B. DON TAYLOR III, Crimes against humanity in the Former Yugoslavia, in R. BELLELLI (ed. by), International criminal justice. Law and practice from the Rome Statute to its review, ed. Ashgate Publishing, Farnham, 2010, pp. 285-294.

[36] ICJ, Croatia v. Serbia, op. cit., para. 148. A. ZIMMERMANN, C.J. TAMS, K. OELLERS-FRAHAM, The Statute of the International Court of Justice. A commentary, op. cit.

[37] First Additional Protocol which entry into force on 18 March 1954. For further details see: B. RAINEY, W. WICKS, C. OVEY, Jacobs, White and Ovey: The European Convention on Human Rights, op. cit., J.P. COSTA, La Cour europèenne des droits de l'homme. Des juges pour la libertè, op. cit., F. TIMMERMANS, Fundamental rights protection in Europe before and after accession of the European Union to the European Convention on Human Rights, op. cit., pp. 225ss. D. HARRIS, M. O'BOYLE, C. WARBRICK, Law of the European Convention on Human rights, op. cit., pp. 372ss. A. SEIBERT-FOHR, M.E. VILLIGER, Judgments of the European Convention of Human Rights. Effects and implementation, ed. Nomos, Baden-Baden, 2017.

[38] The Nagorno-Karabakh region is one of the most disputed in the entire Caucasus since the late nineteenth century. Currently, the most interesting legal profiles with respect to Nagorno-Karabakh concern the proclaimed independence of Azerbaijan, which we should

al. v. Armenia and Sargsyan and others v. Azerbaijan cases were treated by the Court simultaneously because the territorial link was the same. However, here we will focus on Chiragov, where the profiles of conduct attribution of private individuals to the State are more detailed.[39]

The case arises from the application of six Azerbaijani citizens who complain about the violation by Armenia of art. 1 of the First Additional Protocol and of art. 8 of ECHR.[40] According to the applicants,

---

not discuss here. However, a brief historical note is necessary. The Nagorno-Karabakh region has always been a transit ground and, therefore, ethnically mixed. At the end of the nineteenth century, the Russian domination on the territory favours the Armenian presence on the one hand and on the other foments the intolerance of Azerbaijan, which does not enjoy a privileged treatment on the part of Russians and does not have a fully efficient central apparatus. The first independentist ambitions date back to 1918, the period of October revolution during which Russia concentrated on internal problems partially lost control over the Caucasian area. The decision of the Russian central government in 1920 to include Nagorno-Karabakh in the territory of Azerbaijan, definitively sanctioned by USSR Constitution, represents the turning point in the history of the region. The claims by Armenia continue and take hold in 1988, thanks to the moment of confusion within the Soviet power. Thus began a civil war in the disputed territory between Armenia and Azerbaijan that culminates in the declaration of independence of Nagorno-Karabakh in 1994. The Republic of Nagorno-Karabakh is self-proclaimed in compliance with the combined law of the Secession and the Constitution of the Soviet Union. Leaving aside the issues related to the conformity of secession with current domestic law, the creation of Nagorno would probably not have occurred without the Armenian support, given the size of the region and the strength of the movement. Nagorno-Karabakh was not recognized by most members of the international community, and the diplomatic dispute between Armenia and Azerbaijan was mediated by OSCE and the Group of Minsk, without however having produced results. The three Representatives of the USA, France and Russia Group proposed in 2007 a series of Basic Principles for the settlement of the dispute. Among the proposals, the restoration of Azeri control over the territory of Nagorno in exchange for granting an interim status to the Nagorno-Karabakh entity until the final decision to be taken with a referendum. No formal agreement based on these principles has yet been signed. See: H. KRUGER, V. WALTER, Self-determination and secession in international law, Oxford University Press, Oxford, 2014, pp. 214-220.

[39]The main distinction between two judgments concerns the status of territories in which the violations took place. In Chiragov the area of reference is the Lachin, a strip of Azeri land that separates the country from Armenia, but controlled by the secessionist body Nagorno-Karabakh. In Sarsygan, however, the complaints relate to properties in the district of Gulistan, an area almost deserted after the clashes of 1992-1994. It is, in fact, a border territory between Azerbaijan and Nagorno, probably mined and with armed groups stationed on the border line. For the first time, the Court has to deal with a territory where it is not only unclear whether the authorities of the respondent State have effective access, but above all where individuals do not live. In this sense, see the concurring opinion of Ziemele judge in Sarsygan v. Azerbaijan, in particular on the concepts of limited liability and presumption of jurisdiction under the ECHR, para. 2-5. For further details see: C. GRABENWARTER. European Convention on human rights: ECHR, op. cit.

[40]C. GRABENWARTER. European Convention on human rights: ECHR, op. cit.

Armenia occupying the district of Lachin would have prevented them from regaining possession of the abandoned properties due to the outbreak of the Nagorno-Karabakh conflict in 1992. Hence the applicants complain that the damage was not compensated.[41] Alongside the primary violation, the violation of articles 13 (lack of effective remedies) and 14 (discrimination on an ethnic and religious basis) is outlined. ECtHR has welcomed Chiragov and others allegations considering that Armenia had no reason to deny the applicants access to the properties located in Lachin without providing a fair satisfaction in return.

ECHR violations are part of a situation typical of international law, such as the conflict between state agencies and armed groups or, more generally, conflicts over disputed territories. Although ECtHR is faced with a question of public international law tout court,[42] operating within ECHR, it must first verify that at the time of the infringement there was exercise of defendant state jurisdiction in the territory in question, pursuant to art. 1 of the Convention.[43] This is an essential preliminary verification, since it serves as a basis for the assessment of any breach of positive or negative obligations. As already mentioned, in fact, in the framework of the protection of human rights, ECHR requires states parties to refrain from engaging in behaviours that may generate an infringement, or to act to protect individuals under their jurisdiction from violations.

1.7. Effective control of the separatist body as proof of jurisdiction exercise

According to the appellants, the exercise of Armenian jurisdiction over Lachin derives (i) from state direct control and support towards Nagorno-Karabakh forces, or alternatively, (ii) from the exercise of authority of part of the Armenian forces present in the territory of Nagorno. Already here, we introduce a fundamental theme to understand the jurisprudence of the Court with respect to separatist bodies, i.e. the link between attribution and

---

[41]Chiragov and others v. Armenia, op. cit., par. 1-25. Specifically, the applicants claimed that their Azeri-Kurdish mixed ancestors had lived in Lachin for hundreds of years. They had been forced to take refuge in Baku with the outbreak of the conflict in Nagorno. Since then, the presence of Armenian armed forces had prevented them from returning home.

[42]ECtHR, Behrami and Beherami v. France and Saramati v. France, Germany v. Norvegia of 31 May 2007, para. 122. Bankovic and others v. Belgium of 12 December 2001, para. 57. F. MARCHADIER, Convention européenne des droit de l'homme et des libertès fondamentales, op. cit., pp. 679-694.

[43]S. TALMON, The responsibility of outside powers for acts of secessionist entities, op. cit., pp. 493-512.

jurisdiction. Starting from the jurisdiction, the central point of the appeal of Chiragov et al. it is the extraterritorial application of ECHR, as consolidated in particular in Al-Skeini et al. v. GB,[44] Ilaşcu and others v. Moldova and Russia[45] and Catan and others v. Moldova and Russia[46] cases.

The term jurisdiction ex. art. 1 of the Convention must be interpreted first of all in a territorial sense. Progressively, however, the Court has elaborated some exceptions to this interpretation, both in cases where the violations took place in disputed territories and in the event of war occupation. [47] When ECtHR enters the merits in Chiragov, it immediately dismisses the hypothesis of the exercise of authority by Armenian officials directly on the territory. [48] On the other, it is the question of having to prove effective control in order to establish the responsibility of Armenia for the violation of ECHR. [49] In this sense, ECtHR already anticipates the setting of its argument, suggesting that it will oscillate between jurisdiction and attribution. As proof of this interpretation, reference can be made to Jaloud v. the Netherlands case:[50] Although ECtHR does not dwell on the point in the device, in attribution and jurisdiction sentence are clearly defined different institutes,[51] contra Chiragov.

In determining jurisdiction exercise, ECtHR does not consider it necessary to ascertain exactly how many Armenian soldiers are present in

---

[44]Al Skeini and others v. GB, 7 July 2011, para. 149-150.

[45]Ilaşcu and others v. Moldavia and Russia, 8 July 2004.

[46]Catan and others v. Moldavia and Russia, 19 October 2012.

[47]In this sense see the case: ECtHR, Loizidou v. Turkey, (preliminary objections) of 23 March 1995, par. 62. Loizidou v. Turkey, (merits) of 18 December 1996, par. 52. Cyprus v Turkey of 4 July 2001, par. 76; Bankovic and others v. Belgium, op. cit., par. 70. Ilaşcu, op. cit., par. 314-316. Al-Skeini v. United Kingdom, op. cit., par. 138. C. TEITGEN COLLY, La Convention europèenne des droits de l'homme: 60 ans et après?, op. cit.

[48]Chiragov, op. cit., para. 169. "The Court first considers that the situation pertaining in Nagorno-Karabakh is not of the Armenian state agents exercising authority and control over individuals abroad."

[49]Chiragov, op. cit., "the issue to be determined on the facts of the case is whether the Republic of Armenia exercised and continues to exercise effective control over the mentioned territories and as a result may be held responsible for the alleged violations (...)."

[50]ECtHR, Jaloud v. The Netherlands of 20 November 2014.

[51]ECtHR, Jaloud v. The Netherlands, op. cit., par. 154, "the test for establishing the existence of "jurisdiction" under article 1 of the Convention has never been equated with the test for establishing a state responsibility for an internationally wrongful act under general international law." For further details: J.M. ROONEY, The relationship between attribution and jurisdiction after Jaloud v. Netherlands, in Netherlands International Law Review, 62, (3), 2015, pp. 407.

Nagorno-Karabakh,[52] despite this being the subject of contention between the parties. Leveraging on the report of International Crisis Group[53] that testify the Armenian military presence and funding for Nagorno territory management activities, as well as on the presence of former Armenian officials among the political figures in Nagorno-Karabakh, [54] ECtHR concludes that NKR and its administration survive by virtue of the military, political, financial and other support.[55] Referring only to the exercise of a "domination over the territory"[56] ECtHR avoids deploying on the side of war occupation or control over a subordinate authority. This, according to Gyulumyan judge, is the primary fault of the sentence. Not distinguishing the type of control exercised on the territory prevents ECtHR from developing a well-argued ratio decidendi.[57] It is also true, however, that more than one element in the sentence seems to suggest the presence of a subordinate local administration. The court also mentions other sources of financial support for Nagorno-Karabakh, such as those from the United States or the Armenian diaspora.[58] In this sense it cannot be understood that the Azerbaijani region has been annexed or placed under occupation. The Court refers to Nagorno-Karabakh as an institution, a contracting party to 1994 Cooperation Agreement with Armenia. Therefore, it seems that Nagorno has a fair degree of autonomy, otherwise ECtHR could have limited itself to talking about groups armed or separatist movements.[59] Moreover, since the ruling on North Cyprus, [60] ECtHR had not excluded

---

[52]Chiragov, op. cit., par. 180.

[53]International Crisis Group (ICG), Report, Nagorno-Karabakh: Viewing the Conflict from the Ground, 14 September 2005, 9-10.

[54]Chiragov, op. cit., par. 181, "integration of the two entities is further shown by the number of politicians who have assumed the highest offices in Armenia after previously having held similar positions in the NK Republic."

[55]Chiragov., op. cit., par. 186.

[56]Chiragov, op. cit., par. 168.

[57] Chiragov, op. cit, and the dissenting opinion of judge Gyulumyan, par. 50, "the fundamental problem lies in Court's failure to distinguish situations where the control over the territory is established through "a subordinate local administration" from situations where control is established through "the contracting State's own armed forces." And this is not simply a difference in fact. It is a difference in law, since both situations are concerned with different rules of attribution (...)."

[58]Chiragov, op. cit., par. 185.

[59]In the dissenting opinion, judge disputes the fact that by not indicating the degree of control, the court leaves ample room for maneuver to oscillate between the application of articles 4 and 8 of the Project. However, on closer inspection, the Court does not go so far. With due caution, it can be said that if the Court defines Nagorno as an entity and not an Armenian armed wing, it leaves room at least implicitly for the application of art. 8.

[60]Loizidou v. Turkey, (preliminary objections), op. cit., par. 62. Loizidou v. Turkey, (merits),

that in addition to the occupation of war there could be other situations such as to justify the exercise of effective control over the territory, indicating explicitly the presence of a subordinate administrative authority.[61] However, precisely because it is talking about a subordinate authority it is necessary to prove the attribution.

1.8. Test standards and attribution in Chiragov and others v. Armenia

The need to establish what kind of control a third State exercises over a non-state body was set for the first time following the creation of North Cyprus. In Loizidou, ECtHR described the Turkish control in terms of an effective authority that gave an effective overall control.[62] Leaning on the extensive evidence of Turkish occupation, as well as on the Security Council resolutions[63] which demanded not to recognize the illegitimate occupation of North Cyprus, the attribution to Turkey of Turkish Cypriot acts was proven. [64] In Chiragov, however, Armenia status is not comparable to that of Turkey. Specifically, one could say that there are elements such as the massive deployment of armed forces which suggest that the creation of Nagorno-Karabakh took place in 1992 with the indispensable support of Armenia. However, it is very difficult to establish the importance of maintaining this support over time, with the progressive strengthening of Nagorno-Karabakh forces. Above all, the non-position taken by the international community weighs heavily. There are no binding documents that go beyond the observation of a high Armenian presence in the territory. The Security Council resolutions do not directly refer to the Armenian occupation, as is noted by the fact that the withdrawal of troops is requested through the generic "demands the withdrawal of all occupying forces."[65]

op. cit., par. 52.

[61]If this interpretation is accepted, however, it is not clear why the Court has included in the part of the law the four Geneva conventions and the Hague conventions, an element which adds strength to the thesis of the relative ambiguity of the sentence on the subject.

[62]Loizidou v. Turkry (merits), op. cit., par. 52-56; Cyprus v. Turkey, op. cit., par. 77. A variant of the effective overall control was proposed in Issa et al. v. Turkey, where the Court referred to the control of the Turkish mission in northern Iraq used the "temporary effective overall control" formula. See also: Issa and others v. Turkey of 16 November 2004, par. 74.

[63]Resolutions of Security Council, n. 541(1983) of 18 November 1983, par. 1-2 and 7 and n. 550(1984) of 11 May 1984.

[64]Support for the Court's findings in Loizidou v. Turkey we find it also in the Commentary to the Project of articles of the ILC, op. cit., Regarding the application of the art. 8.

[65]Security Council of UN, Resolution n. 822 (1993) of 30 April 1993. Council of Security,

In Chiragov the Court gives extensive weight to the report of Human Rights Watch,[66] statements of Armenian officers and military cooperation agreement signed by Armenia and Nagorno in 1994. The use of reports by non-governmental organizations and declarations is not an established practice in the jurisprudence of Strasbourg. In Loizidou as in Ilaşcu, the Court considered it necessary to base itself on the work of the committees of inquiry.[67] Pursuant to art. 38 of ECHR, ECtHR can proceed to the examination of witnesses or organize the same inquiries. The committees of inquiry are a rather rare practice.[68] By virtue of the role of last resort of the Court, it is not surprising that this jurisdiction is refractory to the organization of inquiry committees.[69] However, in the event that there are substantial divergences concerning the reconstruction of facts, the Court proceeds to set up a Commission, both in the admissibility decision and during the procedure. In Ilaşcu the delegation of four judges who had interviewed numerous witnesses in Moldova had provided considerable support for the elaboration of the Court's device.[70] Hence, in Chiragov and others, Armenia had requested to provide more information through a Commission of inquiry,[71] but the Court held that it was not necessary.[72] By contrast, ICJ in Nicaragua v. USA had outlined a very scrupulous test evaluation model. The model gave particular relevance to disinterested statements by representatives regarding criticisms of their

---

Resolution n. 853 (1993) of 29 July 1993, operative 8, "(...) urges the government of the Republic of Armenia for the Nagorno Karabakh Resolution 822." To have a more direct stance against Armenia one must look at the General Assembly Resolution A/RES/62/243 of 14 March 2008, operative 2, "demands the immediate (...) withdrawal of all Armenian forces from all occupied territories of the Republic of Azerbaijan (...)."

[66]Human RightsWatch, Report, Seven Years of Conflic on Nagorno-Karabakh, 8 December 2004.

[67]On the point v. the Dissenting Opinion of Judge Gyulumyan, par. 43. The judge notes in particular how art. 19 of the Convention puts to the Court the duty to "ensure the observance of the engagements undertaken by the High Contracting parties." The Court, in other words, would have been asked in this case in relation to the legal obligation to set up a Commission of inquiry, above all to be able to express itself on the merits of the case.

[68]C. GRABENWARTER. European Convention on human rights: ECHR, op. cit.

[69]P. LEACH, Taking a case to the European Court of Human Rights, op. cit., pp. 55. See also the Klaas v. Germany case of 22 September 1993, par. 29. A. AUST, Handbook of international law, Cambridge University Press, Cambridge, 2010, pp. 230ss.

[70]Press Release of 18 March 2003 concerning Ilaşcu v. Moldova and Russia.

[71]Chiragov, op. cit., Grand Chamber Hearing, 22 January 2014.

[72]To be honest, however, it is good to note that the decision to open a fact-finding mission is also influenced by temporal reasons. In Tanli v. Turkey, the Court, considering that it had been too long since the deeds of judgment had been carried out, it was not useful to proceed with its own investigation. ECtHR, Tanli v. Turkey of 10 April 2001, par. 7.

own State, while little weight is given to the testimony of military officers.[73] It must be said, however, that Court's scrupulousness was strengthened by the fact that US support on the activities of contras was widely proven.[74]

ECtHR's approach to the military agreement between Armenia and Nagorno-Karabakh is of particular interest compared to documents. The text seems to suggest far more than an involvement. In the argument of the Court one of the supporting elements is art. 4 of the agreement,[75] which provides for the right of the armed forces of the two contracting parties to carry out part of the military service in one of the two countries. However, to note is also art. 5 (1), according to which if Nagorno soldiers in training in Armenia commit crimes, they will be tried under Nagorno-Karabakh jurisdiction. Exercising jurisdiction is perhaps the most striking proof of effectivity on a territory.[76] If he pursued this line, however, ECtHR would probably have to admit the ability to exercise the jurisdiction of Nagorno-Karabakh, going against its own ruling because if it is Nagorno to exercise jurisdiction, it cannot be Armenia. Hence Court's view on the status of Nagorno-Karabakh is deducible from the interpretation of the agreement. ECtHR does not claim that Nagorno-Karabakh and Armenia are a single body, but finds its own interpretation. He believes that Nagorno-Karabakh militias are more than just a rebel movement inside Azerbaijan, but the Court nevertheless claims that NKR forces could not have operated without Armenian support. From here, the judgment can pass to attribution issues.

1.9. A deductive approach to conduct attribution

With respect to conduct attribution, the Court stands on the defensive by stating that the material at its disposal does not allow it to know precisely what the composition of the armed forces in Nagorno-Karabakh is. This does not however prevent it from determining the

[73]P. REICHLER, The impact of the Nicaragua case on matters of evidence and fact-finding, in Leiden Journal of International Law, 25 (1), 2012, pp. 152ss. E. SOBENES ORREGON, B. SAMSON, Nicaragua before the International Court of Justice: Impacts on international law, op. cit.,

[74] The US Congress, for example, had specifically legislated on the financing of paramilitary groups in Nicaragua. Nicaragua v. USA, op. cit., par. 152.

[75]Chiragov, op. cit., par. 74-75.

[76] M.G. KOHEN, Possession contestèe et suverainetè territoriale, Graduate Institute Publications, Geneve, 1997, pp. 191-212.

Armenian responsibility for the violations committed in Lachin. However, we do not directly find any reference to act attribution.[77] Rather, the court seems to infer that the alleged violations are to be attributed to Armenia. Consider effective control as a matter of fact[78] and create the link between jurisdiction and violation in par. 186, when it claims that Nagorno-Karabakh and Armenia are highly integrated.[79] From here, the attribution vanishes from the arguments. One might think that in reality the Court does not need to argue about attribution, because it determines Armenia responsibility for violation of its positive obligations. In this sense, however, the Court should have better grounded its verification of the exercise of jurisdiction. Although in Chiragov appears clearer, the less stringent approach to jurisdiction could be glimpsed already in Ilaşcu and especially in Catan.

1.10. Ilaşcu and others v. Moldova and Russia

In Ilaşcu, legal issues related to attribution are not dealt directly and in detail. The court has at its disposal multiple probative elements that demonstrate Russian control to express itself in a less in-depth way from the theoretical point of view. Russia's responsibility for acts in Transnistria is verified on the "decisive influence" standard[80] and as overall control over an area outside its national territory. Although it is an evaluation standard that recalls that ICTY is focused on the overall control of the third State on the armed movement, the Court refers scrupulously to the activities to which Russian agents themselves participated. In fact, for its argument, the Court has clear evidence of Russian participation and command over the violations committed during the detention of the applicants.[81] In this sense, if the attribution profiles are clearer, the Court does not allow to understand whether the acts of separatists in Transnistria are also attributed to Russia or if the focus is only on Russian activities.[82]

---

[77]The terms "attribution" or "imputability" are in fact almost absent, not only in Chiragov but in the recent jurisprudence of the Court. In Catan, for example, the term attribution is used only when the ruling contains ICJ jurisprudence applicable to the present case, para. 76.

[78]Chiragov, op. cit., par. 107.

[79]Chiragov, op. cit., par. 186, "the two entities are highly integrated in virtually all important matters and that this situation persists to this day. (...) Armenia, consequently, exercises effective control over Nagorno Karabakh and the surrounding territories, including the district of Lachin (...)."

[80]Ilaşcu and others v. Moldavia and Russia, op. cit., par. 392.

[81]Ilaşcu and others v. Moldavia and Russia, op. cit., par. 393.

[82]Ilaşcu and others v. Moldavia and Russia, op. cit., par 385, "in Court's opinion, all of the

1.11. Exercise of jurisdiction and attribution from Catan to Chiragov

In Catan, ambiguity reproduces, but the evidence is not as clear as in Ilaşcu. First of all, the Court states that jurisdiction and attribution are two different institutions,[83] but Russia's responsibility is proven on the Ilaşcu model. Catan indeed opens the way to Chiragov to the extent that the two pronunciations share some elements. The first is the temporal connection. The Court has to do with violations occurring in a temporal space different from that of Loizidou or Ilaşcu. In fact, it is not a question of events that occurred at the time of the birth of an institution or in an armed conflict between central government and separatist groups. The reference period in Catan is after the formation of Transnistria, just like the period of time in which the appellants in Chiragov complain about ECHR violations. With the passage of time and the establishment of a paramilitary group in a given territory, it is likely that the support of the third State decreases, or in any case assumes different traits that require the scrupulous test of individual act attribution to the third State. In this context, the verification of jurisdiction only on the basis of some NGO reports and official statements is incomplete.

The second common element concerns the burden of proof. In Chiragov the court seems to define a probative standard that revolves around expressions like "it could not be expected" or "it is hardly conceivable" that Nagorno-Karabakh, an entity with a population of less that 150000 ethnic Armenians, was able, without the substantial military support of Armenia, to set up a defense force in early 1992.[84] Court interlocutor seems to be more the defendant, who has the burden of subverting a predictable result, so to speak. This suggests a reversal of the onus probabandi, which brings to trial in Catan, when the Court upheld its position against Russia stating that it had failed to prove that jurisdiction conditions for extraterritorial exercise had changed after Ilaşcu.[85]

---

acts committed by Russian soldiers with regard to the applicants, including their transfer into the charge of the separatist regime, in the context of the Russian authorities' collaboration with that illegal regime, are capable of engaging responsibility for the acts of that regime." ECtHR, Costello-Roberts v. United Kingdom of 25 March 1993, par. 23-28.

[83]Catan and others v. Moldavia and Russia, op. cit., par. 115, "the test for establishing the existence of jurisdiction under article 1 of the Convention has never been equated with the test for establishing a state responsibility for an internationally wrongful act under international law (...)."

[84]Catan and others v. Moldavia and Russia, op. cit.

[85]Catan and others v. Moldavia and Russia, op. cit., par. 149-150.

Hence, if we want to find a precedent in court attitude in Chiragov, this seems to be above all Catan.

1.12. Concluding remarks

Based on what has been highlighted so far, multiple reflections are possible. A first general note concerns the impact of very different jurisprudential lines on the fragmentation of law. The tendencies of ICJ and ECtHR seem to consolidate each one in its own dimension and become rigid. This certainly does not favor the uniform interpretation of law.[86] Regarding ICJ, the adoption of penalties in the field of state crime of genocide leaves perplexing. If on the one hand it is a shareable choice given the available information of the Court on the conflict in Ex-Yugoslavia and given the gravity of the offense, there remains a line of interpretation that threatens to weaken the applicability of 1948 Convention. In fact, it is important not only the goal of preventing but also of punishing. Intersecting two individual and state liability-criminal regimes-does not appear to be the purpose of ECHR. ECtHR approach is more pragmatic, but it can be to the detriment of sound legal arguments. One might think that the Court tries to fill the void created by the lack of agreement on the disputed territory, on the one hand, and on the other, the possible normative vacuum[87] in the system of protection of human rights established by ECHR. Would you then face a lex specialis on attribution in ECHR, where the level of control recalls the overall control test elaborated by ICTY and the attribution is deducted?[88]

One could say yes, with the necessary caution, however. In general, ECtHR seems to us to be acceptable, especially in terms of protecting the individual. If anything, it is a question of refining the method of scrutiny. Defining control in a variable way from effective to overall, to decisive

---

[86]L. LINDROOS, Addressing norm conflicts in a fragmented legal system: The doctrine of lex specialis, op. cit., pp. 27-66. G. CONWAY, The limits of legal reasoning and the European Court of Justice, Cambridge University Press, Cambridge, 2012, pp. 156ss. V. JEUTNER, Irresolvable norm conflicts in international legal dilemma, Oxford University Press, Oxford, 2017. N. WALKER Intimations of global law, Cambridge University Press, Cambridge, 2014, pp. 66ss.

[87]Cyprus v. Turkey, op. cit., par. 78. Critics on this point in the partially absent and dissenting opinions are both Judge I. Ziemele, in par. 11, which Judge A. Gyulumyan in par. 58-59.

[88]A. BERKES, The Nagorno-Karabakh cases before the European Court of Human Rights: Pending cases and certain forecasts on jurisdiction and State responsibility, in The Military Law and Law of War Review, 52, 2013, pp. 415ss. A. VAN AAKEN, I. MOTOC, The ECHR and general international law, op. cit.

influence, can also be seen in a positive sense. Although generally accepted, the Nicaragua test has always been elaborated within a specific situation. Therefore, one could consider whether a single test is useful to judges, given that the existence of a certain degree of control depends on the specificity of each case.[89] ECtHR adopts a method of mixed scrutiny, which weaves overall control and evidence of jurisdiction. This is because it is faced with entities with a frozen legal status, against which the international community is unable to take a common position. The ultimate goal does not seem to be to derogate from the existing regime or to create a specific procedure, but to respond to a vacuum of the international system itself in individual's interest. As pointed out by Ziemele, there is no doubt that Court's aim to provide compensation to those who forcibly had to abandon their possessions is shareable.[90] It is extremely understandable that this right must also prevail in the face of a stalled international community. Moreover, the Articles Project did not remain blind to the existence of bodies seeking to control disputed territories. Article 10 establishes that an insurrectionary movement once it has become a State is itself responsible for the conduct of its individuals. Paragraph 3, however, does not affect conduct attribution to a third State, governed by the combined provisions of articles from 4 to 9, which must be interpreted and applied according to the established jurisprudence.[91]

In Jaloud, Raimondi and Spielman judges in their competing opinion considered the attribution of a non issue.[92] Such a consideration seems risky. Establishing jurisdiction does not imply that any act suspected of constituting a violation of the Convention is attributable to the State in question. The attribution is a relevant legal issue in any case before the

---

[89]This argument was proposed, for example, by the vice president of ICJ Al- Khasawneh in Bosnia v. Serbia, noting that there are not only different degrees of control but that the Bosnian Serbian group presented one "unity of goals, unity of ethnicity and a common ideology, such that the effective control over non-state actor would not be necessary." ICJ, Bosnia v. Serbia, op. cit., dissenting opinion of judge Al-Khasawneh, par. 37. A. ZIMMERMANN, C.J. TAMS, K. OELLERS-FRAHAM, The Statute of the International Court of Justice. A commentary, op. cit.

[90]Chiragov, op. cit, dissenting opinion of judge I. Ziemele, par. 1.

[91]Project of articles, op. cit., art. 10, "1. The conduct of an insurrectional movement which becomes the new government of a State shall be considered an act of that State under international law. 2. The conduct of a movement, insurrectional or other, which succeeds in establishing a new State in part of the territory of a pre-existing State or in a territory under its administration shall be considered an act of the new State under international law. 3. This article is without prejudice to the attribution to a State of any conduct, however related to that of the movement concerned, which is to be considered an act of that State by virtue of articles 4 to 9 (...)."

[92]Jaloud v. Netherlands, op. cit., dissenting opinion of D. Spielman and G. Raimondi, par. 7.

Court, because the States act because of individuals. A more flexible approach can be accepted if the Court focuses on states obligations to protect individuals under their jurisdiction from violations. In other words, two hypotheses are found: On one side (i) the issue of attribution is not raised because, being the suspect a de jure organ, there is no need for further proof. On the other, (ii) one might think that in the context of a treaty on the protection of human rights, positive obligations do not make the precise attribution of the necessary act.[93] In this last case, however, the proof of jurisdiction becomes fundamental. The high integration between two bodies on the basis of generic findings and in a very broad period of time such as the existence of Nagorno-Karabakh is not sufficient. We need clearer references, perhaps from specific committees of inquiry, that protect the Court from the criticism of uncertain arguments and excessive activism in similar cases that will arise, such as Georgia v. Russia or Ukraine v. Russia.

[93]M. MILANOVIC, Extraterritorial application of human rights treaties, op. cit., pp. 136-142. C. HARRIS, Extraterritorial application of human rights treaties, Oxford University Press, Oxford, 2012.

CHAPTER 2

Complicity of States in the framework of regulatory activities of international organizations

2.1. Introduction

The subject of this chapter is the complicity of the State in the offense committed by an international organization in the exercise of its regulatory function. The framework in which the case in question unfolds logically presupposes that the complicit State is part of the agreement of the body which is the author of the main conduct.

In the first place we will carry out the examination of a question that takes on a preliminary character with respect to the one we intend to address in the following pages. This is the possibility that the main crime is supplemented by a regulatory act.

Secondly, we will examine the conditions under which the concurrence in the resolution of a third degree legislative act must be qualified in terms of complicity pursuant to art. 58 DARIO.

We will examine the way in which art. 58 DARIO in the hypothesis of conduct held by the States within the UN Security Council. For the purposes of our analysis, the decision adopted by this body based on art. 41 of the Statute of the organization can be taken as a useful model for the reconstruction of some general criteria. First of all, these are normative acts that can fly the international obligations that are incumbent on the organization. Furthermore, in the panorama of international organizations, as we have seen in the previous paragraphs, is very common to find a body with a limited composition to which the Member States have delegated the exercise of certain functions. There is also another aspect of a structural nature which suggests taking the advice, for example, of a body in which the case of complicity can be integrated as for art. 58. Some members benefit from a differentiated legal position which in our opinion can constitute a valid prerequisite for assigning these States of responsibility as a competition with the international organization.

2.2. Configurability of the unlawful act by regulatory norm

The qualification of a datum made as an illicit depends on the norm establishing the international obligation, so that depending on the content of obligation. The violation of this will be constituted by the conduct of a legislative, administrative, or a judicial body. In our opinion it is necessary to move from this premise to the assessment of responsibility of international organizations for regulatory acts. From ILC's codification works, it can easily be deduced that under certain conditions the responsibility of an international organization may arise as a result of a regulatory act having binding effect in contrast with an obligation of the entity itself.[94] The following considerations apply.

In the first place, the principle for which the conduct of any administrative or judicial legislative body is suitable for engaging the international state responsibility is now widely accepted.[95] In his third report on the subject rapporteur Ago, had proposed a provision specifically defining this principle,[96] which was then merged without particular

[94] W. WENGLER, Recours judiciaire à instituer contre le dècisions d'organes internationaux: rapport et projet de rèsolution, in Annuaire de l'Institut du Droit International, 1952, pp. 224ss. M. VIRALLY, La notion de fonction dans la thèorie de l'organization internationale, in G. ABI-SAAB, La communautè internationale. Mèlanges offerts à Charles Rousseau, op. cit., pp. 286ss. E. BUTKIEWITCZ, The premises of international responsibility of intergovenrnmental organiation, in Polish Yearbook of International Law, 11, 1981-1982, pp. 132ss. M. PEREZ GONZALEZ, Les organizations internationale et le droit de la responsabilitè, in Revue Gènèrale de Droit International Public, 92, 1988, pp. 67ss. C. DOMINICÉ, La responsabilitè internationale des Nations Unies, in J.P. COT, A. PELLET, M. FORTEAU, La Charte des Nations Uines-commentaire aricle par article, Economica, Paris, 2005, pp. 142ss. A. REINISCH, Veerfahrensrechtliche Aspekte der Rechtskontrolle von Organen der Staatengemeinschfat in R. HOFMANN, A. REINISCH, T. PFEIFFER, S. OETER, A. STADLER, Berichte der Deutschen Gesellschaft für Völkerrecht: Die Rechtskontrolle von Organen der Staatengemeischaft; Vielfalt der Fericht-Einheit des Prozessrecht?, C.F. Müller, Heidelberg, 2007, pp. 44ss. P. KLEIN, The attribution of acts to international organizations, in J. CRAWFORD, A. PELLET, S. OLLESON, K. PARLETT, The law of international responsibility, op. cit., pp. pp. 300ss.

[95] R. AGO, Le dèlit international, op. cit., pp. 465ss, I. VON MÜNCH, Das Völkerrechtliche Delikt in der Modernen Entwicklung der Völkerrechtsgemeinschaft, P. Keppler Verlag, Frankfurt, 1963, pp. 170ss.

[96] R. AGO, Troisième rapport sur la responsabilitè des États. Le fait internationalement illicite de l'État, source de responsabilitè internationale, op. cit., pp. 267, "article 6: Irrelevance of the position of a State organ in the distribution of powers and internal hierarchy. For the purposes of determining whether the conduct of a State organ is an act of the State in international law, the questions whether that organ belongs to the constituent legislative, judicial or other power, whether its functions are of an international

modifications, in art. 6 of the project of articles on state responsibility approved in (first reading) 1996. The aforementioned rule established that: "The conduct of an organ of the State shall be considered to the constituent, legislative judicial or other power (...)."[97] It should be emphasized that ICJ in the advisory opinion of the Commission on human rights found that the rule under examination was of a customary nature.[98] This is a provision that is also located in the draft articles approved in second reading in 2001. According to art. 4, par. 1, "the conditional of any state organ is considered an act of that State under international law, whether the organ exercises legislative, executive, judicial or any other functions."[99] What is highlighted in the briefly illustrated provisions is the question of imputability of the conduct carried out by legislative state bodies. This is a principle acquired so much that in the codification process it did not have to be listed among the motivated norms in terms of the progressive development of international law. The principle of unity of the State with respect to international order constitutes the shared basis on which even the most recent doctrine has argued in the sense indicated lastly,[100] in the assumption that the internal normative acts are mere facts before international law, made that are relevant if the order contained in them is such as to require the State to behave contrary to its international

law an internal character and whether it holds a superior or a subordinate position in the hierarchy of the State, are irrelevant."

[97]in Yearbook of International Law Commission, vol. II, p. 193.

[98]ICJ, Difference relating to immunity from legal process of special rapporteur of the Commission on human rights, op. cit., p. 29, par. 62. orientations which is affirmed also in the case: Application of genocide convention (Bosnia v. Herzegovina v. Serbia), op. cit., p. 202, par. 385. A. ZIMMERMANN, C.J. TAMS, K. OELLERS FRAHAM, The Statute of the International Court of Justice. A commentary, op. cit.

[99]ARSIWA, par. 40.

[100]C. EAGLETON, The responsibility of states in international law, op. cit., pp. 60ss. E.M. BORCHARD, The diplomatic protection of citizens abroad. The law of international claim, op. cit., pp. 181ss. A. VERDROSS, Règles gènèrales de droit de la paix, in Recueil des cours, ed. Brill, Bruxelles, vol. 30, 1929, pp. 272ss. G. DAHM, Völkerrecht, op. cit., pp. 185ss, R. AGO, Troisième rapport sur la responsabilitè des États. Le fait internationalement illicite de l'État, source de responsabilitè internationale, op. cit., pp. 261-262, in particular the reference to the codification Conference of 1930 that established in art. 6 of the resolution that state responsibility may well arise as a result of commissions or omissions of the legislative power. In this sense, the internal practice that the material limits of the present work do not describe in detail is also evident. There are some cases that deserve to be quickly mentioned. See for example from the ECtHR. Dudgeon v. United Kingdom of 22 October 1981, par. 41, in which the ECtHR considered that the mere validity of legislation incompatible with the ECHR in itself incorporated the responsibility of the respondent State regardless of its unlawful application.

obligations.[101] It is also hardly necessary to point out that the thesis[102] which excluded this form of responsibility due to the sovereign character of the legislative activity, since this characteristic is common to most of the state activities, no longer seems sustainable.

Once is established that under the subjective profile the legislative act is attributable to the State, it must then be verified whether the conduct objectively establishes the violation of an international obligation. It is the provision that establishes the obligation to determine whether the legislative act constitutes a violation, so that for example the obligation for a State to issue certain rules in its internal system is violated by the omission of the tax activity.[103] If this last consideration is well founded, it must be assumed that the examination relating to any illegal act deriving from a legislative one must be carried out on a case by case basis due to the nature of the violated obligation, as is not necessary for the actual execution of the act in question.[104]

In the second place, assuming third-degree sources in the same way as normative acts does not mean ignoring the differences between international and legislative acts of domestic law. What is relevant in our perspective is the common regulation of the acts in question. The very notion of normative act implies the concurrence of a double structural element. It must be a juridical act with the exclusion of mere legal facts.

---

[101] C. DE VISSCHER, La responsabilitè des Etats, in Bibliotheca Visseriana, vol. II, ed. Brill, Leiden, 1924.

[102] O. HOIJER, La responsabilitè internationale des États, Les Éditions Internationales, Paris, 1930, pp. 31ss.

[103] The internal law may constitute in certain circumstances an international illicit. In this perspective, in addition to the damage, there is also the element of guilt, considering that the legislative act integrates an offense only if you are negligent or if the national legislator has not taken into due consideration those elements of fact which should have been taken into account. That the analysis of liability by legislative act must take into account the nature of the violated obligation also results from the distinction between norms that impose a specific conduct and rules that oblige the achievement of a certain result distinction that the doctor had already correctly set in his general terms. What comes to the fore is that the content of the law is inherently illegitimate since in the case in which on the basis of an internally unimpeachable law were issued acts contrary to illicit international obligations would be the acts of emanation and not the law itself.

[104] The mere emanation of a state regulation in itself contrary to the international obligations of the State is not sufficient to integrate an illegal place that the State exercises its power at the time of coercion or when coercion is likely or imminent rather than through the mere emanation of a law that does not have or does not have a gap or possibility of being applied in practice. If it is true that the international offense is perfected in most cases only with the execution of the law it is necessary that the injured State is used to raise protests or complaints from the moment of the approval of a law which, if executed it would produce unjust harm to them.

Secondly, the content of the act must be classifiable as normative, consisting of one or more provisions suitable to act as rules of conduct in the life of a relationship. The first of the two structural elements mentioned above is widely known that in the international order between the various subjective juridical acts, there are some that rise to the category of juridical acts because of the role that the subject of the will assumes in them. In this regard it is hardly necessary to point out that for our purposes the requirement of subjective imputation is satisfied by the circumstance assumed by way of a logical premise that the organizations in question are subject to international law. As for the second of the two elements, it has already been observed that some functional bodies are authorized to carry out regulatory activities which give rise to third-degree sources.

These are expressions of will of the subjects of the legal system in which the competence to dictate rules of behaviour by means of deeds, which produce legal norms that have the force conferred on them by law, is recognized. That then the law is the prototype of the normative act is completely irrelevant if we consider it necessary. In the general theory of law the extension of the notion of normative act to those of the international order is authoritatively accepted, whose sources pose autonomous rules and commands rather than heteronomous inter or even super partes. Hard core in our opinion is the effect produced by the normative act, whether internal or international. Each in the context of his own legal system and in compliance with his own forms of regulatory production is able to innovate the legal situations of the respective subjects, resulting in a change in existing legal conditions. Within the international order the third degree sources are able to innovate Member States' juridical position on the basis of the will expressed by them by means of the establishing agreement.

In light of these considerations, we must understand the analogy with the normative acts of domestic law, not wanting to assert that international organizations are endowed with legislative powers. These are capable of affecting the juridical situation of individuals who in our perspective are subjects of a different ordering and distinct from the international one.

2.3. (Follows) Responsibility of an international organization resulting from a third degree source

A further evaluation is indispensable, which we believe strongly argues in favor of the considerations briefly traced concerning the responsibility of functional bodies for deliberative activities. In terms of imputation, art. 4 DARIO undoubtedly allows to configure the normative acts in the same way as conduct, in principle referable to a functional entity. This rule must then be coordinated with art. 17, par. 1 that in our opinion consistent with the entire international liability regime establishes that an international organization: "Incurs international responsibility if it circumvents one of its international obligations by adopting a binding decision to Member States or international organizations to commit an act that would be internationally wrongful if committed by the former organization." The par. 3 of the same provision clarifies that the aforementioned law is applicable "whether or not the act in question is internationally wrongful for Member States or international organizations to which the decision (…) is addressed."[105] As is evident from the literal side of art. 17 distinguishes expressis verbis the hypothesis of a binding act (decision) from that of an act with authorization and non-binding content regulated instead by par. 2 of the same article. The assumption of the rule in question is well summarized in the words of the Austrian delegate to the VI Committee of the UN General Assembly for which international organizations cannot evade the rules on responsibility "by outsourcing its actors."[106] In the shared assumption of ILC[107] and Gaja[108] the execution of decisions by Member States does not raise the organization from the responsibility for the illicit that derives from it. But what we want to highlight for the purposes of our analysis is that this responsibility arises independently from the actual execution of the act by the States they are addressed to. The general tenor of art. 17, par. 1 indeed "does not stipulate as a precondition, for the international responsibility of an international organization to arise that the required act be committed by Member States."[109] Therefore, since the execution of the decision by these States "is to be expected the likelihood of a third party being injured would then be high."[110] According to ILC regulations, the organization's responsibility is determined in similar circumstances due to the mere fact of having adopted the decision, a circumstance that legitimizes "the third party that would be injured to seek

[105]DARIO, pp. 40-43.
[106]UN Doc. A/C.6/59/SR.22, par. 24.
[107]DARIO, p. 40, par. 5.
[108]G. GAJA, Third report on responsibility of international organizations, op. cit., pp. 16, par. 36.
[109]DARIO, par. 41.
[110]DARIO, par. 41.

a remedy even before the act is committed."[111]

The criterion with which to evaluate the actual occurrence of the case described in par. 1 of art. 17 consists of the margin of discretion available to States in the fulfilment of what is imposed by the decision of an international organization. The parameter in question also emerges as a criterion for assessing Member States responsibility which, in order to carry out a third degree source, put violations on the obligations incumbent on them thanks to general international or contractual law. Here it must be emphasized that if the deed contains a command determined in all its elements and therefore does not leave to its addressees no margin of discretion either with regard to whether, when or how its execution[112] and contextually is contrary to an international obligation of the institution that approved it.[113] Gaja specifies that in the hypothesis of the institution in question the states have a certain degree of discretion, since the responsibility of the organization that has deliberated the act cannot be invoked.[114]

Consequently, a decision that requires States to behave in a specific way in order to fulfil the obligations contained in it entails an international unlawful act of the organization that adopted it regardless of its actual execution. In such circumstances the organization exercises a regulatory control,[115] on its Member States, which would give rise to a form of indirect responsibility in the case of the same entity.[116] That the absence of discretion for the members implies the imputation of conduct

---

[111]N. NEDELSKI, A. NOLLKAEMPER, Responsibility of international organizations, in "connection with acts of states," in International Organizations Law Review, 9, 2012, pp. 33ss.

[112]ARIO, p. 41.

[113]G. GAJA, Third report on responsibility of international organizations, op. cit., p. 12, par. 30.

[114]A. TZANAKOPOULOS, Disobeying the Security Council. Countermeasures against wrongful sanctions, op. cit., pp. 39ss. N. VOULGARIS, Rethinking indirect responsibility. A study of article 17 of the draft articles on the responsibility of international organizations, in International Organizations Law Review, 11, 2014, pp. 17ss. It must be emphasized that this criterion differs from the traditional canon of factual control, precisely from art. 17 ARSIWA that the same project of 2011 assumes as criterion of attribution of responsibility in art. 15 (and specularly in art. 59). In this case, centered on regulatory control, it is not required that the fact be unlawful even for the controlled party. It is integrated regardless of the existence of the subjective element of the organization that exercises the control in question.

[115]A. TZANAKOPOULOS, Disobeying the Security Council. Countermeasures against wrongful sanction, op. cit., pp. 33ss.

[116]N. VOULGARIS, Rethinking indirect responsibility. A study of article 17 of the draft articles on the responsibility of international organizations, op. cit., pp. 34ss.

to the deliberating organization is a datum now widely acquired by the doctrine[117] and consolidated in practice.

In this last profile, it should be noted that in the well-known CJEU, C-175/84, Krohn v. The European Commission case of 26 February 1986,[118] CJEU in that time after having ascertained that the nature of the Community act executed by the German authorities was such as not to leave them any margin of maneuver. It concluded that the unlawful act enclosed by the applicant in support of its right the compensation is attributable not to the BALM, which was required to comply with the Commission's instructions, but precisely to the latter. That is because of the criterion indicated the same CJEU had reached a conclusion of opposite sign C-133/79, Ducrimez and Westzucker v. Commission case of 27 March 1980,[119] where the Luxembourg judge rejected the claims for damages since the alleged injury had been put in place by the national authorities in execution of the non-binding act of the Commission. An orientation of a third degree source can also be found in the well-known C-184/95, Dorsch Consult v. Council case of 28 April 1998.[120] The general

[117]J.P. RITTER, La protective diplomatique à l'egard d'une organization internationale, op. cit., pp. 442ss. G. GAJA, Some reflections on the European Community international responsibility, in H.G. SCHERMERS, T. HEUCKLES, P. MEAD, Non-contractual liability of the European Communities, op. cit., pp. 172ss. M. HIRSCH, The responsibility of international organizations toward third parties. Some basic principles, op. cit., pp. 83ss. P. KLEIN, La responsabilitè des organizations internationales dans les ordres juridiques interne set droits de gens, op. cit., pp. 386ss. D. FRANK, Verantwortlichkeit für die Verletzung der Europäischen Menshenrechtkonvention durch internationale Organizationen, Helbing & Lichtenhahn, Basel, 1999. A. TZANAKOPOULOS, Disobeying the Security Council. Contermeasures against wrongful sanction, op. cit., pp. 24ss. N. VOULGARIS, Rethinking indirect responsibility. A study of article 17 of the draft articles on the responsibility of international organizations, op. cit., pp. 34ss.

[118] CJEU, C-175/84, Krohn v. European Commission of 26 February 1986, ECLI:EU:C:1986:85, I-00753. It was an action of non-contractual liability brought by a German company Krohn & Co. Import/Export for the prejudice suffered following the refusal by the Bundesanstalt für Landwirtschaftliche Marktordnung (BALM) of Frankfurt to implement a Commission regulation, to issue to that company certain import licenses. The problem of imputation was underlined in the same way as a preliminary question, given that the jurisdiction of the Community judge with regard to actions involving non-contractual liability exists only if the damage was caused by an institution of the Union. If, on the other hand, the damage was caused by the state authorities, even if due to the application of a Community act, the jurisdiction falls to the national Court. In the same spirit see also the case: C-101/78, Granaria v. H. v. A., of 13 February 1979, ECLI:EU:C:1979:38, I-00623, par. 13-14.

[119] CJEU, C-133/79, Ducrimez and Westzucker v. Commission of 27 March 1980, ECLI:EU:C:1980:104, I-01299, parrr. 13-25. C-217/81, Interagra SA v. Commission of 10 June 1982,ECLI:EU:C:1982:222, I-02233, parr. 7-11.

[120]CJEU, C-184/95, Dorsch Consult v. Council of 28 April 1998, ECLI:EU:C:1998:74, I-

Court given the appeal to annul the Regulation n. 2340/1990 adopted for the purpose of implementing the Resolution no. 661/1990 of the UN Security Council held that the damage complained of by the appellant should be considered attributable to this Resolution, whose content imposed precisely the conduct object of the complaint. Similar reasoning can be found in the well-known kadi and Yusuf sentence of 21 September 2005 in which the EU Council implemented the Resolution no. 1267/1999 of the UN Security Council. The judgments under consideration together with the second degree sentence of the CJEU (Kadi and Yusuf judgment) have raised some substantive legal issues extensively explored by the doctrine[121] that cannot be explored in this context. It should only be emphasized that the general Court has enhanced the circumstance for which, by adopting the contested regulation, the Community institutions had acted on the basis of a bounded competence having no margin of discretion as regards the execution of the measures imposed by the aforementioned resolution. On the contrary, where the same Court has recognized the existence of discretion, was finally reached a different solution. In T-282/02, Organization des modjahedines du peule d'iran v. Council sentence of 12 December 2006 has partially accepted the applicants' arguments, believing in part that the present case was different from the previous Yusuf and kadi decision for a decisive reason. In these proceedings a community act was contested which constituted the exercise of binding powers on the part of EU Council, which had confined itself to transposing the measures imposed by Security Council into Community law. On the contrary, in the Organization des Modjahedines case the conduct of EU Council constituting the exercise of its own power, even if finalized to the fulfilment of an obligation of result imposed by a Resolution of the Security Council exposed itself to the Union judge in the same way as do EU law.

Even some pronunciations by ECtHR seem relevant to the profile

00667. For further details see: K.LENAERTS, I. MASELIS, K. GUTMAN, European Union procedural law, op. cit., M.DERLÉN, J. LINDHOLM, The Court of Justice of the European Union. Multidiciplinary perspectives, op. cit., A.BOUVERESSE, D. RITLENG, L'effectivitè du droit de l'Union europèenne, ed. Larcier, Bruxelles, 2018. L.CLÊMENT-WILZ, Le rôle politique de la Cour de justice de l'Union europèenne, ed. Larcier, Bruxelles, 2019.

[121]E. CANNIZZARO, A machiavallian moment? The UN Security Council and the rule of law, in International Organizations Law Review, 3, 2006, pp. 190ss. J. RIDEAU, C. GREWE, L. BALMOND, A. ARCARI, Sanctions ciblèes et protection juridictionnelle des droit fondamentaux dans l'Union europèenne. Équilibre et dèsèquilibre de la balance, ed. Anthemis, Bruxelles, 2010.

examined here. It appears to be significant the Nada v. Switzerlancd case of 12 September 2012. The normative act although at the origin of the grievance was the same that had given rise to the Kadi case, i.e. Resolution n. 1267/1999. ECtHR has accepted the appeal based on the topic for which the State "enjoyed some latitude which was admittedly limited but nevertheless real, in implementing the relevant Resolution of the UN Security Council."[122] Regardless of the criticism that can be addressed to this reasoning, the centrality seems to be the Al Dulimi v. Switerland case of 26 June 2016. ECtHR attributes decisive importance to the topic for which Resolution no. 1483/2003 of Security Council[123] at the origin of the state conduct object of the grievance "do not confer on the States concerned any discretion in the implementation of the obligations arising there."[124]

The responsibility of an international organization for legislation from art. 17, par. of the 2011 project follows the approach for which the normative act abstractly contrary to international law is not sufficient to integrate the responsibility of the subject that adopted it in the absence of its concrete application. This rule governs the responsibility of an organization that authorizes Member States to perform an act "that would be internationally wrongful if committed by that organization" but subordinates the arising of this responsibility to the effective and concrete execution of what is authorized.

2.4. Participation in the deliberative procedure as a hypothesis of complicity. The need to "isolate" state behaviour from the outcome of the procedure

Given the conditions under which a legislative act is suitable to integrate the responsibility of an international organization, is necessary to dwell on the possible involvement of Member States with respect to the categories of conduct examined. It is a matter of assessing the circumstances under which the behaviour of Member States is able to carry out the case of complicity in relation to the main crime constituted by the regulatory act of the functional entity itself. To this end, it must be

[122]N. VOULGARIS, Rethinking indirect responsibility. A study of article 17 of the draft articles on the responsibility of international organizations, op. cit., pp. 38ss.
[123]S/RES71483 (2003), 22 May 2003, par. 23. F.L. KIRGIS, Security Council Resolution 1483 on the rebuilding of Iraq, in American Journal of International Law, 97, 2003.
[124] F.L. KIRGIS, Security Council Resolution 1483 on the rebuilding of Iraq, op. cit.

emphasized that the conduct of individual members is susceptible to a separate assessment with respect to that relating to the regulatory act that they contribute to determine.

As noted by PCIJ in the advisory opinion of 1925 on art. 3, par. 2 of the Treaty of Lausanne [125] the delegates within the organ of an international organization commit the responsibility of the respective States. The conduct held by a delegate within an organ is always attributable to the State on whose behalf it acts without prejudice to the fact that the decision is attributed to the organization. Useful indications can be obtained from the judgment of 5 December 2011 by which the ICJ ascertained the responsibility of Greece for having opposed NATO within the admission of the former Federal Republic of Macedonia.[126] In this case, the responsibility of the defendant state was based on the violation of an obligation imposed on it in the same way as the provisional agreement concluded between the parties on 13 September 1995. ICJ's ruling is inscribed in the complex framework of the dispute between former Yugoslav Republic of Macedonia (FYROM), on the one hand and Greece on the other concerning the use of the name Macedonia as part of the first State. During the NATO summit in Bucharest (2008), a decision was made not to invite the state actor to start preliminary negotiations on the admission to the organization, until "a mutually acceptable solution to the same issue" is reached. [127] How the ICJ has easily ascertained the conclusion reached in the course of the summit constituted a direct consequence of the Greek facilitated pressures due to the particular nature of the admission procedure foreseen by the Treaty of Washington of 1949. The appeal of FYROM focused on the alleged violation by Greece of the obligation contained in art. 11, par. 1 of provisional agreement not to oppose the admission of the former in international organizations of which

[125]CPIJ, Consultative opinion of 21 November 1925 relative to art. 3, par. 2 of the treaty of Lausanne (Frontier between Turkey and Iraq) in collection of advisory opinions, series B-N 12, p. 29, where the UN Council "is composed of representatives of members that is to say of persons delegated by their respective governments, from whom they receive instructions and whose responsibility they engage." See also in argument: C. SÖFKER, Durch die Besatzungsmacht geprägte Neuordnungen besetzter Staaten: Welche Auswirkungen haben Völkerrechtlich verbotene Angriffsriege und die Reichweite der Kompetenzen von Besatzungsmächten Untersucht am Beispiel des Irak-krieges, H. Utz Verlag, München, 2014.

[126] ICJ, Application of the interim accord of 13 September 1995, op. cit., A. ZIMMERMANN, C.J. TAMS, K. OELLERS-FRAHAM, The Statute of the International Court of Justice. A commentary, op. cit.

[127]Bucharest Summit Declaration issued Heads of State and of governments participating in the Meeting of the North Atlantic Council on 3 April 2008.

the second phase was a member. ICJ accepted the appeal stating that Greece by obeying the admission of the former Republic of Macedonia to NATO has breached its obligation under article 11, par. 1 of the interim accord of 13 September 1995.

The case just mentioned is outside the scope of our investigation since the responsibility of Greece will not be integrated by participation in the offense of others but exclusively by the violation of the obligation pending on it to hold a certain behaviour within the decision-making body. It seems useful to us to dwell on the orientation adopted by ICJ with regard to certain issues that are relevant to our investigation. Firstly, it attributes to Greece the conduct it has held that such conduct can be assessed independently of NATO's decision. ICJ therefore rejected the Greek defense argument. It was not able to separate the position of the Greek delegate from the collective resolution adopted by the Atlantic Council. It raised that the object of Macedonian appeal concerned the alleged violation of an obligation incumbent exclusively on the agreed State and not on NATO.[128] Secondly, and this is probably the decisive aspect for ICJ, the primary rule relevant in the present case established a specific duty of conduct suitable for imposing itself on Greece and binding its activity even when the latter found itself acting within the decision-making body of an international organization.

2.5. (Follows) The conditions set by art. 58 DARIO to the complicity of States in the offense deriving from the legislative act

According to a first orientation, simple participation in the vote, although not decisive for the purpose of adopting the regulatory act, can commit the responsibility of Member State to complicity.[129] In the opinion

[128]The ICJ assessed the Greek conduct legally independent of the content of the Resolution of the Atlantic Council with the precise indication that the rights and obligations of NATO and other Member States do not come to the fore in resolving the dispute in question, so the argument based on the principle of gold money is to be considered misplaced. A. ZIMMERMANN, C.J. TAMS, K. OELLERS-FRAHAM, The Statute of the International Court of Justice. A commentary, op. cit.

[129]P. KLEIN, La responsabilitè des organizations internationales dans les ordres juridiques interne set droits de gens, op. cit., pp. 592ss. J. KATZ COGAN, I. HURD, I. JOHNSTONE (eds), The Oxford handbook of international organizations, Oxford University Press, Oxford, 2016. P. KLEIN, The attribution of acts to international organizations, in J. CRAWFORD, A. PELLET, S. OLLESON, K. PARLETT, The law of international responsibility, op. cit., pp. 308, which the author appears to be reviewing its position arguing the need for the contribution of the State to be detrimental to the adoption of the

of another part of the doctrine, this offense is produced only under the "very special circumstances,"[130] which occur if and to the extent that the state conduct has made it possible to the Commission of the unlawful act by the organization.[131] Otherwise it is observed, it would deny any allegiance to the distinct legal personality of the organization that adopted the act. The solution accepted by art. 58 DARIO is attributable to this orientation as can be seen from the letter of the provision and from the comment that the ILC itself provided. In ILC's opinion "the possibility that aid or assistance could result from conduct taken by the State within the framework of the organization cannot be totally excluded."[132] In even clearer terms Gaja emphasized in his fourth report that the relevant conduct for the purposes of state complicity "could not simply consist in

---

act. See also: D. SAROOSHI, International organizations and state responsibility, in M. RAGAZZI, Responsibility of international organizations. Essays in memory of Sir Ian Brownlie, Martinus Nijhoff Publishers, Leiden, Boston, 2013, pp. 86ss, Member States incur complicity when they facilitate the adoption of a normative act "that mandates the Commission of the internationally worn act." According to the author the participation in the decision-making process by a Member State exposes the latter to the attribution of responsibility due to the deliberative organization. This position is based on the assumption that the Member States exercise a form of control over the normative conduct of the institution. The jurisprudence expressed by the People's Republic of China within the VI Committee at the General Assembly during the discussions on DARIOs seems to be related to this orientation "since the decisions and actions of an international organization were, as a rule, under the control or reliant of the support of Member States, i.e. those Member States that voted in favour of the decision in question or implemented the relevant decision, recommendation or authorization should incur a corresponding international responsibility," Sixth Committee, summary record of the 11th meeting, in GAOR 23 November 2005, Doc. A/C.60/SR.11, p. 10, par. 543, for the Chinese position see also the comments of: H. QUIAN, Chinese practice in public international law, in Chinese Journal of International Law, 5, 2006, pp. 460ss.

[130] J. D'ASPREMONT, Abuse of the legal personality of international organizations and the responsibility of member states, in International Organizations Law Review, 4, 2007, pp. 109ss.

[131] A. GESLIN, Rèflexions sur la repartition de la responsabilitè entre l'organization internationale et ses États membres, op. cit., pp. 550ss. A similar position, even if not expressly framed in the case of complicity, can be found in I. SEIDL-HOHENVELDERN, Responsible of member states of an international organization for acts of that organization, in A.A.V.V., Le droit international à l'heure de sa codification, op. cit., pp. 420, which the author considers the responsibility of a Member State for the Organization's decisions "should depend on the fact whether or not the Member State, by participating in the decision of the Organization, would be able to prevent the adoption of the decision concerned." In this perspective the provision contained in art. 12, par. 2 of the Charter of economic rights and duties of the States which imposes on the organization and the respective Member States "a duty to ensure that the policies of the organization concerned correspond to the provisions of this Charter."

[132] DARIO, p. 91, par. 4.

participating in the decision making process in the implicit assumption that participation in the vote may well be configured as an aid or assistance pursuant to art. 58."[133]

The configurability of the case in question is subject to the condition post from par. 2 in art. 28 based on which: "An act by a Member State of an international organization done in accordance with the rules of the Organization does not as such engage the international responsibility of that State under the terms of this article." It can be deduced that the physiological participation in the regulatory activity of the institution is in itself not suitable to impose the responsibility provided for by the same provision in par. 1.

It seems possible to conclude that Member States' conduct within the framework of a third-degree regulatory procedure must qualify as an unlawful act of complicity only if is a necessary condition for the occurrence of the main crime.[134] The causal link between accessory and main fact in the specific hypothesis assumes the form of conditionality having to verify from time to time if the damaging act could have been adopted without the favourable vote of the State in consideration. In the event of a positive response, it should be excluded the application of art. 58. The solution adopted by ILC and supported by the majority doctrine, takes into consideration both the nature of international organizations and the need to guarantee their normal and ordinary functioning. On the one hand, in the exercise of legislative activity, organizations' will is to varying degrees influenced by the will of individual Member States. For this reason the decision-making process that is established in organs with a state composition cannot reasonably be considered as originating, in the same way as the legislative procedure of a State. On the other hand, it is in the decision-making process that the existence of a will distinct from that of Member States is tested. In the situation contemplated by art. 58 the will and consequent normative activity of the organization is determined with the contribution of that of Member State without for this reason the second overlaps or replaces the first one.

It has been argued that through par. 2 of art. 58 DARIO, ILC would have set a cause of exclusion of the illegality different from those codified both in ARSIWA and DARIO constituted by the fulfilment of the internal rules to the organization to which the illegal regulatory act is

---

[133]G. GAJA, Fourth report on responsibility of international organization, op. cit., p. 5, par. 62.

[134]P. KLEIN, Les articles sur la responsabilità des organizations internationales: Quel bilan tirer de travaux e la CDI?, op. cit., pp. 19ss.

attributed.[135] It seems that art. 50 requires an assessment of the complicity in the regulatory act by reason of the contribution that each State lends within the deliberating body, without excluding that the accessory fact comes into being even in situations that comply with the internal law of the functional body. In other words, even the institutional framework in which the main crime is produced can play a decisive role in assessing the circumstances of the case. It is undeniable that the nature of the body to which this offense is attributable together with the possibly differentiated position of some Member States with respect to others are elements that contribute to determining the contribution of each State with respect to the damaging act.[136] The project itself expressly admits that "the size of membership and nature of involvement will probably be decisive."[137] These observations make it possible to apply the provisions of art. 58 to the conduct held by some members of the Security Council with respect to the decisions taken by this body on the basis of art. 41 of the Charter that are in contrast with the international UN obligations.[138] In addition to the weight in the decision-making process, other factors must also be taken into account, such as the role played by each member in the preparation of the resolution or in the organization of the procedure for its adoption.

It is necessary to add about the material element of complicity in the adoption of an illicit regulatory act that the same can be supplemented by an illegal behaviour in itself.[139] For example, consider the conduct of Member State which is in contrast with the general obligation of good faith in participating in the voting procedures[140] or to the due diligence. According to ILC would require states to guarantee the lawfulness

---

[135]V. LANOVOY, Complicity and its limits in the law of international responsibility, op. cit., pp. 123ss.

[136]I. SEIDL-HOHENVELDERN, Responsibility of member states of an international organization for acts of that organization, in A.A.V.V., Le droit international à l'heure de sa codification, op. cit. pp. 421ss, which the author with reference to art. 12, of the Charter of economic rights and duties of Members States that the liability regulated therein: "Should be determined in the light of the right given by constitution of the organization to the consent of the State concerned, when reaching such a decision."

[137]DARIO, p. 91, par. 4.

[138]V. LANOVOY, Complicity and its limits in the law of international responsibility, op. cit., pp. 129ss. J.M. CORTÉS MARTIN, Las organizaciones internacionales: Codificatiòn y desarrollo progresivo de su responsabilida internacional, ed. Tirant, Sevilla, 2008, pp. 30ss.

[139]V. LANOVOY, Complicity and its limits in the law of international responsibility, op. cit.

[140]G. FITZMAURICE, The law and procedure of the International Court of Justice, in British Yearbook of International Law, 23, 1952, pp. 28ss. R. KOLB, La bonne foi en droit international public, op. cit., pp. 510ss.

of decisions of the body of which they are members.[141] Likewise, the obligation for Member States of the Executive Board and Board of Executive Directors to ensure that IMF and World Bank's actions respectively produce effects incompatible with the rights enunciated by the International Covenant of Economic, Social and Cultural Rights.[142]

As for the subjective element of complicity, it is believed that its assessment is in most cases easy, given that in practice the voting procedures are always preceded by statements in which the Member States express the reasons for their determinations showing full awareness of the consequences of their vote.[143]

2.6. (Follows) States' participation in UN illicit

The hypothesis of states complicity in the regulatory act of the Security Council assumes that it cannot be the object of further study in this place for which a decision of this body is likely to violate the parameters that regulate the UN activity determining thus the international responsibility.[144]

---

[141]V. LANOVOY, Complicity and its limits in the law of international responsibility, op. cit., pp. 128ss.

[142]A.S. BARROS, Member states and the international legal (dis)order, in International Organizations of Law Review, 12, 2015, pp. 334ss. The obligation in question is supplemented by way of example to indicate that certain categories of rules, including those of a contractual nature, may impose themselves on States acting in the framework of international organizations. The problem that arises with specific regard to international organizations that perform functions in economic and financial matters, such as typically the IMF and the World Bank seem prima facie to be outside the subject of our investigation. First of all because there is no unanimity of coming, for example, in the configuration of the activity carried out by these organizations as strictly normative in the sense seen in the introduction to part II of this work. Secondly, because even to admit its normative character there is more than one doubt about the nature of the act with which, for example, the financial assistance takes place, given that some consider it a unilateral act and others as an agreement with the international State. We can consider that, at least with regard to the world bank, state support activities normally take place following the conclusion of an agreement with the Organization. In such situations, a first degree of complicity could be posed in the first approximation to that developed in this work. We refer to the possibility of examining the activity of this organization in the offense committed by States.

[143]V. LANOVOY, Complicity and its limits in the law of international responsibility, op. cit.

[144]G.H. OOSTHUIZEN, Playring the devil's advocate: The United Nations Security Council is unbound by law, in Leiden Journal of International Law, 12, 1999, pp. 562ss. K. DOWHERING, Unlawful resolutions of the Security Council and their legal consequences, in Max Planck Yearbook of United Nations Law, 1, 1997, pp. 92ss. A. REINISCH, Developing human rights and humanitarian law accountability of the Security Council for the imposition of economic actions, in American Journal of International Law, 95, 2001,

The involvement of Member States with respect to a harmful act put in place by the Security Council must be evaluated according to the particular nature of this body. Art. 58 DARIO attributes a decisive role to the characteristics of the organ and type of membership in determining the complicity of States in the act of the body in question. We have also seen that art. 58, par. 2 establishes as a general rule that the activity normally exercised by States within the framework of the organs does not in itself apply to integrate the case of complicity but at the same time clarifies that in some borderline cases,[145] state involvement can give rise to illicit complicity with respect to an act attributable to the organization. In these cases it can be easy to verify the actual contribution given by the individual Member State with respect to the main crime. The UN Security Council seems in our opinion to be among the borderline cases generically reported by ILC.

First of all, we specify that the composition of the Security Council based on art. 23 of the Charter presented a restricted membership with a differentiated legal position for the benefit of permanent members. This is a widely known aspect on which therefore it does not seem necessary to dwell. What is important to highlight is that the exercise of veto by art. 27 places permanent members to prevent the adoption of acts that prima facie is in contrast with the international UN obligations. The material element in this case would be constituted by an omissive conduct whose normative basis should be sought in the positive obligation of members to ensure that the decisions of the body do not conflict with international law. Furthermore, the negative vote of permanent members against the revocation of sanctions adopted pursuant to art. 41 of which the incompatibility with the regulatory parameters limiting the action of the Council is proven, is an accessory fact of a Commission type. It should be noted that even the mere threat of the use of the right of veto can take the form of illicit assistance in the same way as art. 58 on the responsibility of the organizations that it comes within the same Council. The fact is that this behaviour is in itself completely lawful because is allowed in art. 27 of the Charter. The forms of legal assistance do not to present any profile of opposition with respect to the obligations of the accomplice. Rather, the lawfulness of the behaviour in question, that is the exercise or threat of

---

pp. 852ss. C. DOMINICÉ, The international responsibility of the United Nations for injuries resulting from non-military enforcement measures, in M. RAGAZZI, Responsibility of international organizations. Essays in memory of Sir Ian Brownlie, Martinus Nijhoff Publishers, Leiden, Boston, 2013, pp. 367ss.

[145]DARIO, p. 91, par. 4.

exercising the right of veto, serves as a descriptive criterion that excludes that this conduct reintegrates the case of management and control over organization's crime.[146] If it is true that the exercise of the right of veto by a permanent member of the Security Council constitutes a lawful measure and as such does not represent a valid title of concurrent responsibility in the head of said State,[147] it cannot be excluded that this hypothesis will constitutes illegal assistance pursuant to art. 58.[148]

Secondly, in the cases where the decision or the absence of a decision should be in contrast with erga omnes obligations, Security Council Member States' conduct should, in our opinion, be assessed in the light of art. 58 and 42, par. 1 DARIO. Permanent members who are made aware of the circumstances and consequences of a legislative act on erga omnes obligations should work to prevent the adoption of the same act. If the violation has already occurred and continues over time, the further obligation imposed by art. 42, par. 1 DARIO by virtue of which all Member States of the Security Council and, a fortiori, permanent ones must prepare all lawful measures in order to put an end to "a serious breach of obligation arising under a peremptory norm of general international law." The aforementioned provision is highlighted in particular in the hypothesis

---

[146] J. D'ASPREMONT, Abuse of the legal personality of international organizations and the responsibility of member states, op. cit., pp. 98. The case of management and control that would give rise to a joint and concurrent responsibility would be supplemented by an overwhelming control exercised by some Member States on the decision-making process of the body of which they are part. The latest unspecified statement would occur only in the presence of forms of pressure not envisaged by the trust act of the entity in question.

[147] Contra in this position: J. D'ASPREMONT, Abuse of the legal personality of international organizations and the responsibility of member states, op. cit., pp. 110ss.

[148] It should be noted that the exercise of the power of veto can be considered an abuse of rights at least to the extent that the thesis in the exercise of the rights deriving from the membership of the bodies of the UN is considered by each Member State "legally bound to the principle of good faith, to give effect to the purposes and principles of the UN and to act in such a manner as not to involve any breach of the Charter." Dissenting opinion of judges Basdevant, Winiarski, Sir Arnol McNair and Read, Conditions of admission of a State to membership in the UN (article 4 of the Charter), advisory opinion, 28 May 1948, ICJ Reports, 1948, p. 57Ss, par. 21. See also: A. PETERS, The responsibility to protect and the obligation to give reasons for a veto, in J. HOFFMANN, A. NOLLAEMPER, Responsibility to protect. From principle to practice, Palas Publication, Amsterdam, 2012, pp. 205ss, according to which this circumstance occurs where the Security Council does not endeavour to face the serious violation of human rights, violating the rule that according to this perspective would be imposed by the responsibility to protect. Precisely leveraging the comment on art. 58 of the project on the responsibility of international organizations, the author states that: "The boundary line between lawful participation in the Security Council's decision making on the one hand and the assistance (or control) amounting to an unlawful act seems to be overstepped in cases of an abuse of the veto (...)."

that a decision in contrast is maintained as obligations of the type considered. Art. 42, par. 1 in the hypothesis under examination imposes on each of the 15 Member States the obligation already noted by the doctrine a basis for partially different assessments to bring to the attention of the Security Council the situation detected[149] and above all to activate within this body in order to induce him to revoke the unlawful decision by resorting more precisely to the instruments permitted by the Charter and rules of procedure. It must be assumed that otherwise state responsibility will result in the violation of the obligation of cooperation enshrined in art. 42, par. DARIO.

It seems clear that the five permanent members constitute the prototype of States with respect to those the obligation of cooperation assumes in the words of Gaja, the content of a stricter duty, as they can make a decisive contribution in the indicated perspective. It must therefore be concluded that in the hypothesis envisaged the exercise of the right of veto by the permanent members intact through the abuse of law that the doctrine links to other cases a violation of art. 42, par. DARIO.

The practice in this regard is very small. Nevertheless, we must cite a case often referred to in the doctrine that supports the thesis of complicity in the context of deliberative activities.[150] This is the conduct held by the permanent members of the Security Council and in particular from United Kingdom, i.e. the framework of the sanctioning measures against the former Yugoslavia in the early nineties of the last century. We refer to the Resolution n. 713 of 25 September 1991[151] with which the Security Council imposed an arms embargo and Resolutions n. 757 of 30 May 1992[152] and n. 787 of the following 16 November with which a trade

---

[149] K. DOEHRING, Unlawful resolution of the Security Council and their legal consequence, in Max Planck Yearbook of United Nations Law, 2, 1997, pp. 92ss, stating that the author links the obligation to inform the Security Council of the right of all UN Member States not to apply a resolution contrary to jus cogens.

[150] P. KLEIN, La responsabilitè des organizations internationales dans les ordres juridiques interne set droits de gens, op. cit., pp. 470ss. P. KLEIN, The attribution of acts to international organizations, in J. CRAWFORD, A. PELLET, S. OLLESON, K. PARLETT, The law of international responsibility, op. cit., pp. 308ss.

[151] For further analysis see: K. SEAMAN, UN-tied Nations: The United Nations, peacekeeping and global governance, ed. Routledge, London & New York, 2016. E. PAPASTAVRIDIS, Interpretation of Security Council Resolutions under Chapter VII in the aftermath of the Iraqi crisis, in International and Comparartive Law Quarterly, 56 (1), 2007, pp. 84ss. R. OLALEKAN YUSSUF, A critical evaluation of the UN Security Council's power in form of article 39 of the United Nations Charter: Interpretation, invocation and the morder threat to international peace and security, in Independent Student Journal Law, 2018 (1), pp. 7-9.

[152] For further analysis see also: L. VAN HERIK, Research handbook on UN sanctions and

embargo was decreed.[153]

Resolution n. 713 which forbade the transfer of arms to the Federal Republic of Yugoslavia would have substantially deprived Bosnia of its right to legitimate defense protected by art. 51, UN Charter.[154] The organization of Islamic countries, in that circumstance, declared the illegitimacy of the Resolution specifying that the Member States would not have fulfilled the additional obligations deriving by the decision.[155] It should be noted that the General Assembly recommended to the Security Council: "(...) To exempt the Republic of Bosnia and Herzegovina from the embargo imposed on the Former Yugoslavia under Security Council Resolution 713,"[156] sharing in such a situation the need to guarantee to Bosnia the availability of the military means necessary to exercise the legitimate defense even if in principle it affirmed the exclusive competence of the Security Council in order to revoke the sanctioning measures.[157] Regarding the legal consequences of Resolution no. 713 is worth remembering the position expressed by the judge Lauterpacht during the proceeding brought by Bosnia against Serbia concerning the alleged violations of the 1993 genocide Convention. After having noticed that a decision of the Security Council is able to put itself in contrast with the cogent right. Judge Lauterpacht believed that he could see a violation of the prohibition of genocide in the Resolution. More precisely, according to this opinion, the material impossibility for Bosnia "to fight back against the Serbs and effectively to prevent the implementation of the Serbian policy of ethnic cleansing is at least in part directly attributable to the fact that Bosnia-Herzegovina's access to weapons and equipment has been severely limited by the embargo." So that having prevented Bosnia from exercising its right to legitimate defense Resolution no. 713 would have

---

international law, Edward Elgar Publishing, Cheltenham, 2017, pp. 241-243. R. HIGGINS, P. WEBB, D. AKANDE, J. SLOAN, S. SIVAKUMARAN, Oppenheim's international law: United Nations, Oxford University Press, Oxford, 2017.

[153] L. VAN HERIK, Research handbook on UN sanctions and international law, op. cit., R. HIGGINS, P. WEBB, D. AKANDE, J. SLOAN, S. SIVAKUMARAN, Oppenheim's international law: United Nations, op. cit., C. HENDERSON, Commissions of inquiry. Problems and prosepcts, Bloomsbury Publishing, New York, 2017.

[154] R. HIGGINS, P. WEBB, D. AKANDE, J. SLOAN, S. SIVAKUMARAN, Oppenheim's international law: United Nations, op. cit.,

[155]See the following resolutions of the conference of foreign ministers: Res. 6/22-P (10-12 December 1994), par. 7; res. 7721-P (25-29 April 1993), res. 6723 P (9-12 December 1995), parr. 12-15. See also the OIC Heads of State and government declaration on Bosnia and Herzegovina, 7th Islamic summit conference, 13-15 December 1994.

[156]Res. 47/121 (1992).

[157] A. ORAKHELASHVILI, Peremptory norms in international law, op. cit., pp. 474ss.

imposed on UN Member States "to become in some degree supporters of the genocidal activity of Serbs and in this manner and to that extent to act contrary to a rule of jus cogens."[158]

Bosnia and Herzegovina announced its intention to institute contentious proceedings before the ICJ against UK on 15 November 1993 "for violating the terms of the 1948 Convention on the prevention and punishment of the crime of genocide; of the 1965 international Covenant on the elimination of all forms of racial discrimination; and of the other sources of general international law set forth in article 38 of the international Court's Statute." It is important to underline that according to Bosnia the behaviour in contrast with the mentioned international obligations would have been attributable to UK "while acting in its capacity as a permanent member of the UN Security Council." In this context and acting in violation of the right to self-defense against Bosnia, UK would have facilitated the violation of the prohibition of genocide "by actively opposing al of the efforts by other States to lift this illegal arms embargo."[159] Among the disputed behaviours were the fact that they had concurred with their own vote in the adoption of sanctions and the threat that for the revocation of the embargo decreed by the Resolution n. 713. The proceeding feared by the Bosnian party did not take place since the 20 December 1993 the parties issued a joint declaration, by which the Bosnian government renounced to the jurisdictional action following an agreement that served to extinguish the controversy in question. [160] However, assuming by hypothesis that the Bosnian claim was legally founded, a dual responsibility could be reconstructed for UK. On the one hand, this State would have contributed with its vote to the adoption of a measure that in various respects was in contrast with international obligations and conversely, could not have been adopted if the permanent members, in compliance with the rule of the two stage coaches, had prevented the adoption of the act in question. From this point of view it

[158] Application of genocide convention, op. cit., provisional measures, order of 13 September 1993, in ICJ Reports, 1993, p. 325ss. And the separate opinion of judge Lauterpacht, p. 407, par. 102. A. ZIMMERMANN, C.J. TAMS, K. OELLERS-FRAHAM, The Statute of the International Court of Justice. A commentary, op. cit.

[159]See statement of intention of the Republic of Bosnia and Herzegovina to institute legal proceedings against the United Kingdom before the International Court of Justice, 15 November 1993, par. 1.

[160]C. GRAY, Application of the convention on the prevention and punishment of the crime of genocide (Bosnia and Herzeovina v. Yugoslavia (Serbia and Montenegro)), orders of provisional measures of 8 April 1993 and 13 September 1993, in International and Comparative Law Quarterly, 43, 1994, pp. 704ss.

could be considered integrated the case of art. 58 DARIO. On the other hand, by preventing the cessation of the serious offense deriving from the sanctioning measures, the British conduct would have been in contrast with the obligation of cooperation sanctioned by art. 42, par. 1 DARIO.

2.7. Responsibility profiles and compliance with arms transfer agreements. International state responsibility for provisions violation prohibiting arms transfers

As we know, the internationalist doctrine does not exclude the Commission of illicit or international crimes through violation of the provisions governing international arms transfers.

The profiles of responsibility that will be explained below concern both the States, or the main actors of the "trade" in arms and the individuals, i.e. those who act as public officials of the State, as well as of those acting in a completely private capacity.

Arms transfer activities are typically implemented through exchanges between States. This is admissible because of the commercial monopoly established by the States as regards both the production phase and the sale of armaments, as well as on the basis of an opinio juris progressively formed starting from the end of World War I.

Indeed, the need to "trade" armaments is linked to that to protect oneself or to defend oneself against possible threats of the use of armed force. Arms transfers, although dictated by legitimate self-defense purposes, nevertheless represent a threat to international security.

Moreover, the doctrine maintains that the preservation of international stability goes hand in hand, at least recently, with the respect of certain normative categories, which regulate the conduct carried out by the States in arms transfers, among which human rights, international humanitarian law and obligations arising by the UN Charter, in particular the observance of Security Council resolutions regarding restrictive measures imposed on certain States, are found.[161]

On this point, the recent Treaty on Trade in Armaments (hereinafter ATT) of 2013 was a useful starting point for most of the

---

[161] G. BASTID-BURDEAU, Le commerce international des armes: de la sécurité à la défense de l'éthique et des droits de l'homme?, in Journal du droit international, 2 (4), 2007, par. 7.

doctrine for analyzing the profiles of responsibility in international law.[162]

The doctrine is substantially unanimous in affirming that articles 6 and 7 of the Treaty serve as the central pivot of the entire discipline, as they establish innovative constraints with respect to the previous and fragmented legislation. The scholar finds (in article 7) a prohibition of authorization to transfer following a positive assessment of the likelihood of committing offenses (overriding risk).[163] This evaluation, to use the terms of art. 7, must be done in advance, through, for example, the keeping of registers and the consultation of the same (as required by art. 9), or by drawing up a special list listing any State or not subjects, to which is associated with the Commission of offenses and the ascertained violation of international standards.

There must be not only an evaluation of the recipient of the transfer. According to the doctrine, the obligation of observance of general international law, which also refers to UN Security Council's resolutions which establish embargoes for arms, hangs not only on the State exporter, thus violating an erga omnes obligation,[164] but also on destination.[165]

First of all, there is the general problem of concrete imputability for illicit arms transfers. Where the provisions do not clarify this profile, according to the scholar, it should always be possible to bring the responsibility back to the State, as the subject to whom is attributed the general duty of observance of international law, and especially of human rights.[166] Scholars see this approach emerge from specific obligations, such as that prescribed by art. 5 of ATT, which requires the establishment by state governments of adequate control systems which allow the prevention of illicit arms transfers. Furthermore, the responsibility of other national actors (whether public or private) involved in the transfer, at least in terms of domestic law, is not excluded.

The violation of international law can take place through a

---

[162]G. BASTID-BURDEAU, Le commerce international des armes: de la sécurité à la défense de l'éthique et des droits de l'homme?, op. cit.

[163]M. BRANDES, "All's well that ends well" or "much ado about nothing?" A commentary on the arms trade treaty, in Goettingen Journal of International Law, 5 (2), 2013, pp. 399-429.

[164]A. BELLAL, S. CASEY-MASLEN, D. GIACCA, Implications of international law for a future arms trade treaty, UNIDIR Resources, 2012, pp. 13ss.

[165]It is underlined that this type of "two-faced" responsibility is determined by the letter of the text of art. 6, § 2 ATT, where it indicates that the State violates international law when it engages in activity of transfers included in art. 2 of the agreement, or both export and import documents.

[166]Artt. 1(3), 55 and 56 of the charter of the UN. A. BELLAL, S. CASEY-MASLEN-D. GIACCA, Implications of international law for a future arms trade treaty, op. cit.

considerable number of activities. This would depend, according to the prevailing orientation, on the terminological breadth that is attributed to the term transfer, which is broader than the mere sales or supplies, considered a specification of the first category.

With regard to the protection of human rights, there are no international rules that prohibit prima facie illicit transfers. The main purpose of the human rights treaties is to ensure that States respect and observe the fundamental rights of the subjects, outside as well as within the sphere of jurisdiction.[167] The violation of these rules can derive from the transfer of certain weapons, subsequently used by unauthorized subjects to possess such weapons. It is believed that this would involve at least an obligation to investigate these ends, in the light of national law, as well as of the (poor) international law.

Again with reference to the ATT, art. 6, para. 2 establishes an additional obligation for the States, placed in relation to that on the control of transfers, both in an active (for the seller State) and passive (for the acquiring State) sense. "We consider the case of a State that does not use, by choice or by necessity, adequate resources to ensure its citizens enjoy the right to food, health, be treated humanely in detention (…). The same State would be obliged not to authorize the passive transfer (i.e. the purchase) of conventional arms, if this involves the use of resources that could otherwise be used to allow full respect of those rights, at least when the purchase is not justified from national security needs (...)."[168]

The doctrine, therefore, believes that there would not only be human rights immediately damaged by the use of weapons in the course of an armed conflict, but also those rights connected to the economic and social life of a nation, which are identified in the performance of the essential public services, financed with state funds. A possible "distraction" of the funds for these services, motivated by exceptions to the rights (which may be that of national defense)[169] but not legitimized in the light of existing instruments of international law, could constitute a violation by one State and the subsequent configuration of responsibility for the same.[170]

---

[167]A. BELLAL, S. CASEY-MASLEN-D. GIACCA, Implications of International Law for a Future Arms Trade Treaty, op. cit., pp. 8ss.

[168]A. BELLAL, S. CASEY-MASLEN-D. GIACCA, Implications of International Law for a Future Arms Trade Treaty, op. cit.

[169]L. DOSWALD-BECK, Human rights in time of conflict and terrorism, op. cit., pp. 67ss.

[170]This situation is found, for example, in agreements to offset debts (offset agreements), often stipulated on the occasion of a defense procurement in arms. With these agreements, two States establish a compensation compromise between the purchase sum of the arms

With reference to violations of international humanitarian law, in doctrine these can be configured when the arms trade, if carried out unlawfully, can adversely affect the principle of respect and observance of the conduct to be followed during an armed conflict.[171] Furthermore, the violation may also derive from transfers that have been prohibited.

The responsibility would be further aggravated, when it was ascertained that the State and its organs have knowledge that the transfer of arms could entail a serious risk of committing international crimes. Therefore, it is underlined how this approach is well exposed in art. 6, para. 3, ATT, which, for scholars, would have an innovative character. The types of responsibility would be configured either for the State, for helping the Commission of an offense by another State (on the model of art. 16 of the Draft Articles on Liability in 2001), or to an individual, for complicity in an international crime.

However, the doctrine also points to interpretative difficulties arising from the reference to the term "knowledge." While admitting its penalistic matrix, and even wanting to ascertain the fact that knowledge, with respect to "awareness," prefigures a lesser psychological element, the scholar does not share the choice to use this term also in reference to State responsibility.

On the contrary, to ensure that this approach exists, it would be necessary to admit that the knowledge possessed by the public official who physically transfers the load of arms is the same possessed by the State of belonging or classification. This statement lends itself to obvious

and any previous debts of the purchaser, and in which both the main transfer services and the military supply and assistance are determined, which are perfected in the mere maintenance of weapons (carried out principally or exclusively by the selling State), the training of local armed forces and can even establish services not immediately related to the service of military supply and assistance aimed at favouring the investments of supplier companies, or take advantage of the natural resources of the purchaser's territory on an entirely exclusive basis. The compensation, therefore, would also have the purpose of endorsing any further economic interests on the part of the seller towards the buyer, which has the opposed interest in reducing its debts towards the former. This, evidently, involves a considerable "distraction" of resources on the part of the purchasing State (normally, a developing country).

[171] Art. 1 common to the 4 Geneva Conventions, 12 August 1949, in the Final Record of the Diplomatic Conference of Geneva of 1949, Vol. I, Federal Political Department, Bern pp. 205-224; art. 1 (1) of the 1st Additional Protocol to the Geneva Conventions of 12 August 1949, relating to the protection of victims of international armed conflicts, 8 June 1977, Official Records of the Diplomatic Conference of the Armed Conflicts, Bern, Federal Department of Foreign Affairs, 1978. This approach has been confirmed by jurisprudence (International Court of Justice, Military Activities, para. 220) and practice (ICRC Statement on IHL criteria in Arms Trade Treaty, New York, 2010.

criticisms: For the doctrine, the main difficulty lies in the fact that the delivery process qualifies as an administrative activity, and therefore put in place by several people, who form a "chain of transfer."

If we consider that state administrations are organized hierarchically, the hypothesis proposed would be to configure the responsibility of the "chain" in the light of the joint criminal enterprise. An analogical reference to this institute, however, could give rise to a contrast with the ban on analog application. Therefore, not being able to resort to penal institutions by analogy, the need to decide on the question of individual responsibility incidentally in the judgment of state responsibility is revealed by the doctrine, but for the latter there would be no application of the test standard of the "beyond any reasonable doubt "typical of the criminal trial.

So what would be the correct criterion? The doctrine provides an interpretative solution, basing the characterization of the conduct conducted as attributable to the State as an apparatus. Indeed, it would be impossible to disregard the role of public official in the delivery of arms, and it would be equally impossible to disregard the classification of this subject acting within the bureaucratic-administrative structure of the State as a whole.

Therefore, it becomes easier to configure the responsibility of the State based on the reasons recognized by the doctrine, or because of the assistance of a State in the Commission of an international offense by another State, and therefore having as reference the requisites required by art. 16 of the draft of articles on the international responsibility of States, which mentions the "awareness, on the part of the assistant State, of the circumstances of the offense."[172]

So what would be the correct criterion? The doctrine provides an interpretative solution, basing the characterization of the conduct as attributable to the State. Indeed, it would be impossible to disregard the role of public official in the delivery of arms. It would be also equally impossible to disregard the classification of this subject acting within the bureaucratic-administrative structure of the State as a whole.

Therefore, it becomes easier to configure state responsibility based on reasons recognized by the doctrine, or because of the assistance of a State in the Commission of an international offense by another one, and therefore having as reference the requisites required by art. 16 of the draft of articles on the international responsibility of States, which

---

[172]A. BELLAL, S. CASEY-MASLEN-D. GIACCA, Implications of international law for a future arms trade treaty, op. cit.

mentions the "awareness, on the part of the assistant State, of the circumstances of the offense."[173]

Although we have previously insisted on the prevalence of the author's awareness with respect to the knowledge possessed by the same, the orientation under examination confirms the impossibility of applying the concept of awareness through recourse by analogy to state responsibility. In fact, the having awareness here assumes the meaning of "being aware," with the addition of an "intent" to assist in the Commission of the offense. This last requirement can generate further problems of interpretation and procedural nature. The proof of the end achieved through the transfer of armaments, even in view of a mere circumstance of exchange, could not coincide with the intent to commit international crimes, or international illicit actions such as aggression or unauthorized use of force. This is because, as explained above, the main purpose of the "trade" of arms for each State, to be presumed to be ab origine, is to avoid succumbing to a possible armed attack, therefore to defend itself. The burden of proof, according to doctrine, should be reversed in favor of the State due to a failure to foresee its fault within the discipline of responsibility.

"The very idea of "complicity" of an internationally wrongful act of another [State] necessarily presupposes an intent to collaborate in the Commission of an act of this kind and, hence, in the cases considered, knowledge of the specific purpose for which the State receiving certain supplies decides to use them. Without this condition, there can be no question of complicity."[174]

Ago, therefore, highlights the non-necessity of a specific dolus, when armaments are transferred to another State, but only the malice of its collaboration and the subsequent representation of the consequences that may derive from it, accompanied by the intent of trasfer.[175]

The proof of this knowledge can be provided in various ways: Through an ex post facto presumption, or subsequent to the Commission of the offense, or with one operates ex ante, such as the objective

---

[173]Para. ii).

[174] Seventh Report on State Responsibility by Mr. Roberto Ago-The internationally wrongful act of State, Source of International Responsibility, A/CN.4/307, in Yearbook of International Law Commission, 1978, vol. II, Part One, p. 58, §. 72.

[175]A. BELLAL, S. CASEY-MASLEN-D. GIACCA, Implications of international law for a future arms trade treaty, op. cit. pp. 21ss, states that, in the light of ICJ jurisprudence on the prevention of genocide, taking the formulation of a general rule "en connaissance de cause" of the Commission, even if only potential, of some international crime can raise some doubts.

knowledge of reports of verification of serious violations of law international humanitarian or human rights, or even through mere factual circumstances.

This reasoning can be done, according to part of the doctrine, also with reference to the Commission of the crime of genocide and to the relationship with the complicity in the same. Taking into consideration ICJ jurisprudence,[176] scholars argue that complicity in crime must result from a Commission or positive action, both for States and for other actors other than the State.[177] The doctrine also claims that the general obligation to prevent the Commission for the crime rests on the State. Therefore, it can be highlighted when the transfer is to be considered a material contribution.[178]

2.8. International criminal liability for crimes committed following arm transfers

However, as far as the individual responsibility is concerned, it should be pointed out that this is outlined when there are penal or administrative rules which punish the illicit transfer of armaments. Part of the doctrine believes that in international law there is still no provision for criminalizing these behaviours although it may be considered an illegal act, arms trafficking lacks of its own configuration as an international crime, and the choices of States to criminalize such conduct are well founded on the mere impulse of domestic politics.

In this regard, another part of the doctrine argues that such a gap would depend on the mere "exhortative" character of international norms, where the same "impose" on States an obligation to do, that is, to foresee, through domestic law, these behaviours as unlawful.[179] But this type of obligation, which also translates into an obligation of result for the States, is immediately considered applicable to individuals, since doctrine qualifies it as an obligation having a customary nature.[180] Indeed, "the

[176]Application of the Convention on genocide, op. cit., par. 432.

[177]A. BELLAL, S. CASEY-MASLEN-D. GIACCA, Implications of International Law for a Future Arms Trade Treaty, op. cit.

[178]A. BELLAL, S. CASEY-MASLEN-D. GIACCA, Implications of International Law for a Future Arms Trade Treaty, op. cit.

[179]Article 5 (b) of the 2001 Protocol cited above; art. 10, on the activity of brokering, and 11, on the distraction of transfers, of the treaty on the arms convention.

[180]On the possibility of applying a general international standard to individuals, see the Interlocutory Decision on the Applicable Law: Terrorism, Conspiracy, Homicide, Perpetration, Cumulative Charging, in the case of Ayyash et al., Special Tribunal for Lebanon, Chamber of Appeal, 16 February 2011, STL-11-01 / I, para. 145 et seq. In

criminal liability of individuals in relation to conduct contrary to the rules on arms transfers could be ascertained directly under international law. In particular, we refer to the possibility of sanctioning the activity of individuals (...) involved in arms transfers, in the event that the arms transferred are used to commit international crimes."[181]

Therefore, what can be relevant in domestic law is the possibility that individuals, held responsible for trafficking in arms with other States, are judged on the basis of the institution of complicity in the Commission of crimes (aiding and abetting), as such subjects: "Provides [to] another person (s) useful for committing the crime, therefore he becomes liable in criminal matters in that with his conduct he helps [no] or knowingly favors the material author of an international crime, although not necessarily sharing its intentions."[182]

---

particular, in the decision cited above, we note how the notion of terrorism applicable before the STL, and consequently its configuration as an international crime, derives above all from the customary nature of the phenomenon. In doctrine see: C. RAGNI, The contribution of Special Tribunal for Lebanon to the notion of terrorism: Judicial creativity or progressive development of international law, in N. BOSCHIERO, T. SCOVAZZI, C. PITEA, C. RAGNI, International courts and the development of international law. Essays in Honour of Tullio Treves, T.M.C. Asser Press-Springer, The Hague, 2013, pp. 671ss.

[181]The Guus Kouwenhoven case, as with other internal judicial events, will be taken into account later during the preparation of this work.

[182]The juridical formula is taken into consideration by a large part of international jurisprudence, including the judgment of 18 May 2012 of the Special Chamber for Sierra Leone in the Prosecutor v. Charles Taylor case, SCSL-03-01-T. Former president of Liberia, Charles Taylor was convicted of inciting and supporting the Commission of international crimes in Sierra Leone, through the supply of arms to the Rebel United Front (RUF) rebels. This appears to be the only ruling of an international court that directly takes into consideration the issue of aiding and abetting through the supply of armaments at the international level. The situation with regard to the Akayesu sentence issued by the Tribunal for Rwanda is different (ICTR-96-4, sentence of 2 September 1998, para. 533-37). In this case, there was the supply of armaments for the Commission of an international crime (specifically, genocide), but the transfer took place within the national territory. Furthermore, the Furundžija (ICTY, IT-9517 / 1.T, sentence of December 10, 1998, para. 249) sentence takes into account a different territory than the locus commissi delicti, or rather the one of carrying out the armed conflict, as the supply in itself it had occurred outside the space of the supplier or broker, but the final result of the transfer was however the facilitation in the Commission of international crimes. For further details see: M.J. KELLY, The parameters of vicarious corporate criminal liability for genocide under international law, in A. BYRNES, C. HAYASHI-MICHAELSEN, International law in the age of globalization, ed. Brill, The Hague, 2013. R. BEHRENS, J. HENNAM, Elements of genocide, ed. Routledge, Taylor & Francis, Glass House Book, New York, 2013, pp. 194ss. Y. BEIGBEDER, International Criminal Tribunals, op. cit., M.J. KELLY, The debate or genocide in Darfur, Sudan, op. cit., pp. 208ss. C. LINGAAS, Imagined identities: Defining the racial group in the crime of genocide, op. cit., pp. 82ss. D.S. BETTWY, The

As for the requirement of knowledge, which allows to impute state responsibility, so also for the imputability of complicity in international crimes, according to this orientation, a degree of knowledge would be required, understood as: "(...) The mere awareness of the subject who provides the assistance of the criminal purposes of the principal responsible and who with his actions assist him in the Commission of the crime."

According to this point of view, it would not only be necessary to achieve the object of incorporating information that allows the subject to set a mental framework, in which the Commission of international crimes is highly prefigurable. Individual criminal liability would further require that this information be processed by the aider, who, in turn, will have to come to an awareness of the probable Commission of the crime. This logical process is considered the minimum requirement for attributing assistance in the Commission.[183]

Even the reconstruction of psychological element lends itself to further criticism. The doctrine illustrates how in some cases the substantial effect was put forward,[184] which takes the form of a contribution that is essential for the Commission of the crime, facilitating or accentuating its effects.[185] In others, on the other hand, the requirement of intent was emphasized, establishing that it should be specifically oriented (specific

---

genocide Convention and unprotected groups: Is the scope of protection expanding under customary international law?, op. cit., pp. 102ss. S. MOUTHAAN, Sexual violence against men and international law. Criminalizing the unmentionable, in International Criminal Law Review, 13, 2013, pp. 668ss. P. KIRBY, How is rape a weapon of war?, Feminist international relations, modes of critical explanation and the study of wartime sexual violence, in European Journal of International Relations, 18, 2012. J.R. MCHENRY, The prosecution of rape under international law: Justice that is long overdue, in Vanderbilt Journal of Transnational Law, 35, 2002, pp. 1310ss. N. LAVIOLETTE, Commanding rape: Sexual violence, command responsibility and the prosecution of superiors by the international criminal Tribunals for the Former Yugoslavia and Rwanda, in The Canadian Yearbook of International Law, 36, 1998, pp. 94ss. J.A. WILLIAMSON, Some consideration on command responsibility and criminal liability, in International Review of the Red Cross, 90, 2008, pp. 306ss. D.A. NEBESAR, Gender-based violence as a weapon of war, in U.C. Davis Journal of International Law and Policy, 4, 1998, pp. 148ss. I. PICCOLO, The crime of rape in international criminal law, International Courts Association, 2013.

[183]See, for example, the Furundžija cases, para. 249; Prosecutor v. Blaškić, IT-95-14, 1.T, sentence of 3 March 2000, para. 286; Taylor, §§ 6904, 6947-6952.

[184]ICTY, The Prosecutor v. Furundžija, op. cit.

[185] A. LEANDRO, Arms transfer and complicity in war crimes, in F. POCAR, M. PEDRAZZI, M. FRULLI (eds.), War crimes and the conduct of hostilities, Edward Elgar Publishers, Cheltenham, Northampton, 2013, pp. 225ss, considers that this criterion reflects customary law, with particular reference to arms transfers.

direction) to commit international crimes, when there was geographical, material or other proximity between the activities of the supplier and those of Commission of crimes.[186]

2.9. Criminalization of illicit brokering and deviation of the arms load (diversion)

As seen above, arms transfers would take place, internationally, even by individuals, who would act as intermediaries between supplier and receiving party. This brokerage, in the common opinion, if not authorized by the selling State or the buyer, or even if totally prohibited by international standards, is considered illegal. The issue of illicit brokering more directly affects the ATT, where it establishes that States must adapt their internal regulations in order to adequately sanction those who provide an unauthorized intermediation service.

In doctrine, it is believed that this type of activity, connected with the main ones of transfer, is sustained in the provision of a service by individuals or juridical persons, such as companies of war production.[187] On this point, the 2007 Report of the UN Panel of Experts on Illicit Brokerage,[188] took place, explaining what functions should be performed through the brokering service, namely:-Seeking business opportunities between several parties; - put two or more parts in contact; -provide any kind of assistance possible to facilitate the conclusion of the agreement, or

[186]Prosecutor v. Perišić, IT-04-81, judgment of the Chamber of Appeal of February 28, 2013, § 36. This last configuration of the requirement contrasts well with the psychological element of the crime, understood as a single knowledge (Thus also in art. 25 (3) of the Statute of the International Criminal Court of 17 July 1998, in UN Treaty Series, vol. 2187, pp. 3). Unlike this perspective, the normative formula used by art. 6, § 3, of the Arm Convention Treaty, which can be used to define the mens rea of the physical subject acting in the transfer of arms, and configure its responsibility. For further details see: J. SUBOTIĆ, Legitimacy, scope, and conflicting claims on the ICTY: In the aftermath of Gotovina, Haradinaj and Perišić, in Journal of Human Rights, 13(2), 2014, pp. 172ss. M. OSTOJIC, Between justice and stability: The politics of war crimes prosecutions, Ashgate Publishing, Farnham, 2014. D.F. ORENTLICHER, Some kind of justice, the ICTY's impact in Bosnia and Serbia, op. cit., J. GOW, R. KERR, Z. PAJIC, Prosecuting war crimes, lessons and legacies of the International Criminal Tribunal for the Former Yugoslavia, ed. Routledge, Abington & New York, 2014.

[187]B. WOOD, International initiatives to prevent illicit brokering of arms and related materials, in Disarmament Forum, 2009, n. 3, pp. 5-16. E. KEPPLER, Preventing human rights abuses by regulating arms brokers: The US. Brokering amendment to the arms export control act, in Berkeley Journal of International Law, 19 (2), 2001, pp. 381-411, 386ss.

[188]Report of the Group of Governmental Expert on Illicit Brokering in Arms Transfers, 30 August 2007, A/62/16, § 9.

assist the parties in the bargaining, preparation of meeting places, means to facilitate exchanges and related services; - assist the parties in the steps related to the preparation of the fundamental documentation (including end-user certificates, including falsified ones) and in the execution of the payment; - Finally, prepare a service for the supply or sale of weapons to third parties.

Another form of brokering can be identified, according to the panel's explanation, among those after-sales assistance activities, such as the preparation of a training service for the use of weapons, supply of spare parts, or even advice on the possibility of putting in practice, an offset agreement, in order to reduce costs or amortize them in subsequent periods.[189]

The Report also takes into account the nationality of the broker and the illicit nature of the activity performed. With reference to the first point, the broker can be of the nationality of one of the contracting parties, or it can be a third party, and the activity that it provides can be provided in one of these three States, while is not certain that the transfer of arms it takes place in the State of nationality or in the contracting one, as also is not clear if the broker assumes, albeit for a limited period of time, the title of ownership of the arms transferred.[190] The character of illegality, on the other hand, according to the Panel, derives from that of qualification that a State gives of such activity through its own regulations, both as regards the activities as a whole and taken individually.[191]

This broad consideration of what the activities are, and the various events they can take on, is identified, on one side of the doctrine, as a systematic approach to the world of arms supply, where the supply and transfer chain could take unknowable paths, or outside the regulatory framework that has been established, thus facilitating the spread of illicit practices in the sale of weapons

The indication of the Panel on what are the relevant activities for the brokering would not seem to have been fully regulated, according to a large part of the doctrine, within the ATT. In fact, art. 10 states that States must adapt their internal regulations, based on the obligations of universal or regional international law, in order to adequately regulate and take various types of measures (both criminal and administrative) to counter

[189]Report of the Group of Governmental Expert on Illicit Brokering in Arms Transfers, op. cit., par. 10.
[190]Report of the Group of Governmental Expert on Illicit Brokering in Arms Transfers, op. cit., par. 11.
[191]Report of the Group of Governmental Expert on Illicit Brokering in Arms Transfers, op. cit., par. 13.

the phenomenon of illegitimacy brokering. This seemed to be a step backwards from what had been established in a soft law instrument, such as the Program of Action against the proliferation of SALW.

Otherwise, a minority of the doctrine believes that, despite the lack of a prohibition expressed in the Treaty, the common opinion has spread that regulate and control the intermediation activity, allowing it only by subjects or bodies that have adequate authorizations, it would have the purpose to prevent that the weapons end up to people different from those indicated in the certificates of final user, and that the use for purposes different from those indicated is prevented.

Transfer activities may also be subject to a deviation from the set route, which may be classified as lawful or illegal, depending on the provisions contained in national or international regulations. This could happen in cases where there are no effective controls, which can be applied to end-user certificates, and which can also be ignored, or even not released, and thus facilitate arms trafficking. The problem of deviation (or diversion) is therefore relative to the inadequacy of controls.

The prevailing orientation highlights two types of diversion: The unauthorized deviation of arms loads (specifically SALW) that are sold lawfully, due to the lack of effective controls at the exit or entry of States, and that they are even less effective during the journey made by the weapons, or the deviation that would occur due to the lack of adequate controls by the companies or those that deal with the production and sale of arms on behalf of States.

For scholars, diversion can take place at any stage of the transfer, including the phase following the arrival at the destination of the load and the screening of the regular documentation possessed for transport. It can also take the form of a report of disappearance or theft of the load, tending to associate this act with criminal complicity of the company. More often it can take the form of a diversion accomplished through the re-exportation of the cargo, which can be performed in cases where no specific clause has been provided in the exchange agreement, or when there is no provision of domestic law that prohibits it, or finally when the coordination between the various national authorities in charge of controls acts ineffectively, making these controls tamquam non essent.

Government and public law subjects may also be involved in the diversion of the load. In particular, according to statistical reconstructions, reported by the doctrine, is above all the military and state defense branches that commit such an offense, given the availability to them of both the load of armaments, and the certificates of use of the same, and finally due to the possible configuration of corruption phenomena to which they can adhere.

A significant example of the importance of diversion in international law is found in relation to the deviations of planes (and therefore of the related cargo).

Aircraft hijacking is described by the Institute of International Law as "acts of seizure or an exercise of control of aircraft in flight." If such types of conduct were to be carried out, the doctrine considers it necessary that the States, in whose jurisdiction the perpetrator of the crime is located,[192] take action to pursue the same, without prejudice to the possibility of proceeding with the extradition.[193] To this is added the specific obligation of States to assist with any means possible the aircraft diverted into the territory of the same, subject to the consent of the owner and the flag State,[194] as well as the due diligence obligations regarding the preparation of effective controls to land.

By applying these considerations to the loads of armaments,[195] is possible to find the typical conduct that authoritative doctrine defines as "skyhijacking," from which the definitions of "hijacking" derive for "profit" and "sky bandits."[196]

According to scholars, this would take place because of the end manifested during this type of activity, or the hijacking of the aircraft, as well as the seizure of the load of weapons, presumably takes place in order to take possession of a "sensitive" commodity, to profit from it directly (through its sale) or indirectly (by perpetrating various types of criminal offenses).[197]

Even with reference to the case of diversion, the doctrine strongly criticizes the choice made by art. 9, ATT would have granted ample discretion to States both in deciding which activities should be considered as deviation of the load of arms, and in providing the most suitable means to foresee the illegality of such conduct, with the risk of nullifying the objective set by the treaty.

---

[192]Convention on International Civil Aviation, firmed in Chicago on 7 December 1944, art. 1 et seq.

[193]Resolution IV/1971, op. cit., par. I.

[194]Resolution IV/1971, op. cit., par. II-2.

[195]E. MCWHINNEY, The illegal diversion of aircraft and international law, Sijthoff, Leiden, 1975, pp. 10.

[196]E. MCWHINNEY, The illegal diversion of aircraft and international law, op. cit., pp. 11.

[197]E. MCWHINNEY, The illegal diversion of aircraft and international law, op. cit., pp. 1-2.

2.10. Tools for compliance with the required obligations

A last, but fundamental, reference must be made to the control mechanisms present in the context of international discipline of arms control, in particular drawing on general ideas from the observations on existing compliance mechanisms.

This paragraph will aim to illustrate first of all the meaning of constraint set by most of the arms control agreements, and in particular we analyze the legal influence of political value of these agreements. Later, any observance resulting from the provisional application of the agreements will be considered. Finally, the analysis will focus on the exposition of the main control and fulfilment mechanisms of the treaties.

2.11. Political significance of arms control agreements

To "agreements" establishing a control on the proliferation of weapons is recognized the value of international agreement.[198] Their ability to bind the signatory States, however, does not depend on the nature or value, but on the value that is attributed to this type of agreement. Most of the doctrine underlines, in this regard, how there is a general political will to stipulate, but also is recognized the discipline of arms control based on principles of international law, such as the prohibition of armed aggression and respect for international peace,[199] as set out in the UN Charter.[200]

In light of these rules, the doctrine emphasizes the willingness of States to enter into such agreements in order to drastically or greatly reduce their armaments, or limit their acquisitions, and thus protect international peace and security. The manner in which these agreements are stipulated is identified in political negotiations that lead to the

[198]C. AHLSTRÖM, The status of multilateral export control regimes: An examination of legal and non-legal agreements in international cooperation, Iustus Forlag, Uppsala, 1999. G. DEN DEKKER, The law of arms control. International supervision and enforcement, Martinus Nijhoff Publishers, Dordrecht, 2001, pp. 50ss.

[199]Art. 2 (4) of the Charter, to which is added the principle of equalization of States in the international community and the prohibition of interference in internal affairs, enucleated in art. 2 (1).

[200]G. DEN DEKKER, The law of arms control. International supervision and enforcement, op. cit., pp. 18-19.

conclusion of agreements.[201] Moreover, the doctrine would support the belief perceived by the States of a discipline of arms control as functional and instrumental to the pursuit of certain international political aims, or "to achieve the objective of improved security and, through that, to reduce the chance of war."[202]

Furthermore, part of the doctrine has subsequently been questioned about the opportunity that States have to stipulate non-binding agreements on armaments. In this sense, we highlight three characteristics, which are found in most agreements of this type.

The first would be found in the flexibility of these types of agreements, by virtue of the changing nature of certain situations that must be regulated and the need to have an instrument adaptable to the situation that arises. Moreover, the need to have a flexible agreement would also be identified in the possibility of renegotiating the terms of the agreement at a later time, thus avoiding the rigidity typical of most binding agreements of international law.[203]

The second characteristic would be identified in the rapidity of stipulating these types of agreements, or a State would be more inclined to conclude them where is not necessary to follow any solemn procedure.[204] This, however, is also considered in the light of domestic law, which differs from State to State in the regulation of transposition and adaptation methods to these types of agreements.[205]

The third, finally, would be identified in the confidentiality that is generated by agreements of this type, or the need not to make the results of transparent, at least internally, negotiations in order to avoid the intervention of the legislative power, which could, in some cases, deciding to authorize parliamentary ratification of the agreement just signed.[206]

---

[201]G. DEN DEKKER, The law of arms control. International supervision and enforcement, op. cit., pp. 22. It is commonly accepted that there is not a substantial distinction between the various types of agreements, ending up also considering the minutes of negotiations that have been validly signed as binding (International Court of Justice, Maritime Delimitation and Territorial Questions, Qatar v. Bahrain, judgment on jurisdiction and admissibility of 1st July 1994, in I.C.J. Reports, 1994, pp. 122ss).

[202]G. DEN DEKKER, The law of arms control. International supervision and enforcement, op. cit., pp. 23.

[203]C. AHLSTRÖM, The law of arms control. international supervision and enforcement, op. cit.

[204]C. AHLSTRÖM, The law of arms control. International supervision and enforcement, op. cit., pp. 68-69.

[205]In this sense see: art. 26 VCLT.

[206]C. AHLSTRÖM, The law of arms control. International supervision and enforcement, op. cit., p. 71.

Political significance can also be deduced from the classification of arms control agreements. In particular, part of the doctrine holds that a greater distinction should be made between treaties for which there has been a voluntary entry or accession by States and those having a “coercive” nature, such as ceasefire agreements or peace treaties. With specific reference to the first category, the types of agreement are identified according to general models, that is distinguishing between bilateral treaties,[207] multilateral agreements and accessory documents or annexes to treaties. As regards conventional arms, the treaties open to regional distribution are important, which, according to the common opinion, would have a typical structure of multilateral treaties for arms control. A short text of a treaty nature, a series of attachments and related documents, in addition to the possibility of issuing derivative documents, for example where an institutional set-up has been provided.[208]

Most of these agreements, however, would produce, according to the doctrine, a series of documents with merely programmatic value, which can easily address the future behaviour of States. The political nature of these agreements, therefore, would favor the accession of States to programs set up for arms control.

But in addition to a more direct function control, these instruments have a fundamental role in directing future negotiations of agreements for control, as well as establishing a basic procedure for negotiation.[209] Furthermore, there are also those who maintain that these agreements would enjoy more the application of the principle of good faith, due to the future expectations of international community for the observance of the discipline of this sensitive subject.[210]

2.12. Provisional application of arms control agreements

An argument of little debated in the doctrine, but that has a fundamental function, can be found in the provisional application, established with specific clauses, of agreements that regulate aspects

---

[207]. In which we understand above all the agreements for the limitation of nuclear proliferation, such as the SALT I and II agreements and the START Agreement.

[208]As the periodic meeting of a conference of the States Parties, or as informal meetings for regulatory needs (eg, the Wassenaar Agreement).

[209]G. DEN DEKKER, The law of arms control. International supervision and enforcement, op. cit., p. 60.

[210]C. AHLSTRÖM, The law of arms control. International supervision and enforcement, op. cit., pp. 272-274.

relating to the control of weapons.

This need would seem to have arisen, as doctrine emphasizes, in the 1990s, when most of the disarmament agreements were stipulated. The need that has been found at the base of this progressive discipline, and consequent provisional application, is the urgency of application and fulfilment of such agreements, where is believed that the discipline in question must find an immediate application before the attainment of the number of ratifications needed.[211]

The possibility of having recourse to these clauses is found in the connection that one has between the necessary urgent application and the weightings that must be had internally, or rather one must take into account above all the requirements of domestic law, the adjustment in progress, the costs that must be addressed, as well as the ratification authorization processes that must be completed in order for the agreement to be applied in the ratifying States.[212] "Political" considerations are also extended to the possibility of including certain States that have a particular technological and military advancement in the field governed by the single treaty. This, therefore, would be read, by the States and by doctrine, as a conditional requirement, to which the ratification of the treaty will be subject.[213]

The provisional application would, in fact, also have legal implications of no small importance. In fact, given the political significance of many agreements, as seen above, the parties will take into consideration the fact that every type of act, carried out by a single contractor and that is in contrast with the object and purpose of the agreement, can produce negative future consequences for other parts. For this reason, in the interim period between the opening to the signing and the entry into force of the agreement, the provisional application would also have the function of avoiding any conflicting attitude, by virtue of the application of the principle of good faith in international agreements.[214] And this principle would also be addressed by the minority doctrine as a more stringent obligation in the field of disarmament and arms control, given the sensitivity of subjects dealt with and the close connection with

---

[211]A. MICHIE, The law of arms control. International supervision and enforcement, in Journal of Conflict and Security Law, 10 (3), 2005, pp. 345-377.

[212]A. MICHIE, The law of arms control. International supervision and enforcement, op. cit., pp. 348.

[213]A. MICHIE, The law of arms control. International supervision and enforcement, op. cit., pp. 349.

[214]Art. 18 VCLT. A. MICHIE, The law of arms control. International supervision and enforcement, op. cit., pp. 352ss.

the preservation of international peace and security.[215]

2.13. Compliance with agreements and mechanisms

Since most of the arms control agreements are characterized by a lack of constraint, are there possibilities to enforce the obligations set by these agreements or understood in full?

A large part of internationalist doctrine tried to answer this question, when it approached with a critical evaluation of these treaties. A prevalent orientation has tended to affirm that these agreements have established a sort of "international cooperation law," where it was necessary to regulate, through multilateral channels, common problems of the international community, and in particular the threat of a nuclear explosion or the proliferation of conflicts worldwide.[216] In this regard, this orientation underlines how the compliance of a State with the obligations provided by the treaty to which it is a part is not only an abstract aspect and of, so to speak, "moral" nature in international law, but is even in the interest of parts of the treaty. Therefore, it would be the basis of the establishment of compliance mechanisms, or fulfilment, of the treaties concerning arms control.[217]

On the other hand, it has been argued that ensuring compliance and adaptation to this type of agreement would not be possible, given the overriding political nature of the constraint assumed and the possibility for states not to feel bound by such provisions.[218]

---

[215] International Law Association, Final Report of the Committee-International And National Legal Regulation for Arms Control and Disarmament, Berlin, 2004, para. 5. This would seem true at least in the case of nuclear weapons and mass destruction in general. Such an obligation would not be present or verifiable in the context of conventional arms, where the Report itself (§ 11 et seq.) mentions only the exhortative character of the instruments of international law and the role of implementation and consultancy that NGOs carry out in this field.

[216]G. ULFSTEIN, T. MARAHAUN, A. ZIMMERMANN (ed. by), Making treaties work. Human rights, environment, arms control, Oxford University Press, Oxford, 2007, pp. 3ss.

[217]C. AHLSTRÖM, The law of arms control. International supervision and enforcement, op. cit., pp. 276ss. G. DEN DEKKER, The law of arms control. International supervision and enforcement, op. cit., p. 88ss.

[218]R. L. WILLIAMSON, Jr., Is international law relevant to arms control? Hard law, soft law and non-law in multilateral arms control: Some compliance hypotheses, in Chicago Journal of International Law, 4, 2003, pp. 59ss. W. SANDHOLTZ, C.A. WHYTOCK, Research handbook on the politics of international law, Edward Elgar Publishers, Cheltenham, 2017. S. HARAMOTO, H. SAKAI, A. SHIBATA, L'être situè. Effectiveness and purposes of international law. Essays in honour of Professor Ryuichi Ida, ed. Brill,

More specifically with regard to individual mechanisms, the prevailing doctrine identifies three main instruments for compliance, namely the procedures for the peaceful resolution of disputes, the infringement and for the implementation procedures, fulfilment and verification of the obligations of the treaty.[219]

With regard to the first instrument, its diffusion was considered central at the beginning of the 20th century, when the Hague Conferences established the principle of peaceful resolution of international disputes to replace the use of force in international relations.[220] Generally, few recent examples of clauses for the resolution of disputes concerning the interpretation or application of an arms control treaty are known, and the doctrine tends to evaluate this lack of provision as a repulsion for a "repressive" instrument of States' behaviour, who continue to feel unconstrained in treaties of this type. Recently, however, a minority orientation of the doctrine would have supported the need to resolve disputes on the matter through the institution of arbitration.

Preferable, according to the doctrine, would seem the instruments of the second type, or fulfilment clauses, between which the procedures for the application and observance of the treaty are found. For the first type, the prevailing doctrine holds that such predictions cannot be lacking in arms control treaties, since they would have the function of preventing the dispute from degenerating into harmful effects for the application of the treaty, even compromising future compliance with the agreement.[221]

These would also appear to be accompanied by tools of the third

---

Bruxelles, 2015, pp. 223ss. M.J. BOWMAN, D. KRITSIOTIS, Conceptual and contextual perspectives on the modern law of treaties, op. cit., pp. 165ss.

[219] T. MARAHAUN, Dispute resolution, compliance control and enforcement of international arms control law, in G. ULFSTEIN T. MARAHAUN, A. ZIMMERMANN (ed. by), Making treaties work. Human rights, environment, arms control, op. cit., pp. 243ss.

[220] J. G. MERRILS, International dispute settlement, Cambridge University Press, Cambridge, V ed., 2011, pp. 4ss.

[221] G. MARAHAUN, T. MARAHAUN, A. ZIMMERMANN (ed. by), Making treaties work. Human rights, environment, arms control, Oxford University Press, Oxford, 2007, pp. 267ss. G. DEN DEKKER, The law of arms control. International supervision and enforcement, op. cit., pp. 110ss. From a historical point of view, however, the first tendency towards disarmament was to attribute a specific power to the Security Council, due to the sensitivity of the matter treated and the possible assimilation as a threat to national peace and security. This tendency would seem to have been arrested on the basis both of the impossibility of adopting sanctioning measures, given the Council's blockade during the Cold War, and on the basis of a clear desire by the States to create specific and self-managed control systems. On the self-sufficiency of international regulatory regimes, see the Report of the Study Group of the International Law Commission on the fragmentation of international law, A/CN.4/L.682, of 13 April 2006.

type, namely the procedures for verification, inspections and controls, typically found in treaties for the control of weapons of mass destruction,[222] whose function would be to make transparent situations considered illegal, and therefore would have the possibility to highlight, through the reconstruction and analysis of facts, the unlawfulness of which one complains.

As regards the distinction between this type of mechanism (very similar to inquiry or consultation) and the judicial resolution of disputes, the doctrine is not uniform in laying down a precise distinctive sign between the two. This is mainly due to what should be considered a controversy in the area of arms control. In this sense, the doctrine would not be uniform in considering what mechanism is necessary to apply to a given situation. A first orientation maintains that the resolution of disputes is experienced when an interpretation relating to the fulfilment of the obligations of a treaty cannot be achieved through the sole experiment of a verification, which, as just illustrated, would be limited to an assessment of the disputed facts , and not even to provide a decisive interpretation.[223]

According to a minority orientation,[224] in the arms control treaties it would also be possible to carry out countermeasures, which do not have

---

[222]An example can be found in the art. 9 of the Convention on the prohibition of the development, production, storage and use of chemical weapons and on their destruction, signed in Paris on 13 January 1993, in UN Treaty Series, 1997. vol. 1975, n. 33757, pp. 470ss.

[223]G. DEN DEKKER, The law of arms control. International supervision and enforcement, op. cit., p. 108. P. TRIMBLE, Beyond verification: The next step in arms control, in Harvard Law Review, 102, 1989, pp. 885-912, which clearly explains the difference between the instrument of the investigation and the other means of resolving disputes, arguing that the former would have a mere ascertainment function, becoming very often instrumental to the latter where there is uncertainty about a mere fact to be ascertained for the purpose of a negotiation, or when it is necessary to resolve a dispute judicially.

[224]Agreements of this type are considered by the doctrine as self-sufficient regimes, where institutional systems for control are envisaged, and consequently provisions are provided for the resolution of any disputes (for example, the cited Chemical Weapons Convention, or the Convention on non-compliance, proliferation of nuclear weapons in 1978, which established the International Atomic Energy Agency, a body responsible for verifying the fulfilment of the States that develop nuclear energy programs). It is not infrequent, however, that, following the non-fulfilment of the provisions, the States decide the application of economic countermeasures, or even resort to the collective security system provided for by the UN Charter. Given the potential threat to international peace and security that these types of weapons hold, the Security Council would be entitled to intervene. This is the case of Iran, subjected to penalties for failure to comply with the IAEA obligations between 2002 and 2015. As regards the area of conventional arms, such measures would not be envisaged, therefore having to support the sole possibility of resolution peaceful settlement of disputes between States Parties.

the nature of retaliation, such as also withdrawing, denouncing or ending the treaty, where “extraordinary events”[225]occur that prevent the continuation of the contractual relationship and therefore determine the termination of the execution of the treaty. Where the treaty is multilateral, the doctrine still supports the possibility of suspending the agreement for a serious violation of the treaty, based on art. 60 (2) (c) of the Vienna Convention, which would be applied beyond its express formulation, as it was considered a general rule.[226]

Finally, it is generally considered that the sanctions of the UN Security Council are admissible, where the compliance mechanisms are not effective and there are no further remedies for violations. The Council, therefore, will have a power of intervention, when the situation generated may be likely to threaten international peace, pursuant to art. 39 of the UN Charter.[227] This power, in fact, would seem to be considered residual, since the States themselves regulate the matter and expressly provide for compliance mechanisms.[228]

2.14. Concluding remarks

The complicity of States in acts carried out by international organizations within the framework of the regulatory activities is based on the assumption that a third-degree source of the order is likely to integrate an illicit fact. In our opinion, this hypothesis can be seen in the decisions taken by the functional bodies that are not only binding on their recipients but also have the characteristic of imposing specific conduct obligations without leaving any margin of discretion with regard to their execution. Determining whether or not an obligation to conduct has been violated appears to be rather simple. A violation will occur whenever the conduct known to you is active or omitted will not comply with the one imposed by the law to nothing, detecting the effects of misconduct.

We have seen how the examination of these profiles is conditioned by the difficulty of separating the conduct of the organ from that of

---

[225]This expression is reported in art. IV of the Limited Test Ban of 1963, and is placed in relation to the supreme interests of the State that intends to withdraw, denounce or terminate the treaty.

[226] T. MARAHAUN, Dispute resolution, compliance control and enforcement of international arms control law, in G. ULFSTEIN, T. MARAHAUN, A. ZIMMERMANN (ed. by), Making treaties work. Human rights, environment, arms control, op. cit., pp. 246ss.

[227] A. HENRIKSEN, International law, op. cit.,

[228] T. MARAHAUN, Dispute resolution, compliance control and enforcement of international arms control law, in G. ULFSTEIN, T. MARAHAUN, A. ZIMMERMANN (ed. by), Making treaties work. Human rights, environment, arms control, op. cit., pp. 243ss.

individual states that compose it. In this regard, ICJ's jurisprudence seems to dispel any doubt, pointing out that the conduct of individual members is susceptible of a separate legal assessment with respect to that relating to the normative act that they combine to determine. In particular, the responsibility of these States for the vote expressed within a given body can be based on at least two different legal titles. In fact it can be determined by the violation of a primary obligation that binds the individual member, as shown by the FYROM v. Greece case of 2001. The second legal title is relevant in our investigation, namely the hypothesis in which the vote expressed by the Member State integrates an accessory fact based on art. 58 DARIO. We have tried to highlight how this specific case of complicity is conditioned on the one hand by the reported need to distinguish the will and activity of the State from that of the body of which the latter is a part and on the other by the need to guarantee the ordinary functioning of the organization as an independent subject by Member States.

The solution formulated by ILC in art. 58 DARIO. In our opinion, the equilibrium point between the aforementioned autonomy of the functional entities and the need for the regulation to sanction the social disvalue represented by the conduct of Member States of these bodies is configured. The norm on complicity is therefore declined here in partially different terms from those reconstructed in chapter II of this work. The fundamental difference lies in the causal link between the accessory fact, constituted by members vote and the main fact constituted by the act approved by the organization and attributable to it. This requirement appears to be in terms of conditionality in the sense that is considered satisfied if the main act would not have taken place without the intervention of the accessory conduct. In assessing the factual circumstances, the actual contribution of the Member State is relevant, which can also be measured in light of the weight assigned to it by the internal law of the principal responsible organization.

As a paradigm of this hypothesis, the role played within the UN Security Council by the permanent members who, based on UN rules, are able to influence the adoption or not the decisions of the board on the basis of Chapter VII of the UN Charter.

CHAPTER 3

Complicity of States in the framework of operational activities of international organizations

3.1. Introduction

International organizations also carry out functions of an operational nature with respect to which is necessary to evaluate the possible involvement of Member States. At the outset it must be reiterated that this kind of activity is susceptible by its nature to generate illicit acts with respect to which the assistance of various international subjects and third States can be configured. This last hypothesis, even if fully theoretical, appears to be of little relevance to the practical point of view, if only with regard to the cases that we will examine in this chapter.

The preliminary aspect that must be evaluated is that of the imputation of material conduct, having regard to both the criteria elaborated by ILC and international practice that is abundant and widely explored in international doctrine. We will have regard only to the organized operational activities managed and controlled from the political and strategic point of UN view. We will use the peace-keeping operations carried out by this organization as a reference model. Excludes from our analysis any activity that is already in principle due to the States possibly involved. We refer to military missions authorized by the UN. The behaviours carried out in this context are in principle attributable to the State or States involved, except for verifying the existence of suitable elements for the attribution of the international delegating responsibility.

We will then proceed to examine the thesis according to which under certain conditions the unlawful act committed during the operations in question should be simultaneously imputed to the organization and supplier State of the contingent who physically committed the conduct.

Finally we will try to illustrate the conditions under which state responsibility that contribute to the mission can be configured as complicity.

3.2. Peace-keeping operations. The reference model

Peace-keeping operations represent the privileged instrument to which the functional bodies make recourse in order to deal with situations likely to endanger international peace and security. The doctrine has long debated about the juridical foundation of such an operation having particular regard to the UN that, due to the impossibility of making the collective security system governed by VII Chapter of the UN Charter have established peacekeeping missions, the whose normative basis does not coincide notoriously with the speech of articles 43 and following of the Statute.[229] It should be noted that the operations in question have undergone considerable development in the organization's practice, giving rise to a model that was substantially used also by regional organizations[230] such as EU. The evaluations carried out in this chapter can therefore be considered in principle applicable to peacekeeping operations carried out by these organizations.

For the purposes of this investigation is appropriate to examine the imputation profiles of the illegal conduct that may be implemented in the context of such operations. To this end, it is necessary to trace the characteristics that the military contingents are made available to the organization concerned by some Member States following a complex legal transaction.[231] The practice developed within the UN provides useful elements for the reconstruction of characteristics just mentioned. First of all, the decision to set up a peacekeeping operation is taken by the Security Council, which delegates to the general secretary the task of mechanism of stand by arrangements, the UN Member States provide to train part of their armed forces according to possible peacekeeping operations.[232] This

---

229 M. BOTHE, Peace-keeping, in B. SIMMA, The charter of the United Nations. A commentary, Oxford University Press, Oxford, 2002, pp. 648ss.

230 M. BOTHE, Peacekeeping forces, in Max Planck Encyclopedia of Public International Law, 2016, par. 51.

231 M. BOTHE, Peace-keeping, in B. SIMMA, The charter of the United Nations. A commentary, op. cit., pp. 260ss.

232 P. KLEIN, Le panel consultatif des droits de l'homme (human rights advisory panel) de la MINUK: une étape dans le processus de responsabilization des Nations Unies?, in M. KOHEN, R. KOLB, D.L. TEHINDRAZENARIVELO, Perspectives du droit international au 21e siècle-Liber Amicorum Christian Dominicé, ed. Brill, Leiden/Boston, 2012, pp. 226ss. P. KLEIN, Panels, médiateurs et mécanismes informels de controle des activités des organizations internationales: entre accountability et responsibility, in Select Proceedings of the European Society of International Law, vol. 3, Oxford University Press, Oxford, 2010, pp. 228ss. P. BODEAU-LIVINEC, Les faux-semblants de la lex specialis: l'exemple

mechanism allows the Peace Operations Secretariat Department to schedule the availability of contributing States. These contingents are then placed under the command of the General Secretary through an agreement specifically entered between supplier State and UN. From the military point of view, the contingents thus constituted are placed under the operational control of a commander appointed by the General Secretariat who, accompanied by a military councilor, exercises the strategic direction of the peace force. The operational commander holds "full command and authority of the force" in the field and is always responsible for operations "for the performance of all functions assigned to the force by the UN and for the deployment and assignment of troops placed at the disposal of the force."[233] This contributes to forming a strongly centralized command structure, in which the supreme commander of the force translates the decisions taken by the Security Council and by the General Secretary into operational orders through a chain of command that it himself designates. For the entire period in which the mission takes place, each national contingent can be considered as part of the personnel placed under the UN authority.[234] The illegal conduct possibly put in place by these troops would in principle be attributable to the organization.

3.3. Liability for facts committed during peace-keeping operations in ILC and in practice prior to DARIO adoption

Examination of the practice relating to the various operations attributable to UN shows several cases in which this organization has taken on exclusive responsibility for unlawful conduct of the peacekeeping forces, but this occurred only on the basis of the assumption that it united in itself and the political control that the operational command of the mission,[235] i.e. elements that contribute to the indictment of any illegal

de la résolution 52/247 de l'assemblée générale des Nations unies sur les limitations temporelles et financières de la responsabilité de l'ONU, in Revue Belge de Droit International, 117, 2013, pp. 118ss.

[233]See the regulation of mission UNEF of 20 February 1957, UN Doc. ST/SGB/UNEF 1, art. 11: Identical provision in the regulation of ONUC of 15 July 1963 (UN Doc. ST/SGB/ONUC 1 art. 11) and of INFICYP of 25 April 1964 (UN Doc. ST/SGB/UNFICYP 1 art. 11).

[234]R.C.R. SIEKMANN, National contingents in United Nations peace-keeping forces, ed. Springer, Dordrecht, 1991, pp. 112ss. M. HIRSCH, The responsibility of international organizations toward third parties. Some basic principles, op. cit., pp. 66ss.

[235]M. HIRSCH, The responsibility of international organizations toward third parties. Some basic principles, op. cit., pp. 66ss. B.D. TITTEMORE, Belligerents in blue helmets:

behaviour, now shared by the majority doctrine[236] and established in practice, so much so as to be received by the project on the responsibility of international organizations definitively approved in 2011.

The picture briefly outlined so far must be completed by a further relief that appears to be decisive in examining the profiles of responsibility that are of interest for the purposes of this investigation. These are the well-known circumstances for which the national contingents who use the body for the entire period of the mission do not cease to be simultaneously the organs of the sending State. The dissenting opinion of judge Koretskly focused precisely on this fact in the ICJ advisory opinion on certain expenses of the UN concerning the financing of the mission in Congo in 1962. According to the judge: "Les forces armèes mises à la disposition du Conseil de Sècuritè demeureraient des forces armèes des membres de l'organization et ne deviendraient pas celle de l'organization" being at most able to assimilate to the armed forces of an alliance or a coalition and therefore to a common organ, "sans pour autant former une armèe distincte des forces armèes nationales."[237] In fact, although the members of such forefathers constitute in the indicated period "international personnel under the UN authority and subject to instructions of the commander through the command chain,"[238] each supplier State preserves important prerogatives on its own quota both on organizational and on a strictly

---

Applying international humanitarian law to United Nations peace operations, in Stanford Journal of International Law, 33, 1997, pp. 80ss. K.M. LARSEN, C.G. COOPER, G. NYSTUEN, Searching for a principle of humanity in international humanitarian law, Cambridge University Press, Cambridge, 2013. Y. DINSTEIN, War, aggression and self-defence, Cambridge University Press, Cambridge, 2017, pp. 184ss.

[236]J.P. RITTER, La protective diplomatique à l'egard d'une organization internationale, op. cit., pp. 442ss. B. AMRALLAH, The international responsibility of the United Nations for activities carried out by UN peacekeeping forces, op. cit., pp. 62ss. M. HIRSCH, The responsibility of international organizations toward third parties. Some basic principles, op. cit., pp. 65ss. P. KLEIN, La responsabilitè des organizations internationales dans les ordres juridiques interne set droits de gens, op. cit., pp. 379-380. M. PEREZ-GONZALEZ, Les organizations internationales et le droit de la responsibilità, op. cit., pp. 83ss. C. PITSCHAS, Die Völkerrechtliche Verantwortlichkeit der Europäischen Gemeinschaften und ihren Mitgliedstaaten, Duncker & Humblot, Berlin, pp. 51ss. A. BERGMANN, Zur Souveränitatskonzeption des Europäischen Gerichtshofs: Die Autonomie des Unionsrechts und des Völkerrecht, Mohr Siebeck, Tübingen, 2018.

[237]Certain expenses of the UN (article 17, par. 2 of the Charter), advisory opinion of 20 July 1962, in ICJ Reports, 1962, p. 151ss. Dissenting opinion of judge koretsly, p. 257. A. ZIMMERMANN, C.J. TAMS, K. OELLERS-FRAHAM, The Statute of the International Court of Justice. A commentary, op. cit.

[238]For example art. 6 of the regulation of UNFICYP.

disciplinary level such as for example the military police functions,[239] the remuneration and career advancement of the units employed and above all the exercise of career jurisdiction of the units employed and the exercise of criminal jurisdiction.[240] This is an element of no minor importance, according to which Gaja sustained: "The question of attribution is not clear-cut" although peacekeeping forces are normally classified as subsidiary UN organs.[241] The relationship between organization and State that provides the contingent falls within the legal category of the loan of organs that ILC had already outlined in the codification of state responsibility. In his third report, Ago pointed out that in the hypotheses in which a body acts simultaneously as a state organ of belonging and a body performing functions on behalf of the beneficiary, it will be necessary to ascertain "for the compte de qui et sous l' authorite de qui l'on aura commis une action ou omission dèterminèe."[242] What is relevant, therefore, is the actual authority under which the harmful conduct took place, given that looking at such a criterion of imputation constitutes a corollary of the more general principle of effectiveness,[243] which informs itself of the same structural characteristics of international order. Relying on the practice concerning the loan of state military bodies to international organizations, the rapporteur saw the decisive criterion for the correct configuration of responsibility in the specific circumstances in which the unlawful conduct occurred. The responsibility of the beneficiary is integrated in other terms if the harmful conduct has taken place under its direct control with the important clarification that the principle in question can be deduced in unequivocal terms from international practice and that in any case, "il s'emposerait dèjà sur la base même de la logique juridique, de rèflecivitè et de l'èquitè."[244]

---

[239]For example art. 13 of the regulation of INFICYP.

[240]Art. 34 of UNEF Regulation, art. 33 of ONUC Regulation and art. 29 of UNFICYP Regulation.

[241]G. GAJA, Second report on responsibility of international organizations, UN Doc. A/CN.4/541, p. 11, par. 35.

[242]R. AGO, Troisième rapport sur la responsabilitè des États. Le fait internationalement illicite de l'État, source de responsabilitè internationale, op. cit., p. 285, par. 201.

[243]R. AGO, Troisième rapport sur la responsabilitè des États. Le fait internationalement illicite de l'État, source de responsabilitè internationale, op. cit., p. 285, par. 206.

[244]R. AGO, Troisième rapport sur la responsabilitè des États. Le fait internationalement illicite de l'État, source de responsabilitè internationale, op. cit., p. 273-274, par. 214. The rapporteur proposed a provision, art. 9 section: Attribution à l'Etat, sujet de droit international, des faits d'organes mis à sa disposition par un autre Etat ou par une organization internationale, in the base of "est de même considèrè comme un fait de l'Etat sur le plan d droit international le comportement d'une personne ou d'un groupe de

And indeed international practice seems to testify precisely in favour of the criterion of effectiveness (in the utmost ut res magis valeat quam pereat),[245] briefly outlined. As is known, the first case in which the question of responsibility for the conduct of state bodies placed at the disposal of the UN is raised is that relating to certain offenses occurring within the ONUC mission in the Congo framework. After an initial uncertainty the UN assumed responsibility for some conduct detrimental to the rights of private parties established in December 1961 by the personnel of the multinational force.[246] With an exchange of notes on 20 February 1965, the UN General Secretariat and the Belgian Foreign Minister reached an agreement stating that the organization "ne se soustrairait pas à sa responsabilitè s'il ètait ètabli que des agents de l'ONU ont effectivement fait subir un prèjudice injutifiable à des innocents."[247]

Equally significant are the figures that can be obtained from the Nissan case, relating to claims for damages by a British citizen against the United Kingdom for the victims of the British troops integrated in the UNFICYP mission. The story originated from the occupation of a hotel in Cyprus owned by the applicant of the British contingent. As a result of some damage to the building, the appellant turned to the British Court for civil compensation. Although this was a claim for damages, the preliminary determinations of the judge regarding the immutability of the harmful conduct are reported here. In the first instance judge Stephen of

---

personnes qui ont la qualitè d'organes dans le cadre de l'ordre juridique d'un autre État ou d'une organization intrnatonale et qui ont ètè mis à sa disposition, à codition que ces organes relèvant effectivement de l'autoritè de l'État à la disposition duquel ils se trouvent et agissent selon des instructions èmanant de ce dernier (...)."

[245]According to the ICJ in opinion of 18 July 1950 on the Interpretation of Peace Treaties with Bulgaria, Hungary and Romania (second phase), I.C.J. Reports, 1950, p. 229, this principle "cannot justify the Court in attributing to the provisions (...) a meaning which (...) would be contrary to their letter and spirit (...)." A. ZIMMERMANN, C.J. TAMS, K. OELLERS-FRAHAM, The Statute of the International Court of Justice. A commentary, op. cit.

[246]In a first phase, the organization decided to pay the families of the victims a pretty sum without assuming any legal responsibility for the disputed facts. See in argument. F. SEYERSTED, United Nations forces in the law of peace and war, A.E. Sijthoff, Leyden, 1966, pp. 194ss. In a letter sent to the Belgian foreign minister the general secretariat stated that the UN would not escape: "A' sa responsabilitè morale s'il est ètablie que ces agents (...) ont effectivement fait subir un prèjudice ingiustifiable (…) des innocents." J. SALMON, Les accords Spaak-U Thant du 20 fèvrier 1965, in Annuaire Français de Droit International, 11, 1965, pp. 479ss. M. BOTHE, Le droit de la guerre et le Nations Unies à propos des incidents armès au Congo, in Etudes et travauz de l'Institut Univeritaire des Haute Etudes Internationales, 5, 1967, pp. 208ss.

[247]. J. SALMON, Les accords Spaak-U Thant du 20 fèvrier 1965, op. cit., pp. 496ss.

the Queen's Bench Division after examining the various instruments relating to the establishment of the mission and the chain of command of the same came to the conclusion that British troops "derived their authority to occupy the hotel no longer from Her Majesty but from the UN and occupied it as agents of the UN."[248] For these reasons the conduct at the origin of the appeal was not ascribable to the United Kingdom but at least in principle to the UN. The same orientation was followed at the appeal stage where Lord Denning pointed out that the English troops were at the time of the damaging conduct "under the UN command."[249] According to Lord Danckwerts: "The responsibility for their acts fall on the UN, and the acts of the troops were no longer those of the British Crown (...)."[250]

The House of Lords has overturned the reconstruction provided in the two degrees of judgment just mentioned. In the assumption that state sovereignty prevails in any case over the control exercised by the organization, it was to be considered ascribable to the United Kingdom and not to the UN.[251] In the opinion of Lord Morris of Borth-y-Gest even though they were subjected to the organization's urge: "The British forces continued therefore to the soldiers of Her Majesty" place that members of the multinational force "elsewhere subject to the exclusive jurisdiction of their respective national States in respect of any criminal offences committed by them in Cyprus."[252]

The orientation of the House of Lords has to a large extent depended on the opinion expressed by various members of the same for which the UN is not actually an autonomous institution, but rather an "instrument of collective policy" in the context of which "each member still retains its own sovereignty."[253] The ruling of the House of Lords is probably the only significant exception to the general orientation which, as stated, lays in the sense of the UN responsibility for offenses committed in the context of peacekeeping missions.[254] It has confirmation from

[248]Nissan v. Attorney General, Queen's Bench Division, in All England Law Reports, 1967, vol. 2, p. 220.
[249]Nissan v. Attorney General, Court of Appeal, in All England Law Reports, 1967, vol. 2, p. 1244.
[250]Nissan v. Attorney General, Court of Appeal, in All England Law Reports, 1967, vol. 2, p. 1247.
[251]Nissan v. Attorney General, House of Lords, in All England Law Reports, 1969, vol. 1, p. 647ss.
[252]Nissan v. Attorney General, House of Lords, in All England Law Reports, 1969, vol. 1, p. 646.
[253]Nissan v. Attorney General, House of Lords, op. cit., opinion of Lord Pearce, p. 647.
[254]M. WÄHLISCH, Peace making power-sharing and international law. Imperfect peace, Hart Publishing, Oxford, Oregon, Portland, 2019.

another case or invoked by the doctrine in support of the exclusive UN responsibility decided by the Oberlandesgerich of Vienna on 26 February 1979. The case originated from the damage suffered by a member of the Austrian contingent integrated in the UNDOF (United Nations Disengagement Observer Force) mission established by the UN in the Golan Heights in 1974 and still in operation.[255] More specifically, the appellant had suffered financial loss from another soldier who was also a member of the Austrian contingent and had brought an action for compensation against the State before the Vienna Court. The Court of first instance dismissed the appeal on the assumption that the decisive aspect for the imputation of the conduct was not the authority that under the general organizational profile controlled the mission but the one under which the organ acted at the time of production. of the damaging event.[256] In the appeal proceedings, the Oberlandesgericht of Vienna upheld the first instance sentence with substantially similar arguments. According to the appeal judge, the harmful conduct had occurred in a time frame in which the body that had put it in place was ascribable to the UN by not being able to qualify at all as an organ of the Austrian State.

Similar evaluations regarding the imputation to UN of illegal conduct under its effective control[257] can be deduced from the complex

---

[255]P. SANDS, P. KLEIN, Bowett's law of international institutions, ed., Sweet & Maxwell, 2009. J.E. SCHWARTZBERG, Transforming the UN system designs for a workable world, Brookings Institution Press, Tokyo, New York, Paris, 2016.

[256]See from the Superior Provincial Court of Vienna the case: N.K. v. Austria of 26 February 1979, in International Law Review, vol. 77, 1979, p. 470-472. For further details see: M. KANETAKE, The UN security Council and domestic actors: Distance in international law, ed. Routledge, London & New York, 2017.

[257]The concept of "effective control" is decisive for the purpose of attributing action to the organization also in another type of UN intervention in the field of peacekeeping and international security, or in the context of joint military operations a joint responsibility may arise, for example, in the UNAMID operation in Darfur case conducted jointly by UN and AU Resolution 1769 (2007) of the Security Council states that "there will be unity of command and control which, in accordance with basic principles of peacekeeping, a single chain of Command means is formed (Resolution 1769, 31 July 2007, par. 7). In fact, the operation has a Special Representative who is placed under the command and unified control of the Commander of the Force. The latter is appointed by the African Union in consultation with the UN, but responds directly to the Joint Special Representative, where they work simultaneously body of state forces made available to the UN and support forces belonging to other States (the joint mission of the UN (MONUSCO). The Congolese army (FARDC) can be cited to restore peace and security conditions in the eastern region of the Congo in January 2015 threatened by the activities of the National Liberation Forces. As stated in the famous Report drawn up in 1996 by the then General Secretary Kofi Annan (Financing Report)," [t]he international responsibility of UN for combat-related activities is premised on the assumption that the operation in question is under its exclusive

command and control (…). In joint operations, international responsibility for the conduct of the troops lies where operational command and control is vested according to the arrangements establishing the modalities of cooperation between the State or States providing the troops and UN. In the absence of formal arrangements (...) responsibility would be determined in each and every case according to the degree of effective control exercised by either party in the conduct of the operation. In these cases, a "joint responsibility" may arise where the action of the parties is in some way related, although the likelihood of this hypothesis actually occurring is somewhat remote (ILC, "Report of the International Law Commission Fifty-sixth session," op. cit., A/59/10, p. 110, § 4.). A third type that can be found in practice, in addition to the case of peace-keeping missions and joint operations, is that in which a military operation is conducted by states authorized to act by the Security Council in the regulatory framework outlined in Chapter VII of the UN Charter. In this case, the international responsibility for the conduct of armed forces is not attributable to UN, but to the various sending states, since the effective operational control of the troops is in the hands of the individual national governments. As we read, in fact, within the same Financing Report, "[w]here a Chapter VII-authorized operation is conducted under national command and control, international responsibility for the activities of the force is vested in the state or states conducting the operation." In light of the foregoing, it emerges that the criterion of attribution of international responsibility adopted by UN institutions in recent years is that of "effective control," whose existence derives from the verification of the presence of certain factual elements, between the general control exercised by the Security Council, the operational control of the General Secretary and the Commander of the Force and the powers reserved to the sending States. The current practice demonstrates, however, how the test is difficult to decide in order to attribute an unlawful UN conduct, since the contingents used in the missions are not totally "subordinated" to the directives given, at various levels, by the UN organs, but they must also indirectly submit to the command of their own sending States, which retain ample decision-making powers within the Organization and the concrete functioning of an operation. In this sense, albeit with the difficulties associated with its use, the hypothesis of dual attribution of conduct can be considered, which, as we shall see below, has also been taken into consideration by a certain international jurisprudence. The dual responsibility must necessarily also be based on a dual conduct attribution. The CDI admitted this possibility, specifying however that it "may not frequently occur in practice." The only example reported by the CDI in which there may be a double attribution of conduct is that in which two international organizations establish a joint body that operates for both, this situation obviously cannot come to light with reference to the CSDP. According to the doctrine, as we have seen, a dual attribution can occur when the conduct is carried out by an individual or entity to which it applies to more than one attribution rule, or in the cases in which it acts on behalf of more than one entity at the same time. A multiple attribution of conduct in the practice of EU missions could arise, for example, in cases where the contingent "lent" to the organization is subjected both to the directives coming from its own sending State, and to those issued, at various levels, by EU institutions and bodies. In this case, the decisive element lies in the "double belonging" of the body in question, which acts both on behalf of its sending State and of EU. A problematic aspect, however, consists in establishing the criteria on the basis of which to evaluate this "double belonging:" Should one use formal or organic criteria? or to factual criteria, as for the application of the "effective control" test. In the latter case, what kind of control must be exercised on such individuals so that there can be attribution of conduct? In other words,

affair concerning the activity of UNOSOM II, a mission established by the Security Council with the Resolution n. 814 of 26 March 1993,[258] in order

what is the "minimum threshold" of control required? These questions have not yet received a convincing answer in doctrine, nor can we obtain indications from jurisprudence. In the case, in fact, in which a body acts on behalf of more than one legal entity at the same time, as, for example, the de facto organ of one and the de jure organ of the other, it is possible to speak of a double attribution of conduct or should article 6, which instead provides for an exclusive attribution to the international organization, be considered applicable? In our opinion, the 2011 Project is not, at present, able to answer these questions, since it is strongly oriented to the unambiguous attribution of conduct. A possible way could be to use the hypothesis of dual attribution as a sort of "default attribution rule" in all those cases in which it is not possible to find the presence of the attribution elements outlined in articles 6 and 7 of the 2011 Project. We have seen, in fact, that if the conduct is not carried out by an organ or agent, in law or in fact, of an international organization, nor is it subjected to the "effective control" of the latter, it must presumably be attributed to the sending State. In this scenario, the dual attribution could find space, especially in the residual cases of article 7, in which it is ascertained that the organization has not exercised an "effective control" on the specific conduct, but has in any case, in some way, influenced the occurrence of this unlawful fact. However, it is inevitable to observe how every effort to configure a multiple attribution in cases of CSDP operations and, more generally, for military operations conducted under the aegis of international organizations, clashes, on the one hand, with the lack of clear normative references and, on the other, with a jurisprudence still extremely timid and, in our opinion, not always convincing. In essence, the multiple attribution remains till now a pure theoretical hypothesis. For further analysis see: P. KOUTRAKOS, The EU Common Security and Defense Policy, Oxford University Press, Oxford, 2013. F. NAERT, International law aspects of the EU's Security and Defense Policy, with a particular focus on the law of armed conflicts and human rights, Hart Publishing, Oxford & Oregon, Portland, 2010. P. EECKHOUT, The EU's Common Foreign and Security Policy after Lisbon: From pillar talk to constitutionalism, in A. BIONDI, P. EECKHOUT, S. RIPLEY, (eds.), EU Law after Lisbon, Oxford University Press, Oxford, New York, 2012, pp. 265-291. R.A. WESSEL, Division of international responsibility between the EU and its Member States in the area of Foreign, Security and Defense Policy, in Amsterdam Law Forum, 3 (3), 2011, pp. 34-48. Ö.F. DIREK, Responsibility in peace support operations: Revisiting the proper test for attribution conduct and the meaning of the "effective control" standard, in Netherlands International Law Review, 61, 2014, pp. 7ss. D. SAROOSHI (ed.), Remedies and responsibility for the actions of international organizations, Martinus Nijhoff Publishers, The Hague, 2014, pp. 444ss. H. KRIEGER, Addressing the accountability gap in peacekeeping. Law-making by domestic courts as a way to avoid UN reform?, in Netherlands International Law Review, 62, 2015, pp. 262ss. C. RYNGAERT, Apportioning responsibility between the UN and member states in UN peace-support operations: An inquiry into the application of the effective control standard after Behrami, in Israel Law Review, 45, 2012, pp. 152ss. N. VOULGARIS, Rethinking indirect responsibility: A study of article 17 of the Draft Articles on the Responsibility of International Organizations, in International Organizations Law Review, 11, 2014, pp. 8ss. D. WHITTLE, The intervention brigade, Monusco, and the application of international humanitarian law to UN forces, in Georgetown Journal of International Law, 6, 2014-2015, pp. 838ss.

[258] For further details see also: J. GINIFER, Beyond the emergency: Development within

to face the complex situation created in Somalia in the first half of the nineties. Following the killing of 25 members of mission, on 5 June 1993 the Security Council set up a Commission of inquiry with the task of clarifying the factual elements of the whole affair.[259] As far as our investigation is concerned, the Commission of inquiry was able to evaluate UNOSOM II's conduct and in particular the respect of international humanitarian law by the mission itself. It is interesting to note that according to the Commission of inquiry, several national continents available to UNOSOM escaped a careful examination of the UN chain of command and received orders from their respective national commands. So since many operations carried out under the aegis of the organization "were totally outside the command and control of the UN,"[260] the conduct examined by the Commission of inquiry could not be attributed to the UN.[261] Moreover, the recommendation formulated by the Commission for which it would have been appropriate to pay compensation to the injured parties[262] was followed only by some of the states whose quotas were involved in the damaging actions and not even by the UN.

The UN practice lays down in sufficiently clear terms in the sense of organization responsibility itself with regard to that conduct carried out in the framework of military missions of the type examined on which the institution exercises effective control. It seems that this practice is accompanied by the opinio juris expressed on several occasions by the main UN organs. It is useful in this regard to recall the report of the general secretary on the financing of peacekeeping operations.[263] In the cited document UN international responsibility for the harmful conduct put in place by the forces is subject to the assumption that "the operation in question is under the exclusive command and control of the UN." In the report, care is taken to specify that in the absence of "formal arrangements for the cooperation of the State and UN," the responsibility will be determined "in each and every case" due to the degree of control

UN peace missions, Frank Cass, London, Portland, OR, 1997, pp. 85ss. F. MCCONNELL, T. MOREAU, J. DITTMER, Mimicking state diplomacy: The legitimizing strategies of unofficial diplomacies, in Geoforum, 43 (4), 2012, pp. 806ss.

259S/RES/885 (1993), par. 1.

260UN Doc. S/1994/653, p. 45, parr. 243-244.

261In this sense DARIO, p. 22, par. 8, the ILC concerning the effective control that the criterion of imputation of the unlawful conduct and the behaviours carried out by the UNOSOM personnel had to be more properly attributed to the individual sending States.

262UN Doc. S/1994/653, par. 264, which is affirmed that: "Ex gratia payments should be considered for those innocent Somali civilians who suffered injury as a consequence of UNOSOM II's implementation of Security Council resolution 837 (1993)."

263UN Doc. A/51/389 (1996).

effectively exercised by each party "in the conduct of operation."[264]

3.4. (Follows) The criterion adopted by art. 7 DARIO

In consideration of the quickly illustrated practice, ILC has correctly set the problem of imputation of the offense according to the criterion to which the conduct harmful to state organs lent to an international organization refers to the subject who exercises on the same conduct effective control. First of all it is a criterion that evidently relies on elements of a factual nature, detecting the formal qualification of peacekeeping missions as subsidiary UN organs or the circumstance for which the organization itself "insists on claiming exclusive command and control over peacekeeping forces."[265] Precisely similar considerations have imposed on ILC during the works related to the responsibility of organizations the elaboration of a norm that governs the case of the loan of organs not considering adequate for this purpose the provision contained in art. 6 of the project. According to this article the conduct of an organ or agent of an international organization in the performance of its duties "shall be considered an act of that organization under international law, whatever position the organ or agent holds in respect of it."[266]

According to ILC, the aforementioned regulation covers the behaviour of bodies only in the hypothesis in which the latter are fully subjected to the authority of the relevant organization.[267] This last circumstance does not apply in the case of military bodies that States make available to international organizations because of the prerogatives that the former maintain on their respective quotas. In the opinion of Gaja, widely shared by ILC, the link between each State and its regiment prevents it from being configured as a "fully placed at the disposal" organ of the organization and above all "may have consequences with regard to the attribution of conduct."[268] In addition to configuring itself case by case with regard to the authority under which the harmful conduct took place, the subjective element of the offense must be reconstructed also due to the type of conduct and the nature of the violated obligation. This last consideration assumes a decisive role in our opinion. Each state of

---

[264]UN Doc. A/51/389 (1996), parr. 17-18.
[265]DARIO, p. 22, par. 9.
[266]DARIO, p. 22,
[267]DARIO, pp. 19-20, par. 1.
[268]G. GAJA, Second report on responsibility of international organizations, op. cit., p. 12, par. 38 and DARIO, p. 20, par. 7.

dispatch maintains for the entire period of the mission the exclusive competence in criminal matters regarding crimes attributable to its military personnel. In this regard, Gaja cites as an example the position expressed by the UN Legal Affairs Office originally to the fulfilment of obligations established by the 1973 agreement on the trade of animal and plant species at risk of extinction.[269] Since the agreement just mentioned does not see UN between contracting parties and each sending state maintains the criminal jurisdiction over its military. "The responsibility for enforcing the Convention rest with those troop contributing States which are parties to it."[270] Control over conduct must also be assessed on the basis of power that each supplier exercises "in the relevant respect,"[271] that is to say, according to the content of the obligation possibly flown by the operating units. This is an aspect of no minor importance. The complex of juridical (passive) situations referring to each of them remains to the fore, of the supplier States, to nothing revealing the circumstance for which the military organs are, temporarily in the availability of the receiving organization. If this approach is correct, each State participating in peace-keeping missions having to comply with its international obligations also within the framework of these missions, may incur independent international responsibility as a result of the violation of obligations incumbent upon it. The foregoing assumes importance with regard to the obligations provided for by international humanitarian law,[272] most of which can only be fulfilled by the states regardless of the well-known circumstance for which the contractual instruments which constitute the Aja and Geneva law are formally inaccessible to non-state lawyers. It should be remembered that the obligations under discussion presuppose an apparatus and even legal structures of which only the States currently have. It goes without saying that in a reverse perspective with respect to the one outlined so far the state responsibility ultimately indicated would be excluded if the assumptions did not occur, that is to say the effective control over the conduct and above all the recipient of the obligation violated at state level in reason for the material affiliation of this obligation

[269]G. GAJA, Second report on responsibility of international organizations, op. cit., p. 12, par. 38.

[270]Question of whether the UN should be held responsible for violation of the convention on international trade in endangered species in wild fauna committed by servicemen of UNOSOCM II, in United Nations Judicial Yearbook, 1994, pp. 450ss.

[271]DARIO, p. 21, par. 7.

[272] A. ABI-SAAB, Human rights and humanitarian law in internal conflicts, in D. WARNER, Human rights and humanitarian law. The quest for universality, op. cit., pp. 98-112.

to exclusive competences such as those in criminal matters, which the States retain for the entire duration of the mission.

These considerations explain the reasons for which ILC drafted a specific rule within the draft of articles on the responsibility of international organizations, art. 7 in order to regulate the imputation of conduct carried out by state bodies made available to a functional entity. The conduct of the body that in ordinary conditions should be imputed to the State is exceptionally attributed to the organization due to two circumstances which must cumulatively occur for the purposes of the application of the law. On the one hand, the state body must be in the availability of the organization; on the other, the latter must exercise effective control over the conduct in question. If these conditions are not met the organ's behaviour must qualify as a fact of the sending status. In similar circumstances, in other words, the presumption on which the entire codification enucleated is based in art. 4 par. 1 ARSIWA for which: "The conduct of any State shall be considered an act of that State under international law."

3.5. Application of the criterion adopted by ILC practice. ECtHR jurisprudence

The provision contained in the current art. 7 proposed by Gaja already in his second report of 2004 he has known an almost immediate and sometimes improper application, both in international and in the internal jurisprudence. The ECtHR particularly interpreted and applied the law in question with reference to behaviours carried out by state contingents integrated in the NATO-Kosovo force mission (KFOR) which, as is known, the Security Council had authorized with the Resolution of 10 June 1999 n. 1244. The leading case is represented by the decision given on 2 May 2007 in Behrami and Saramati v. France,[273] Germany and

---

[273]According to our opinion the ECtHR would naturally have had to resort to the criterion of effective control (to be interpreted as operational control) and ask which subject had possibly ordered not to remove unexploded cluster bombs: NATO, through the Com-KFOR and/or France, through its own national authorities? Such an operation would certainly not have been easy to carry out, because the scarce information available would not have allowed to easily establish whether the omissive conduct had been the result of decisions taken by the Com-KFOR, or had been caused by indications given to the French contingent by its own command national or, even, had arisen from a choice taken jointly by the international and national command. It is superfluous to recall that, in the first case, the omissive conduct should have been attributed to NATO, in the second, to France and, in the third, to both subjects It is good to specify that everything that can be disputed with the Court is the hasty definition of the mandate of KFOR and UNMIK in relation to de-mining

Norway[274] with which the ECtHR declared inadmissible the individual appeals filed against some ECHR Member States certain claims of human rights occurred in the autonomous province of Kosovo which as is known is placed under the UN provisional administration.[275]

A line of jurisprudence includes the cases of exclusive attribution of the violation to the sending State. An example of this is the recent ruling issued by the Court of First Instance of Belgium in the Mukeshimana-Ngulinzira v. Belgium, more commonly known as the Kigali case,[276] originated from the appeal presented by some Rwandan applicants before

activities, which led her to consider only UNMIK and not KFOR involved in the aforementioned activities; in any case, in light of the factual data as determined by the Grand Chamber, the attribution of the conduct of UNMIK is correctly determined. For further analysis see: G. VERDIRAME, Breaches of the European Convention on Human Rights resulting from the conduct of international organizations, in European Human Rights Law Review, 8, 2008, pp. 220ss. K.W. WATSON, Behrami v. France: Constructive blue helmets protect KFOR nations from accountability, in Tulane Journal of International and Comparative Law, 16, 2007-2008, pp. 576ss. Also in this case, a "univocal" interpretation of the attribution of conduct prevails, which leads to attributing solely to the UN the responsibility for violations of international law committed during the operation. The Nuhanović case, however, contains an element of greater openness with respect to the Behrami and Saramati sentences. The Court, in fact, envisaged the possibility that, as part of a peacekeeping operation, under certain circumstances, the Dutch government could be held responsible for illegal conduct by acting in a position of "effective control" over UNPROFOR troops. In particular, the judges pointed out that if it is established, it is a violation of the factual basis on which the attribution is based to the UN rests. The Court therefore acknowledged that the Netherlands could have "effective control" over the contingent and consequently respond internationally to its conduct, in the event that the troops had received orders from the Dutch government to contravene an order deriving from the chain of UN command (hypothesis of the cutting-across orders).

[274]A. SARI, Jurisdiction and international responsibility in peace suport operations: The Behrami and Saramati cases, in Human Rights Law Review, 8, 2008, pp. 152ss. P. KLEIN, Responsabilitè pour les faits commis dans le cadre d'opèrations de paix et ètendue du pouvoir de contrôle de la cour europèenne des droits de l'homme: quelques considèrations critiques sur l'arrêt Behrami et Saramati, in Annuaire Français de Droit International, 53 (1), 2007, pp. 44ss. P. LAGRANGE, Responsabilitè des Etats pour actes accomplis en application du Chapitre VII de la Charte des Nations Unies, in Revue Gènèrale de Droit International Public, 112, 2008, pp. 86ss. T. DANNENBAUM, Translating the standard of effective control into a system of effective accountability: How liability should be apportioned for violation of human rights by member state troop contingents serving as United Nations peacekeeping, in Harvard International Law Journal, 51, 2010, pp. 115ss.

[275]In particular the applicants complained of the violation of art. 2 of the ECHR (law of life) by the French contingent integrated into the KFOR and the violation of art. 5 (right to freedom and security), 6 (fair trial) and 13 (right to an effective appeal) attributable to Norway, France and Germany.

[276]Court of First Instance of Belgium, Mukeshimana-Ngulinzira and others v. Belgium, Mukeshimana 04/4807/A and Ngulinzira 07/15547/A, 8 December 2010.

the Belgian Court of First Instance in order to obtain compensation from Belgium for the unlawful acts committed by its military during the UNAMIR peacekeeping operations carried out in Rwanda.[277] In particular, the plaintiffs accused Belgium of having abandoned a building (the École Technique Officielle) in which some Tutsi individuals were refugees, among which there were some relatives of the applicants, later killed by Hutu militias and, therefore, of not having offered them adequate protection, withdrawing their own contingents from that area. After noting that the decision to evacuate the country had been taken by Belgium without any authorization from UNAMIR, the Court ruled that having obeyed orders does not relieve the military of their responsibility, if such risk allow the Commission of war crimes, such as those that occurred in Rwanda.

In essence, the fact that the decision was taken by the Belgian Chief of Staff without prior consultation or authorization by the UNAMIR military command was considered sufficient to attribute the conduct to Belgium rather than to UN. In this case, therefore, there is an even more rigorous application of the "effective control" criterion, since the Court focused on the effectiveness of the orders given, going beyond the simple fact that the operation had been established by UN. In our opinion, the reasoning on which the Court relies to argue that there may be a "double attribution," indeed that more than one entity can exercise "effective control" over the conduct of a group of individuals at the same time, does not correspond to the content of article 7 of the 2011 Project. We have seen, in fact, that this concept is characterized by a series of elements, including the causal link between control and Commission of the offense and the fact that this control it must be exercised on a specific action, which make it logically impossible to configure a situation of "double effective control." This hypothesis is also contrary to provision's purpose and would make the ascertainment of international responsibility even more uncertain and difficult. In fact, the article configures a sort of "exception" with respect to the organic model of attribution of conduct, in which the behaviour of state bodies, such as those taking part in crisis management missions conducted under the auspices of an international organization, should normally be attributed to the State pursuant to article 4 of the 2001 Project, which provides that "[the] behaviour of a state body will be considered as

---

[277]UNAMIR was a peace-keeping operation established by the UN in October 1993 with Resolution n. 872 of 1993. The objective of the mission was to eliminate ethnic tensions in the country, in particular those between the Hutu and Tutsi ethnic groups. Commander Luc Marchal had effectively managed the withdrawal of troops.

an act of the State under international law, whether that body exercises legislative, executive, judicial or other functions, whatever position it has in its organization and whatever its nature is as an organ of the central government or of a territorial unit of it."[278] Only in the presence of an "effective control" on the conduct of such bodies by the international organization, this must be attributed to the latter. Therefore, to affirm that this "effective control" can be simultaneously exercised also by the State would, in our opinion, be tantamount to emptying any meaning of article 7. In other words, the "effective control" test configures, as mentioned above, a scenario of attribution of conduct that is exclusively "univocal." If the presence of such a type of control is ascertained, the possibility of having a double attribution, consequently, lapses nevertheless, the sentence marks a particularly important precedent since, for the first time, a state government has been held responsible on the international level for the conduct of its troops operating under UN mandate.[279]

Basing its decision essentially on general international law and recalling for this purpose the draft articles on the responsibility of international organizations, the ECtHR considered that the acts whose litigation was challenged in the course of proceedings were attributable to UN as placed in by the KFOR contingents and from the staff of UNMIK. For these reasons, it has declared its incompetence ratione personae. Art. 7 of the project on the responsibility of international organizations was only relevant with regard to the case that the nature of the UN's subsidiary UNMIK, which could be attributed to the deeds object of the Behrami appeal, was such as to configure the responsibility of the organization in the same way as articles 4 and 6 of the same project. According to the

[278]E. SOMMARIO, Responsibility under international law for human rights violations committed by UN peacekeepers: Reconsidering issues of attribution, in A. DE GUTTRY, E. SOMMARIO, L. ZHU (eds.), China's and Italy's participation in peacekeeping operations: Existing models, emerging challenges, Lexington Books, London, 2014, pp. 369-397. N. ACHTEN, Compensation claims of individuals for violations of rules on conduct of hostilities. Comment on a judgment of the District Court of Bonn, Germany-LG Bonn 1 0 460/11, 11 December 2013, in Humanitares Volkerrecht, 28, 2015, pp. 35ss. C. AHLBORN, The use of analogies drafting the articles on the responsibility of international organizations: An appraisal of the "copy-paste approach," op. cit., pp. 54ss. C. AHLBORN, To share or not to share? The allocation of responsibility between international organizations and their member states, in Die Friedens-Warte, 88, 2013, pp. 46ss.

[279]Liesbeth Zegveld, the Dutch lawyer who defended the interests of the victims, said that "to U.N. flag does not give (...) immunity as a state or individual soldier." Thanks to the sentence, two Bosnian families were able to claim compensation for damages to the Netherlands.

ECtHR, in fact "UNMIK was a subsidiary UN body created under Chapter VII of the Charter so that the impugned inaction was in principles attributable to the UN in the same sense."[280] The Saramati case will be dealt with as conduct attributable to the military contingents integrated into the KFOR. It is reconstructed by the ECtHR, applying art. 7 of the project. According to the judge of Strasbourg, the consideration for which "KFOR was lawfully exercising delegating Chapter VII powers of the UN Security Council, so that the impugned action was in principle attributable to it (...)."[281] The ECtHR after observing that "the key" question is whether the Security Council authority and control so that operational command was only delegated,[282] concludes that in the present case, the Security Council would have maintained such control throughout the duration of the mission. More precisely, the delegation contained in Resolution no. 1244 in setting the objectives and mandate of the international security presence provided at the same time to identify the limits. Therefore, according to the ECtHR, it is the Security Council that exercises effective control over the entire mission although it has delegated to NATO the task of establishing the security force and of assuming the operational command. Starting from these premises the ECtHR sees in the case a specific hypothesis of responsibility of an international organization for conducts of state organs placed at its service. This same orientation was reiterated by the ECtHR in two other cases such as Kasumaj v. Greece of 7 July 2007 and Gajić v. Germany of 29 August 2007 in which the conduct object of grievance was attributable to the military personnel integrated in the KFOR.

ECtHR jurisprudence lends itself to various critical considerations. First of all, ECtHR uses the provisions of art. 7 of the project with regard to hypotheses that do not fall within the scope of application of the same rule. The institution of organ loan and the relative criterion of effective control are only relevant in cases of military operations established and controlled directly by an international organization, provided that the subjective element of the offense always depends on the actual authority under which the behaviour actually took place. In any case, the cases attributable to military operations authorized by the Security Council,[283] fall outside this regulatory framework, which certainly includes KFOR.

---

[280]ECtHR, Behrami and Saramati v. France, Germany and Norway of 2 May 2007, par. 143.

[281]ECtHR, Behrami and Saramati v. France, Germany and Norway, op. cit., par. 141.

[282]ECtHR, Behrami and Saramati v. France, Germany and Norway, op. cit., par. 133.

[283]G. GAJA, Second report on responsibility of international organizations, op. cit., p. 10, par. 32.

Having made this clarification, what is interesting to note here is that the ECtHR has adopted an extremely broad notion of control over conduct such as to depart, in decisive terms, from the letter of art. 7 and above all from the authentic interpretation of the same rendered by the ILC in the relative comment.[284] What would be worth according to this perspective to configure the attribution of the conduct in question to UN is not in fact actual and concrete control over them in the same way as art. 7 but the circumstance for which the Security Council through Resolution n. 1244 "retained ultimate authority and control"[285] on KFOR, considered as a whole. Article 7, on the other hand, requires an examination aimed at identifying the individual who has actually and concretely exercised control over the allegedly illegal conduct, case by case. Moreover, ILC did not fail to highlight the difference between the content of the cited standard and the imputation criterion used by the ECtHR in the cases illustrated "since the later hardly implies a role in the act in question."[286]

Partly similar considerations concern international and internal sentences regarding actions attributable to the multinational force deployed in Iraq in 2004 and authorized by the Security Council with Resolutions no. 1511 and 1546 of the same year. These are the Al-Jedda v. United Kingdom and Al-Skein v. United Kingom cases of 13 June 2007. Since these are offenses related to the activity of military forces authorized by the Security Council and as such attributable to the individual authorized States, the cases just mentioned are outside the scope of our investigation. It is however useful to underline for our purposes how the first time the national judges called to ascertain the responsibility of the defendant State have attributed the conduct object of grievance to the UN in the assumption that the authorization of the Security Council was worth to configure the control of this last on the offenses in question. With the sentences handed down on 7 July 2011, instead, the large chamber of the ECtHR accepted the appeals believing that the conduct at the origin of the appeals was attributable to the United Kingdom and that in a prodromal

---

[284]P. KLEIN, Responsabilitè pour les faits commins dans le cadre d'opèrations de paix et ètendue du pouvoir de contrôle de la cour europèenne des droits de l'homme: quelques considèrations critiques sur l'arrêt Behrami et Saramati, op. cit., pp. 56ss. K.M. LARSEN, Attribution of conduct in peace operations: The "ultimate control and authority test," op. cit., pp. 522ss.

[285]ECtHR, Behrami and Saramati v. France, Germany and Norway, op. cit., par. 133. E. DE WET, The governance of Kosovo: Security Council Resolution 1244 and the establishment and functioning of EULEX, in American Journal of International Law, 103 (1), 2009, pp. 85ss.

[286]DARIO, p. 23, par. 10.

perspective with respect to the questions before it, the invasion of Iraq could in no way be qualified as a UN operation.[287]

---

[287]The Al-Skeini v. The United Kingdom case it originated from the appeal brought by six Iraqi nationals who died during British operations in southern Iraq. With the sentence of 13 June 2007, the House of Lords had recognized the UK jurisdiction as art. 2 ECHR only with reference to one of the deaths in question since it occurred in a British reason in Iraq. The other alleged violations having occurred in Iraq on which the regulatory coverage of Resolutions nos. 1511 and 1546 of the Security Council should have been considered attributable to UN. In front of the ECtHR the United Kingdom has substantially reaffirmed these arguments by claiming that since the family members of the applicants "had been killed after the adoption of UN Security Council Resolution 1511 (...) the acts which led to their deaths were attributable to UN and not to the United Kingdom" (par. 96). ECtHR rejected the British arguments that in the part that notes to our facts, considering that: "It is a question of fact whether a contracting state exercises effective control over an area outside its own territory" (par. 139) and that the conduct in question were attributable to it (par. 142ss). In the Al-Jedda v. The United Kingdom case the applicant also of Iraqi nationality complained of the violation of art. 5 ECHR by the United Kingdom that would have illegally detained him in one of his prisons in Iraq. Also in this case the conventual State maintained that the applicant's detention was attributable to UN and that consequently his jurisdiction under art. 1 ECHR. ECtHR noted that: "The invasion of Iraq by the US led coalition forces in March 2003 was not a UN operation" (para. 71). The ECtHR stated that the authorization to establish a multinational force contained in Resolution n. 1511 of the Security Council in no way implied imputation to UN of the acts performed within the framework of the force in question. According to ECtHR: "The language of the UN Security Council Resolution 1511 did not support government's interpretation" (par. 72). According to our opinion the House of Lords ended up contradicting what was claimed in the Saramati case. On the contrary, the House of Lords declared that MNF actions were attributable to participating States, and not to UN, only because in relation to the Iraqi case "the analogy with the situation in Kosovo breaks down (...) at almost every point," and not by virtue of the fact that the attribution of the conduct of authorized forces to the authorizing organization was conceptually incorrect. In other words, for the British Supreme Court are the circumstances of the species that make the national, not the latter, approach incorrect in the Al-Jedda case. The House of Lords therefore suggests that if the Iraqi situation had been similar to the Kosovar situation, the actions/omissions of MNF would have been attributed to UN, according to what happened in the Saramati case. Now, the distinction between the Kosovar case (NATO mission authorized by the Security Council) and the Iraq one (multinational force predominantly Anglo-American authorized by the Security Council) drawn by the British Supreme Court seems artificial. Therefore seems possible to affirm that the mentioned distinction between the Kosovar and Iraqi context has been specially delineated by the House of Lords, in order to depart from jurisprudence without being openly rejected. Although, therefore, the Al-Jedda sentence should be considered a further confirmation of the fact that international practice lays down in the sense of not attributing the actions of forces authorized to the Organization, the attitude of the House of Lords remains criticizable. Instead of unconvincingly distinguishing the Iraqi situation from the Kosovar situation, the British Supreme Court could, more simply, have distanced itself from its predecessor. Although it is true, that the authoritativeness enjoyed by the European Court of Human Rights makes it extremely difficult for an internal jurisdictional instance to be in open contrast with the

According to the constant jurisprudence of the Court, art. 5 ECHR does not allow the State to internally or detain dangerous persons when there is no intention to formalize an indictment and initiate a criminal trial within a reasonable period of time, and after noting that the British State has not formalized any declaration of derogation to art. 5 pursuant to the aforementioned art. 15 ECHR In relation to its military mission in Iraq, the Grand Chamber notes that pursuant to art. 1 of the Charter, UN has the task not only of maintaining peace and security among nations, but also of fostering international cooperation to "promote and encourage respect for human rights and fundamental freedoms."[288] For its part, art. 24 of the Charter requires the Security Council to comply, in adopting its resolutions, with the "aims and principles of the UN," as sanctioned by the aforementioned art. 1. From this derives, at least, the Grand Chamber acutely states an interpretative rule according to which it must be presumed that the Security Council does not intend to impose on the UN Member States any obligation to violate the fundamental principles of human rights, whenever the text of the resolution is not unique in this sense. In the framework of such a "human rights compliant interpretation," the ECtHR will therefore have to "choose the interpretation that is most in harmony with the requirements of the Convention and that avoids the emergence of conflicts of duties"[289] with regard to States Parties to the two international organizations.

In light of this interpretative criterion, the resolutions of the Security Council that are taken into consideration in the case of species, which merely authorized the armed forces of the coalition to "adopt all the necessary measures" to maintain security and stability in Iraq cannot be interpreted as authorizing, or even imposing (according to the reading made by the British government and by the House of Lords itself), to adopt a policy of preventive detentions without time limits and jurisdictional guarantees of suspicions terrorists, in violation of international obligations to respect human rights affecting the coalition of Member States, and in particular of those arising by art. 5 ECHR. All the necessary measures must therefore be read as implicitly limited by the respect of the international obligations in question, and in particular by those concerning

---

Strasbourg judges, and equally undeniable that the ECtHR sentences they do not have the value of real stare decisis for national courts. Therefore, despite the final outcome of the House of Lords regarding the attribution of the conduct is appreciable, it cannot be said the same for the motivations underlying the sentence of the Supreme Court, which demonstrate how difficult it can be to get rid of the inheritance left by the Saramati jurisprudence.

[288] A. HENRIKSEN, International law, op. cit.

[289]The Al-Skeini v. The United Kingdom, op. cit.

the protection of personal freedom. That is also in consideration of the repeated positions taken by the same UN representatives in Iraq against the practice of preventive detentions, implemented on a large scale by the Anglo-American armed forces. The conclusion of the majority of the ECtHR in the Al-Jeddah case is, therefore, that the detention of the applicant for over three years in a British prison in Basra, without any jurisdictional guarantee and without trial, constituted a violation of article 5 par. 1 ECHR. This conclusion, on which the very succinctly motivated dissent of judge Polaelungi is recorded, who instead agrees with the judgment of the House of Lords according to which the resolutions of the Security Council here under discussion imposed, at least implicitly, the appeal to preventive detentions of suspected terrorists as "necessary" measures to maintain security and stability in Iraq, moreover in conformity with a consolidated international practice in situations of armed conflict and subsequent military occupation.

Precisely on the ambiguity of the ratio assumed as basis of today's decision and on the consequent state of obscurity in which the ECtHR jurisprudence still pays in the matter of art. 1 ECHR, is not by chance that the reservations expressed in the two concurring opinions by judges Rozakis and Bonello are pointed out. In this last, articulated opinion is argued in particular the opportunity for the Court to embrace in the future a new test, of a functional nature, intended to overcome the current artificial antinomy between the "space" (effective control over an area) and "personal" (effective control over a person by a State agent) criterion. More specifically, a test according to which the State would exercise its "jurisdiction" pursuant to art. 1 ECHR whenever it is in its power to carry out at least one of the five functions in which the "respect" of conventional rights is declined-refrain from direct violations through its own agents, prevent violations by third parties, investigate violations committed, sanctions responsible of them, and compensate the victims. In simple words, according to the Maltese judge, "a State has jurisdiction pursuant to art. 1 whenever the observance or violation of any of these functions falls within its power and control."[290] The "jurisdiction" does not derive only from the democratic exercise of powers of government. It can also derive "from the mouth of a firearm" "apart from the situations of firefighting, whoever is in the range of a gun is in the authority and in control of those who keep it in sight."[291] Such a reconstruction naturally assumes as obvious the "divisibility" of human rights recognized by the

[290]The Al-Skeini v. The United Kingdom, op. cit.
[291]The Al-Skeini v. The United Kingdom, op. cit.

Convention, in front of contrast with respect to the dictum of Bankovic v. Belgium of 19 December 2001 from which now the entire Grand Chamber, as noted above, has also considered distancing itself. State jurisdiction which sends its soldiers on a military mission abroad will thus extend only to those conventional rights which, in those particular conditions, the State will be in factual conditions to respect. In short, the soldiers will have to respect the lives of people who are within the range of their rifles; but their government cannot be held responsible for the guarantee of the right to education or to free elections of the population residing in the territory in which the mission takes place, since these are tasks normally reserved for civil governments that will regain their full functions once ended the emergency phase in which the military mission takes place.

Against the background of this competing lively argument, full of controversial ideas against the English government, is the firm conviction, repeatedly reiterated by judge Bonello, of the universality of human rights, in diametric contrast to concerns, surfacing even in the opinions of the judges of the House of Lords, of "imperialism of human rights" connected to the application of the Convention beyond its natural regional juridical espace. The hypocritical nature of such an argument in relation to a case such as the one at issue here is denounced by the judge with sarcastic accents. And not wrongly is not at issue here, for example, the imposition of a "Western" concept of family or sexual morality on a society in which Islamic Sharia is in force, but the principle according to which the soldiers of a State they must, first of all, refrain from violating with their own conduct the most fundamental rights among those who have committed themselves to respecting it by adhering to the Convention, including first of all the life of every person subjected to the range of their guns. "I believe," concludes Bonello, just on the eve of his retirement after a long service as a judge at ECtHR, that those who export the war should also be concerned about exporting the guarantees against the atrocities of the war. And then, if necessary, they should also have the strength to endure being labeled "imperialist human rights." For my part, I want to make my diversity public. At my age, it may no longer be elegant to have dreams. But the dream of being branded perpetually as an imperialist of human rights, I recognize that it sounds particularly seductive to my ears and certainly very far from the spirit of history and ILC projects.

3.6. Internal jurisprudence. The Nuhanović and Mustafić v. the Netherlands cases

Some cases decided by the Dutch Courts regarding the conduct attributable to the Dutch contingent deserve careful analysis. The Dutschbat integrated into the UNPROFOR mission in Bonsia Herzegovina. These are both cases related to the Srebrenica massacre of July 1995, H.N. (Hasan Nuhanović) v. the Netherlands and Mustafić v. the Neherlands.[292] The facts of the appeal concern the murder of the applicants' relatives by the Bosnian Serb militias led by Ratko Mladić, which was part of the genocide established by the ICTY[293] and ICC.[294] In the opinion of the applicants the death of their relatives was made possible by some commissive and omissive conduct carried out by the Dutchbat, which would have allowed the expulsion of the victims by the compound UNRPOFOR while awaiting the evacuation of refugees from the same military base. The applicants therefore acted in compensation against the Dutch State to which the conduct object of the complaint should have been attributed. The district Court of the Hague, in the first judgment of 10 September 2008 rejected the appeal on the assumption that the conduct the object were attributable to the UN, the head to which was found "the operational command and control" on the troops provision of UNPROFOR.[295] The line of argument followed by the district court seems to attribute an exorbitant importance to the generic control over the operation rather than to the actual control over the relevant behaviours and from this point of view it seems to be inscribed in the line traced by ECtHR in the Behrami and standby case.[296]

In the application initiating the appeal, Nuhanović employed as a translator in the service of the Dutch contingent intended to enforce Netherlands' responsibility on the basis that the Dutchbat had the possibility but had not included the names of its relatives in the UN staff

---

[292]Case n. 265618/HA ZA 06-1672, 10 September 2001. See also the sentence of appeal of 5 July 2001: Hasan Nuhanović v. The Netherlands, court of appeal in the Hague, civil law section, case n. 200.020.174/01, Mustafić v. The Netherlands, Court of appeal in the Hague, civil law section, case n. 200.020.173/01. B. BOUTIN, Responsibility of the Netherlands for the acts of Dutchbat in Nuhanović and Mustafić: The continuous quest for a tangible meaning for "effective control" in the context of peacekeeping, in Leiden Journal of International Law, 25, 2012, pp. 522ss.

[293]Judgment, Krstić, IT-98-33, appeals chamber, 19 April 2003, par. 37.

[294]Application of the convention on the prevenion and punishment of the crime of genocide, op. cit., p. 166.

[295]H.N. (Hasan Nuhanović) v. The Netherlands, district court in the Hague, op. cit., parr. 4.9-4.11.

[296]In this sense: T. DANNENBAUM, Translating the standard of effective control into a system of effective accountability: How liability should be apportioned for violation of human rights by member state troop contingents serving as United Nations peacekeeping, op. cit., pp. 115ss.

list so as to prevent them from being taken by Bosnian Serb troops. Secondly, in the immediate aftermath, the soldiers had not intervened at the time of deportation of victims in question and above all they had not reported to the general command of UNRPOFOR on the incident and the probable and imminent execution of their relatives. According to the applicants, UN responsibility was not such as to exclude that of the respondent state itself. More precisely, according to the actors, in Dutchbat he had compiled a list of people who should have been evacuated "together with its own troops." In this regard, the commander of the Dutch battalion had rejected the applicant's request to include the names of his relatives on the list, who were later killed in the Srebrenica massacre, although the Dutchbat was fully aware of the imminent danger faced by the male individuals present at the interior of the Compog of Potogori. When that last circumstance became emotionally verified, the Dutchbat did not intervene to prevent the deportation of the victims without informing the general command of what was happening. The facts just described included, in the opinion of the appellants, the violation of article 2 and for ECHR articles 6 and 7 of the international Covenant on civil and political rights as well as the serious violation of humanitarian law obligations in the field of protection of civilians in wartime and of the Convention on repression of the genocide of 1948 "by making insufficient efforts to prevent genocide." The district Court moves from the shareable observation that the case in question imposes a preliminary examination of the imputation profiles of its disputed conduct. On this point after recalling that the Dutchbat was integrated into a mission set up by the Security Council pursuant to UN Charter VII, the district Court reconstructs the factual and legal framework in which the Dutch contingent was operating in July of 1995. In this regard the district Court finds that the peace-keeping operations established by the Security Council presuppose that the organization has "operational command and control" on the mission. At the same time, it acknowledges that this form of command and control does not extend to the "personnel matters of the troops and the material logistics of the deployed detachment,"[297] which remain direct responsibility of the individual sending State. This last observation allows the district Court to construct the first step of the argument aimed at rejecting the appeal if it is true that the organizational and disciplinary aspects remain in exclusive competence of the contributing States. It is also true that the applicant's relatives were not part of the Duchbat staff so that the lack of protection they suffered "has

[297]Par. 4.9.

not bearing on personnel matters reserved to the Netherlands or on the power reserved to the latter to decide whether to withdraw Dutchbat from the UN authority."[298]

Furthermore, the right of the Netherlands to withdraw its contingent from Bosnia and Herzegovina must not be confused according to the district Court with the right/power to decide on the education of the units integrated in the UNPROFOR which belonged exclusively to the UN. This leads the district Court to say of a state body made available to UNRPOFOR: "Should to be attributed strictly, as matter of principle, to the UN."[299] In this respect, the district Court does not differ from the general orientation indicated above, so that the imputation of the offense to one of the two parties involved excludes ex se the simultaneous assignment of the same conduct to the other subject. The argumentative path followed by the district Court seems to reduce the scope of the last-mentioned principle decree and at the same time reveals its substantial weakness. The district Court still presumes the exclusive imputation to the UN to the petitum of parties in which there was no trace of arguments of different tenor. "No submission were made possible without this rule of exclusive attribution (...) so that the Court assumes none occurred."[300] This reasoning leads the district Court to affirm that the rule identified by it in the matter of imputation is applied regardless of the content of the primary norm violated so that since the conduct in question was attributable to the UN it must be considered that "even gross negligence or serious failure of supervision (…) must in principle be attributed exclusively to this organization."[301] On the other hand, the district Court asserts that the imputation of the UN conduct in the terms indicated would cease only if the Dutch government had given orders to its quota contrary to those issued by the UN, circumstance that did not occur in the present case.

With the sentence of 5 July 2011 the Court of Appeal of the Hague, on the contrary, moving from the first instance judge to the assumption that the criterion of imputation of conduct carried out by the peacekeeping forces could be found in art. 7 DARIO detects the responsibility of the Dutch State in organs for acts performed by the Dutchbat described above.[302]

It is interesting to note that the Court of appeal reaches this

---

[298]Par. 4.10.
[299]Par. 4.11.
[300]Par. 4.12.
[301]Par. 4.13.
[302]A. NOLLAKAEMPER, Dual attribution: Liability of the Netherlands for conduct of Dutchbat in Srebrenica, op. cit., pp. 1144ss.

conclusion after having ascertained the omissive behaviour of the defendant State consisting in not having exercised the power that the circumstances of fact made very concrete to prevent the occurrence of the harmful conduct. In order to verify if the behaviours object of the grievance were attributable to the UN, the Netherlands "or possibly both," the Court of appeal will reconstruct the relevant factual and regulatory context in the case in question. First, it notes that the Dutchbat was integrated into the UNPROFOR force placed under the command of the UN. According to this last circumstance it is completely irrelevant that "the decisive criterion for attribution is not who exercised command and control but who actually had possession of effective control" citing in this regard the current art. 7 of the project.[303] And it is on this point that the fulcrum of the argument under consideration is grafted. Control effectiveness over the conduct must be measured by reason of the concrete possibility of preventing the production of the same conduct. This reconstruction seems very close to the thesis of those in the doctrine who interpret the criterion adopted in art. 7 to bring back the conduct of the subject who is in a position to prevent certain violations of human rights.[304] From this point of view, the criterion of effective control assumes the force of a preventive power, rather than a direct control over the damaging action, a deduction that appeared from the first comments to the decidedly untrusted sentence with respect to law provisions.[305] The district Court of appeal thus arrives at the co-imputation of the deeds deducted in Court also in consideration of the changed circumstances of fact for which the conduct object of grievance would have been object of decision shared between the UN the Dutchbat.[306]

With the judgment of 6 September 2013, the Dutch supreme Court substantially confirmed the orientation of the second instance judge, believing that the conduct of the Dutchbat was attributable to the State in accordance with art. 7 DARIO and in a measure not

---

[303]Parr. 5.7-5.8.

[304]T. DANNENBAUM, Translating the standard of effective control into a system of effective accountability: How liability should be apportioned for violation of human rights by member state troop contingents serving as United Nations peacekeeping, op. cit., pp. 158ss.

[305]A. NOLLAKAEMPER, Dual attribution: Liability of the Netherlands for conduct of Dutchbat in Srebrenica, op. cit., pp. 1148ss, observes that where this interpretation of art. 7, the conduct of the peacekeeping forces would be "almost by definition" attributable to the sending States.

[306]Where the district council explicitly refers to the possibility that "more that one party has effective control." As noted this solution seems to serve the Court in order to apply art. 7 DARIO to the conduct of the defendant State.

better specified by art. 8 ARSIWA.[307]

Secondly, the supreme Court adheres to it specifying its content to the approach for which the project on the responsibility of international organizations does not exclude that in the case of the loan of organs there may be a double imputation of the same conduct. The normative basis of this conclusion should be derived according to the Dutch supreme Court from the combined provisions of articles 7 and 8 par.4, DARIO.[308]

3.7. (Follows) The Srebrenica v. Netherlands mother case

The facts behind Srebrenica v. The Netherlands case decided by the district Court of the Hague on 16 July 2014 are substantially the same as seen in the previous paragraph. It is necessary to point out some aspects of this pronunciation. First, the districtual Court notes that the Dutch contingent "was (...) placed under UN orders and operated as a contingent of UNPROFOR" [309] with the important clarification that the State concerned "attached no conditions to the transfer of command and control

[307]The state of the Netherlands v. Hasan Nuhanović, Supreme Court of the Netherlands, First Chamber, 12/03324, 6th September 2013.

[308]Par. 3.11.2.

[309]See ex multis in argument: O. SPIJKERS, The immunity of the United Nations in relation to the genocide in Srebrenica in the eyes of a Dutch District Court, in Journal of International Peacekeeping, 9, 2009, pp. 197ss. T. HENQUET, international organizations in the Netherlands: Immunity from the jurisdiction of the Dutch courts, in Netherlands International Law Review, 49, 2010, pp. 267ss. B.E. BROCKMAN-HAWE, Questioning the UN's immunity in the Dutch Courts: Unresolved issues in the Mothers of Srebrenica litigation, in Washington University Global Studies Law Review, 10, 2011, pp. 727ss. J. TAVERNIER, La responsabilité des Etats au regard de la Convention européenne des droits de l'homme pour la mise en oeuvre de résolutions adoptées dans la cadre du chapitre VII de la Charte des Nations Unies, in Revue Générale de Droit International Public, 117, 2013, pp. 102ss. R. PAVONI, Human rights and the immunities of foreign states and international organizations, in E. DE WET, J. VIDMAR, Hierarchy in international law: The place of human rights, Oxford University Press, Oxford, 2012, pp. 71ss. E. DE BRABANDERE, Immunity of international organizations in post-conflict international administrations, in International Organizations Law Review, 7, 2010, pp. 79ss. C. TOMUSCHAT, The European Court of Human Rights and the United Nations, in A. FØLLESDAL, B. PETERS, G. ULFSTEIN, Constituting Europe: The European Court of Human Rights in a national, european and global context, Cambridge University Press, Cambridge, 2013, pp. 334ss. C. ECKES, S. HOLLENBERG, Reconciling different legal spheres in theory and practice: Pluralism and constitutionalism in the cases of Al Jedda, Ahmed and Nada, in Maastricht Journal of European and Comparative Law, 20, 2013, pp. 218ss. G. VERDIRAME, The United Nations and human rights. Who guards the guardians?, Cambridge University Press, Cambridge, 2011, pp. 354ss. J. KRUMREY, Die Immunität der Vereinten Nationen: Verantwortlichkeit für Friedenswissenshaft, Mohr Siebeck, Tübingen, 2018, pp. 312ss.

over Dutchbat to the UN."[310] The presumption that it should result for which any harmful conduct put in place by the contingent should be attributed to the UN could be lost according to the Dutchbat. It should the sending State interrupt the chain of command that is part of the organization by means of orders contrary to those given by the latter.

The Dutchbat accepts the appeal on the basis of the decisive importance that the defendant State would have shared with the UN the decision which would then trigger the order to evacuate the compound.[311]

---

[310]Mothers of Srebrenica v. The state of the Netherlands, The Hague District Court, 295247/HA ZA 07-2973, 16th July 2014. For further analysis see: K. SCHMALENBACH, Preserving the gordian knot: UN legal accountability in the aftermath of Srebrenica, in Netherlands International Law Review, 62, 2015, pp. 313ss. J.J. PAUST, The U.N. is bound by human rights: Understanding the full reach of human rights, remedies, and non immunity, in Harvard International Law Journal, 51, 2010, pp. 4-9.

[311]Final decision of 19 July 2019 (ECLI:NL:HR:2019:1284). According to our opinion the two main reasons that categorically exclude that art. 8 DARSIWA regulate the attribution in the peacekeeping operations case. Absurdly, the argument of the Dutch Supreme Court founded on that rule seems to put on the same level state contingents lent to the UN in the sphere of peacekeeping operations and paramilitary groups such as the contras in Nicaragua. It does not seem to have to linger any further on this parallelism, except to point out that, although it is nevertheless open to criticism, a particularly strict standard of attribution appears justified when the conduct is carried out by subjects who have no organic relationship with the State. But in this case the conduct is carried out by state organs, which maintain their status even when they are loaned to UN and even continue to receive orders and instructions from their governments. Why, therefore, did the Supreme Court use this argumentation scheme? An answer can (perhaps) be found in paragraph 3.3.5. (...) It should be noted that in these proceedings, unlike in the (Nuhanovic) and (Mustafic) judgments (...) the question of whether making Dutchbat available to UN implies that Dutchbat's conduct can be attributed to UN, or to the dual attribution (attribution to both UN and state) is possible, is not at issue. Nuhanovic and Mustafic judgments that the latter was the case. This is why the provisions in DARIO concerning the attribution of conduct to an international organization are not directly relevant to these proceedings (...) (para. 3.9.1 et seq.). The passage, indeed very obscure, seems to reveal how the Court did not intend to make use of DARIOs because no attribution profile to UN was under discussion. The explanation seems reasonable only up to a certain point. It is understandable that the attribution of conduct to the state is evaluated through DARSIWA rules and not through DARIO ones. This can happen when, pursuant to art. 7 of the DARIO, UN does not exercise sufficient control over the conduct in question that at that point would be attributed to the supplier state of the troops on the assumption that these are (are) to be considered their own de jure organs pursuant to art. 4 of DARSIWA. The reasoning just developed stimulates two conclusions: - admitting that DARSIWA are the regulatory framework for the attribution, it is art. 4, not 8; -in any case we do not see how we can ignore art. 7 DARIO, even if only to show that the UN exercises or does not exercise a form of control over national contingents, thus excluding the attribution to the state or justifying it pursuant to art. 4 DARSIWA. The explanation provided by the Supreme Court in paragraph 3.3.5, therefore, does not hold. All that remains is to try to go beyond the reasons given by the Supreme Court, looking at the judicial case as a whole and, again, the Nuhanovic and

This conclusion is based on art. 7 DARIO although as has been observed this provision concerns exclusively the imputation of the illicit fact to the organization that manages the mission.[312]

Mustafic cases. Indeed, it is perhaps the sentences of the Supreme Court in these last two cases to help find the right interpretation. While acknowledging the responsibility of the Dutch government for the omissions of the Dutchbat during the evacuation of UNPROFOR compound following the fall of Srebrenica, the Supreme Court had outlined two possible scenarios during a peacekeeping operation: 1) The normal scenario, in where national contingents are part of the UN chain of command; 2) a "pathological" scenario, such as, for example, the final phase of an operation, in which the UN chain of command withdraws in favor of the national ones. The outcome of the judicial case initiated by the Srebrenica Mothers tells us therefore that in the first scenario the standard of attribution to the State must be more severe than in the second. It is necessary to prove the existence of orders that interrupt the UN chain of command, the mere ascertainment of a certain influence by the supplier state of the troops is not enough. Article 8 DARSIWA and the caudine forks of the effective control elaborated by ICJ have been assumed to standards of attribution also in the context of a peacekeeping operation because functional to the objective, although the choice is not justifiable in the light of the international law. It is more than legitimate to doubt the appropriateness of using such a strict attribution standard. The reality of peacekeeping operations is made up of continuous consultations with national governments, which it is possible that they do not materialize in actual "orders." Some of these consultations may well influence the conduct of peacekeepers, as we have seen in connection with the abandonment of checkpoints in Srebrenica. In light of this, it is so certain to believe that if the Minister of Defense gives a general instruction to give priority to the safety of the personnel and if such instruction induces the troops on the field to hold a contrary behaviour to a endowment order from the UN chain of command, is it always the latter organization that exercises effective control? On the other hand, is it not reasonable to assume that with regard to such conduct it is the state that exercises control? Or that at least one can doubt that the organization is in full control of troops receiving instructions from their governments? And if, as a result of such conduct, some individuals see their fundamental rights violated, it is not reasonable to assume that those individuals may attempt to obtain relief from the national courts of the troop-supplying states, since it is impossible, cause immunity, criticize the UN? The answers to these questions will probably need to be reflected again. The result, for now, is that the spaces to invoke responsibility for human rights violations in the context of peacekeeping operations have been drastically restricted.

[312]In this sense and in the same orientation we could say that while the ECtHR was examining its first case concerning state responsibility in peace operations, in 2004 the Queen's Bench Division adjudicated a case concerning the liability in compensation of the UK for the killing, the wounding and the illness caused to two Kosovar Albanians who were shot by UNMIK British forces in 1999 (Queens Bench Division, Bici and Bici v. Ministry of Defence, EWHC 786, 7 April, 2004). The plaintiffs were travelling in a car in the streets of Pristina during the "Kosovo National Day." One of the victims was sitting on the roof of the car and, according to the findings of the Court, had fired his gun in the air during the gathering of that celebration day; the other claimants were sitting inside the car. The British soldiers, who were defending a building while the car was passing by fired back at the car in alleged self-defence. The gunfire resulted in the killing of the person sitting on the car's roof, in the injuring and in the psychiatric illness of the other two

plaintiffs seated in the car. The sentence, which found the UK liable in compensation, touched upon the issue of attribution of wrongful conduct quite succinctly. In fewer than 40 words on the subject, the findings reported a very interesting opinio iuris of the UK on the attribution of conduct of its forces seconded to a UN-led mission, expressed in the following terms: "[T]he defendant has conceded that it is vicariously liable for any wrongs committed by any of the soldiers. The Crown retained command of the British forces notwithstanding that they were acting under the auspices of the U.N. In other words, the UK has accepted its liability in compensation for the wrongful acts committed by its soldiers. Moreover, it has stressed the requirement of national command exercised over the forces, implicitly refusing the theory of UN-led mission as UN subsidiary organs and the related exclusive attribution to the Organization. It is well known, however, that the UK has significantly changed this approach by claiming before the Strasbourg Court in several occasions the exclusive attribution to the UN of wrongful conducts occurring not only in UN-led, but also in UN-authorised, operations (Behrami, Al Saadon, Al Jedda, Al Skeini. It is interesting to note in the Al Skeini case the UK was expressly estopped by the Court to formulate this objection as it was never brought before national Courts while exhausting local remedies, see Al Skeini case, par. 100). Another example of this change can be found in the Mohammed case, where the UK maintained the exclusive attribution to the UN of conduct of its soldiers in Afghanistan (Mohammed v. Ministry of Defense et al. and Secretary of State v Mohammed et al., Court of Appeal, EWCA 3846, 30 July 2015. See also the Supreme Court Judgment that eventually upheld the crown of State act defence, while not dealing with attribution issues, n. 2017 UKSC 1, 17 January 2017). The claim concerned the illegal detention of the plaintiff by British Forces participating in ISAF, the first case dealing with the responsibility of the UK for alleged violations occurred during their presence in Afghanistan. In Queen's Bench division, judge Leggatt, carried out a careful analysis of the facts and of the legal precedents to respond to the government's argument, investigating, on the one hand, whether the conducts of ISAF were generally attributable to the UN and, on the other hand, whether the impugned actions were attributable to the ISAF or solely to the UK. In order to inquire the attribution link between ISAF and the UN, judge Leggatt looked into the chain of command and control of ISAF, stressing that since August 2003 "overall operational command had been vested with NATO" (beforehand ISAF had been under the alternating leadership of the UK, Turkey, and, jointly, Germany and The Netherlands). The impugned acts occurred in April 2010, hence in the context of NATO-led ISAF, that is to say of a UN-authorised mission, as opposed for example to UNMIK which was a UN-led operation. The judge was convinced that the chain of delegation of command for ISAF is essentially similar to the chain of delegation and command for KFOR, as described in the judgement of the European Court in the Behrami and Saramati cases. From this premise, the judge drew another unfortunate parallelism with the Behrami case, maintaining that "the UN Security Council has "effective control" (and "ultimate authority and control") over ISAF in the sense required to enable wrongful conduct of ISAF to be attributed to the UN." As a consequence, judge Leggatt, stated that should the detention of Mr Mohammed be authorised by COMISAF (ISAF Commander), the wrongful act would be attributable to the UN, similarly to the detention of Mr Behrami that was authorised by the COMKFOR (KFOR Commander) and hence attributed to the UN by the ECtHR. In the Court's reasoning it was thus crucial to determine which entity authorised the detention, whether the UK or COMISAF, or both. To resolve this pivotal issue, judge Leggatt relied again on the mission's chain of command and control, this time with a special focus on existing policies and special arrangements for detention. The evidence before the Court showed that since November 2009 the UK operated in Afghanistan according to its national detention policy, which implied, on the one hand, that the applicable laws and regulations were set forth not in ISAF standards but rather in UK national standards; on the other hand, the authority to detain was vested in the UK national chain of command and not with COMISAF. In other words, prisoners detained by UK forces participating in ISAF were under UK authority, through the Commander of Joint Force Support who reported to the UK Permanent Joint Headquarter and finally to the Ministry of Defence; whereas the relationship between the UK and ISAF on the issue of detention was "of liaison and coordination only." Furthermore, the Standard Operating Procedures of detentions of UK forces differed significantly from those of ISAF. Under the latter, an individual can only be detained for 96-hours, afterwards she or he had to be released or handed over to Afghan authorities. A possible extension can only be authorised by COMISAF. The UK applied a caveat to NATO ISAF guidelines stating that the detention regime was the troop contributing nation's "sovereign business and based upon UK national sovereignty." Accordingly, the UK had informed NATO of its intention to detain individuals for longer than 96 hours based on the main concern that the time lapse foreseen in NATO standards was too limited to grant effective information-gathering, which was deemed essential to the mission. Due to the lack of objection from NATO, the judge inferred that the caveat had been eventually accepted by the Organization. Once the general detention-policy framework in Afghanistan was depicted, the Court ascertained that in the circumstances of the case the capture and the detention of Mr Mohammed was authorised and periodically revised by the UK and that his internment took place in the military base of Camp Bastion, under the "full and exclusive de facto control of the UK." Hence judge Leggatt concluded that the impugned acts were only attributable to the UK as the conduct took place solely under the national chain of command and control. Differently said, the wrongful acts are not attributable to ISAF as no authorization concerning Mr Mohammed detention had been sought by COMISAF. Accordingly, no attribution to the UN could be envisaged, lacking a previous attribution of conduct to ISAF. As to the conduct's wrongfulness, the Court concluded that the plaintiff's detention beyond the initial 96 hours was arbitrary, as no power to detain beyond that period was entrusted to the respondent country, neither under the UN mandate nor under ISAF mandate, or under Afghan law, or even under international humanitarian law. Consequently, the Ministry of Defense has incurred liability for violations of art. 5 of the European Convention on Human Rights and of section 6 of the Human Rights Act. The Court's findings have been confirmed in the appeal. The impact of this case law on the interpretation of attribution under international law is a mixed blessing. The judgement's main shortcomings lie with the application of the rules on international responsibility as the domestic judge seems more familiar with the ECtHR jurisprudence rather than with the DARIO. While the sentence relied extensively on the Behrami approach, it only resorted to the DARIO in a brief consideration on ultra vires acts.Furthermore, a major inconsistency in the Court's reasoning lies with the use of the effective control test, that has been interpreted both in a normative and in a factual fashion. In the first part of his analysis, judge Leggatt determined that the UN SC had "effective control" and "ultimate authority and control" over ISAF for the purposes of attributing conducts of ISAF to the UN. The inference was therefore that the impugned conduct would be attributable to the UN insofar as it would be attributable to ISAF. In the second part of the judgement, in order to determine whether the wrongful acts were attributable to ISAF, the judge included a very detailed factual analysis of the chain of command and control of the mission in general, and also of the impugned detention in

The Court of appeal of the Hague substantially confirmed on 27 June 2017 the first instance sentence with regard to state responsibility of the defendant one, but ordered a compensation in favour of the victims in a decidedly lower amount than what was requested in the appeal. The reasoning of the appellate judge proceeds from this point of view in hypothetical terms based on the premise that the conduct of the Dutch military would probably have guaranteed the relatives of the applicants to survive the Srebrenica massacre. The Court of appeal has estimated this probability to the extent of 30% and has ordered the compensation amount based on this assessment.[313]

3.8. (Follows) Effective control in Brussels. The Mukeshimana-Ngulinzira case

The Court of first instance of Brussels was asked to adjudicate the liability in compensation of the Belgian State and of two Belgian high officers for the actions and omissions of the Belgium contingent of the Mission des Nations Unies pour l'Assistance au Rwanda (MINUAR). The case was brought by nine survivors and next of kin of those killed in the mass killing of Tutsi and moderated Hutu that sought refuge in a school in Kigali that was then the headquarter of the Belgium contingent participating to MINUAR, in the context of 1994 Rwanda genocide. After Belgium decided to withdraw its troops from the mission, including the contingents in the school that became a de facto refugee camp in April 1994, most of the refugees-about two thousand people-were killed by the Hutu's militias during the genocide. Only some hundreds people managed to escape the massacre.[314] The claimants maintained that the killings were

particular. The Court resorted extensively to military concepts, as well as to military documents and to the witness of several military high-ranking officers. Hence, in this section of the judgement the criterion of effective control was intended as a factual test (inquiring which entity had authorised the detention within the mission's chain of command and control) and not as normative standards (the "ultimate authority and control" test), although the term "effective control" was never used in this part of the sentence. In sum, the Mohammed judgement constitutes another meaningful example of the existing tension between the normative and the factual interpretation of attribution criteria. Despite the inconsistencies highlighted so far, this case provides for an extremely accurate analysis of how a factual effective control test can be applied to peace operations, focusing on the chain of command and control that was followed to carry out the internationally wrongful act at hand.

[313]Mothers of Srebrenica v. The state of the Netherlands, 27 juin 2017, C/09/295247/HA ZA 07-2973.

[314]Court of First Instance of Brussels, Mukeshimana-Ngulinzira et al. v Belgium et al., RG No 04/4807/A, 07/15547/A, 8 December 2010.

a direct consequence of the evacuation of the Belgium contingent and therefore the Belgium State and the respondent commanding officers failed to fulfil the mission's mandate to protect civilians. The judgement, which is just an interim decision, tackled several issues including the question of statute of limitations under Belgian law. For the purpose of the present analysis it is particularly interesting to highlight the Court's findings as to jurisdiction and to attribution of conduct. The respondent State contented that the Court lacked jurisdiction because in order to adjudicate the claim it would have had to assess the responsibility of the UN and of the other Member States participating in the mission. In the State's reasoning, the Court would have clearly been precluded to do so due to the jurisdictional immunity of the Organization. The Court did not share this view and positively affirmed its jurisdiction stressing that only the liability of Belgium and of two Belgian nationals was at issue because the impugned acts were attributable exclusively to the State. The inquiry conducted by the Court showed that the decision to evacuate the Belgium contingent from the camp was taken exclusively by the Belgium State in the exercise of its full command. In fact, Belgium at that time had not only withdrawn troops from the school-camp but had withdrawn its whole participation from MINUAR. Hence the Court determined that: (...) La thèse défendue par les parties demanderesses est précisément que le contrôle des troupes stationnées à l'ETO [the compound] a été retiré à la MINUAR et placé sous la responsabilité exclusive de l'ETAT BELGE lequel aurait commis seul les fautes reprochées, entraînant une responsabilité qui lui est propre (...) comme le précisent les demandeur, "les faits reprochés à l'Etat belge ne relèvent pas de son action en qualité d'Etat participant à la MINUAR."[315] It should be noted that the Court did not make any explicit reference to the provisions of the DARIO, but it is quite evident that it endorsed to a certain extent the effective control test and, more precisely, a factual interpretation thereof, by looking into the chain of command of the contingent's withdrawal from the refugee camp (In this sense see the comment to the sentence by Ryngaert in Oxford Reports on International Law, ILDC 1604 (BE 2010), and of the same author "Apportioning Responsibility Between the UN and Member States in UN Peace-support Operations.)"

---

[315] Court of First Instance of Brussels, Mukeshimana-Ngulinzira et al. v Belgium et al., RG No 04/4807/A, 07/15547/A, op. cit.

3.9. Member States position and thesis of double imputation of conduct in peacekeeping missions

The criterion for imputing unlawful conduct committed within the framework of peace-keeping missions is such as to constitute the responsibility of the organization to which the states lend their military continents on condition that the same conduct takes place under the effective control of the functional body that manages the operation itself. If the criterion indicated is commonly considered by the doctrine of title of exclusive responsibility of the beneficiary loan organization,[316] there is no lack of opinions of a different sign that without denying the responsibility of the functional bodies reach the conclusion for which the imputation to the latter, of the significant behaviour does not serve to exclude the responsibility of the supplier States. The authors who support this thesis start from the common assumption for which the troops used by the international organizations do not cease to be contextually organs of the respective sending States.[317]

Part of the doctrine in question considers with particular reference to peacekeeping operations managed by the UN that the blue helmets are good to look at "des agents doubles, in ce sens qu'en eux cohabite a double rattachement (..) un double statut organique." [318] According to this perspective, although the members of the multinational forces are to be considered for the duration of the mission to the truce of UN agents. It should be noted that at the same time their legal status as (military) organs of the respective sending States remains. The principle of double imputation of the same conduct should be applied as a general rule so as to generate the international responsibility of both subjects, the organization and the state of belonging to which the material author of the offense is bound by an organic bond to the military forces employed by the UN in the missions here under consideration are always subject to the authority and control of the supplying States and represent the instrument for the exercise of prerogatives of "puissance publique" as much of the UN as of those States.[319]

---

[316]F. SEYRSTED, United Nations forces in the law of peace and war, op. cit., pp. 428ss. C. AMERASINGHE, Principles of the institutional law of international organizations, Cambridge University Press, Cambridge, 2005, pp. 244ss.

[317]C. LECK, International responsibility in United Nations peacekeeping operations. Command and control arrangements and the attribution of conduct, op. cit., pp. 346ss.

[318]C. LECK, International responsibility in United Nations peacekeeping operations. Command and control arrangements and the attribution of conduct, op. cit.

[319] C. LECK, International responsibility in United Nations peacekeeping operations.

Another part of the doctrine moving from a substantially analogous line of reasoning centered on the link that exists between each contingent and its sending status highlights the substantial unsuitability of the prevailing thesis which, as said, lays in the sense of the exclusive responsibility of the receiving organization to configure the position of the supplier States.[320] According to this orientation, the control exercised by the organization over the state contingents is at least in principle full with the clarification that such control extends only to the political and operational aspects of the mission.[321]

On the organizational level, according to this perspective the sending States compete with the functional body in the exercise of powers of direction and supervision over the respective troops, thereby maintaining a considerable degree of control over their military organs. The double organic connection would operate exclusively with regard to the organizational profiles with respect to which the configuration of the double imputation of the illegal conduct possibly put in place by the national contingents should more properly be limited.

The appeal sentence in the Nuhanović case was favourably received by the authors for whom in the context of peacekeeping operations the conduct of the military organs lent by a State to the organization could simultaneously be attributed one to the other.[322]

3.10. (Follows) Considerations regarding the double imputation theory

The arguments set out in the previous paragraph, although decidedly persuasive as concerns the premises from which they move, lend themselves to certain critical considerations with regard to the conclusions to which they are based. In the first place, as has been repeatedly emphasized, the possibility of the double attribution of the same unlawful conduct is certainly conceivable if only in abstracto. Already at regulatory

Command and control arrangements and the attribution of conduct, op. cit.

[320] C. LECK, International responsibility in United Nations peacekeeping operations. Command and control arrangements and the attribution of conduct, op. cit.

[321] K. SCHMALENBACH, Die Haftung Internationaler Organizationen im Rahmen von Militäreinsätzen und Territorialverwaltungen, ed. Peter Lang, Frankfurt am Main, 2004, pp. 249, which is observed that: "den Vereinten Nationen ist das Handeln der Peace-keeping-Soldaten zuzurechnen, da sie während der Einsatzes unter dem operativen Kommando der Vereinten Nationen stehen."

[322] F. MESSINEO, Attribution of conduct, in A. NOLLKAEMPER, I. PLAKOKEFALOS, Principles of shared responsibility in international law. An appraisal of the state of the art, op. cit., pp. 95ss.

level, this is confirmed both in the article on state responsibility and the project on responsibility of international organizations. It must be noted on the one hand how the practice seems decidedly oriented towards the exclusive imputation to a single subject among those involved[323] and on the other how difficult is to reconstruct and demonstrate the circumstances in the presence of which two subjects of the order share on an equal level at all the realization of an offense so that the latter can be simultaneously attributed to both.

In fact the 2001 Project contemplates the case in question with regard to those situations in which "the latter organ of one State acts on the joint instructions of its own and another State," since "the conduct in question is attributable to both States."[324] The provisions of art. 47, par. 1 of the mentioned instrument under which "where several States are responsible for the same internationally wrongful act the responsibility of each State may be invoked in relation to that act."[325] In quite similar terms, the article on responsibility of international organizations envisages the hypothesis in which the same unlawful conduct can be attributed both to the organization and to one or more of its Member States. It seems that the ILC presents an eventuality as already mentioned on a purely theoretical level, considering that "dual or even multiple attribution of conduct cannot be excluded," although "it may not frequently occur in practice."[326] The approved 2011 project therefore regulates the legal consequences deriving from the double imputation, establishing in art. 48, par. 1, which: "Where

[323] C. LECK, International responsibility in United Nations peacekeeping operations. Command and control arrangements and the attribution of conduct, op. cit., pp. 358ss.

[324] ARSIWA, p. 44, par. 3. the passage cited is treated by the comment to the art. 6 which regulates the imputation of conduct carried out by organs lent to one State to another State. In the aforementioned paragraph the ILC takes care to exclude from the scope of application of art. 6 all those situations in which the body that materially carries out the harmful conduct acts under the shared control between the two States involved.

[325] A. NOLLKAEMPER, I. PLAKOKEFALOS, Principles of shared responsibility in international law, op. cit.

[326] DARIO, p. 16, par. 4. C. LECK, International responsibility in United Nations peacekeeping operations. Command and control arrangements and the attribution of conduct, op. cit., pp. 361s, the comment of art. 7 affirms that: "Seemed to leave little away for dual or multiple attribution based on dual or joint control of the conduct concerned." The co-allocation of the same conduct constitutes a mere conceptual abstraction is also supported by P. KLEIN, The attribution of acts to international organizations, in J. CRAWFORD, A. PELLET, S. OLLESON, K. PARLETT, The law of international responsibility, op. cit., which is observed that "the existence of parallel international responsibility as between an international organization and one or more of its members therefore continues for the present to be of a purely hypothetical kind; however nothing appears to prevent it from a theoretical standpoint."

an international organization and one or more States or international organization are responsible for the same internationally wrongful act, the responsibility of each State or international organization may be invoked in relation to that act." The indications that can be drawn from the comments to the cited rules seem to confirm the strict scope of application. The comment to art. 47 takes as examples of shared responsibility, the joint action on the one hand and the unlawful conduct put in place by a common body on the other.[327] In our opinion, the first of the two hypotheses is configurable where each of the States, rectius of the subjects involved, acts through its own organs and instruments. This seems to be the perspective closest to the factual reality, with reference at least to the examples to which the doctrine which intends to examine an illegal conduct of the type considered. In the case of military operation, contrary to the prohibition of the use of force, carried out by two States, [328] the international responsibility of the latter normally derives from a joint action but that they tend to compete on an equal footing to finalize as said through their own organs. The Anglo-American aggression against Iraq in 2003 could be cited in this sense. The second of the two hypotheses mentioned, that focused on the institution of the common organ is equally to be excluded if only because the military contingents employed in peace-keeping missions are formally sending state organs. Even if they were considered qualified in the official UN documents or access to the thesis that reveals their possible assimilation to the de facto body,[329] these contingents would

---

[327]ARSIWA, p. 124, par. 2.

[328]C. DOMINICÉ, Attribution of conduct to multiples states and the implication of a state in the act of another state, in J. CRAWFORD, A. PELLET, S. OLLESON, K. PARLETT, The law of international responsibility, op. cit., pp. 282ss.

[329]C. DOMINICÉ, Attribution of conduct to multiples states and the implication of a state in the act of another state, in J. CRAWFORD, A. PELLET, S. OLLESON, K. PARLETT, The law of international responsibility, op. cit., C. KRESS, L'organe de facto en droit international publi. Rèflexions sur l'imputation à l'Etat de l'acte d'un particulier à la lumière des dèveloppements rècents, in Revue Gènerale de Droit International Public, 105, 2001, pp. 126, defined as: "Le noyay de la notion d'organe de facto." The 2001 project defines and distinguishes between organs and individuals who act on behalf of the state acquires its own independent meaning. The quality of organ would refer to the existence of a particularly close connection between the individual agent and the state would be exhausted in the fact of the instruction given or of the direction and control exercised by state organs towards that individual. It must be asked whether a reconstructive approach that purports to accurately identify the relevant factual elements for the purpose of attributing excessively rigid attribution criteria that are not able to adequately account for the variety of situations that may arise in practice. A criticism of this kind in fact to be addressed towards the draft of articles adopted in first reading, having given importance to these exclusively to the hypothesis of the individual acting behind the instructions of state

organs did not seem to provide an adequate reading key to interpret those cases of the practice in which the behaviour of individuals who were connected to it by a de facto relationship based on elements different from the instructions or from the control on the specific conduct was attributed to the State. The same objection can also be moved towards the solution proposed by the chambers of appeal of the ICTY in the Tadić and Ilaşcu and others v. Moldova and Russia case of 8 July 2004 by ECtHR which has made similar considerations in relation to the problem of the traceability to Russia of the acts put in place by the separatist regime established in the Moldovan region of Transdniestria. The ECtHR avoids qualifying the separatist regime as a subordinate local administration of Russia, the applied attribution criterion appears to be the same used in the Loizidou v. Turkey case (I. PETCULESCU, Droit international de la responsabilitè et droits de l'homme, in Revue Gènèrale de Droit International Public, 109, 2005, pp. 590ss. M.P. SCHARF, How the Tadić appeals chamber decision foundamentally altered customary international law, in M. STERIO, M. SCHARF, The legacy of ad hoc tribunals in international criminal law. Assessing the ICTY's and the ICTR's most significant legal accomplishments, Cambridge University Press, Cambridge, 2019). The argument was developed to argue that in order to attribute to the State the conduct of paramilitary groups, it is always necessary to ascertain that state organs had effective control over the work of these groups. To confirm this thesis, he referred to ICTY ruling in the Hadžihasanović case in which the ad hoc court to establish the responsibility of a Bosnian commander for the crimes committed by a paramilitary group was not limited to finding that this group was based to an act of domestic law formally part of the army of that state but had also ascertained the existence of an effective control over the work of this group. It is not clear how the principle established in this ruling may have some relevance even in terms of attribution for the purposes of state responsibility unless one wishes to support a thesis that appears to be totally unfounded, namely that the quality of body based on internal law not sufficient for the attribution of the conduct of this to the State, being in any case necessary in addition to the existence of a formal link of internal law between the individual or the group and the State, proof of effective control over the unlawful conduct. See for comments: M. SPINEDI, State responsibility v. individual responsibility for international crime: Tertium non datur?, in European Journal of International Law, 13, 2002, pp. 896ss. In the same orientation, think of opinion no. 9/1998 of the working group on arbitrary detention of the UN Human Rights Commission (UN Doc. E/CN/2000/4 28 December 1999, par. 11-18) concerning abuses committed in the detention center of Al- Khiam subject to the authority of the army of South Lebanon (SLA) where, for the purposes of a legal qualification of this militia, the Commission traces these offenses to Israel solely on the basis of an overall control of Israel over the military formation in question to regardless of a certain relationship with the specific disputed torts. The criterion of global control can constitute a valid criterion of attribution in relation to the type of situation contemplated in that case. It does not seem able to provide an adequate foundation with respect to other hypotheses in which the behaviour of individuals united to this can be attributed to the state from a factual relationship (F. DOPAGNE, La responsabilitè de l'Etat du fait des particuliers: les causes d'imputation par les articles sur la responsabilitè de l'Etat pour fait internationalement illicite, in Revue Belge de Droit International, 34, 2001, pp. 522ss. L. CONDORELLI, L'imputations à l'Etat d'un fait internationalement illicite: solutions classiques et nouvelles tendances, op. cit., pp. 102ss). One can certainly imagine the situation in which a State recognizes as its own a conduct that would not otherwise refer to it to the general rules of attribution. In this case it does not seem that there is need to resort to the notion of

not in any case fall within the notion of the common body which presupposes the presence within it of elements attributable to it, i.e. to the authority of one or more States participating in it and acting through it in a uniform and simultaneous manner. Consider, for example, an inter-allied commander or an agency in charge of managing a watercourse, made up of individuals appointed by two States. In other words, the recognizable organic link in the military contingent here has an exclusive character so that it must be configured as a state organ that de jure and de facto is in the availability of the receiving organization. As a result of these observations, it seems possible to conclude that the joint imputation of illegal conduct by national troops integrated in peacekeeping missions, even if theoretically possible, is indeed a hypothesis.[330]

---

attribution to explain why the state is obliged to answer for the conduct in question. The obligation of the State can be seen as the consequence of the unilateral act, by which the State has recognized this as its own conduct. In our opinion, any global control exercised by a State over private individuals should favour the recognition of its overall responsibility for the activities of the latter, which can be qualified as its de facto organs. The choice of the state not to directly involve its own bodies even to escape an immediate dispute about its responsibility necessarily implies the assumption of a certain risk for the activities carried out by private persons legally extraneous to its own organizational structure but on whose behaviour could actually have affected. In our opinion, the approach aimed at attributing to the controlling state the entirety of the unlawful actions produced by the group in question leads to the same substantive conclusions that lead to some cases commonly considered as examples of hypotheses of de facto organs. The circumstance according to which the major openings towards the recognition of more flexible criteria aimed at widening the possibilities of attribution to a state of acts of groups made up of private individuals, is essentially from courts competent to judge on the violations of humanitarian law and from bodies committed to safeguarding human rights. The importance of complicity as a specific imputation criterion of the international crime in the State implies that the object of consideration is the active or omissive behaviour of the organs of the State which contributes with proven effectiveness and with full psychology awareness to the execution of an at least materially illicit fact for international law (M. CHERIF BASSIOUNI, Legal control of international terrorism, in Harvard International Law Journal, 43, 2002, pp. 84ss. K. DALACOURA, Islamist movements as non-state actors and their relevance to international relations, in D. JOSELLIN, W. WALLACE, Non-state actors in world politics, ed. Palgrave, London, New York, 2001, pp. 236ss). Where international subjectivity is denied to the individual, it is equally possible to speak of complicity, even if only in a technical sense, in order to indicate the existence of an alternative criterion of attribution of state responsibility, with respect to which the private act represents a given purely factual, which allows it to emerge similarly to what happens in the event of non-compliance with due diligence obligations. Compared to this case, the attribution of complicity on the side of understanding would imply a more serious responsibility of the state than that deriving from the omission of suitable preventive and repressive measures: The act of the private would indicate precisely the material content of the offense committed by the State.

[330]C. DOMINICÉ, Attribution of conduct to multiples states and the implication of a state

Coming then to the ruling of the appellate or the Hague and the Dutch Supreme Cerourt in the Nuhanović case it does not seem that the picture changes decisively. Dutch judges expressly admit the possibility of co-imputation of the conduct at the origin of the appeals but it seems that this happens mainly on the basis of a different reconstruction of the facts, which starts from the consideration that at the time of consummation of the conduct disputed the situation to the context so much so that according to the Court after 11 July 1995 the mission to Srebrenica had clearly failed. In other words, in our opinion the co-imposition mainly relies on the fact that the evacuation order was issued by mutual agreement between UN and Dutchbat, so that according to the Court of appeal the Dutch government "participated in that decision-making at the highest level."[331] Moreover, the legal title invoked by the Court of appeal in support of the double attribution of its object, that is to say art. 7 DARIO. This provision governs the hypothesis in which the conduct of a state body can be attributed to an international organization. This eventuality occurs only the conditions set by art. 7 otherwise it assumed that the conduct in question is due to the sending State. In other words, attribution to one or the other subject arises as an alternative,[332] as seems to be deduced from the comment of art. 7 DARIO[333] and the Mukeshimana-Ngulinzira and others v. Belgium sentence of 8 December 2010 with which the Court of first instance of Belgium attributed to Belgium the conduct of the Belgian contingent engaged in the UNAMIR mission in Rwanda.[334] Then another

in the act of another state, in J. CRAWFORD, A. PELLET, S. OLLESON, K. PARLETT, The law of international responsibility, op. cit., pp. 283ss.

331Even more explicit is the court's conclusion to par. 5.17, which is affirmed that "on 11 July 1995 the Dutch government took the decision to evacuate dutchbat together with the refugees."

332For which art. 7 DARIO would not be incompatible with the possibility of a double attribution of unlawful conduct.

333"The criterion for attribution of conduct either to the contributing State or organization or to the receiving Organization is based according to article 7 on the factual control," DARIO, p. 20, par. 4.

334The facts at the origin of the appeal had taken place in the course of the UNAMIR mission, established from the Security Council with Resolution no. 872/1993. In April of 1994, the Belgian contingent integrated into the mission decided to evacuate a refugee camp mainly of Tutsi ethnicity. As a result of this decision, most of the unprotected refugees were killed by militias of the Hutu ethnic group. Some survivors of the massacre presented against Belgium at the Brussels Court of first instance. The latter attributes the object of grievance to the state of dispatch due to the fact that the national leader "n'hèsitait pas par ailleurs à passer outre the avis de la MINUAR" interrupting the chain of command that was headed by the UN (Mukeshimana-ngulinzira and others v. Belgium RG N. 04/4807/1, 07/15547/A, ILDC 1604 (BE 2010), 8th December 2010, Belgium, Brussles; Court of First

consideration seems possible. The appeal ruling considered the requirement of effective control to be satisfied due to the power/duty of the sending State to prevent the event suffered by the family members of the applicants presumably of the order's primary rule. This reading of art. 7 in addition to making the imputation to state conduct committed in the context of peacekeeping missions almost automatic, it does not seem compatible with the factual nature of the criterion adopted by the ILC which seems tended to determine the link between a subject and actual course it events regardless of the primary obligation with which to assess the lawfulness of the conduct. If the assessment regarding the behaviour that the state body should have held in a given situation does not integrate a criterion of imputation of conduct, it may nevertheless form the basis of a different international responsibility title which we will try to reconstruct in the following paragraphs.

3.11. Law application on complicity to cases of offenses committed in the context of peacekeeping operations

The relief for which the military contingents continue to be military organs of the respective sending States, as such subjected in any case to the authority of the latter and which according to the orientation described above serves as a presupposition of co-imputation, constitutes to our notice the basis for a different solution to the legal question under consideration. More precisely, the criterion set forth in art. 7 of the project on the responsibility of international organizations described above represents a parameter for imputing the offense to the subject who has exercised effective control over it. This does not exclude the possibility that such an offense is assisted by an act consisting of the participation of another subject, being able to configure the former as main offense, the latter as behaviour that integrates a form of complicity based on the general rule set forth in articles 16 ARSIWA ad 58 DARIO. So if it is assumed that in art. 77 DARIO the responsibility of the organization that manages the mission the position of the State of nationality of the contingent that materially implements the harmful conduct can be assessed in the light of the rules governing the institution of assistance to the crime of others. In our opinion, the last perspective indicated is in our opinion a

Instance in ORILDC, 2010). The court did not mention art. 7 DARIO but seems to entice it to the contrary. Given that the effective control of the UN on the unlawful conduct was not evident (...).

legislative confirmation in the provisions of art. 58 DARIO. As already noted by the doctrine that supports in general terms the thesis of co-attribution of the offenses put in place in the organizational phase of the peacekeeping missions the material element of complicity could result satisfied by the circumstance for which the sending State by making available the contingent to which the injurious conduct is actually attributable provides a contribution to the occurrence of the principal offense. As for the subjective element of the relevant assistance pursuant to art. 58 according to this opinion, the due diligence obligation that in itself binds every State that takes part in the mission could be highlighted. According to this orientation the case of complicity would be integrated if the sending status being aware of the main crime does not make use of all the appropriate measures to prevent its realization.

The argument just reported seems to be substantially acceptable, even if it lends itself to observation. There seems to us to be a breach of the duty of diligence as well as constituting an independent illicit,[335] could contribute together with the loan of the quota to integrate the material element of complicity in the hypotheses we are considering. The threshold of applicability of the rule from a subjective point of view would be reached by the awareness of the imminent occurrence of the principal offense which in the case of peacekeeping operations carried out under the UN command is to be presumed due to the intimate and structured consultations that continuously take place between the force commander, i.e. NCCs (National Contigent Caommanders) on the employment of their contingent.[336] The distinction between the case of assistance to the illicit of functional body and violation of the due diligence obligation of Member States seems to be reflected, in the Report of ILA of 2004 where it is stated that the responsibility of an international organization does not excludes that: "Any separate or concurrent responsibility of a State which participated in the performance of the wrongful act or which has failed to comply with its

[335]This circumstance is also highlighted because it is an obligation in its own right, the violation of which implies the attribution to the States of a responsibility connected to that attributed to the organization.

[336] C. LECK, International responsibility in United Nations peacekeeping operations. Command and control arrangements and the attribution of conduct, op. cit., pp. 357ss. See also Department of peacekeeping operations, Department of field support, UN peacekeeping operations. Principles and guideliness, approved by J.M. Guèhenno, USG/DPKO, 2008, in part., p. 52, par. 4.3, where expressly the Department underlines the centrality of a constant consultation with the contributing States "at the key stages in the life of a UN peacekeeping operation."

own obligation concerning the prevention of that wrongful act."[337]

3.12. (Follows) Violation of humanitarian law as a material element of complicity

The line of reasoning just traced leads to another observation that starts from the observation that the material element of complicity can be integrated by a fact that is in itself illegal. Due to the factual context in which peacekeeping missions take place and above all the military nature of the state bodies in question, the regulatory regime of international humanitarian law could be highlighted. State involvement with respect to unlawful acts of the type analyzed is, in our opinion, susceptible of evaluation in light or art. 1 common to the four Geneva conventions of 1959.[338] The following considerations apply.

The aforementioned law which according to part of the doctrine constitutes the normative nucleus of a system of collective responsibility,[339] establishes that the high contracting parties undertake to respect and enforce the obligations contained in the Geneva conventions in all circumstances. [340] The centrality of the law in question was

---

[337]ILA, Report o accountability of international organizations, op. cit., p. 28, sex. 2, par. 4.

[338]N. TSAGOURIAS, A. MORRISON, International humanitarian law: Cases, materials and commentary, op. cit.,

[339]L. CONDORELLI, L. BOISSON DE CHAZOURNES, Common article 1 of the Geneva conventions revisited: Protecting collective interests, in International Review of Red Cross, 82, 2000.

[340]"The High Contracting Parties undertake to respect and to ensure respect in all circumstances" (in English version); "les Hautes Parties contractantes s'engagent à respecter et à faire respecter la prèsente Convention en toutes circonstances" (in French version). Identical provision according to the Additional Protocol of 1977 relating to non-international armed conflicts does not contain provisions of a similar standard. P. BENVENUTI, Ensuring observance of the international humanitarian law: Function, extent and limits of the obligation to ensure respect for IHL, in Yearbook of the International Institute of Humanitarian Law, 1989-1990, pp. 27ss. F. KALSHOVEN, The year at the international humanitarian law, ed. Brill, Bruxelles, 1997, pp. 48ss. B. KESSLER, The duty to "ensure respect" under the common article 1 of the Geneva conventions: Its implications on international and non-international armed conflicts, in The German Yearbook of International Law, 44, 2001, pp. 507ss. V. CHETAIL, Permanence et mutation du droit des conflits armès, op. cit., Moreover, this orientation is reflected in the Nicaraguan v. United States in which the ICJ identified in art. 1 common to the Geneva Conventions the obligation of the United States "not to encourage persons or groups engaged in conflict in Nicaragua to act in violation of the provisions of article 3 common to the four 1949 Geneva convention" (par. 220). A. ZIMMERMANN, C.J. TAMS, K. OELLERS-FRAHAM, The Statute of the International Court of Justice. A commentary, op. cit.

underlined already by the most recent doctrine for which the protection system provided for by the Convention requires that the contracting parties: “Fassent ègalement tout ce qui est en leu pouvoir pour que les principes humanitaires qui sont à la base de la convention soient universellement appliquès.”[341] Article 1 of which ICJ has established the customary nature,[342] therefore imposes a specific obligation on each State that is part or less of the conflict: “D’agir oar tout moyen appropriè afin que ces règles soient observès par tous, et en particulier par les autres Etats.”[343] This

---

[341] J. PICTET, Commentaire-IV La Convention de Genève relative à la protection des personnes civiles en temps de guerre, ICRC, Genève, 1956, pp. 21ss.

[342] According to military and paramilitary activities in and against Nicaragua sentence, merits, op. cit., p. 114, par. 120, which ICJ affirmed that “such an obligation does not derive only from the convention but from the general principles of humanitarian law to which the conventions merely give specific expression.” See also in argument: L. CONDORELLI, L. BOISSON DE CHAZOURNES, Quelques remarques à propos de l’obligation des Etats de “respecter et faire respecter” le droit international humanitaire “en toute circonstances,” in C. SWINIARSKI, Études et essais sur le droit international humanitaire et sur le principes de la Croix-Rouge en l’honneur de Jean Pictet, Martinus Nijhoff Publishers, Genève, The Hague, 1984, pp. 18ss. T. RENSMANN, Die Humansierung des Völkerrects durch das ius in bello. Von der Marten’schen Klausel zur Responsibility to protect, in Zeitschrift für ausländisches Recht und Völkerrecht, 68, 2008, pp. 120ss. J.M. HENCKAERTS, L. DOSWALD-BECK, Customary international humanitarian law, Cambridge University Press, Cambridge, 2005, pp. 510ss. A. ZIMMERMANN, C.J. TAMS, K. OELLERS-FRAHAM, The Statute of the International Court of Justice. A commentary, op. cit.

[343] L. CONDORELLI, L. BOISSON DE CHAZOURNES, Quelques remarques à propos de l’obligation des Etats de “respecter et faire respecter” le droit international humanitaire “en toute circonstances,” in C. SWINIARSKI, Études et essais sur le droit international humanitaire et sur le principes de la Croix-Rouge en l’honneur de Jean Pictet, Martinus Nijhoff Publishers, Genève, The Hague, 1984, pp. 24ss, the authors highlight how the wording of the norm focused on obliquity to enforce humanitarian law has been repeated without difficulty, during the Geneva Conference in the editorial office of art. 1 of I Additional protocol, thus demonstrating how the participating states were perfectly aware: de la signification juridique de cette obligation (...). The law in question asks a closer look at the simple faculties of the contracting states to demand the respect for humanitarian law in the course of an armed conflict of which they are not parties. C. FOCARELLI, Common article 1 of the 1949 Geneva Conventions: A soap bubble?, in European Journal of International Law, 21, 2010, pp. 126ss, which leads the author to reduce the actual legal scope of art. 1 common to the Geneva conventions, if only because of the application that this rule has known in practice. See also in argument: R. KOLB, Ius in bello. Le droit internationale des conflits armès, Helbing & Lichtenhahn, Basel, 2003, pp. 244ss. A.J. BELLAMY, Responsibility to protect, polity, Cambridge University Press, Cambridge, 2009. N.F. DASTOOR, The responsibility to refine: The need for a Security Council Committee on the responsibility to protect, in Harvard Human Rights Journal, 22, 2009, pp. 25ss. A. ORFORD, Jurisdiction without territory: From the holy roman empire to the responsibility to protect, in Michigan Journal of International Law, 30 (3), 2009, pp. 982ss. S.P. ROSENBERG, Responsibility to protect: A framework for prevention, in Global Responsibility to Protect, 1, 2009, pp. 442ss. J. SARKIN, The responsibility to protect and

interpretation was confirmed in the Resolution adopted following the Teheran Conference on human rights in 1968 where express reference is made to the responsibility of States: "To ensure the request of these humanitarian rules in all circumstances by other States, even if they are not themselves directly involved in an armed conflict."[344]

The decisive aspect for the purposes of our investigation lies in the fact that all States hold a particularly qualified legal interest consisting in demanding the fulfilment of the norms of humanitarian law by all the subjects of the order who are recipients of it. Most of these regulations establish erga omnes obligations designed to protect the fundamental interests of the international community as a whole.

The above is confirmed by ICTY jurisprudence in the Kuprekić and others case of 2000 which is affirmed that: "As a consequence of their absolute character these norms of international humanitarian law or not pose synallagmatic obligations (…) they lay down obligations towards the international community as a whole with the consequence that each and every member of the international community has a legal interest in their observance and consequently a legal entitlement to demand respect for such obligations."[345]

In our opinion, it can be said that the law in question entails for the States that participate in a peacekeeping mission the obligation to demand respect for humanitarian law by the receiving international organization. More precisely, the aforementioned obligation requires the

---

humanitarian intervention in Africa, in Global Responsibility to Protect, 2, 2010, pp. 371ss. A. PETERS, The Security Council's responsibility to protect, in International Organizations Law Review, 8, 2011, pp. 4ss. B.E. VALLEJO FRANCO, La responsabilidad de proteger. Una nueva dimensión de la soberanía, in Oasis, 15, 2011, pp. 8ss. C. FOCARELLI, Ahead to the past? Responsibility to protect and the global system, in Groningen Journal of International Law, 1, 2012, pp. 4ss. J. HOFFMANN, A. NOLLKAEMPER (eds.), Responsibility to protect: From principle to practice, Pallas, Amsterdam, 2012. L. GLANVILLE, The responsibility to protect beyond borders, in Human Rights Law Review, 12, 2012, pp. 4ss. P. HILPOLD (ed.), Responsibility to protect (R2P): A new paradigm of international law?, ed. Brill Martinus Nijhoff Publishers, Leiden-Boston, 2015. J. SARKIN, Is the responsibility to protect an accepted norm of international law in the post-Libya era? How its third pillar ought to be applied, in Groningen Journal of International Law, 3, 2012, pp. 12ss. B. POMMIER, The use of force to protect civilians and humanitarian action: The case of Lybia and beyond, in International Review of the Red Cross, 93, 2011, pp. 1063ss. D. KUWALI, F. VILJOEN, By all means necessary: Protecting civilians and preventing mass atrocities in Africa, Pretoria University Law Press, Pretoria, 2017.

[344]International Conference on Human Rights, Teheran, 1928, Res. XXIII, 12 May 1968.

[345] C. FOCARELLI, Ahead to the past? Responsibility to protect and the global system, op. cit.

supplier States to ensure that their quotas are used in accordance with what is prescribed by armed conflict law. Nor is the objection that functional bodies are extraneous to the sphere of application of humanitarian law. It no longer seems to be in question that they are recipients at least of the customary norms of this right. In this respect, the UN position is decidedly peculiar, given that this organization appears to be the recipient of a definitely broader spectrum of norms falling within the scope of humanitarian law.[346]

The proposed thesis draws inspiration from the arguments put forward by the doctrine, albeit in an upside-down perspective with respect to what is intended to be outlined in the present investigation. This is the opinion for which the responsibility for offenses committed during

---

[346] It should be remembered that before the adoption of the Bulletin of the Secretary-General (UN Doc. ST/WGB/1999/13) the applicability of the humanitarian right to UN forces is particularly problematic at least under formal and technical terms. In practice, an attempt is made to overcome the problem by inserting a standard formula in the regulations of multinational forces on the basis of which "the force shall observe and respect the principles of a general international conventions applicable to the conduct of military personnel." This circumstance led the doctrine to admit the applicability to the forces of peace at least of an essential nucleus of norms of humanitarian law. For further analysis see also: B.W. BOWETT, A legal study of United Nations practice, The Lawbook Exchange, London, 1964, pp. 484ss. C. GREENWOOD, International humanitarian law and United Nations military operations, in Yearbook of International Humanitarian Law, 1, 1998, pp. 18ss. A. RYNIKER, L'application du droit international humanitaire et les opèrations militaires organisèes en vertu de la Charte des Nations Unies, in International Review of Red Cross, 86, 1999, pp. 796ss. U. PALWANKAR, Applicability of international humanitarian law to United Nations peacekeeping forces, in International Review of Red Cross, 81, 1993, pp. 228. The aforementioned Bulletin is a legal document adopted by the general secretary of the UN for the purpose of "setting out fundamental principles and rules of international humanitarian law" to be applied to operations carried out under the command and control of the UN. The legal nature of the Bulletin cannot be assimilated to a standardization act in the light of the fact that the general secretary limiting himself to the lex lata simply specified the content of rules that already bound the UN, according to which it must be assessed on the basis of the position of the general secretariat in the context of peacekeeping operations, which this body is the strategic-operational summit. According to this perspective, however, the Bulletin reveals some innovative aspects due essentially to the rapid transformations undergone by the humanitarian law which led to coining the expression coutume-grad-vitesse according to the author: L. CONDORELLI, La Cour pènale internationale. Un pas de gèant (pourvu qu'il soit accompli), in Revue Gènèrale de Droit International Public, 111, 1999, pp. 12ss. See also in argument: R. KOLB. Droit international et opèrations de paix internationales, Helbing & Lichtenhahn, Genève, 2002, pp. 20ss. N. HAJJAMI, Que signifie l'expression "prendre toutes les mesures nécessaires" dans la pratique du Conseil de Sécurité des Nations Unies?, in Revue Belge de Droit International, 46, 2013, pp. 232ss. A. HAMONIC, Les relations entre l'Union europèenne et l'ONU dans le domaine de la gestion des crises, ed. Bruylant, Bruxelles, 2018.

operations authorized by the Security Council which is incumbent on the authorized States does not exclude the possibility of configuring UN responsibility for violation or art. 1 common to the Geneva conventions in the part in which this rule requires the enforcement of humanitarian law.[347] The other terms according to this reconstruction when the UN authorizes some Member States to resort to armed force in order to protect a collective interest on the organization remains the obligation of: "Veiller à ce que l'emploi de la force par les Etats (…) se fasse dans le stricte respect de toutes les règles pertinentes" among which are certainly the norms of international humanitarian law. [348] In our opinion this same order of arguments is applicable, even if as said in an inverse perspective to peacekeeping operations managed directly by the UN, in consideration of two fundamental findings. First, if the obligation contained in art. 1 common to the conventions of Geneva binds the organization, it must be assumed that such obligation operates at least in the same terms with regard to the contributors due to their address not only substantial but also formal of the rules in question. Secondly, the obligation contained in art. 1 assumes at the head of these States a quite peculiar content due to the organic constraint that each of them maintains with their military contingents made available to the UN. This last circumstance causes the States involved to find themselves in the material conditions of requiring the receiving organization that their troops are employed in compliance with the obligations set by humanitarian law.[349]

For the same reasons the violation of obligation indicated above could constitute the legal basis of an illegal assistance given by the states concerned to a conduct contrary to the humanitarian law attributable to the organization due to the criterion of actual control. In such circumstances the ascertainment of subjective element of complicity could be easy

---

[347]N. TSAGOURIAS, A. MORRISON, International humanitarian law: Cases, materials and commentary, P. BUIRETTE, Le droit international humanitaire, op. cit., E. DAVID, Principles de droit des conflits armès, op. cit.,

[348] A. RYNIKER, L'application du droit international humanitaire et les opèrations militaires organisèes en vertu de la Charte des Nations Unies, op. cit.

[349]In other words, the supplying States find themselves in the de facto conditions to which according to the most cautious doctrine regarding the real extent of art. 1 the power to enforce the humanitarian law available to States in the same way as the aforementioned provision is limited. The ultimate power is not a legal, but rather a condition of fact. It refers to what a State can factually do not legally do. According to: C. FOCARELLI, Common article 1 of the 1949 Geneva Conventions: A soap bubble?, op. cit., pp. 150ss, while adhering to this approach as said very skeptical, it seems to us that what is claimed in the text is not contradicted by the circumstance for which the power of which the sending States have is a factual one.

considering the line of communication that normally exists between the chain of command that belongs to the UN and the States that contribute to the multinational force.

In doctrine the emphasis has often been placed on the coordination between art. 1 common to the Geneva conventions must be coordinated and the general discipline regarding the participation of others crime.[350] It should be noted in this regard that the study conducted on behalf of the international committee of the Red Cross expressly leverages art. 16 ARSIWA in support of the customary nature of the Rule 44.[351] According to a widespread opinion, art. 1 common to the Geneva conventions imposes to all signatory States the prohibition to lend help or assistance to the state party of a conflict that acts the violation of obligations deriving from the same conventions,[352] as well as to assist this State in the maintenance of said violation.

It has also been argued that in the hypotheses in which behaviours suitable for integrating the case of participation in the violation of humanitarian law are established, the relationship between art. 1 common to the Geneva conventions on the one hand and art. 16 ARSIWA on the other should be framed the terms of lex specialis to lex generalis.[353]

This thesis does not seem entirely persuasive. It does not seem to us that they relate to the relationship between art. 1 common to the Geneva

---

[350]H.P. AUST, Complicity in international law, op. cit., pp. 387ss.
[351] B. KESSLER, Die Durchsetzung der genfer Abkommen von 1949 in nicht-internationalen bewaffneten Konflikten auf Grundlage ihres gemeinsamen Art. 1, Duncker & Humblot, Berlin, 2001, pp. 108ss.
[352] D. SCHINDLER, Die erga-omnes Wirkung des humanitären Völkerrecths, in U. BEYERLIN, M. BOTHE, R. HOFMANN, Recht zwischen Umbruch und Bewährung. Festschrift für Rudolf Bernhardt, ed. Springer, Berlin, 1995, pp. 200ss. M. SASSÓLI, State responsibility for violations of international humanitarian law, in International Review of Red Cross, 84, 2002, pp. 414ss. B KESSLER, Die Durchsetzung der genfer Abkommen von 1949 in nicht-internationalen bewaffneten Konflikten auf Grundlage ihres gemeinsamen Art. 1, op. cit., pp. 504ss. A. IMSEIS, Critical reflections on the international humanitarian law aspects of the ICJ wall opnion in American Journal of International Law, 99, 2005, pp. 102ss. A. FELDER, Die Beihilfe im Rect der völkerrechtlichen Staatenverantwortlichkeit, op. cit., pp. 150ss. C. FOCARELLI, Common article 1 of the 1949 Geneva Conventions: A soap bubble?, op. cit. pp. 146ss, it is not clear what measures can be exercised by third States that intend to enforce humanitarian law. The ultimate author notes that the adoption of lawful measures such as the unassisted and the non-recognition is confined to a literal interpretation of art. 1 while clarifying that such "proves hardly satisfactory" interpretation (par. 149). A. ZIMMERMANN, C.J. TAMS, K. OELLERS-FRAHAM, The Statute of the International Court of Justice. A commentary, op. cit.
[353]M. SASSÓLI, State responsibility for violations of international humanitarian law, op. cit., pp. 414ss.

conventions and the general rule on complicity of the conditions for the former to prevail by way of specialty on the latter.[354] First of all there is a difference in the structure and the respective modes of operation between the two standards under consideration. It is sufficient to point out from this point of view that the illicit fact regulated by art. 16 ARSIWA and 58 DARIO exists only on condition that the main unlawful act has been carried out. On the contrary, the obligation set by the Geneva conventions can be violated regardless of the actual non-compliance of the humanitarian law by the assisted subject. It seems to us that the rule that is considered special sets a positive obligation which is susceptible to infringement "where the action or omission found to have occurred is in fact not in conformity with the conduct specifically required of the responsible organ for the action or omission." The violation exists in this hypothesis regardless of the circumstance for which it originated: "Consequences that were actually harmful."[355] Moreover, as observed by the supporters of this thesis, the rule contained in art. 1 common to the Geneva conventions would apply to a wider spectrum of cases than those provided by art. 16 ARSIWA and 58 DARIO.[356] In other words, it does not seem that the first rule is linked to the second by a relationship of logical inclusion in the sense seen in Chapter 1. The violation of art. 1 of Geneva conventions is integrated by behaviours that in themselves would not fall within the scope of application of articles 16 ARSIWA[357] and 58 DARIO. As noted by the ICJ[358] in fact art. 1 implies ex se the prohibition to

---

[354]N. TSAGOURIAS, A. MORRISON, International humanitarian law: Cases, materials and commentary, P. BUIRETTE, Le droit international humanitaire, op. cit., E. DAVID, Principles de droit des conflits armès, op. cit.,

[355]In Yearbook of International Law Commission, vol. II, part 2, p. 15, it is the comment to art. 20 of the project on state responsibility approved in the first reading on the conduct of obligations. The circumstance indicated in the text is one of the distinctive elements of this type of illegal with respect to that resulting from the violation of an obligation to prevent a given event, which the same project provided for in art. 23, in the Yearbook of International Law Commission, vol. II, part. 2, p. 81ss.

[356]D. TURNS, Implementation and compliance, in E. WILMSHURST, S. BREAU, Perspectives on the ICRC study on customary international humanitarian law, Cambridge University Press, Cambridge, 2007, pp. 354ss. H.P. AUST, Complicity in international law, op. cit., pp. 388ss.

[357]M. SASSÓLI, State responsibility for violations of international humanitarian law, op. cit., pp. 414ss, where the author notes as an example art. 1 common to the Geneva conventions prohibits the transfer of arms to a State of which the systematic violation of data obligations of humanitarian law is known even if the circumstances let presume a licit use of those weapons.

[358]See also in argument: C. FOCARELLI, Common article 1 of the 1949 Geneva Conventions: A soap bubble?, op. cit. pp. 169ss, where he believes that the obligation not

encourage conduct contrary to humanitarian law, so that the aforementioned provision would be violated by merely instigating behaviours while this circumstance does not integrate the case of complicity under international general law.

This being clarified, it can be concluded that even though it does not constitute a special norm concerning complicity, art. 1 common to the Geneva conventions[359] may nevertheless be considered as part of the material element of the case provided for in articles 16 ARSIWA and 58 DARIO.

3.13. (Follows) Complicity model with reference to UNPROFOR conduct

The procedural procedure relating to the facts of Srebrenica offers the opportunity to envisage the application of the rule on complicity to the offenses ascribable to the UNPROFOR mission, even in purely hypothetical terms.

It must first be observed that it seems to us to share the opinion that the tragic events at the origin of the appeal were closely related to a plurality of subjects posed that "not a single conduct or omission caused the injury." Dutch judges used art. 7 DARIO in order to attribute the conduct object of grievance to the defendant State, considering the criterion of effective control satisfied due to the power/duty of the State to prevent the event suffered by the family members of the applicants. This solution does not seem to be compatible with the rationale of the provision in question which is intended to impute what actually happened rather than what should have taken place. If the power to prevent the serious events in question could not have been enough to establish a different and autonomous title of responsibility to the Netherlands. In the first place, it could be assumed that the responsibility in this State could have been due to the violation of the positive due diligence obligation, consisting in the duty to prevent the occurrence of the events subject to grievance. In view of the fundamental norms of international humanitarian law relating to the protection of civilians in time of war, the provision of art. 1 common to

to encourage violations of humanitarian law which can be understood as a specification of the obligation not to render assistance, is not attributable to art. 1 common to the Geneva Conventions which instead prescribe passive conduct.

[359]N. TSAGOURIAS, A. MORRISON, International humanitarian law: Cases, materials and commentary, P. BUIRETTE, Le droit international humanitaire, op. cit., E. DAVID, Principles de droit des conflits armès, op. cit.

the Geneva conventions.[360] The above argument seems to be confirmed by the orientation of Gaja according to whom, besides the possibility of joint imputation of the same conduct, one can well configure the hypothesis in which the illicit fact is attributed "to either the State or the UN, while omission of any to the required measures is attached to the other subject." [361] The same conclusions referring to serious violations of humanitarian law are, according to the rapporteur, extensible to all the offenses committed by personnel of the peace forces in violation of other regulations protecting fundamental rights.[362]

Secondly, supposing by hypothesis that the evacuation order of the compound was attributable to the ordinary chain of command of UNPROFOR and UN, the Dutch negligence ascertained both from the appeal and supreme Court of the Hague could have integrated the case in point of complicity in the organization's crime. Consider that in the course of the first instance judgment it emerged that the Dutch government had been informed of the situation in Srebrenica so much that it had advised the Dutchbat to ascertain: "That the men were under no circumstances treated as a separate group." [363] In our opinion, awareness of the circumstances of the offense allows us to envisage the application of art. 58 DARIO to the case in question, it being possible to hypothesize that in the present case an accessory feature of character could be discerned as omissive.[364]

---

[360]N. TSAGOURIAS, A. MORRISON, International humanitarian law: Cases, materials and commentary, P. BUIRETTE, Le droit international humanitaire, op. cit., E. DAVID, Principles de droit des conflits armès, op. cit.

[361]G. GAJA, Second report on responsibility of international organizations, op. cit., pp. 12-13, par. 42. P. BENVENUTI, Le respect du droit international humanitaire par les forces des Nations Unies: la circulaire de Secrètaire gènèral, in Revue Gènèrale de Droit International Public, 105, 2001, pp. 373ss.

[362]G. GAJA, Second report on responsibility of international organizations, pp. 12-13, par. 42.

[363]Hasan Nuhanović v. The Netherlands, court of appeal in the Hague, op. cit., 2.10. As stated by the Court of first instance, the evacuation order of the compound had been issued by the UNPROFOR command of Saràjevo to the chief of staff stationed in Srebrenica who was acting simultaneously on behalf of the UN and on behalf of the Dutch government to which it was bound by organic bond. C. BAKKER, Dual attribution of acts committed by a UN peacekeeping force: An emerging norm of customary international law? The Dutch Supreme Court's judgments in Nuhanoviç and Mustafić, in Italian Yearbook of International Law, 23, 2013, pp. 288ss.

[364]P. BENVENUTI, Le respect du droit international humanitaire par les forces des Nations Unies: la circulaire de Secrètaire gènèral, op. cit.

3.14. Effective control as a summation of the authority to issue orders and prevent the occurrence of harmful conduct

By virtue of the shared fears mentioned above, i.e. the approach aimed at identifying the subject exercising effective control over the subject with the capacity to prevent damaging conduct and to approve ma cum grano salis. In other words, it does not seem correct to claim that the segment of authority that comes into relief to determine the attribution of the conduct of the "blue helmets" must in all circumstances be the ability to prevent the conduct in question. In fact, it is not clear why, if the conduct complained of arises from the implementation of higher orders, it should not be attributed to the entity that imparted the same. On the other hand, it seems that the valid interpretation of the criterion of effective control aimed at making the latter coincide with the ability to prevent is more functional in determining the attribution of those conducts that have not been implemented higher orders.[365]

In other words, the impossibility of establishing peacekeepers' conduct, is determined by the effective equal to operational control. This must not necessarily lead to rejecting in full a meaning of effective control which considers the control in question to be the authority to issue instructions. The aforementioned impossibility should rather lead to the belief that effective control is not exclusively based on the supply of orders. It also extends to other forms of authority, such as, for example, the ability to prevent. If, therefore, effective control coincides with both the authority to give orders to troops, and with the ability to prevent, by virtue of the need to adopt an interpretation of effective control that allows coherently to determining the attribution of all the actions and omissions that the peacekeepers have performed in the exercise of official functions (both those deriving from the implementation of directives received, and those carried out in the absence of higher orders), it is necessary to adopt a double-step approach. According to this the criterion of effective control takes the form, first of all, of the authority to give orders to the troops and, secondly, of the capacity to prevent the alleged harmful conduct. In order to identify the body to which the conduct of "blue helmets" is attributed, it will therefore be necessary to ask, first of all, which subject has given orders to the military and, once the absence of higher orders has been

[365] A. NOLLKAEMPER, Dual distribution, in Journal of International Criminal Justice, 9, 2011, pp. 1144ss.

identified, it will be necessary to ask which subject would have been better able to prevent the occurrence of harmful conduct.

3.15. (Follows) Necessity to attribute ultra vires actions of peace forces to the respective sending States

The usefulness of adopting an approach that, in the absence of higher orders, identifies the subject exercising effective control in the entity with the capacity to prevent the harmful and immediately evident conduct if the ultra vires acts of the peacekeepers are taken into consideration. That is to say those actions/omissions carried out by the "blue helmets" not in compliance with higher orders, but carried out in contravention of these, or in excess of authority (i.e. going beyond the instructions received), regardless of the fact that the these orders were given by one or other entity exercising operational control.[366] If the ultra vires deeds are by definition the result of personal military initiatives and do not derive from the implementation of orders received, is evident that in such circumstances one wonders who instructed the troops in order to identify the subject exercising effective control is not of any utility. If, on the other hand, we asked which subject would have been able to prevent the conduct in question, assuming that the exercise of effective control is not based solely on operational control but also extends to the ability to prevent harmful conduct, is possible to identify a subject to whom to attribute the ultra vires actions/omissions of peacekeepers.

Indeed, if, on the one hand, we bear in mind the fact that (by virtue of the full command of exercise of which they remain invested) the supplying States maintain an exclusive competence with regard to a whole series of aspects (including the exercise of the criminal jurisdiction and discipline on troops, as well as the performance of administrative functions such as the selection and training of the military), and if, on the other hand, the nature of the ultra vires acts (actions/omissions deriving from personal initiatives of undisciplined soldiers who do not exercise their authority within the limits found in the instructions given to them or disregard such instructions), then is logical that the subject able to prevent ultra vires actions (thus showing effective control on the

---

[366]With regard to the concept of ultra vires, reference is made to what was drafted by the UN's international law Commission in the context of art. 7 of the draft of articles on the responsibility of States, and of the art. 8 of the one concerning the responsibility of the organizations.

same) and the sending State of militaries.[367]

States can in fact work, ex ante, to provide military personnel who will subsequently be employed in the field of peace operations with adequate training in respect of codes of conduct, international legislation for the protection of human rights, international humanitarian law and so on, even arriving to wait for their troops under observation, in order to choose to employ those soldiers in the missions that prove to be more reliable, responsible, and capable.[368] Ex post, States can punish with disciplinary sanctions, and/or penalties in the measure in which the action in question integrates an hypothesis of crime, those soldiers who have acted in contravention of the instructions received or in excess of authority.[369] The sending State is therefore the only person who has the necessary tools to exercise control over ultra vires, both upstream and downstream.

In light of the considerations just made, is clear that the actions taken by peacekeepers in excess of authority or in breach of the instructions received should be attributed to the respective sending State. The latter is in fact the only person invested with the relevant skills to prevent ultra vires, while the UN has no authority either ex ante or ex post, in order to prevent similar actions.

3.16. (Follows) Impossibility of determining the attribution of the ultra vires conduct of the peace forces pursuant to art. 8 of the draft articles on the responsibility of international organizations

The reasoning we have just implied naturally implies that, due to the peculiar legal status of the "blue helmets," the attribution of acts that they have performed ultra vires cannot follow the general rule codified in art. 8 of the Draft Articles on the Responsibility of International

[367] T. DANNENBAUM, Translating the standard of effective control into a system of effective accountability: How liability should be apportioned for violations of human rights by member state troop contingents serving as United Nations peacekeepers, op. cit., 2010, pp. 114ss.

[368] T. DANNENBAUM, Translating the standard of effective control into a system of effective accountability: How liability should be apportioned for violations of human rights by member state troop contingents serving as United Nations peacekeepers, op. cit.

[369] T. DANNENBAUM, Translating the standard of effective control into a system of effective accountability: How liability should be apportioned for violations of human rights by member state troop contingents serving as United Nations peacekeepers, op. cit.

Organizations, which prescribes that the conduct that organs and agents of an organization put in place in contrast with instructions received or in excess of authority should be attributed to the organization itself.[370] With such a statement it does not seem to contradict the ratio of the aforementioned rule, because the peacekeepers are neither organs nor agents of the UN but, precisely because of the exclusive prerogatives maintained by their sending States in criminal and disciplinary matters, they qualify as organs, state authorities only partially available to the organization, and therefore art. 8 is not applicable to them.

Nevertheless, the difference between the assignment of the ultra vires acts put in place by the organs/agents of an international organization and those carried out by the state organs 'lent' partially to the organization has not been properly addressed in Project's articles.[371] On the contrary, in the context of the Commentary to the aforementioned art. 8, the Commission has suggested that the ultra vires acts of the "blue helmets" should be attributed to UN.

The Commission carried out an incomprehensible reasoning. First, it has reproduced in its entirety in the aforementioned Commentary the paragraph of a document adopted by the UN in which the Organization denies that it can be attributed the acts put in place by peacekeepers outside the exercise of official functions, immediately afterwards, the Commission stated the following: "[W]hile the "off-duty" conduct of a member of a national contingent would not be attributed to the organization, the "on-duty" conduct may be so attributed. One would then have to examine whether the ultra vires conduct in question is related to the functions entrusted to the person concerned."[372] From what has just been mentioned, it seems possible to deduce that ILC attributes to the UN ultra vires acts of the 'blue helmets' deriving from the fact that the organization refuses to see itself attributed the actions performed by the latter off-duty; otherwise said, from the refusal of the UN to see itself attributed only the acts put in place by the members of the peacekeeping force as private individuals.

---

[370]T. DANNENBAUM, Translating the standard of effective control into a system of effective accountability: How liability should be apportioned for violations of human rights by member state troop contingents serving as United Nations peacekeepers, op. cit.

[371]"The conduct of an organ or agent of an international organization shall be considered an act of that organization under international law if the organ or agent acts in an official capacity and within the overall functions of that organization, even if the conduct exceeds the authority of that organ or agent or contravenes instructions:" DARIO, art. 8.

[372]T. DANNENBAUM, Translating the standard of effective control into a system of effective accountability: How liability should be apportioned for violations of human rights by member state troop contingents serving as United Nations peacekeepers, op. cit.

The Commission deduces, on the contrary, all the acts that the members of the peacekeeping force put in place in the exercise of official functions, including the ultra vires deeds.

Such a conclusion is unacceptable because, in addition to being confusedly argued, it arises in direct contrast to the position that the UN itself assumes with regard to the subject under consideration. UN considers that the ultra vires actions of the 'blue helmets' do not give rise to any legal responsibility for the organization. It is clear that if the UN does not consider its responsibility in the face of ultra vires acts of the peacekeepers, this means that the organization does not consider such acts likely to be attributed to it. Moreover, in this sense the MODEL MoU also serves as the basis for the conclusion of participation agreements between UN and Member States taking part in the operations. In fact, in the context of this document is stated that the responsibility to pay compensation to third parties harmed by the actions of the mission rests on the organization[373], but is also specified that, in the event of "loss, damage, death or injury arising from gross negligence or wilful misconduct of personnel provided by the government,"[374] UN reserves the right to bring an action for recourse against the supplier State. Now, although it is true, as the Commission points out, that "[t]he agreement appears to deal only with distribution of responsibility and not of conduct."[375] This does not mean that the underlying rationale for such a provision is that for which the organization deems necessary to attribute the ultra vires deeds to the supplying States. The deeds put in place with gross negligence or wilful misconduct are in fact by definition made in contravention of the instructions received.

In light of what has just been said, the Commission's position aimed at attributing to UN the ultra vires acts enacted by the "blue helmets" does not seem sustainable. We therefore reiterate that the latter

[373]"The United Nations will be responsible for dealing with any claims by third parties where the loss of or damage to their property, or death or personal injury, was caused by the personnel or equipment provided by the Government in the performance of services or any other activity or operation under this Memorandum:" see, MODEL MoU 1997, art. 9. B. OSWALD, H. DURHAM, A. BATES, Documents on the law of UN peace operations, Oxford University Press, Oxford, 2010, pp. 52ss.

[374]B. OSWALD, H. DURHAM, A. BATES, Documents on the law of UN peace operations, op. cit., T. DANNENBAUM, Translating the standard of effective control into a system of effective accountability: How liability should be apportioned for violations of human rights by member state troop contingents serving as UN peacekeepers, op. cit.

[375]T. DANNENBAUM, Translating the standard of effective control into a system of effective accountability: How liability should be apportioned for violations of human rights by member state troop contingents serving as UN peacekeepers, op. cit.

should be attributed to the respective sending States.[376]

Of course, this conclusion applies only to the ultra vires of military personnel. On the other hand, the general rule set forth in art. 8 of the Project. The conduct they hold in excess of authority or in breach of the instructions received will, consequently, be attributed to the organization.

In the end we can say that although from the formal point of view the respective spheres of competence of the supplying States and organizations are generally outlined (the organizations are invested with the exercise of operational control, while the States continue parallel to exercise the so-called full command towards of its own military personnel, maintaining exclusive prerogatives with regard to disciplinary and criminal matters), from a factual point of view the States frequently end up being involved in the exercise of the operational control that is de jure and entrusted to the International Commander, arriving in some cases to completely cancel the authority of the latter. With regards to the constituent elements in which the standard of effective control is deemed to be, in the present study it was proposed to adopt a double step approach in light of which the identification of the person exercising such control must be determined as follows. First of all, it is necessary to ask whether, the operational control was exercised by the supplying States and/or receiving organizations, which amounts to asking whether in the above circumstances the first and/or second were to give orders to the forces of peace. If, then, it is recognized that the specific conduct adversely affecting and accruing in the absence of superior directives, it becomes necessary to ask whether the supplying States and/or the receiving organizations could have prevented the conduct in question, which means asking whether one of the subjects involved, or both, they could have acted differently and prevented from occurring. This is the rest of the notion of effective control that seems to emerge from the systematic analysis of the articulated (even if sometimes not very linear) indications that the ILC has provided on the attribution of the conduct of the peace forces. A similar interpretation of effective control seems, however, to have the advantage of making it possible to determine the attribution not only of the conduct that the military contingents have held in implementation of instructions received, but also of the acts that they have performed ultra vires. It is therefore

---

[376] J. CRAWFORD, A. PELLET, S. OLLESON (eds.), The law of international responsibility, Oxford University Press, Oxford, 2010. M. ODELLO, R. PIOTROWICZ (eds.), International military missions and international law, op. cit., C. RYNGAERT, H. BUCHANAN, Member state responsibility for the acts of international organizations, op. cit., pp. 132ss.

evident that, if the attribution of the conduct carried out by the peacekeeping forces in the execution of the mandate entrusted to them must be determined in the light of the effective control (which must in turn be understood as a segment of authority coinciding above all with the operational control and secondly with the ability to prevent the alleged harmful conduct), the actions and omissions of the armed contingents will be attributed only to the receiving organization or to the supplier State to the extent that one of the subjects in question exercises operational control exclusively while, in the event that in the individual case the operational control is exercised jointly, the conduct can only be attributed to both.

If instead the peacekeeping forces were to act ultra vires, exceeding the instructions received or putting themselves in contrast with them, their actions and omissions should be attributed only to the respective sending States, by virtue of the fact that the latter continue to exercise on an exclusive basis on its military personnel, disciplinary and criminal duties, that is to say those segments of authority that are primarily in relief to prevent the occurrence of a harmful conduct that has not been implemented superior directives.

It is beyond doubt, then, that the meaning of effective control suggested in the present work determines the impossibility of attributing to the authorizing organization the actions and omissions that take place in the context of missions purely authorized by the UN Security Council , both in the case of peace missions set up by regional organizations, as well as in the one dealing with operations conducted by multinational forces. Moreover, in this direction the most recent jurisprudence also appears, despite the alarming indications in the opposite direction of which the ECtHR had promoted some years ago.

3.17. Concluding remarks

In this chapter we have analyzed the case of complicity of States in the offense committed by functional bodies in the exercise of operational activities assuming as a model of analysis the violations of international law attributable to peacekeeping missions. It has been noted that the profiles of imputation of similar ones are conditioned by the circumstance for which the organization employs military personnel that is made available by the Member States. The forces in question act under the authority and control of the organization but retain their status as organs of the sending state. Art. 7 DARIO establishes that the organization is responsible only for the conduct committed under its actual control. Outside of this hypothesis it can be considered that the unlawful act is to be attributed to the State of dispatch of the agent body according to what established by art. 4, par. 1 ARSIWA.

Secondly, how the peculiarities of the offense under consideration have led a part of the doctrine to formulate the thesis in virtue of which in the situations under consideration a double attribution of the offense can be configured, that is the imputation of the same sending State and the international organization. It was noted that this approach, although fully valid from a theoretical point of view, is difficult to achieve in practice.

Finally, an attempt was made to show that the imputation of the offense to the international organization based on art. 7 DARIO does not exclude that the responsibility of States contributing to the mission may arise, the responsibility based on art. 58 DARIO. In this hypothesis the material element of the case could result from the circumstance for which the status of sending by making available the continent to which the possible harmful conduct is concretely attributable provides a contribution to the occurrence of the main crime. The material element could be supplemented by an offense fact. This circumstance occurs when the sending status violates the positive obligation to ensure that the international organization to which it has provided its quota does not commit a violation of international humanitarian law. As for the subjective element, it seems to us that the requirement of knowledge of the circumstances of the main fact is set by art. 58, par. 1 a) can be considered satisfied in a wide range of hypotheses in consideration of the bridge of constant communication that during the operations between the organization and each contributing State.

3.18. Outlook

The governing rule of complicity in the international offense has begun to mature in international relations since the second half of the last century, acquiring a customary nature in the period immediately following the definitive notion of the analysis project of articles on state responsibility. As noted above, this case has certain characteristics that can be distinguished from multiple points of view by the ordinary structure of the international crime. The conduct of the accomplice State is characterized by its accessory nature compared to the unlawful act of others and by being made up of two elements-material and subjective-which necessarily had to occur for the purposes of integrating the responsibility provided for by articles 16 ARSIWA and 14, 58 DARIO.

Beginning with the accessories we have seen that the behaviour of the complicit State integrates an unlawful fact only to the extent that it accesses the main conduct: As long as the latter is not materially in place, the act attributable to the assisting State cannot be qualified as an illegal act of competition. The responsibility of the complicit State wants the actual perpetration of the principal behaviour finding in its own subsistence. However, the accessory fact constitutes an act distinct from the conduct which carries out the principal offense with respect to which it receives an autonomy from the legal classification. This aspect is central to the theoretical reconstruction of the case studied in this work and has a decisive impact on the content of the relationship of responsibility that is established between accomplice State and injured party.

As seen from the codification works and the practice it emerges that in principle any material conduct is suitable to integrate the accessory fact. Consider the provision of financial aid, of arms of logistic facilities useful for the violation of the prohibition of the use of force or of obligations regarding human rights or even the participation in a regulatory procedure which gives rise to a legal act in contrast with international organization's obligations that adopts it. The only condition set by ILC consists in the requirement that the conduct in question must produce the effect of facilitating the realization of the principal offense. Therefore the causal efficiency-declined in terms of facilitating causality-is the only parameter for identifying the accessory pipeline. This means that the conduct of the matter may be specific and by abstraction of the principal licit or illicit fact in the first case it does not violate any obligation other than that laid down by the law on complicity. In the second case the complicit State commits two violations. The first is integrated by the contrast between material conduct and an obligation imposed by a primary rule, the second is supplemented by the violation of the norm on complicity and derives, as already mentioned, from the facilitation of the main fact. In this case the first violation constitutes an integral part of the second one. Starting from these considerations we have identified different types of accessory act.

In first place there is the accessory fate in itself lawful which occurs when a certain action is suitable to assist the other person's conduct, although isolated from the latter, is not prohibited by any international norm. To the category of the accessory fact which is in itself illegal, on the other hand, we have brought back both the commissive and omissive facts. The former undoubtedly represent the most common complicity hypothesis in practice, given that often states assist the illicit of others, in turn violating substantial obligations imposed on them, for example in the case of binding international organizational acts. The omissive accessory act required a deeper study in consideration of two circumstances. On the one hand the position taken in this respect by ICJ with the February 2007 sentence on the application of the Convention on the prevention and repression of the crime of genocide, it has expressly ruled out that an omissive offense could integrate the case of complicity. On the other hand, the orientation of a part of the doctrine according to which a particular category of omission offense, that deriving from the violation of due diligence obligations, performs a function similar to that to which the norm on complicity is ordered. We have tried to demonstrate that complicity can be well integrated by an omissive conduct as it results from the practice and as supported by the prevailing doctrine. what matters is the suitability of the conduct in question to facilitate the execution of the main crime with the clarification that with respect to the simple omission the accessory fact in question is characterized by the awareness at the head of the State that puts it in the circumstances in which carries out the main conduct.

Coming to the subjective element just mentioned, we have seen that the rule encoded by articles 16 ARSIWA and 14, 58 DARIO requires the accomplice to know the circumstances of the main offense. This is an inescapable requirement that distinguishes the complicity from all the other illegal cases regulated by the regulatory regime of international responsibility in which guilt generally plays a marginal role. According to the majority orientation of the doctrine, the existence of this element can be assumed in a considerable number of hypotheses with the specification that the ascertainment of the requisite in question is not entirely independent of objective factors, such as for example the notoriety of the illicit main fact and the historical-factual context in which the State comes into being.

We then focused on the other condition laid down in articles 14 ARSIWA, 14 and 58 DARIO for which the accomplice must be bound by the same primary obligation violated in the main way. This requirement inserted by ILC on the eve of the definitive adoption of the article on state responsibility is susceptible to more than one criticism. First of all, we have emphasized that the mere recipient of a provision for a subject does not in itself apply to prohibiting the latter from assisting others in violation of the obligations deriving from that rule. Moreover, the simple application of the principle pacta tertiis nec nocent nec prosunt to the illicit case in question appears to be markedly problematic and seems to be the prerogative of a markedly contractual conception of international responsibility.

The investigation conducted in this study leads to the conclusion that the general rule concerning complicity is not attributable either to the category of primary norms or to that of secondary norms of international law. In our opinion, it is considered to be supplementary to each primary regulation to the extent that it assists the latter in protecting the legal asset from time to time taken into consideration. This rule applies to conduct that does not carry out the case envisaged by the primary obligation but which nevertheless contributes to damage the interest from the obligation itself.

The supplementary standard of which we have outlined the fundamental aspects operates with regard to conduct that is ancillary to any type of offense. Starting from this consideration, we considered the argument that complicity with serious offenses would be governed by art. 41, par. 2 ARSIWA considered prevalent on art. 16 as a lex specialis. The two provisions in question seem to differ in object and purpose. More precisely art. 41 regulates the consequences of a violation of fundamental norms rather than the complicity in the realization of such illicit. The ban on assistance by art. 41, par. 2 relates to the maintenance of the situation arising from an unlawful act already carried out in respect of which the conduct contemplated by this provision does not place it in an ancillary function.

The accessory fact integrates an international offense distinct from the main one, giving rise to a secondary juridical relationship between the subject who creates it and the injured party parallel to the one established between the latter and the author of the main crime. This means that the accomplice is obliged to provide adequate compensation to the injured party. However, the picture just traced must be measured against the peculiarities of the offense in consideration that make some forms of repair difficult to configure already from a theoretical point of view. It must be borne in mind that the two unlawful cases determine a single prejudice for the injured party. It will be necessary to ascertain the causal efficiency of each of them with respect to the injury in question. This operation appears particularly complex with regard to the repair by equivalent which involves the application of specific rules relating to the calculation of the sum due as compensation, which is itself problematic even in simple cases in which the damage is caused by a single illicit fact. It seems to us that satisfaction is the most appropriate form of repair in most cases of complicity. Equally problematic is the configurability of countermeasures against the accomplice State. Although admissible from a theoretical point of view the use of these self-protection measures could prove difficult from a practical point of view. It may not be easy to identify the obligation capable of being violated as a countermeasure, despite the relative discretion that the project attributes to the injured party with respect to this assessment.

The second part of this investigation was dedicated to a form of complicity rendered in many cases peculiar by the relationship between accomplice State and author of the main crime. Our analysis has in fact concentrated mainly on the international organization responsible for the main fact. From this angle of view we have found that the regulatory framework, together with the elements of this bankruptcy case, present few but significant peculiarities with respect to the discipline outlined in the first part. Firstly, after reiterating our concerns, the order to the condition set by art. 58, par. 1 b) DARIO we stressed that even if it were to adhere to the general law, it would not operate in the hypothesis under consideration. In our opinion, the Member States of an international organization cannot be considered completely extraneous to the contractual obligations entered into by the organization with third parties. The complicity of application of art. 58, par. 1. Secondly we have tried to reconstruct the case of Member States complicity in the violation by the functional body of obligations placed to protect collective legal assets. It seems to us that in general international law there is a rule that establishes a duty for States to ensure that the institutions to which they belong do not commit violations of the rules on environmental protection or legal assets of similar value. In our opinion, the violation of these positive obligations may complement the case under art. 58 DARIO provided that the omission of states in consideration is on the one hand accompanied by the subjective element and the other suitable to facilitate the harmful conduct of the functional entity.

The analysis is focused on two profiles that raise legal questions of great interest. On the one hand the complicity of States in acts carried out by international organizations in the exercise of the normative function, on the other the participation in international crimes carried out within the framework of the operating activities of the institution.

The first profile of investigation as we have seen appears to be conditioned by the difficulty of separating the conduct of the organ from that of the individual States that compose it and which contribute with their vote, to the adoption of the normative act that integrates the main crime. In this context, the rule on complicity takes on quite peculiar connotations, with particular regard to the causal link between the accessory fact, constituted by members voters and the main fact constituted by the act approved by the organization and attributable to it. We have seen that the etiological link in question is configured in terms of condicio sine qua non of the main conduct. The reconstruction of the subjective element is carried out according to the ordinary criteria, on the other hand being facilitated instead, is carried out according to the ordinary criteria, moreover being facilitated by the declarations of vote with which, often the States motivate their behaviour within the deliberating body.

The second profile is part of international responsibility for crimes committed in the context of peacekeeping operations managed by international organizations and carried out by military personnel made available by States. In our opinion, the imputation of such offenses to the international organization does not in itself exclude the possibility that the contributing States of the mission may have the responsibility based on art. 58 DARIO. In the light of the reconstruction set out in the relevant Chapter, it seems to us that this case can be supplemented by an accessory omissive fact of the contributing State consisting in the violation of the obligation to make sure that the organization to which it lends its quota does not comment through the latter on violations of international law and in international humanitarian law. In this case the ascertainment of the subjective element could be based on the line of communication that normally occurs between the chain of command that is part of the organization and the States contributing to the multinational force.

CHAPTER 4

Interpretations, thoughts and critics of EU international responsibility in the implementation of Common Security and Defense Policy (CSDP)

4.1. Introduction

The development of a common defense policy and the ever-increasing number of EU operations nevertheless raised some legal problems which, without being presumptuous. Our purpose is to analyze the current status of the EU's foreign and security policy following the entry into force of the Treaty of Lisbon.[377] The latter has, in general, introduced profound changes in the organization's structure, replacing the three old "pillars" that formed a single, all-encompassing and apparently slimmer structure the difficulty in finding some "border," or at least the exact division of "competences" between these two legality circuits, with the one that poses as lex specialis towards the other, makes particularly interesting the analysis of the norms of international law, both general and including the customary law[378] and general principles of law both conventional, such as agreements with third States and decisions of International Organizations, applicable in the Common Security and Defense Policy (CSDP).

The topic and the theme of international responsibility profiles of EU[379] links from the work of conducting CSDP missions.

---

[377]M. CREMONA, Implementation of the Lisbon treaty. Improving functioning of the EU: Foreign Affairs (Brussels: Policy Department C: Citizens' Rights and Constitutional Affairs, European Parliament, 2016).

[378]N. CROQUET, The import of international customary law into the EU legal order: The adequacy of a direct effect analysis, in Cambridge Yearbook of European Legal Studies, 15, 2012-2013, pp. 48ss.

[379]The discourse on the internal legal responsibility of international organizations and, more specifically, of EU is different. It derives directly from the legal personality of domestic law which, together with international subjectivity, all international organizations possess. In fact, the activities of the latter inevitably have importance also at national level,

International responsibility is one of the topics that, in recent years, has aroused greater interest in science, [380] especially following the codification work carried out by the Commission of International Law (ILC),[381] which has come to the adoption of two important Projects of

---

in particular in the legal systems of Member States or third parties; in other words, international organizations also have the capacity of private law, such as that of concluding contracts, of acquiring movable and immovable property, of being in Court (see, for example, article 335 TFEU which states that on each of the Member States, the Union has the widest legal capacity accorded to legal persons by national legislation, and may in particular acquire or dispose of movable and immovable property and stand in court). These capacities are governed, with reference to Member States, by the trust act (the TEU and the TFEU with regard to the EU), while with reference to third States, by national rules or other international agreements, such as headquarters agreements (see article 218 TFEU which provides for the possibility for the Union to conclude international agreements with third States).

[380]Indeed, the doctrine has devoted extensive investigations since the beginning of the last century to the issue of the responsibility of States. One can remember, among others, the contributions made by Anzilotti, Kelsen and Ago, which marked decisive turns in the arrangement of the matter. Moreover, already at the time of the League of Nations, various attempts at codification were made both by scientific institutions (Institut de Droit International, Harvard Law School), and within the Society itself, without leaving much trace. Since 1953 the ILC has undertaken the study of the topic, but a definitive project only came to light in 2001.

[381]The ILC is a subsidiary body of the General Assembly-constituted by the latter with the Resolution n.174 of 21 November 1947-with the task of providing for the preparation of texts for the codification of the customary rules relating to certain subjects, proceeding to studies, collecting data of practice, sending questionnaires to the States and thus preparing projects of international multilateral conventions which then usually either in the General Assembly or in special and solemn state Conferences-are adopted and finally open to ratification and membership by the States themselves. The LC was created in order to perform the functions dictated by art. 13 of the UN Charter towards the General Assembly; the norm, in fact, provides that the latter "undertake studies and make recommendations in order to a) promote international cooperation in the political field and encourage the progressive development of international law and its codification" (UN Charter, article 13, paragraph 1, letter a). The Statute of the ILC, in particular, in articles 15-18 distinguishes between functions of "progressive development of international law" and "codification of international law," by arranging two different procedures. However, the ILC seems to have never practically made this distinction, at least until the beginning of the work on the international responsibility of the organizations. See Statute of the International Law Commission, 1947, A/RES/174 (II), 21 November 1947, U.N. Official Records, Second Session of the General Assembly, Resolutions, 16 September-29 November 1947. On the different modalities of codification of international law by the ILC. See in argument: S. D. MURPHY, Codification, progressive development, or scholarly analysis? The art of packaging the ILC's work product, in M. RAGAZZI (ed.), Responsibility of international organizations-Essays in Memory of Sir Ian Brownlie, Martinus Nijhoff Publishers, Leiden, Boston, 2013, pp. 29-40. N.M. BLOKKER, Preparing articles on responsibility of international organizations: Does the International Law Commission take international

articles, one concerning the international responsibility of the States[382] (Project 2001), the other concerning the responsibility of international organizations[383] (Project 2011).[384] The Statute of the ILC originally envisaged two different types of projects by the ILC: "Progressive development" and "codification" projects.[385] A project that progressively developed the law, by definition, created new rules, in that it addressed subjects which have not yet been regulated by international law or in regard to which the law has not yet been sufficiently developed in the practice of States.[386] The growing attention to the issue of international responsibility of intergovernmental organizations has been fueled, first of all, by the

---

organizations seriously? A midterm view, in J. KLABBERS, A. WALLENDAHL (eds), Research handbook on the law of international organizations, Edward Elgar Publishers, Cheltenham 2011, pp. 313ss. F. HOFFMEISTER, Litigating against the European Union and its member States: Who responds under the ILC's draft articles on international responsibility of international organizations?, op. cit., pp. 724ss.

[382]ILC, Draft Articles on Responsibility of States for Internationally Wrongful Acts, 2001, UN Doc. A/56/10, pp. 31- 143.

[383] ILC, Draft Articles on the Responsibility of international organizations, with commentaries 2011, "Report of the International Law Commission on the Work of its Sixty-third session," General Assembly Official Records, Supp. No. 10 (A/66/10), pp. 69-172.

[384]International Law Commission in its 2011 Articles on the Responsibility of international organizations (DARIO Articles on the Responsibility of international organizations, with commentaries, in Report of the International Law Commission on the work of its sixty-third session, UN Doc A/66/10, in (2011) Yearbook of the International Law Commission vol. II, pt 2. The DARIO (adopted as a Resolution by the UN General Assembly on 9 December 2011, Doc A/RES/66/10) were drafted on the model of the articles on the responsibility of States for Internationally Wrongful Acts (ARSIWA); adopted as a Resolution by the UN General Assembly on 12 December 2001 (International Law Commission, A/RES/56/83).

[385]G. NOLTE, The International Law Commission facing the second decade of the twenty first century, in U. FASTENRATH et al., From bilateralism to community interests, Oxford University Press, Oxford 2011, pp. 782ss. S. VILLALPANDO, Codification light. A new trend in the codification of international law at the United Nations, in Brazilian Yearbook of International Law, 10, 2013, pp. 118ss. Y. CHEN, Structural limitations and possible future of the work of the ILC, in Chinese Journal of International Law, 9, 2010, pp. 478ss.

[386]Art. 15 (ILC Statute) ("In the following articles the expression progressive development of international law is used for convenience as meaning the preparation of draft conventions on subjects which have not yet been regulated by international law or in regard to which the law has not yet been sufficiently developed in the practice of States.") M. WOOD, The General Assembly and the International Law Commission: What happens to the Commission's work and why?, in I. BUFFARD et al., International law between universalism and fragmentation, Martinus Nijhoff Publishers, The Hague, 2008, pp. 373ss. N. JANSEN, The making of legal authority. Non-legislative codifications in historical and corporating perspective, Oxford University Press, Oxford, 2010, pp. 8ss. P. BEHRENS, Diplomatic interference and the law, Hart Publishing, Oxford & Oregon, Portland, 2016.

increasingly incisive and pre-eminent role assumed by these non-state actors in the international community. This phenomenon is evidenced by the extension of the principle that, like the States, they are also required to exercise political and juridical power.[387]

The Laeken Declaration on the Future of the Union, adopted by the European Council on 15 December 2001, repeatedly called for the duty of EU to assume its responsibilities in light of the profound political changes taking place in many areas of the world and the advent of globalization.[388] For its part, the European Security Strategy of the European Council of 12-13 December 2003 emphasizes that the growing convergence of European interests and the strengthening of the EU's mutual solidarity makes us a more credible and effective actor.[389] Europe must be ready to assume its share of responsibility for world security and building a better world.[390] The version adopted in 2009 states that "in the twenty-first century it is more true than ever that sovereignty implies responsibility"[391] and reiterates that Europe must be ready to assume its share of responsibility for world security and in the construction of a better world.[392] These statements, although they have little to do with the responsibility in the legal sense of the term expressing mostly a "soft" concept of political responsibility, nevertheless highlight the centrality of the theme and its importance from the perspective of representation of the role of the Union on the international scene. With the beginning of the work of the ILC on the responsibility of international organizations, the theme of the international responsibility of the Organization has also begun to attract the attention of scholars, both internationalists and pro-

---

[387] K.E. BONN, New directions in responsibility: Assessing the International Law Commission's Draft Articles on the Responsibility of international organizations, in The Yale Journal of International Law, 37, 2011, pp. 4ss. D. SICURELLI, The European Union's Africa policies: Norms, interests and impact, ed. Routledge, London & New York, 2016.

[388] J. KLABBERS, A.WALLENDAHL (eds.) Research handbook on the law of international organizations, Edward Elgar Publishers, Cheltenham, 2011, pp. 314ss.

[389] H. ELSDTRÖM, D. GYLLENSPORRE, Minding the gap between words and needs: Towards a new European Union strategy on security in, in European Foreign Affairs Review, 25, 2015, pp. 6ss.

[390] A Secure Europe in a Better World-European Security Strategy, Bruxelles, 12 December 2003.

[391] A. NOLLKAEMPER, I. PLAKOKEFALOS (eds.), Principles of shared responsibility in international law. An appraisal of the state of the art, op. cit.

[392] M. EVANS, P. KOUTRAKOS (eds.), The international responsibility of the European Union. European and international perspectives, Hart Publishing, Oxford & Oregon, Portland, 2013, pp. 6ss.

Europeans,[393] who had previously never dealt with the issue.[394]

4.2. The sui generis nature of EU and its applicability to the general regime on the responsibility of international organizations

To address the issue of international EU responsibility in the context of CSDP missions, importance must be given to the fact that we are confronted with a subject of international law with particular characteristics in various respects.[395]

First of all, EU legal nature is that of one international organization (IO) with, in part, elements of "supra-nationality" (especially as regards the policies relating to the single market), partly of a type "intergovernmental," therefore with more extensive and articulated skills than the traditional forms of association between States (i.e. in the sector of the Common Foreign and Security Policy (CFSP) and of CSDP), but not such as to be able to speak of a constitutional or federal body. It is above all the element of "supra-nationality" that distinguishes EU from "traditional" International organizations, which, on the other hand, carry out their competences exclusively on the basis of "intergovernmental" cooperation between the governments of their respective Member States. The Member States of the Union, unlike, for example, of what is not in the

---

[393] P. EECKHOUT, The EU and its Member States in the WTO-Issues of responsibility, in L. BARTELS, F. ORTINO (eds.), Regional trade agreements and the WTO legal system, Oxford University Press, Oxford, 2006, pp. 450ss. F. HOFFMEISTER, Litigating against the European Union and its Member States-Who responds under the ILC's Draft Articles on international responsibility of international organizations?, in European Journal of International Law, 21 (3), 2010, pp. 724ss. A. DELGADO CASTELEIRO, The international responsibility of the European Union-The EU perspective: Between pragmatism and proceduralization, op. cit., pp. 564ss. M. SZABÓ, International legal responsibility of the European Union according to the Draft Articles of the International Law Commission, in M. SZABÓ (ed.), State responsibility and the law of treaties, Eleven International, The Hague, 2009, pp. 186ss. V. LANOVOY, Complicity and its limits in the law of international responsibility, op. cit.

[394] P. KLEIN, La Responsabilité des Organizations Internationales dans les Orderes Juridiques Internes et en Droit des Gens, ed. Bruylant, Bruxelles, 1998. M. HIRSCH, The responsibility of international organizations toward third parties, op. cit., M. PEREZ GONZALEZ, Les organizations internationales et le droit de la responsabilité, op. cit., pp. 63-102.

[395] M. HLAVAC, Less than a State, more than an international organizations: The sui generis nature of the European Union, in MPRA paper, 2010. W. PHELAN, What is sui generis about the European Union? Costly international cooperation in a self-contained regime, in International Studies Review, 14 (3), 2012, pp. 368ss.

UN context or WTO, in fact part of their sovereignty in favor of the institutions of the Organization.[396]

Furthermore, the relationship between EU, as a legal entity, and its Member States, as material executors of the various policies, is closer and more penetrating than is the case for all the other existing international organizations. It also has consequences for the theme of the Organization's international responsibility in various aspects. The most important is certainly the one related to the complex issue of the attribution of illicit conduct to the Union and/or to the States that contribute to the implementation of crisis management operations by sending their bodies.

There is good reason to compare the competence of the Union in the CFSP and, more specifically, with reference to the CSDP to a concurrent competency. This provides that both the Member States and the Union can take the necessary measures to implement that policy, but the competence of the former can only be exercised to the extent that the Union has not exercised its own.[397] Although the pre-emption mechanism[398] does not presumably find application in CFSP,[399] it is difficult to admit that international decisions and agreements in this area do not restrict Member States' freedom to act in external relations.[400]

The problem of heterogeneity of international organizations and, in particular, the specific characteristics of EU that cannot be found in other bodies, have characterized the codification work carried out by ILC.[401] One of the major problems faced by the European Commission

---

[396]To this end, they usually set up referendums to decide on access to the Union; on the other hand, the sale of a part of sovereignty "is (...) a politically sensitive matter" according to M. HLAVAC, Less than a State, more than an international organizations, op. cit., p. 12.

[397]Art. 2, par. 2 TFUE. For further details see: A. HATJE, J.P. TERHECHTE, P.C. MÜLLER-GRAFF, Europarechtswissenschaft, op. cit., J. SCHWARZE, V. BECKER, A. HATJE, J. SCHOO, EU-Kommentar, op. cit., M. KELLERBAUER, M. KLAMERT, J. TOMKIN, Commentary on the European Union treaties and the Charter of fundamental rights, op. cit.

[398]It provides that, if the EU decides to adopt a complete and detailed framework in a certain area of shared competence, any intervention by the Member States would be precluded and in certain cases the competing competence of the Union would become, in fact, exclusive.

[399]M. CREMONA, B. DE WITTE, EU foreign relations law-Constitutional fundamentals, Oxford University Press, Oxford, 2008, pp. 65ss.

[400]R.A. WESSEL, Division of international responsibility between the EU and its Member States in the area of foreign policy, security and defense policy, op. cit., pp. 44ss.

[401]According to the opinion of G. Gaja: "(...) There are considerable differences among States but these have not prevented codification conventions and other instruments from setting forth rules applying to all States. Unlike States, international organizations are established for specific functions which characterize their activities. They are very diverse,

(EC) was, in fact, to find a legal framework that could adapt to all international organizations without distinction, not an easy task because of the diversity in terms of objectives, functions, size, etc. of existing international organizations. In this regard, the EC noted that the one size fits all approach could not work, due to the significant differences between "traditional" international organizations and those, on the other hand, like the EU, regional and economic.[402] To address the problem of the different legal nature of international organizations, with reference, in the first place, to the characteristics of the Union, ILC decided to include in the Project of 2011 a specific provision, article 64 on the lex specialis which establishes: "These articles do not apply where and to the extent that the conditions for the existence of an internationally wrongful act or the content or implementation of the international responsibility of an international organization (IO), or a State in connection with the conduct of an IO, are governed by special rules of international law. Such special rules of international law may be contained in the rules of the organization applicable to the relations between an IO and its members."[403] According to us, it is worth emphasizing that creating lex specialis is not considered a devious and troubling technique or States to evade obligations under general international law. To the contrary, lex specialis offers states a way to achieve more tailored and effective regulation. Thus customary international law and general principles need not categorically bind international organizations the way that jus cogens norms do. In particular the International Monetary Found explicitly framed the argument in terms of lex specialis "(...) when an organization acts in accordance with the terms of its constituent charter, such acts can only be wrongful in relation to another norm of international law if the other norm in question is either a "peremptory norm" (jus cogens) or arises from a specific obligation that has been incurred by the organization in the course of its activities (e.g., by entering into a separate treaty with another subject of international law). However, towards all other norms of international law, both the Charter and the internal rules of the organization would be lex specialis as far as the organization's responsibility is concerned and, accordingly, cannot be overridden by lex generalis, which would include the provisions

given the enormous variety in their size, membership, functions and resources (...)." Articles on the Responsibility of international organizations, Introductory Note, New York, 9 December 2011, pp. 5ss.

[402]ILC, Responsibility of international organizations-Comments and observations received from international organizations, A/CN.4/637, European Commission, p. 7.

[403]ILC, Responsibility of international organizations-Comments and observations received from international organizations, op. cit.

of the draft articles (...)."[404]

The "special" rules of international law referred to in the article may be the constituting instruments of an organization, such as the treaty that gave rise to it, or the rules deriving from them; in turn, these rules may include decisions, resolutions and other acts of the organization, including agreements concluded with third parties.[405] The purpose and the principle underlying the provision are peaceful, that is to better regulate the will of the parties thanks to the specificity and therefore to the greater concreteness and applicability of the special rules, to the detriment of the general ones,[406] in compliance with the criterion according to which the special law derogates compared to the general one. Precisely with regard to this aspect, the 2011 Project has been criticized,[407] since it seems not to

---

[404] Int'l Law Comm'n, Responsibility of international organizations: Comments and Observations Received from international organizations, U.N. Doc. A/CN.4/582, at 5 (May 1, 2007) (statement of IMF).

[405] K. E. BONN, The role of lex specialis in the articles on the responsibility of international organizations, in M. RAGAZZI, Responsibility of international organizations. Essays in memory of Sir Ian Brownlie, Martinus Nijhoff Publishers, Leiden, Boston, 2013, pp. 129ss.

[406] The concept was also expressed by the President of the Study Group entitled "Fragmentation of international law: Difficulty arising from the diversification and expansion of international law" (M. Koskenniemi), which, with reference to the function and purpose of the lex norm specialis and the question of self-contained regimes, he noted that the rule in question - compared to that of a general nature-is more pragmatic and ensures greater clarity and precision; moreover, it can regulate a specific legal question more effectively and efficiently, as it better reflects the will of the parties. Koskenniemi added that although there is no formal hierarchy in the sources of international law, there is however a kind of informal hierarchy "which emerged pragmatically as a" forensic "or" natural "aspect of legal reasoning, preferring the special standard to the (...) more general one." This hierarchy would express the consensual nature of international law, in which the particular rule is preferred, as it best reflects the intent of the parties that are bound to it. ILC, "Report of the International Law Commission Fifty-sixth session" (3 May-4 June and 5 July-6 August 2004), General Assembly Official Records, Supp. No. 10 (A/59/10), pp. 285-286, parr. 305-307.

[407] See the comments of Pambou-Tchivounda (A/CN.4/SR.2801, pp. 75-76, parr. 22-24), Pellet (A/CN.4/SR.2962, p. 6), McRae (A/CN.4/SR.3081, p. 4) and Pellet (A/CN.4/SR.3082, p. 4), all available in Yearbook of International Law Commission, 2006, vol. I. In the same spirit see also the observation from the UN: ILC, Responsibility of international organizations-Comments and observations received from international organizations, 17 February 2011, A/CN.4/637/Add.1, p. 4, par. 1 and from other international organizations in the matter of Responsibility of international organizations-Comments and observations received from international organizations, 25 June 2004, A/CN.4/545: UE (p. 22, par. 5); International Monetary Fund (pp. 22-23, parr. 6-8). See also, A/CN.4/637: international organizations of Labour (p. 8); International Monetary Fund (pp. 9-10), "joint submission" (p. 11, par. 3) and Organization for Cooperation and Economic Development (p. 13). In argument see: A. PELLET, international organizations are definitely not States. Cursory remarks on the ILC Articles on the responsibility of

give enough importance to the element of the specialty, which-as also affirmed by ICJ[408] is a key principle of organizations.[409] In the intentions

---

international organizations, in M. RAGAZZI (ed.), Responsibility of international organizations-Essays in Memory of Sir Ian Brownlie, op. cit., V.J. PROUX, An uneasy transition? Linkages between the law of State responsibility and the law governing the responsibility of international of international organizations, in M. RAGAZZI (ed.), Responsibility of international organizations-Essays in Memory of Sir Ian Brownlie, op. cit., K.E. BONN, "The role of lex specialis" in the articles of responsibility of international organizations, in M. RAGAZZI (ed.), Responsibility of international organizations-Essays in Memory of Sir Ian Brownlie, op. cit., pp. 41-54, 109-120 and 135-145. P. J. KUIJPER, E. PAASIVIRTA, EU international responsibility and its attribution: From the inside looking out, in M. EVANS, P. KOUTRAKOS (eds.), The International Responsibility of the European Union. European and international perspectives, op. cit., pp. 69ss.

[408]"The rights and duties of an entity such as the Organization must depend upon its purposes and functions as specified or implied in its constituent documents and developed in practice." ICJ Reports, 1949, p. 180. See in particular the opinion from the ICJ (Legality of the Use by a State of Nuclear Weapons in Armed Conflict, advisory opinion, 8 July 1966, ICJ Reports, 1996, 78, par. 24), where the ICG stated that the instruments establishing international organizations are international treaties whose purpose is the creation of new legal entities, endowed with a certain autonomy, to which the parties entrust the task of achieving common goals; in the same opinion, the IGC, however, emphasized that international organizations do not possess, as opposed to States, general jurisdiction. In the same spirit see also: Reparation for injuries suffered in the service of the United Nations, I.C.J. Advisory Opinion of 11.4.1949, I.C.J. Reports 1949, p. 174-179. Interpretation of the Agreement of 25.3.1951 between the WHO and Egypt, I.C.J. Advisory Opinion of 20.12.1980, I.C.J. Reports 1980, p. 73, para 37, pp. 89-90. For further details see: R. COLLINS, N. WHITE (eds.) international organizations and the idea of autonomy. Institutional independence in the international legal order, ed. Routledge, London & New York, 2011, pp. 10ss. R.A.WESSEL, S. BLOCKMANS (eds.) Between autonomy and dependence. The EU legal order under the influence of international organizations, T.M.C. Asser Press, The Hague, 2013, pp. 14ss. A. ZIMMERMANN, C.J. TAMS, K. OELLERS-FRAHAM, The Statute of the International Court of Justice. A commentary, op. cit.

[409]In particular, some authors complain that the scope of article 64 appears to be too broad and, consequently, unable to capture the great differences between the various international organizations. On the other hand, it is also true that an operation of "selective codification" of the particular norms of each individual international organizations would not have been possible, as admitted by the Commission itself (Project 2011, 168, par. 2) which therefore opted for an all-encompassing and apparently vague rule in its formulation. Furthermore, according to Ahlborn, the language used by the Commission is imprecise and not entirely correct, since it seems to overlap the concept of lex specialis with that of internal rules of the organization. The law governing relations between Member States and organization, explains the author, is the internal law of the organization and not lex specialis. Consequently, the text of the Project should eliminate the part in which it refers to the "rules of the organization applicable to the relations between an international organizations and its members" as a lex specialis. The position of Ahlborn is, in our opinion, excessively rigid, but shared in substance. See in particular: C. AHLBORN, The rules of international organizations and the law of international responsibility, in ACIL Research Paper (SHARES Series) n. 2, 2011, pp. 28-32.

of ILC,[410] however, the article seems to fit quite well with the characteristics of EU, particularly with regard to the special rules concerning the allocation to the Organization of the conduct of its Member States when they are implementing them to binding acts issued by the same.[411] The ILC, commenting on the article in question, makes extensive reference to the practice arising on the attribution of a given behaviour to EU and its Member States when they have to implement a binding Union decision as a possible example of the existence of a "special rule."[412] In fact, the Project cites some case law cases[413] that would prove the existence of a special rule on attribution "to the effect that, in the case of a EC act binding a Member State, state authorities would be considered as acting as organs of the Community."[414] EU has repeatedly highlighted its peculiarities and the need for the ILC Project to take it into account, sometimes expressing doubts about the possibility of bringing together in a single text rules concerning deeply different international organizations.[415] Following the first work of the ILC on the subject of the responsibility of international organizations, the EC recognized in 2004 that "while it is in many ways

[410]J. D'ASPREMONT, A European law of international responsibility? The Articles on the responsibility of international organizations and the European Union, in ACIL Research Paper (SHARES Series) n. 22, 2013, pp. 7-8.

[411]J.M. CORTÉS MARTÍN, Las organizaciones internacionales: Codificación y desarrollo progresivo de su responsabilidad internacional, op. cit., C. GUTIERREZ ESPADA, La responsabilidad internacional de las organizaciones internacionales a la luz del proyecto definitive de artículos de la Comisión de Derecho Internacional (2011), ed. Comares, Granada, 2012.

[412]Project 2011, pp. 168, par. 2.

[413]European Commission of Human Rights, case: M & Co. v. Germany of 9 February 1990, case n. 13258/87. see also the Report of Panel OMC, European Communities-Protection of Trademarks and Geographical Indications for Agricultural Products and Foodstuff-Complaint by the United States, WT/DS174/R, 20 April 2005. In particular the European Commission of Human Rights came to the conclusion that "(...) the transfer of powers to an international organizations is compatible with the Convention provided that within that organization fundamental rights will receive an equivalent protection (…); and the legal system of the European Communities not only secures fundamental rights but also provides for control of their observance (...)."

[414]C. PITSCHAS, Die volkerrechtliche Verantwortlichkeit der Europaischen Gemeinschaft und ihrer Mitgliedstaaten, op. cit.

[415]ILC, Responsibility of international organizations-Comments and observations received from international organizations, 31 March 2008, A/CN.4/593, p. 4, "as in previous years, the European Commission expresses some concerns as to the feasibility of subsuming all international organizations under the terms of this one draft in the light of the highly diverse nature of international organizations, of which the European Community itself is an example." See also: A/CN.4/637, p. 7, "a principal general comment which has been highlighted throughout previous comments is the need for the draft articles to allow sufficient room for the specificities of EU."

sui generis, it is clear that all international actors, be States or organizations, need to recognize their international responsibility in the event of any wrongful acts."[416] Furthermore, it was careful to state that "the European Community is an IO with special features as envisaged in the founding treaties"[417] and emphasized the need "to address the special situation of the Community within the framework of the draft articles."[418] In particular EC proposed three ways to adapt the issue of responsibility of international organizations to EU characteristics: "(a) Special rules of attribution, so that actions of Member States' organs can be attributed to the organization; (b) Special rules for responsibility, so that the latter can be charged to the organization, even if Member States' organs were the prime actors of a breach of an obligation borne by the organization; (c) Consideration of the possibility that the European Community (...) should benefit from a special exception or of a kind of special savings clause for such an organization."[419]

A few months before the second reading of the Project of ILC, in the commentary on article 63,[420] the EC re-emphasized the peculiar aspects of the organization and welcomed the introduction of this provision, stating that "to the extent that the draft articles, even taking account of the commentaries, at present do not adequately reflect the situation of regional (economic) integration organizations such as the EU, it would seem particularly important for the draft to explicitly allow for the hypothesis that not all of its provisions can be applied to regional (economic) integration organizations (lex specialis)."[421] Lex specialis can refer to "weak" provisions, such as individual provisions or "strong" elements of lex specialis, meaning "self-contained regimes," a term originally coined

---

[416]LC, Responsibility of international organizations-Comments and observations received from Governments and international organizations, 25 June 2004, A/CN.4/545, p. 22, par. 6.

[417]ILC, Responsibility of international organizations-Comments and observations received from governments and international organizations, 12 May 2005, A/CN.4/556, p. 31. K. DAUGIRDAS, Reputation and the responsibility of international organizations, op. cit., pp. 994ss.

[418]J.M. THOUVENIN, Responsibility in the context of the European legal order, in J. CRAWFORD, A. PELLET, S. OLLESON (eds.), The law of international responsibility, Oxford University Press, Oxford, 2010, pp. 862ss.

[419]ILC, Responsibility of international organizations-Comments and observations received from Governments and international organizations, 12 May 2005, A/CN.4/556, p. 31.

[420]Responsibility of international organizations. Comments and observations received from international organizations, 14 February 2011, A/CN.4/637, pp. 37-38, par. 1.

[421]G. GAJA, The relations between the European Union and its Member States from the perspective of the ILC Articles on responsibility of international organizations, ACIL Research Paper (SHARES Series) n. 25, 2013, pp. 3.

by the PCIJ in the SS Wimbledon case.[422] This idea of "self contained regimes" has come to mean specific secondary norms, for example norms contained within the Vienna Convention on Diplomatic Relations.[423]

The EU contested, essentially, the premise on which the work of codification of the ILC was based, or that the acts implemented by the Member States in regard of the guidelines provided by the organization to which they belonged could not in principle be attributed to the latter. The EC, for its part, said that when the EU Member States implement a decision of the Organization, they act almost as organs of it, since they have no margin of discretion. Therefore, according to the EC itself, a given behaviour should in any case be attributed to the EU. The insistence on this position expressed in written statements and interventions made in the discussion of the text of the Project convinced the ILC to include the numerous references to the practice on the assignment to the EU of a conduct put in place by Member States.

In the intentions of ILC, article 64 should cover all the situations delineated by the EC in which different rules regarding attribution[424] or content of the international EU responsibility are required. The provision specifies that "special rules of international law may be contained in the rules of the organization applicable to the relationship between an international organizations and its members."[425] In this regard, the rules on the division of competences between EU and Member States could be

---

[422]Wimbledon case, PCIJ, Series A, No.1 (1923), at pp. 23ss. For further details see: C. RYNGAERT, The European Court of Human Rights' approach to the responsibility of Member States in connection with acts of international organizations, in International and Comparative Law Quarterly, 60, 2011, pp. 998ss. A. ZIMMERMANN, C.J. TAMS, K. OELLERS-FRAHAM, The Statute of the International Court of Justice. A commentary, op. cit.

[423]United States Diplomatic and Consular Staff in Tehran, Judgment, ICJ Reports 1980, at p. 3. For further details see: A. ZIMMERMANN, C.J. TAMS, K. OELLERS-FRAHAM, The Statute of the International Court of Justice. A commentary, op. cit.

[424]According to D'Aspremont, "article 64 allows (theoretically) the emergence of special rules of international responsibility in relation to REIOs (Regional Economic international organizations) like the EU, especially when it comes to attribution of conduct." J. D'ASPREMONT, A European law of international responsibility? The Articles on the responsibility of international organizations and the European Union, op. cit., pp. 8.

[425]C. AHLBORN, The rules of international organizations and the law of international responsibility and the law of international responsibility, op. cit., pp. 29ss. J. D'ASPREMONT, The Articles on the responsibility of international organizations, The Articles on the responsibility of international organizations and the European Union, op. cit. See also the opinion of some critics from some States in ILC, Eighth report on responsibility of international organizations by Mr. Giorgio Gaja, Special Rapporteur, 14 March 2011, A/CN.4/640, pp. 36-37.

highlighted. However these are mere "internal" rules, which in all likelihood cannot qualify as lex specialis under article 64 of Project.[426]

Although the European Union possesses special characteristics that differentiate it from other international organizations in many respects, there is no doubt that the general regime on international responsibility for international organizations applies to it, albeit with certain "adaptations,"[427] which however do not substantially affect the content of the obligations.

4.3. Interpretation of article 340 (2), TFEU

EU law on liability is rather poor and does not seem to concern international responsibility for international organizations. As regards, in particular, the sources of primary law, in particular the Treaties, the most relevant, if not the only, provision is undoubtedly article 340 (2) TFEU, which provides: "In matters of non-contractual responsibility, the Union must reimburse, in accordance with the general principles common to the laws of Member States, damage caused by its institutions or agents in the performance of their duties."[428]

The provision concerns the non-contractual EU liability, namely that which does not concern contracts concluded between the Union and a third party. The provision is related to article 268 of the TFEU, which states that "CJEU has jurisdiction over disputes relating to compensation for damages referred to in article 340, second and third paragraphs."[429] Moreover, article 275 of the same Treaty[430] specifies that "CJEU has no

[426] C. AHLBORN, The rules of international organizations and the law of international responsibility and the law of international responsibility op. cit., pp. 38ss.

[427] N. TSAGOURIAS, The responsibility of international organizations for military missions, in M. ODELLO, R. PIOTROWICZ (eds.) International military missions and international law, op. cit., pp. 246ss.

[428] G. MARHIC, Le régime de responsabilité des operations de paix de l'Union Européenne: quelles règles applicables?, in Revue Belge de Droit International, 117 (1), 2013, pp. 137-145, 140ss.

[429] S. GRILLER, The Court of Justice and the common foreign and security policy, in CJEU, The Court of Justice and the construction of Europe, T.M.C. Asser Press, Bruxelles, 2013, pp. 675ss.

[430] "(...) It must be held that a reading of the law in this sense would lead to the paradoxical conclusion that the Lisbon Treaty instead of strengthening weakened the Court's judicial review (…). It should be emphasized that only CFSP decisions which have restrictive measures are pursuant to article 275, paragraph 2, TFEU (…). The demarcation of the Union's material policies with respect to CFSP has undergone "redeployment" over time. The reconditioning of a certain action within one area that within another was based on a finalistic approach (…). By virtue of such a reconstruction, the adoption of measures based on several legal bases (so-called measures having a cross-pillar dimension) had to be precluded when the objectives falling within the Community competences were prevalent

jurisdiction with regard to the provisions relating to CFSP, nor with regard to the acts adopted on the basis of those provisions."[431] From the combined provisions of the articles, it is clear that the CJEU has no jurisdiction over the compensation for damages related to the operations of CSDP.

---

or equivalent. Article 47 prevented the adoption by the Union, on the basis of the EU Treaty, of a measure that could be validly adopted on the basis of EC Treaty, and the Union could not resort to a legal basis under CFSP to adopt provisions also falling within the scope of the powers conferred by the EC Treaty on the Community (…). So the protection of the person in Union law is fragmentary. If this is the general framework, a fortiori must occur if the jurisdiction of the Court to review only the restrictive measures in CFSP can put forward in the sense that-albeit the general limitations referred to above-the protection of human beings in EU is also equally guaranteed in relation to CFSP acts. If one adhered to such a literal interpretation, it would lead to a reduction in Court's jurisdiction over that which it exercised under the regulatory framework preceding the Treaty of Lisbon. Indeed, article 275 TFEU legitimizes the challenge only of Community acts implementing CFSP measures which adopt restrictive measures against natural or legal persons and only on the part of the latter and not to all the applicants who, ordinarily, under the conditions set out in article 263 TFEU, are entitled to challenge EU acts. Thus, these last acts would continue to be subject to the general power of scrutiny by the CJEU (…) if the implementing measures for CFSP acts were not directly based on CFSP provisions, they did not escape the control of the Court and the provision referred to in article 275 TFEU would prove useless. It would then be appropriate for an interpretative reconstruction under which the acts of execution of CFSP as well as acts which are directly based on the provisions of the common foreign and security policy, are beyond the control of the Court with the exception of restrictive measures taken against natural or legal persons (…). This assumption should lead to the consequence that although the CJEU has no jurisdiction to rule on CFSP acts (with the exceptions mentioned above), it should instead be competent to know all the acts adopted on the basis of the provisions of the TFEU to implement CFSP acts in the event that they should find a conflict between the basic CFSP acts and implementing measures. If this were the case it would be to establish an indirect power of the CJEU for the interpretation of CFSP provisions. Indeed in order to assess the compatibility of a reprehensible measure with regard to CFSP provisions, it is essential that the Court should interpretively reconstruct the scope of those provisions (…). It follows that the reference parameter of the legality of restrictive measures must also be the acts adopted on the basis of CFSP provisions. If this interpretation were correct, the Court would in fact exercise a power of interpretation which, in principle, should be precluded (…). It seems clear that whenever there are spaces that lend themselves to being attracted by the jurisdiction of the Court, this increasingly restricts the terrain of the unappealable. He did so under the previous regime and does so even more in the unified regulatory environment redesigned on the occasion of the last amendment of the Treaties. However, in the face of the deficiencies of the system with regard to the protection of the fights of the person in the field of CFSP, the Lisbon Treaty has brought partial solutions and the protection of the person continues to suffer from important limitations. D. LIAKOPOULOS, Art. 275 TFUE, in P.E. HERZOG, C. CAMPBELL, G. ZAGEL, Smit & Herzog on the law of the European Union, ed. LexisNexis, New York, 2018.

[431]For details see. S. GRILLER, The Court of Justice and the common foreign and security policy, in CJEU, The Court of Justice and the construction of Europe, op. cit.

The problem which arises in relation to article 340, second sub-paragraph, concerns its scope: In particular, the non-contractual liability regime it has set up relates to the international responsibility of the Union, under international public law, or is it only of an administrative, civil or even private international law liability? Some authors have highlighted this aspect,[432] particularly the one linked to the difficulty of analyzing the regime configured by the provision in terms of international responsibility under international "public" law.[433] On the other hand, other scholars consider that the non-contractual responsibility of international organizations corresponds essentially to international responsibility, which is emphasized in the event of illicit and harmful exercise of their competences and, in this sense, article 340 would reflect this reality.[434] The liability regime configured by the provision taking into consideration the fundamental elements that characterize the international responsibility of the organizations, namely the existence of an offense, damage, causal link between the damage and the illicitness,[435] illegality of the conduct of an omission nature, and the effectiveness of the damage referring to the general principles common to the rights of Member States.

These assumptions of the non-contractual liability of the Union have been illustrated by the CJEU.[436] They are always necessary, if they are added other two if the behaviour of the Institutions of the Union consists in the exercise of powers characterized by a wide margin of discretion and, in particular, in the adoption of normative acts involving choices of economic policy (for example, regulations in the framework of the common agricultural policy). In these cases, it is not enough to

---

432 J. SALMON, Les accords Spaak-U Thant du 20 fevrier 1965, op. cit., pp. 479ss.

433 J.M. THOUVENIN, Responsibility in the context of the European legal order, in J. CRAWFORD, A. PELLET, S. OLLESON (eds.), The law of international responsibility, op. cit., pp. 861ss.

434 P. DAILLER, M. FORTEAU, A. PELLET, Droit international public, LGDG, Paris, 2009, pp. 680ss.

435 V. F. CASTILLO DE LA TORRE, Article 340 TFEU on contractual and non-contractual liability of the Union, in P.E. HERZOG, C. CAMPBELL, G. ZAGEL, Smit & Herzog on the law of the European Union, LexisNexis, New York, 2010, pp. 340-347. S. VAN RAEPENBUSCH, La convergence entre les régimes de responsabilité extracontractuelle de l'Union Européenne et des États Membres, in ERA Forum, 12 (4), 2012, pp. 672ss.

436 CJEU, C-4/69, Alfons Lütticke GmbH v. Commission of the European Communities, 28 April 1971, ECLI:EU:C:1971:40, ECR 1971. parr. 10-11. M.RIDDERVOLD, G. ROSÉN, Trick and treat: How the Commission and the European Parliament exert influence in EU Foreign and Security Policies, in Journal of European Integration 38 (6), 2016, pp. 688ss. T. GIEGERICH, Wege zu einer vertieften Gemeinsamen Außen-und Sicherheits-politik: Reparatur von Defiziten als "kleine Lösung," in S. KADEBACH, Die Europäische Union am Scheideweg: mehr oder weniger Europa?, ed. Nomos, Baden-Baden, 2015, pp. 138ss.

demonstrate the mere illegitimacy of the behaviour and the act from which the damage is derived, but it is also necessary, firstly, that the rule violated by the institutions is intended to confer rights to individuals and, moreover, whether it is a serious and manifest violation.

According to our opinion on the basis of article 340 (2), the EU would be constructing, little by little, in accordance with the general principles common to the law of the various Member States and through CJEU jurisprudence, a system of responsibilities whose characteristics they correspond to a large extent to those of the responsibility of international law.[437] Instead, the situation is in some ways more complex and nuanced, since the practice does not seem to indicate with certainty that the EU's non-contractual liability under article 340 TFEU is the same as that of "public" international law, nor can it be fully configured as a responsibility of private derivation. Thus, the provision on non-contractual EU liability, although very elastic and seemingly broad in scope, cannot reasonably refer to the international responsibility of the Organization. Rather, it seems to involve a substantially "private" type of liability[438] concerning only the liability, arising outside the contract practice, of the EU towards individuals within the Union system for damages caused by omissions or actions (culpable behaviour with certain and real damage) by bodies, institutions or agents in the exercise of their functions. Our position is also based on an objective analysis which leads us to observe, as we

[437]M. FORTEAU, Régime général de responsabilité ou lex specialis?, op. cit., pp. 147-160.

[438]In this spirit, the eventual responsibility of the EU will be determined, if the private contractors' conduct can be attributed to it. Article 340.2 TFEU stipulates the non-contractual liability for any damage caused by its institutions and servants, which include private contractors authorised by the Union to fulfil official duties. The contractual liability of the Community is governed by the law applicable to the contract in question. With regard to non-contractual liability, the Community must, in accordance with the general principles common to the laws of the Member States, make good any damage caused by its institutions or agents in the performance of their duties. The second subparagraph shall apply to the same conditions as damage caused by the European Central Bank or by its servants in the exercise of their functions. The personal liability of the agents towards the Community is governed by the provisions establishing their status or the regime applicable to them (...). E. KRAHMANN, C. FRIESENDORF, The role of private security companies (PSCs) in CSDP missions and operation, European Parliament Directorate-General for External Policies, Policy Department, 2011, pp. 6-7. See also: CJEU, C-9/56, Meroni & Co., Industrie Metallurgiche, SpA v. High Authority of the European Coal and Steel Community of 13 June 1958, ECLI:EU:C:1958:7, I-00133, parr. 42-47 and case: C-138/79, Murri Frères v. Commission of the European Communities of 29 October 1980, ECLI:EU:C:1980:249, I-03333, parr. 34ss. O. DE FROUVILLE, Attribution of conduct to the State: Private individuals, in J. CRAWFORD, The law of international responsibility, Oxford University Press, Oxford, 2010.

have already said, how the practice on EU liability for illicit acts at international level is very scarce or almost non-existent, a circumstance which certainly does not play in favour of an "internationalist" view of the regime set out in article 340, second sub-paragraph of the TFEU.

Other provisions that may be noted with regard to EU responsibility are contained in specific decisions and joint actions issued by Council.[439] For example the Council Joint Action 2008/851/CFSP[440] which established the start of Operation Atalanta states that "(...) the conditions of the presence of units belonging to Atalanta aboard merchant ships, in particular those chartered from World Food Program, including privileges, immunity [441] and other guarantees necessary for the good performance of the mission, are established with the flag State of these ships,"[442] while the Council Joint Action 2007/192/CFSP concerning the EUSEC mission in Congo provides that "(...) neither the EU nor the SG/HR (Secretary-General/High Representative) can in any case be held responsible by the contributing Member States for acts or omissions of the Head of Mission in the use of the funds of these States."[443] Furthermore,

439F. NAERT, The international responsibility of the Union in the context of its CSDP operations, in M. EVANS, P. KOUTRAKOS (eds.), The international responsibility of the European Union. European and international perspectives, op. cit., pp. 333ss.

440Council Joint Action 2008/851/CFSP of 10 November 2008 on a European Union military operation to contribute to the deterrence, prevention and repression of acts of piracy and armed robbery off the Somali coast, OJ L 301, 12.11.2008, p. 33-37. L. SIMÓN, No mighty, no right: Europeans must rediscover military power, in Real Instituto Elcano, European Global Strategy Project, EGS 2/2013, 19 March 2013. See also: I.K. DÜSTERHERF, A.I. GERLACH, The successes and failures of the interventions of the European Union, the African Union and neighbouring powers in Somalia, in Sicherheit und Frieden, 31 (1), 2013, pp. 19ss. F. LEONARD, G. RAMSAY, Globalizing Somalia: Multilateral international and transnational recpercussions of conflict, Bloomsbury Publishing, New York, 2013. R. SCHÜTZE, T. TRIDIMAS, Oxford principles of European Union law, Oxford University Press, Oxford, 2018. P. KOUTRAKOS, Judicial review in EU's common foreign and security policy, Cambridge University Press, Cambridge, 2018.

441In its advisory opinion on Differences Relating to Immunity from Legal Process of a Special Rapporteur of the Commission on Human Rights, the same Court pointed out that, if damages incurred as a result of acts performed by the United Nations or by its agents acting in their official capacity, "(...) the UN may be required to bear responsibility for the damage arising from such acts."

442Council Joint Action 2008/851/CFSP of 10 November 2008 on a European Union military operation to contribute to the deterrence, prevention and repression of acts of piracy and armed robbery off the Somali coast, OJ L 301, 12.11.2008, p. 13. Council Decision 2014/827/CFSP of 21 November 2014 amending Joint Action 2008/851/CFSP on a European Union military operation to contribute to the deterrence, prevention and repression of acts of piracy and armed robbery of the Somali coast, OJ L 335, 22.11.2014, p. 19-21.

443 Council Joint Action 2007/192/CFSP of 27 March 2007 amending Joint Action

with regard to the EULEX Operation in Kosovo, the EU has set up a Human Rights Review Panel (HRRP), active since 2010, to accommodate complaints of potential human rights violations committed by the operation personnel in the carrying out its mandate.[444]

A document that may be important with reference to some possible profiles of responsibility is represented by the "Generic Standards of Behaviour for ESDP Operations,"[445] i.e. the guidelines drawn up by the Council in 2005 for the purpose "to ensure that all categories of personnel involved in ESDP (CSDP) operations (…) maintain the highest personal standards of behaviour."[446] Indeed, the document contains directives of a non-juridical nature, the violation of which seems to constitute, more than anything else, a responsibility of an individual, penal or disciplinary nature. In this regard, it provides that "(...) the standards of behaviour are

---

2005/355/CFSP on the European Union mission to provide advice and assistance for security sector reform in the Democratic Republic of the Congo (DRC), OJ L 87, 28.3.2007, p. 22, art. 1 (1).

[444] Agreement between EU and the former Yugoslav Republic of Macedonia on the participation of the former Yugoslav Republic of Macedonia in the EU military crisis management operation in Bosnia and Herzegovina (Operation ALTHEA), OJ 2008 L 188/10; Agreement between the EU and the Republic of Croatia on the participation of the Republic of Croatia in the EU military operation to contribute to the deterrence, prevention and repression of acts of piracy and armed robbery off the Somali coast (Operation Atalanta), OJ 2009 L 202/84. T. PALM, The changing character of EUFOR Althea: Power politics or learning?, in Cambridge Review of International Affairs, 30 (1), 2017, pp. 68ss. N.I.M. NOVÁKY, European Union military operations: A collective action perspective, ed. Routledge, London & New York, 2018.

[445] Doc. of Council 8373/3/05 REV 3, 18 May 2005. For further details see: W. BENEDEK, M.C. KETTEMANN, M. MÖSTL, Mainstreaming human security in peace operations and crisis management: Policies, problems potential, ed. Routledge, London & New York, 2019. M.P. MOELLE, The international responsibility of international organizations: Cooperation in peacekeeping operations, Cambridge University Press, Cambridge, 2017, pp. 119ss.

[446] W. BENEDEK, M.C. KETEMANN, M. MÖSTL, Mainstreaming human security in peace operations and crisis management: Policies, problems, potential, op. cit. The whole process is known as the crisis management procedures and it will culminate with the Operation Plan (OPLAN), and where applicable, the Rules of Engagement (ROE). At the point of development, the OPLAN should clarify the applicable law to the operation, specifying whether international humanitarian law or human rights law is suitable for each context, but this is not always the case. The absence of this kind of exact provision may be reflected in references to applicable rules of international humanitarian law or human rights law, which does not clarify in which circumstances those rules actually are applicable. Consequently, the Operation Commander would have to determine this to some extent. See also in argument: C. MÁRQUEZ CARRASCO, The applicability of human rights instruments to European Union's CSDP operations: Framing the challenges, in Cuadernos Europeos de Deusto, 53, 2015, pp. 60ss.

complementary to the legal obligations of personnel. The latter must apply the provisions of international law, including, when applicable, the law of armed conflict, and the laws of the contributing State. As a rule, personnel will also respect local law unless the execution of the mission requires otherwise" and adds, moreover, that "(...) not adhering to the required standards of behaviour is misconduct and may result in disciplinary measures. This is independent of possible criminal procedures."[447]

Actually, the ESDP became operational in 2003 when the General Affairs and the External Relations Council stated "the EU now has operational capability across the full range of the Petersberg tasks.[448] The entry into force of the Treaty of Nice gave the legal basis for the EU's involvement in military operations by virtue of art. 17 that declared, questions referred to shall include humanitarian and rescue tasks and these of combat forces in crisis management, including peacemaking."[449]

However, the boundary between these different types of responsibility within the CSDP is uncertain and labile and it cannot be ruled out that a violation of these provisions may also give rise to international responsibility on the part of the Organization or one of its Member States, especially where consider the possibility that such offenses have been committed in the performance of official functions.[450] The guidelines also provide that "personnel should report any alleged violations by personnel of human rights and international humanitarian or criminal law" and specify that the rules set out "are not intended to replace,

---

[447]An example of misconduct of EU mission personnel is in the case of sexual abuse and exploitation. In this regard we read that "(...) sexual exploitation and abuse violate universally recognized international legal norms and standards. They constitute acts of serious misconduct and are therefore grounds for disciplinary measures."

[448]Declaration on EU military capabilities, 19-20. V. 2003. 9379/03 (Press 138) p. 2.

[449]Art. 17 contained the so called "Petersberg Tasks." The Petersberg Tasks were set out in the Petersbergs Declaration adopted at the Ministerial Council of the Western European Union in June 1992; Petersbergs Declaration of the Western European Union Council of Ministers, para. II.4, June 19, 1992. see also: P. PONZANO, Mèthode intergouvernementale une mèthode communautiare: Une question sans intèrêt, in Notre Europe. Les Brefs, n. 23, 2011.

[450]This will depend on what scope to attribute to the notion of "functions," as also foreseen by article 6 of the 2011 Project. It is obvious, in fact, that crimes such as sexual exploitation, corruption or trafficking in human beings-provided for within the Generic Standards of 2005-cannot be included among the functions assigned by the EU to the staff, but an extensive interpretation of the concept, in the sense of intending such illicit actions, but nevertheless conducted within the assigned functions (for example, in the event that a contingent with the task of overseeing an area exercises at the same time some form of corruption on the local population) it could trigger the responsibility of the organ/agent and, therefore, of EU.

restrict or extend national regulations."[451] The common foreign and security policy shall include all questions relating to EU security.

4.3 The role of effective control....

The concept of effective control is not used (only) in the military, but has broader and more general scope. It is connected to the degree of control over conduct, which must necessarily be assessed on a case-by-case basis. What does this concept refer to in practical terms? Effective control is essentially equivalent to operational control, which in turn corresponds to the power to direct field operations and which is usually transferred by States to the IO conducting the operation. As a result, an illicit conduct is generally attributed to the IO, since it is usually the latter that exercises operational control. Only the operative level of command can generate an effective control, while other forms of command and control are judged irrelevant. For the same reason we can argue that a conduct must be attributed to the entity that formally holds the operative command, with the consequence that this hypothesis can be refuted if it is the State to exercise this type of command. Effective control does not imply only operational control, but must be interpreted, more generally, as the factor that has led to the implementation of a conduct.[452] There must be a sort of cause-effect link between the control exercised and the resulting action. In military operations, in particular, the conduct must be attributed to the entity that exercises a form of "causally linked" military control over the conduct of the offending party. This approach broadens the scope of effective control, attributing illicit conduct to the entity that, in the absence of operational control, also exercises other types of control, such as the organic command or strategic control, provided that there is a

[451]M.H.A. LARIVÉ, Debating European security and defense policy understanding the complexity, ed. Routledge, London & New York, 2016, pp. 197ss.

[452]N. PEROVA, Disentangling "effective control" test for the purpose of attribution of the conduct of UN peacekeepers to the State and the UN, in Nordic Journal of International Law, 86 (1), 2017, pp. 32ss. In particular we take in consideration as to the precise standard of this overall control-test, the International Criminal Tribunal for the Former Yugoslavia in case: ICTY in Prosecutor v. Tadić, Judgment, Case No. ICTY-94-1-A, 15 July 1999, parr. 185-229, considered as follows "(...) the control required by international law may be deemed to exist when a State (or, in the context of an armed conflict, the party to the conflict) has a role in organizing, coordinating or planning the military actions of the military group, in addition to financing, training and equipping or providing operational support to that group. Acts performed by the group or members thereof may be regarded as acts of de facto state organs regardless of any specific instruction by the controlling State concerning the Commission of each of those acts (...)."

link between this control and occurrence of the unlawful action. This theory seems to be acceptable, as it has the merit of reflecting the real complexity of military operations conducted under the auspices of an IO, where violations of international obligations often derive from the fulfilment of actions that do not fall within the concept of operational control, such as for example an individual unlawful conduct.

The notion of effective control, which has a legal nature, must be distinguished from that of command and control, which instead has a technical meaning, although the two concepts are not mutually exclusive. Article 7, in particular, seems to indicate that, in order to evaluate the effectiveness of the criterion under examination, it is necessary to carry out an analysis of each individual action, using the concept of "control" in a manner similar to how it is used in article 8 of the 2001 Project.[453] However, article 7 only requires that there be a factual link between the given organ and the IO that uses it, not attaching any importance to the existence of an institutional or organic link. ECtHR has repeatedly referred in its judgments to the test of effective control,[454] however, developing this concept in an innovative way.

The general check was used for the first time by the ECtHR in the decision on the admissibility of Behrami v. France and Saramati v. France, Germany and Norway of 2 May 2007 cases.[455] The decision, in fact, seems

[453]According to our opinion, the international organizations will be responsible for the ultra vires acts of its organs/agents under DARIO art. 8 only if they act in the official capacity. Therefore there must be a "close link" between the ultra vires conduct and their official functions. It does not matter whether an ultra vires act is valid or not under the international organizations's rules. The IO may still entail responsibility because, if the attribution of conduct were denied on this ground, it would deprive third parties of all redress, unless the conduct could be attributed to a State. The DARIO Commentary also provides that art. 8 covers situations when the conduct of its organ/agent exceeds the competence of the IO, because "it will also exceed the authority of the organ/agent who performed it." In this spirit an organ/agent must act within the overall functions of organization but may exceed the international organizations's competence for the ultra vires acts to be attributed to the international organizations. The question lies in the distinction between both of the terms. International organizations' functions reflect its responsibility to fulfil the assigned task and may sometimes in constituent instruments of international organizations be referred as "tasks," "purposes," "objects" or "aims." Probably, one potential approach to the definition of ultra vires acts can include acts beyond the ascribed powers and competences but within the attributed functions.

[454]ECtHR, Behrami and Behrami v. France and Saramati v. France, Germany and Norvay of 2 May 2007; Kasumaj v. Greece of 5 July 2007; Gajić v. Germany of 28 August 2007; Berić et al. v. Herzegovina Bosnia of 16 October 2007; Al-Jedda v. United Kingdom of 7 July 2011.

[455]A. SARI, Jurisdiction and international peace support operations. The Behrami and Saramati cases, op. cit., pp. 154ss. B. KNOLL, Rights without remedies: The European

to preclude every possible alternative on the front of imputability, attributing to UN exclusively the activities carried out by the military contingents and, moreover, it affirms in a rather dubious way the absolute prevalence of the peacekeeping regime under the Security Council, with the result of denying access to the control system guaranteed by ECHR to victims of violations committed during missions of peace led by UN.[456] The latter did not fail to criticize the work of the ECtHR, asserting that, based exclusively on the delegation of powers carried out by the Security Council in favour of KFOR as a result of which the former had "ultimate control and authority."[457] Further, the judges of Strasbourg "disregarded the test of "effective command and control" which for over six decades has guided UN and Member States in matters of attribution. Another case in which the Court of Strasbourg used the ultimate control criterion as the basis for the attribution of conduct is Al-Jedda v. United Kingdom.[458] The facts relating to Al-Jedda present numerous similarities with respect to the Saramati case, since it concerned alleged wrongdoing committed in the context of a mission authorized by UN. In the ruling given in the Nada case,[459] the Court of Strasbourg seems to have further restricted the scope of the ultimate control test as a criterion for allocation. Although the facts did not fit into the context of a multinational peace operation, the ECtHR expressly rejected the argument put forward by France, according to which the measures taken by Member States to implement Security Council resolutions under Chapter VII of the UN Charter must always be attributed to UN. In particular, the judges have ruled out that the ultimate control test applies to actions taken by Member States to implement, at national level, a Resolution of the Security Council which imposes restrictive measures against individuals.[460]

Court's failure to close the human rights gap in Kosovo, in Zeitschrift für äuslandisches öffentliches Recht, 68, 2008, pp. 432ss. K. MUJEZINOVI Ć LARSEN, Attribution of conduct in peace operations: The "ultimate authority and control" test, op. cit., pp. 512ss.

[456]D. LIAKOPOULOS, L'ingerenza umanitaria nel diritto internazionale e comunitario, op. cit.

[457] K. ZWOLSKI, The European Union and international security: Developing a comprehensive approach, in C. KAUNERT, S. LÉONARD (eds) European security, terrorism and intelligence, ed. Palgrave Macmillan, London, 2013.

[458]ECtHR, Al-Jedda v. United Kingdom of 7 July 2011.

[459]ECtHR, Nada v. Switzerland of 12 September 2012. L. VAN DEN HERIK, Research handbook on United Nations sanctions and international law, Edward Elgar Publishers, Cheltenham, 2017, pp. 423ss.

[460]G.I. HERNANDEZ, Beyond the control paradigm? International responsibility and the European Union, in The Cambridge Yearbook of European Legal Studies, 15, 2012-2013, pp. 644ss.

The test of the "effective control" as a reference criterion for attributing the conduct to an IO in the context of peace operations. Although the verification of the presence of this type of control is more complex than what can be said for the test of "general control," it has the merit of more equitably assigning an illegal conduct where there are more legal entities involved, since this type of control is exercised by the person who has actually given the precise order of, or issued the authorization to, commit certain actions and who has, at the same time, the power to prevent them. On the other hand, in the face of increasing application, especially with regard to disputes concerning the attribution of crimes committed in the course of military operations conducted by international organizations, the "effective control" test as configured in the Project of ILC does not corroborated, in all likelihood, by a sufficient opinio iuris to be considered to correspond to a norm of customary international law.[461] On the other hand, a sufficient diuturnitas seems to be lacking, to the extent that the provision is applied in different ways, which do not yet allow to configure a constant and uniform repetition of this "behaviour" over time. Even EU, in the work of the ILC, has expressed doubts about the effectiveness of article 7 and its customary nature, stating that "this remains a controversial area of international law."[462] The most problematic aspect, however, concerns the uncertainty that still exists regarding its actual scope and, in particular, the elements that must be taken into consideration to assess its presence.

One of the most interesting aspects of the criterion as formulated in article 7 of the Project of 2011 concerns its "unambiguous" scope, under two different aspects. Firstly, in spite of many of them favourable to a "double use" of the test, it has the purpose of attributing a conduct exclusively to the IO, since it cannot be used "directly"[463] to attribute the conduct to sending State (or States) or another IO.[464] Consequently, it can

---

[461]G.I. HERNANDEZ, Beyond the control paradigm? International responsibility and the European Union, op. cit.

[462]ILC, Responsibility of international organizations-Comments and observations received from international organizations, A/CN.4/637, 14 February 2011, Draft article 6, European Commission p. 22, par. 2.

[463]F. L. BORDIN, Reflections of customary international law. The authority of codification Conventions and ILC draft articles in international law, in International & Comparative Law Quarterly, 63 (3), 2014, pp. 537ss.

[464]In this regard, the language used by the ILC in the commentary on art. 7 is not always clear. In fact, it states that: " (...) The criterion for the attribution of conduct to the fact that the system is based on and that when an organization or agent is placed at the disposal of an international organizations the decisive question. See the Project of 2011, p. 87, par. 4 and p. 89, par. 8. These statements would seem to pave the way for a "two-way" use of the

be assumed that, where illicit conduct at international level does not meet the award criteria established by the provision, it will automatically have to be attributed to the State (or States) or to the IO which made the organ available, which then, in turn, committed the violation. The doubt that may arise with regard to the scenario just configured is whether it is sufficient to hold responsible the State (or the IO) that made the "loan" only on the basis of a "default attribution rule" or if, on the contrary, is necessary to demonstrate the presence of other elements. The Project of ILC does not provide any guidance on this, but in all likelihood, the responsibility of the State will have to be ascertained under the relevant Project of 2001. Secondly, unlike the Court of Appeal in the Nuhanović [465] case, the "effective control" outlined in article 7, in our opinion, can be exercised by a single legal entity at the same time and in relation to the same conduct. In practical terms, this means that the provision does not allow to configure the hypothesis of a dual, or multiple, attribution of conduct.

4.5. Comparative remarks from the praxis of UN and NATO into the sector of foreign defense

With regard to the practice of UN, the organization has the will to respond internationally for any violation committed during the peacekeeping missions, [466] through the implementation of an adequate

"effective control" criterion, but in our opinion the correct interpretation is based on the text of the article, which speaks unambiguously of attribution to the organization, as well as object and purpose of the Project (under article 31, paragraph 1 of the Vienna Convention on the Law of Treaties) and of Chapter II in particular, which is precisely to regulate the question of the attribution of a organization. For a position favourable to the "bi-univocal" interpretation of the "effective control" criterion. See in argument, T. DANNENBAUM, Killings at Srebrenica, effective control, and the power to prevent unlawful conduct, prevent unlawful conduct, in International and Comparative Law Quarterly, 61 (3), 2012, pp. 714ss. A. SARI, UN peacekeeping operations and article 7 DARIO: The missing link, in international organizations Law Review, 9 (1), 2012, pp. 77-85.

[465] Supreme Court, The Netherlands v. Hasan Nuhanović, 12/03324, ECLI/NL/HR/2013/BZ9225, 6 September 2013, parr. 3.11.2 e 3.5.2. Nuhanović v. The Netherlands case number 265618/HA ZA 06, 1672, Mustafić v. Netherlands, appeal judgment, LJN BR5386, Judgment of 5 July 2011; Netherlands (Ministry of Defense and Ministry of Foreign Affairs) v. Nuhanović, Final appeal judgment, ECLI/NL/HR/2013/BZ9225, ILDC 2061 (NL 2013), 12/03324, 6th September 2013, Supreme Court; Claimant 1 et al and the Mothers of Srebrenica v. the State of the Netherlands and the United Nations case, C/09/295247/ HA ZA 07, 2973, Judgment of The Hague District Court of July 16th 2014.

[466] A. NOVOSSELOFF, United Nations-European Union. Cooperation in the field of peacekeeping. Challenges and prospects, in Global Governance Institute, Analysis Paper, June 2012.

reparation to the injured Parties.[467] In this regard, the decades of experience gained in the field of peacekeeping and international security,[468] as well as the primacy in it, is a fundamental aspect, which has led the UN for some decades to develop the awareness that violations of international obligations can be frequent in this type of interventions, so as to act accordingly, thus adopting standards of conduct, issuing statements, concluding agreements that provide for appropriate procedures for the resolution of disputes, etc.

The practice is inclined to attribute responsibility for offenses exclusively to the UN, appearing to be depositing for a widening of the scope of the responsibility of the participating States to military operations, a tendency which we believe to be welcomed. The reason should not be sought only on the basis of legal considerations. It is important to highlight, in fact, the greater number of primary rules of international law applicable to States, rather than to international organizations, as well as the easier judicial assessment of state responsibility, when compared to the difficulty of judging matters concerning the responsibility of an organization, often frustrated by the application of the rules on immunity benefiting these institutions.

With reference to NATO practice,[469] the issue of international responsibility has not yet developed widely. Appeals for violations of international law have been brought against the individual States participating in the mission and not the Organization as a legal entity. Moreover, the international courts called to resolve the issue have never been able to rule on the merits and possibly recognize a state responsibility.

In particular, the next and later operation deployed with recourse to NATO assets and capabilities was operation ALTHEA in Bosnia and

---

467"It has always been the policy of the UN, acting through the Secretary-General, to compensate individuals who have suffered damages for which the organization was legally liable." UN Doc. S/6589, p. 41.

468P. BARRETTE, Croyances et cooperation: Analyse du résau des acteurs de la Politique de sécurité et de défense commune de l'UE, in Swiss Political Science Review, 20 (1), 2014, pp. 118ss. H. BIEHL, B. GIEGERICH, A. JONAS, Strategic cultures in Europe. Security and Defense Policies across the continent, ed. Springer, Wiesbaden, 2013.

469H. KRIEGER, Common European Defence: Competition or compatibility with Nato?, in M. TRYBUS, N.D. WHITE (eds.), European security law, Oxford University Press, Oxford 2007, pp. 174-197. T. STEIN, Kosovo and the international community. The attribution of possible internationally wrongful acts: Responsibility of NATO or of its Member States?, in C. TOMUSCHAT (ed. by), Kosovo and the international community. A legal assessment, op. cit., pp. 182ss. F. TERPAN EU-NATO relations: Consistency as a strategic consideration and a legal requirement, in M. TRYBUS, N.D. WHITE (eds.), European security law, op. cit., pp. 270-294.

Herzegovina in 2004.[470] In this operation, as in CONCORDIA, the Joint Action established recourse to NATO's assets and capabilities, and NATO placed the Deputy Supreme Allied Commander Europe (DSA-CEUR) and the SHAPE at the disposal of EU. The collaboration of NATO in these two operations was also based on the "Concerted Approach for the Western Balkans," which outlined "core areas of cooperation and emphasizes the common vision and determination both organizations share to bring stability to the region."[471]

If we look at the UN and NATO[472] responsibility practice arising from the conduct of crisis management missions, it shows that the violations established and decided by the courts derive almost exclusively from the violation of international humanitarian law rules[473] and on human

---

[470]A. JUNCOS, EU foreign and security policy in Bosnia: The politics of coherence and effectiveness, Manchester University Press, Manchester, 2013. B. POHL, EU foreign policy and crisis management operations: Power, purpose and domestic politics, ed. Routledge, London & New York, 2014. M.E. SMITH, Developing a comprehensive approach to international security: Institutional learning and the CSDP, in J. RICHARDSON (ed) Constructing a policy-making state? Policy dynamics in the EU, Oxford University Press, Oxford, 2012, pp. 254ss. S. BLOCKMANS, M. SPERNBAUER, Legal obstacles to comprehensive European Union external security action, in European Foreign Affairs Review, 18 (4), 2013, pp. 9ss. F. CAMERON, An introduction to European foreign policy, ed. Routledge, London & New York, 2012. A. JUNCOS, EU foreign and security policy in Bosnia: The politics of coherence and effectiveness, Manchester University Press, Manchester, 2013. B. POHL, EU foreign policy and crisis management operations: Power, purpose and domestic politics, ed. Routledge, London & New York, 2014. M.E. SMITH, Developing a comprehensive approach to international security: Institutional learning and the CSDP, in J. RICHARDSON (ed) Constructing a policy-making state? Policy dynamics in the EU, Oxford University Press, Oxford, 2012, pp. 254ss. F. CAMERON, An introduction to European foreign policy, ed. Routledge, London & New York, 2012.

[471]P. PETROV, Early institutionalization of the ESDP governance arrangements: Insights from the operations Concordia and Artemis, in S.VANHOONACKER, D. HYLKE, M. HEIDI (eds). Understanding the role of bureaucracy in the European Security and Defense Policy, in European Integration online Papers, 14 (1), 2010. K. ENGBERG, The European Union and military operations: A comparative analysis, ed. Routledge, London & New York, 2013, pp. 53ss. U. RABI, International intervention in local conflicts. Crisis management and conflict resolution in the cold war, I.B. Tauris Publishers, London & New York, 2010. M. REICHARD, The European Union-NATO relationship: A legal and political perspective, ed. Routledge, London & New York, 2016, pp. 247ss.

[472]In this spirit see also the Ruggie's Framework of 2011, UN Doc. A/HRC/17/31, 21 March 2011 contains a number of principles that help to flesh out the components of a corporate human rights due diligence process, which-should include assessing actual and potential human rights impacts, integrating and acting upon the findings, tracking responses, and communicating how impacts are addressed.

[473] M. ZWANENBURG, The duty to respect international humanitarian law during European union-led operations, in A. SARI, R.A. WESSEL, Human rights in EU crisis

rights. This should not be surprising, when considering the centrality of the aspects related to the use of force and the protection of human rights in carrying out peace operations.[474] However, one of the obstacles that do not allow a full assessment of the international responsibility of these two organizations is the uncertainty about the scope and content of international humanitarian law and human rights applicable in such situations. The same problem emerged with reference to the operations of CSDP of the EU.[475] A clarification of the applicable law in such situations therefore appears opportune and necessary, also in light of the considerable development of the practice in the field of peacekeeping and crisis management.[476]

And a question arises: Should an EU military operation be involved in an armed conflict as combatants, what are the foundations for the application of international humanitarian law? It has been established, even by the EU, that the rules of the Vienna Convention on the Law of Treaties are customary international law[477] and, therefore, they must be applied by all subjects of international law,[478] which refers to the EU, this

---

management operations. A duty to respect and to protect?, T.M.C. Asser Institute, The Hague, 2012.

474F. LACHENMANN, K. WOLFRUM, The law of armed conflict and the use of force, op. cit.

475In addition, the Strategic Framework highlights some areas of action related to CSDP. See Council of the European Union, Strategic Framework and Action Plan on Human Rights and Democracy, 11855/12 (2012).

476D. LIAKOPOULOS, Kritik an friedenserhaltenden/Peacekeeping Operationen und die Entwicklung des Konzepts der Souveränität im Völkerrecht, in International and European Union Legal Matters, 2011

477J. PEJIC, The protective scope of common article 3: More than meets the eye, in International Review of the Red Cross, 93, 2011, pp. 5-7.

478The ICJ in its advisory opinion on the Interpretation of the Agreement of 25 March 1951 between WHO and Egypt ruled that "international organizations are subjects of international law and, as such, are bound by any obligations incumbent upon them under general rules of international law, under their constitutions or under international agreements to which they are parties." Interpretation of the Agreement of 25 March 1951 between The WHO and Egypt, I.C.J. Reports (1980), art. 37. In relation to the applicability of the international humanitarian law to UN, Zwanenburg stated that article 1 (I), 3 and 103 of the UN Charter "together make clear that UN Security Council can derogate from customary law," when acting under the chapter VII of the UN Chapter. For further details and analysis see: M. ZWANENBURG, Toward a more mature ESDP: Responsibility for violations of international Humanitarian Law by EU crisis management operations, in S. BLOCKMANS (ed.), The European Union and crisis management. Policy and legal aspects, T.M.C. Asser Institute, The Hague, 2008, pp. 395ss. A. ZIMMERMANN, C.J. TAMS, K. OELLERS-FRAHAM, The Statute of the International Court of Justice. A commentary, op. cit.

applicability is supported by TEU and EU case law which states "that European Community must respect international law in the exercise of its powers. It is therefore required to comply with the rules of customary international law when adopting a regulation (...)."[479] One of the problems arising from this assertion is the question of which rules are applicable to a conflict in which the EU is involved. The Salamanca Declaration and Framework of Action adopted on 7-10 June 2004, the EU Guidelines on Promoting Compliance with International Humanitarian Law.[480] Both of them might well be considered unilateral acts. However, the absence of one of the requirements for the existence of a unilateral act such as the intent to generate legal effect, when combined with the vague content of the documents as well as the purpose of the second document to "promote compliance with international humanitarian law" among non-Member States, have hampered the classification of these documents as unilateral acts. Council joint actions might be also considered a source of unilateral acts. In relation to EU military operations, in some of the Council joint actions pertaining to operation EUNAVFOR,[481] the EU makes reference to different UN Security Council Resolutions as a basis for its operation. In these resolutions, the Security Council allows the states to enter and use the territorial waters of Somalia to fight against piracy in a manner consistent with relevant International Law, which in the case of an armed conflict would be international humanitarian law. This limitation has also been included in the "whereas" sections of one of the Council joint action. According to this conclusion, it is possible to affirm that the EU is bound

[479] J. CARDONA LLORENS, J. PUEYO LOSA, J.L. RODRIGUEZ-VILLASANTE PRIETO (eds.) Estudios de Derecho Internacional y de Derecho Europeo en Homenaje al Profesor Manuel Pérez González, ed. Tirant lo Blanch, Valencia, 2012, pp. 168ss.

[480] Updated European Union Guidelines on promoting compliance with international humanitarian law (IHL), OJ C 303, 15.12.2009, p. 12-17. In argument see also: A. BRESLIN, Ensuring respect: The European Union's guidelines on promoting compliance with international humanitarian law, in Israel Law Review, 43 (2), 2010, pp. 382ss. T. PFANNER, Various mechanisms and approaches for implementing international humanitarian law and protecting and assisting war victims, in International Law Red Cross, 91, 2009, pp. 280ss. D. PATTERSON, A. SÖDERSTEN, European Union law and international law, ed. Wiley Blackwell, New York, 2016.

[481] Council Decision (CFSP) 2015/778 of 18 May 2015 on a European Union military operation in the Southern Central Mediterranean (EUNAVFOR MED), OJ L 122, 19.5.2015, p. 31-35. H. MERKET, The European Union and the security-development nexus bridging the legal divide, ed. Brill, Leiden, Boston, 2016, pp. 130ss. A.J.BELLAMY, Libya and the responsibility to protect: The exception and the norm, in Ethics & International Affairs, 25 (3), 2011, pp. 263ss. S. CHESTERMAN, Leading from behind: The responsibility to protect, the Obama doctrine, and humanitarian intervention after Libya, in Ethics & International Affairs, 25 (3), 2011, pp. 282ss.

by international humanitarian law.

ILC has also made this criterion in the 2011 Project and this will also be the model to be followed to address the issue of attribution of responsibility in the context of EU crisis management missions. Finally, the practice of UN and, to a lesser extent, NATO has shown that there are different types of international responsibility (direct, shared, secondary), depending on the degree of involvement of the various actors in the Commission of the offense and the relationship between these. However, the state of international law regarding situations in which a liability that is not of an exclusive nature emerges is not yet well established at the present time, in order to determine exactly which of the above hypotheses can be configured in the concrete case.[482]

I disagree with the position that international humanitarian law applies only to the operations authorized by the UN Security Council and led by other States, while not applying to the operations under UN command and control. This is not possible simply because international humanitarian law starts to apply in the situations where there is an armed conflict or an occupation of the territory in fact and does not depend on any justification to use force lawfully or unlawfully coming from jus ad bellum. Accordingly, as soon as a State or IO becomes a party to the armed conflict, they are bound by international humanitarian law. In this spirit in case of peacekeepers participating in hostilities will become combatants. They cannot be considered civilians anymore because their States are in conflict with other parties and they are members of the armed forces. To argue otherwise would lead to unfortunate results, as if they were not considered combatants and still participated in the armed conflict, they would become unlawful combatants with very arguable status under international humanitarian law. When they do not participate in hostilities, their States are not parties to the conflict and they are not considered armed forces and will be civilians of a neutral State. Their participation (representing an international actor) may convert that conflict in an international armed conflict if they participate in hostilities against state armed forces or against an armed group in the State without a government and that group may pretend to act on behalf of it. This position argues for a gradual approach to the application of the law of occupation under Vienna Conventions on the law of Treaties.[483] If protected persons fall in

---

[482] M. P. MOELLE, The international responsibility of international organizations. Cooperation in peacekeeping operations, Cambridge University Press, Cambridge, 2017, pp. 168ss.

[483]E. BENVENISTI, The law of global governance, ed. Brill, The Hague, 2014, pag. 99,

the hands of peacekeepers and the application of any provision of Vienna Conventions on the Law of Treaties is triggered, they must comply with it irrespective of the heading under which the provision is placed in Vienna Convention on the Law of Treaties.[484] The whole system of Vienna Conventions on the Law of Treaties may also apply to the peacekeepers, even if they do not participate in the conflict provided that they exercise the sole authority in the country. In all cases whether international humanitarian law applies or not the troop contributing countries and UN remain bound by international humanitarian law obligations (the UN remains bound by customary international humanitarian law).[485] As a consequence international human rights law does not cease to apply during the application of international humanitarian law, they apply concurrently. In any case of their conflict, it can be solved by interpretation of the one in the light of another. If the peacekeepers commit human rights violations and their conduct is attributable to their respective troop contributing countries will be responsible for that conduct, even though it was committed beyond the territorial borders and territorial control is not needed. The argument is made that the notion of jurisdiction, provided in human rights treaties, is not a condition additional to the attribution of the conduct to States but, in substance, represents the same limitation to state responsibility for the conduct performed abroad. The human rights bodies use the jurisdictional requirement to find state responsibility in the same way as the attribution of the conduct is used to find the responsibility of that State. Therefore, the UN or troop contributing countries can be responsible for the human rights violations committed by peacekeepers during their operations if the conduct constituting human rights violations is attributed to either of them. Regarding individual criminal responsibility of peacekeepers, the thesis argues that the SOFAs which the UN signs with the host states provide blanket exception from the host state jurisdiction for peacekeepers and may lead to the impunity of peacekeepers for the acts committed during peace operations. The host States signing such agreements may violate their obligations under the VCLT.[486] Under those

---

"(...) as an international person, an international organization is subject to general international law. Therefore [IOs] are subject to customary international law and general principles of law (...)."

[484]For details see: O. CORTEN, P. KLEIN, The Vienna Conventions on the law of treaties. A commentary, op. cit.

[485]K. DAUGIRIDAS, How and why international law binds international law, in Harvard Journal of International Law, 57 (2), 2016.

[486] See also: J. OBERMATT, The development of customary international law by international organizations, in International & Comparative Law Quarterly, 66 (2), 2017,

Conventions, the host States are obliged to establish their jurisdiction over war crimes or crime of torture, if a perpetrator of those acts is present in their territory. They are also under obligation to take him into custody and prosecute or extradite. No such possibility is envisaged under the UN SOFAs and when a peacekeeper commits an international crime, the host state will be in violation of its obligations. It can be concluded that the responsibility of the UN, troop contributing countries and peacekeepers depends on the factual circumstances of the Commission of international law violations during PSOs. The troop contributing countries hiding behind the veil of the UN and its immunities cannot avoid international responsibility for those crimes that they were able to prevent. The fact that the troop contributing countries possess more powers than the UN (including disciplinary, prosecutorial and training powers) to prevent violations of international law contributes to their responsibility for those crimes. The UN should not bear the responsibility on its own. The UN should change its position with regarding the SOFAs that it signs with the host States, as by this act it may compel the latter to violate their obligations under international law. Although the UN tries to adopt certain measures and policies directed to prevent unlawful conduct of peacekeepers, it does not change its policy in shielding troop contributing countries and their peacekeepers from any international responsibility and by that contributing to the sense of impunity among them. What should be done is to recognize that the international responsibility for violations of international law committed during peace operations is shared between the UN, troop contributing countries and peacekeepers and neither of them will avoid responsibility by reason of simple collaboration with the UN and authorization by the UN Security Council.

4.6.(Follows) CSDP missions in EU

The hypothesis that the contingents taking part in a military operation of CSDP[487] can be qualified as de jure EU bodies is to be

---

pp. 494ss.

[487]For further analysis see: A. SARI, R.A. WESSEL, International responsibility for EU military operations: Finding the EU's place in the global accountability regime, in B. VAN VOOREN, S. BLOCKMANS, J. WOUTERS (eds.), The EU's role in global governance: The legal dimension, Oxford University Press, Oxford 2013, pp. 128ss. M. ZWANENBURG, Accountability of peace support operations, Martinus Nijhoff Publishers, Leiden, Boston, 2005. A. BILLON-GALLAND, M. QUENCEZ, Can France and Germany make PESCO work as a process toward EU defense?, in Policy Brief, n. 33, Washington, DC: German Marshall Fund of the United States, 2017. S. BISCOP, All or nothing? The EU global strategy and defense policy after Brexit, in Contemporary Security Policy, 37

excluded, since there is no indication to that effect that can be found in deeds, declarations and other soft law instruments issued by EU, or even less, in provisions contained in the Treaties. For similar reasons, even the possibility of configuring such groups as "subsidiary" organs of the organization is groundless. Finally, the hypothesis consisting in considering military contingents de facto organs shows evident difficulties in many ways. Although military contingents transfer part of their command and control structure to EU, the EU does not exercise full command over them. On the other hand, it can be said that only bodies under its "direct" and "exclusive" operational and organizational control are EU bodies, and this criterion can be extended, in general, to all international organizations. In other words, the concept applies only to those subjects on whom the Organization has the "exclusive" authority to impose operational decisions or regarding the appointment of their duties within the mission. This is not the case of personnel participating in CSDP[488] missions.

In our opinion, the quotas that take part in the military operations of CSDP cannot therefore qualify as EU bodies under article 6 of 2011 Project. The application of this provision is, therefore, excluded with reference to the allocation of unlawful conduct during CSDP operations. The absence of specific provisions that set the state quotas as organs of the Organization when they act as part of CSDP operations can be explained by the awareness of the risks related to the Commission of violations of

---

(3), 2016, pp. 432ss.

[488]To date, the EU and CSDP has successfully launched 34 operations and missions: Seven military operations (Concordia, Althea, Artemis, EUFOR DR Congo, EUFOR Tchad/RCA, Atalanta, EUFOR RCA), twelve assistance/supporting missions (EUSEC DR Congo, EU support to AMIS Darfur, EUSR BST Georgia, EUPAT fYROM, EUPT Kosovo, EUSSR Guinea-Bissau, EUNAVCO, EUCAP Sahel Niger, EUCAP NESTOR Horn of Africa, EUAVSEC South Sudan) including the two most recent (EUCAP Sahel Mali and EUAM Ukraine), six police operations (EUPM, Proxima, EUPOL Kinshasa, EUPOL COPPS, EUPOL DRC, EUPOL Afghanistan), three rule of law missions (EUJUST THEMIS, EUJUST LEX, EULEX Kosovo), three border missions (EUBAM Rafah, EUBAM Ukraine/Moldova, EUBAM Libya), and two monitoring missions (AMM and EUMM Georgia). See for further details: A.E. JUNCOS, European Union foreign and security policy in Bosnia. The politics of coherence and effectiveness, Manchester University Press, Manchester & New York, 2015, pp. 145ss. M.E. SMITH, Europe's common security and defense policy: Capacity-building, experimental learning and institutional change, Cambridge University Press, Cambridge, 2017. B. MÖLER, European security. The roles of regional organizations, ed. Routledge, London & New York, 2016. C. MAJOR, Towards an EU peace building strategy: The effects of the Lisbon Treaty on the comprehensive approach of the EU in the area of civilian crisis management, in European Foreign Affairs Review, 18, 2014, pp. 46ss.

international law and, consequently, perhaps also by the will to ensure that, first and foremost, States have to respond internationally to any illegal conduct. On the other hand, it is appropriate to emphasize the large, and in some ways unexplained, asymmetry between 2001 Project and 2011 Regulation concerning the attribution of conduct. This is a "deficient" regulatory framework, in which the (few) provisions concerning the attribution of conduct of the 2011 Project do not seem sufficient to regulate the various situations that may actually occur with reference to the increasingly complex practice of IO.

4.7. EU responsibility related to Member States' acts

Under certain circumstances, the responsibility of an IO may arise in connection with the conduct of a State or another IO, pursuant to arts. 15[489] and 17 of the 2011 Project.[490] Article 15 provides that where an organization directs and controls a State (or another IO) in the Commission of an international offense, it will be responsible for that act, if it does so "with knowledge of the circumstances of the internationally wrongful act" and if the act "would be internationally wrongful if committed by that organization."[491]

This case may take on a certain importance during the CSDP operations. One of the discriminating factors for the attribution of conduct and responsibility is to assess the type of control exercised over a Member State, also with reference to the hypothesis of "related liability" it is fundamental to understand what kind of relationship exists between EU and Member States participants in the missions. In this case, the position of Member States is emphasized, not that of their organs made available to the organization. This aspect must be appropriately taken into account

[489]See, O. KEEFE, C.J. TAMS, A. TZANAKOPOLOS, The United Nations Convention on jurisdictional immunities of States and their property, Oxford University Press, Oxford, 2013, pp. 241ss.

[490]See in argument: C. ALBORN, The rules of international organizations and the law of international responsibility, in international organizations Law Review, 8, 2011, pp. 398ss. P. JACOB, Les définitions des notions "d'organe et d'agent" retenues par la ILC sont-elles opérationnelles?, in Revue Belge de Droit International, 117, 2013, pp. 18ss. Y. KERBAT, Sanctions et contre-mesures: risques de confusion dans les articles de la ILC sur la responsabilité des organizations internationales, in Revue Belge de Droit International, 117, 2013, pp. 105ss. M. MÖLDNER, Responsibility of international organizations-Introducing the ILC's DARIO, op. cit., pp. 285ss.

[491]A. DELGADO CASTELEIRO, The international responsibility of the European Union. From competence to normative control, op. cit.

and may change the conclusions that can be reached. It can be said, in essence, that in the course of a military operation conducted under the aegis of EU, the latter directs and controls a Member State in the Commission of an unlawful act in accordance with article 15 of Project? In our opinion, the hypothesis is hardly feasible in practice, but should not be excluded a priori. The only form of control exercisable by an IO on Member States is achieved through the enactment of binding acts. In this sense, there is no doubt that within CSDP the Member States are obliged to comply with the measures decided and adopted by EU, in particular the Council. In fact, the transactions are initiated through the issue of joint actions, which, pursuant to article 25, lett. b), i, of the TEU, are among the decisions taken by EU to conduct CFSP. The decisions are binding acts issued by the Union, obligatory in all their elements, which may have general scope or, if they designate the recipients, individual scope.

One of the major problems, however, lies in the fact that the management and control in question must be exercised directly on the concrete EC of the unlawful act, or must be functional and closely related to it. Moreover, this control must refer to a real "domination" on the Commission of the deed, while the management must also be factual. The first requirement seems to imply that the Member State cannot have any alternative available except to commit the act.[492] For example, it could be assumed that a Member State is bound by a provision contained in a decision to individuals captured in the course of a military operation to arbitrary arrest and detention, in violation of its obligation under international law of a customary nature. Regarding the second requirement, it seems at first sight easier to consider it satisfied in relation to the subject in question. The term "directs," in fact, refers to an "actual direction of an operative kind"[493] which can be said to exist with regard to CSDP missions. Nonetheless, the control we are referring to is implemented towards state bodies and not by Member States tout court. The latter provide civilian and military capabilities for carrying out the various missions which, in concrete terms, consist precisely of qualified personnel. It is therefore a sort of "three-way relationship:" On the one hand, there is the EU, which leads CSDP and has its full "ownership;" on the other hand, there are the Member States, which provide their necessary resources for the organization, preparation and actual conduct of the missions; finally, in a

---

[492] S. YEE, Member responsibility and the ILC Articles on the Responsibility of international organizations: Some observations, M. RAGAZZI (ed.), Responsibility of international organizations. Essays in Memory of Sir Ian Brownlie, op. cit.
[493] ILC, Project 2011, p. 106, par. 4.

position, so to speak, "intermediate," there are the state bodies made available to the Union, which act as a filter between the two main actors and which, in practice, carry out the activities envisaged by each individual operation. If from a purely practical point of view this situation may appear well defined, the legal uncertainties it poses are not, as we have so far been able to appreciate, of little importance. In particular, since the "control" requirement on States does not seem to be fulfilled, we believe that EU cannot be held responsible for an international offense committed within the framework of a CSDP mission under article 15 of the Project.[494] On the other hand, the relationship between the Member State participating in a mission and EU does not seem to be sufficiently regulated and, even less, the triple relationship that is created between a Member State and its own military contingent, on the one hand, and this last and the Union, on the other.

On the other hand, as regards the circumvention hypothesis (article 17 of the Project), it may be the most suitable for the purpose of configuring the possible international responsibility of EU in the context of CSDP.[495] In fact, in this area of foreign policy, the Union does not have the basic elements to implement proper regulatory control towards Member States, i.e. CJEU jurisdiction over the provisions concerning CFSP. The Member States being excluded would continue to incur liability for issues related to this sector, while EU could incur international liability, not on the basis of a rule on attribution, but exclusively under article 17.[496] This position, although present undeniable connotations of logic, does not seem to be shared in the light of what we say below.

If we apply the provision in question to the operations of CSDP,[497] we can see, in fact, how Member States conduct their actions on the basis of binding decisions issued by the Council. However, two requirements

[494] In argument see: K. BERNER, Subsequent agreements and subsequent practice in domestic courts, ed. Springer, Berlin, 2017, pp. 76ss. P. BEHRENS, Diplomatic interference and the law, op. cit.

[495] M. CORTÉS MARTÍN, The European exceptionalism in international law? The European Union and the system of international responsibility, in M. RAGAZZI (ed.), Responsibility of international organizations-Essays in Memory of Sir Ian Brownlie, op. cit., pp. 190ss.

[496] R.A. WESSEL, L. DEN HERTOG, EU foreign, security and defense policy: A competence-responsibility gap?, in M. EVANS, P. KOUTRAKOS (eds.), The international responsibility of the European Union. European and international perspectives, op. cit.

[497] An international organizations incurs international responsibility if it circumvents one of its international obligations by adopting a decision binding Member States or international organizations to commit an act that would be internationally wrongful if committed by the former organization.

need to be met to hold EU accountable under article 17, par. 1. First of all, it must be shown that, in issuing a decision with regard to Member States, it had the precise intention of circumventing its own international obligation. Furthermore, the decision must not leave any room for maneuver in the hands of the Member State, which must be forced to commit an international offense by implementing that decision. Finally, there is no responsibility of the IO if the authorization is no longer valid and applicable to the circumstances of the case due to changes that have occurred since its adoption.[498] The conditions of applications provided for in article 17 are so restrictive that they jeopardize the usefulness of the whole provision. As regards the first aspect, it is clear that it is difficult to demonstrate that EU wants to circumvent an international obligation which will be free to adopt the measures it deems most appropriate in this regard. On the other hand, in general and theoretical the fact remains that these are official organs and therefore always subject to the supreme command of their sending State.

The hypothesis of the circumference, in fact, implies the presence of the specific element of malice, or the will to cause a certain act, as clarified also by the ILC. This is obviously an element of a subjective nature whose presence cannot be deduced from mere factual criteria. In relation to the second aspect, it is difficult to establish to what extent the States enjoy a certain degree of discretion when they have to implement the measures imposed by EU in the context of CSDP, partly because of the secrecy of certain documents such as those concerning, for example, the rules of engagement. In the Rheinland-Pfalz case,[499] for example, the judges considered that the unlawful conduct was attributable exclusively to Germany, stating that it had a significant influence on the transfer of these subjects.

Since the state organs operating in the context of a CSDP operation are still subject to the general control of their sending State, they enjoy a certain degree of discretion in implementing EU measures. Furthermore, an observation is opportune. Article 17 of the Project assumes that the action taken by the Member State following the decision issued by the organization is illegal for the latter, regardless of whether it is also for the circumvented Member State (or IO). With regard to the

---

[498] J. D'ASPREMONT, The law of international responsibility and multilayered institutional veils: The case of authorized regional peace-enforcement operations, SHARES Research Paper n. 24, 2013, p. 13.

[499] CJEU, 44/79, Liselotte Hauer contro Land Rheinland-Pfalz of 13 December 1979, ECLI:EU:C:1979:290, I-03727, par. 15.

international responsibility deriving from the CSDP operations, we can say that almost all the international standards in this area constitute obligations both for EU and Member States.[500] It follows that, whenever art. 17 is applied to cases of international crimes committed during a CSDP mission, both the EU and the Member State will be responsible internationally. Art. 17 may seem at first indicated to regulate the issues concerning the assignment of international responsibility in the context of CSDP missions. Nevertheless, to a deeper analysis, the fundamental requisites that constitute its application base seem to be missing.

4.8. (Follows) Multiple attribution and responsibility

The hypothesis that an international crime committed during a CSDP operation can be attributed both to EU and to the individual sending States, to varying degrees depending on the case.

An attribution of this type within the scope of CSDP operations can, in our opinion, occur when the "effective control" exercised by EU on the offending conduct[501] is not sufficiently clear, and there is no time for exclusive control by the sending State. At the regulatory level, the Political and Security Committee (PSC) (article 38 TEU)[502] is responsible for the political control and strategic direction of military operations, under the authority of the High Representative for the Common Foreign and Security Policy from the Council. On the other hand, from a factual point of view, the contingents obey the directives of the Commander of the EU Force, but are subjected to the "full command and authority" of their

[500]The only cases where the EU appears to have its own "specific" international obligations are those related to compliance with international agreements concluded with third States participating in the missions or resolutions issued by the Security Council which constitute the legal basis of certain CSDP operations (such as, for example, the 1846 issue of 2008 which calls into question international organizations in order to combat piracy in accordance with international law). Other resolutions, on the other hand, seem to impose obligations only on States. For example, again with reference to the ATALANTA Operation, the Res. 1816 (2008) authorizes States to enter the territorial waters of Somalia to combat piracy in accordance with international law (article 7, letter a). In this case, there are doubts about the applicability of the provisions with regard to EU.

[501] B. KONDOCH, The responsibility of peacekeepers, their sending States, and international organizations, in T.D. GILL, D. FLECK, The handbook of the international law of military operations, Oxford University Press, Oxford, 2010, pp. 524ss.

[502]Political and Security Committee Decision (CFSP) 2017/682 of 29 March 2017 on the appointment of the EU Force Commander for the European Union military operation in Bosnia and Herzegovina and repealing Decision (CFSP) 2016/332 (BiH/25/2017), OJ L 98, 11.4.2017, p. 20-21.

sending State, which, as previously mentioned, retains powers on these disciplinary and jurisdictional measures and can also decide on a number of aspects, such as participation in a particular operation, the withdrawal of troops from the same, the number of men to be made available to the Union, etc. In this scenario, the dual (or multiple) attribution and responsibility hypothesis can be a valid solution for regulating this issue.[503] The difficulty of this approach is, however, to distribute equally the "weight" of responsibility between the sending State and EU. In concrete terms, it will be necessary to assess the damage caused to the victims of the illicit act (where it is quantifiable) and to what extent each party will have to respond internationally.

The dual or joint responsibility situation, it is also foreseen by the 2011 Project in art. 48.[504] The limitation of this provision is that it deals only with the "consequence" of the Commission of the unlawful act, providing that, where an IO and one or more States or IO are responsible for the same offense, "the responsibility of the State or organization may be invoked in relation to that act."[505]

Dual responsibility will necessarily have to be based on an attribution of dual conduct. The ILC has admitted this possibility, stating

---

[503]An interesting application of the dual responsibility theory, in close connection with the concepts of control and command, is provided by the International Law Association (ILA) in relation to the respect of international humanitarian law in the context of peace-keeping missions and of peace-enforcement. In particular, the Final Report entitled Accountability of international organizations provides that: "(...) Troop contributing countries remain responsible for violations of the applicable International Humanitarian Law (IHL), but IO-s bear a coordinate responsibility with troop-contributing with the applicable principles of (IHL) in peacekeeping or other operations under the control or authority of the international organizations." In its commentary, the Report states that "the obligation to abide by (IHL) rests wholly on the State when the armed forces remain under its command and control, while the international organizations has granted the authorization, has the special responsibility to ensure respect for (IHL) by the State. If you are not responsible for the same rules, you will be responsible for ensuring compliance with the IO. In the case of a national control system, choose the targets, both the State and the IO share responsibility for a violation of (IHL). In other words, primary responsibility by way of effective control is always accompanied by independent, secondary obligations (...)." For the ILA, in essence, although as a consequence of the application of the "effective control" criterion one can attribute the conduct to only one of the parties in question, the other also shares a portion of responsibility, deriving from the violation of international obligations secondary. The theory contains valid aspects, but in our opinion it is scarcely supported by praxis. See, ILA, Accountability of international organizations, Berlin Conference, Final Report, 2004, pp. 24.

[504]T. KOMORI, J. WELLENS, Public interest rules of international law: Towards effective implementation, ed. Routledge, London & New York, 2016, pp. 203ss.

[505]A. NOLLKAEMPER, The duality of shared responsibility, op. cit.

however that it "may not frequently occur in practice." The only example reported by the ILC in which there can be a double attribution of conduct is that in which two IO establish a joint body that works for both. This situation obviously cannot be emphasized with reference to CSDP. A dual attribution can occur when the conduct is put in place by an individual or entity to which more than one attribution rule applies, or in cases where it acts on behalf of more than one entity at the same time. A multiple attribution of conduct in the practice of EU missions could arise, for example, in cases where the quota "given" to the organization is subject both to the directives originating from its sending State and to those issued, at the various levels, by the institutions and bodies of the Union. In this case, the decisive element lies in the "double membership" of the body in question, which acts both on behalf of its sending State and on EU. A problematic aspect, however, consists in establishing the criteria on the basis of which to evaluate this "double belonging."[506] Must we use formal or organic criteria? Or to factual criteria, as for the application of the "effective control" test? In the latter case, what kind of control should be exercised on such individuals so that there can be attribution of conduct? In other words, what is the "minimum threshold" of control required?

Another question we consider open concerns, moreover, the overlap of the dual attribution hypothesis with other cases configured by the 2011 Project, such as that of the conduct of organs or agents of the IO (article 6). In fact, in the case where a body acts on behalf of more than one legal entity at the same time, for example, as a de facto body of one and another de iure organ of the other, it is possible to speak of a dual attribution of conduct o should however be considered applicable article 6, which instead provides for an exclusive attribution to the IO? In our opinion, the 2011 Project is not, at present, able to answer these questions, as it is strongly oriented towards the unequivocal attribution of conduct. A way forward could be to use the hypothesis of dual attribution as a sort of "default attribution rule" in all those cases in which it is not possible to find the presence of the attribution elements outlined in articles 6 and 7 of the 2011 Project. If the conduct is not carried out by an organ or agent, in law or in fact, of an IO, or is subject to the effective control of the latter, it must presumably be attributed to the sending State. In this scenario, the dual attribution could find space, especially in the residual cases of article 7, in which it is ascertained that the organization has not exercised an "effective control" on the specific conduct, but has in any case, in some

[506] O. QUIRILO, The international responsibility of the European Union. A basic interpretive pattern, in Hungarian Yearbook of International and European Law, 63, 2013.

way, influenced the occurrence of this unlawful event.[507] However, it is inevitable to observe how every effort to configure multiple attribution in cases of CSDP operations and, more generally, for military operations conducted under the aegis of IOs, clashes, on the one hand, with the lack of clear normative references and, on the other, with a jurisprudence still extremely timid and, in our opinion, not always convincing. In essence, the multiple attribution of conduct, although desirable, remains today a purely theoretical hypothesis.

Regardless of the difficulties in applying the criterion, the attribution to both the EU and to the Member States of the same international illicit fact is certainly an aspect to be taken into consideration in order to provide an effective remedy for victims of such violations of international law. Since the primary objective of the international liability regime is the possibility for the injured party to invoke this responsibility and, above all, to assert it in legal terms, obtaining the reparation of damages under the various forms provided for by international law,[508] in the case in which the victim may have recourse against both the EU and one or more Member States, the probability of obtaining such redress will obviously increase. The dual attribution of an illicit conduct would prevent the States, therefore, from hiding behind the "shield" constituted by the organization (the so-called organizational veil),[509] also providing for them the obligation to furnish an adequate repair and, moreover, it can provide an incentive to EU and the Member States participating in the missions so that they do not commit violations of international law during the operations.

It is clear that it is not possible to establish a general rule, which would allow always to attribute any international wrongdoing to EU. This may be true, in a broad sense, for all those military operations established, managed or authorized by an IO. This leads, once again, to highlighting that the concrete attribution of a particular conduct detrimental to the subjects involved depends on the analysis of the circumstances proper to the specific case. In particular, to consider an action attributable to the

---

[507] B. BOUTIN, Attribution of conduct in international military operations. A causal analysis of effective law, in Melbourne Journal of International Law, 18, 2017, pp. 158ss.
[508] The repair (envisaged by article 31 of the 2011 Project), in all its forms (articles 34-37), is one of the consequences that is produced as a result of international responsibility, together, usually, with the obligation to end of the unlawful act (article 30, letter a) and not to repeat it (article 30, letter b).
[509] J.D'ASPREMONT, The law of international responsibility and multilayered institutional veils: The case of authorized regional peace-enforcement operations, in SHARES Research Paper n. 24, 2013, pp. 9ss.

Organization, we have seen that the "roads" that can be pursued are substantially two: Either the person who has violated the international obligation is a EU agent or organ, or is a state body which acted under the "effective control" of the organization.

The bodies that participate in CSDP operations, even more markedly with regard to the peacekeeping missions of UN, cannot in our opinion, be defined as de facto EU departments, nor much less de jure organs, constituting state ones made available to the organization. They cannot even be framed as EU agents, being first of all those of their own State. Therefore, linking the hypothesis of EU international responsibility in this sector with the dictate of article 6 of the 2011 Project would, in our opinion, be a stretch.

It is certainly correct to say that the personnel, both civil and military, which actually perform CSDP is "made available" to EU by the Member States and, to a lesser extent, by third parties. In particular, these are state bodies that act on behalf of the Organization, but under the "general command" of their sending State. The attribution rule that seems best suited to the situation in question is therefore that contained in article 7 of the Project. The difficulty, quite obvious, is to establish whether or not the Union exercises an "effective control" over the conduct of these national bodies and, to this end, determine under what circumstances such control exists. We have seen, in this regard, that the chain of command can be a useful tool for this purpose, especially if we move on the basis of the UN practice. It clarifies, in fact, what are the functions of each single structure participating in the operations, but has the defect of not being able to determine, when an international obligation is actually violated, if the EU were actually exercising such type of control.[510] As the Atalanta operation demonstrates, in fact, the "effective control" on a specific conduct, understood as the specific order to perform a given act and therefore the ability to concretely influence the occurrence (or the non-occurrence) of that event, it can also be exercised by a different body than the one to which this control was originally assigned. Consequently, in order to hold EU accountable internationally, it will be necessary to take into account the specific act, contrary to a requirement of international law, and to ascertain who has given the precise order to accomplish it and, as established from the Hague Court of Appeal in the Nuhanović case, had the power to prevent it.

---

[510]G. FERNÁNDEZ ARRIBAS, International responsibility of the European Union for the activities of its military operations. The issue of effective control, in Spanish Yearbook of International Law, 18, 2013-2014, pp. 58ss.

As far as military operations are concerned, the EU holds the command and control of the operation through a chain of command that originates from the Council and arrives up to the Operation Commander, who exercises command and strategic control at the narrowest level, under the authority of EUMC and COPS. This transfer of authority from national governments to EU can be interpreted as an exercise of effective control by the Union,[511] especially when one considers that in the case of UN recognized its international responsibility, a similar mechanism took place, as it was the Force Commander to exercise command and control in the field on behalf of UN. In the case of ONUC[512] mission, the chain of command originated from the Secretary General under the authority of the Security Council and from General Assembly passed through the officer in charge and reached up to the Commander of the Force. On the other hand, the concepts of general "command" and "control" are not sufficient to establish who exercises the "effective control" on a given conduct pursuant to article 7 of the 2011 Project. For this purpose, it is necessary to evaluate what is the authority that exercises control when the violation takes place, or the authority from which the order is issued which, in turn, causes the occurrence of the unlawful conduct. This can only be done by carefully assessing, on a case-by-case basis, all the details of the offending case.

Since this operation can be very complex with reference to the still poor EU practice, one possibility could be that of setting up a "dual attribution" of an illegal conduct, either to EU or to the most sending States that concretely commit the violation of an international obligation, evidently in proportion to the type of offense committed. This operation would also give rise to a dual international responsibility and, therefore, to that for the injured party to take legal action against both parties. Although it is undeniable the difficulty of distributing the weight of each (part of) responsibility equally and the lack of adequate normative references. This approach appears at the moment, in our opinion, the most responsive way to the real modalities of CSDP operations. In order to simplify the distribution of responsibilities under the scenario just outlined, a viable

---

[511]S.Ø. JOHANSEN, Accountability mechanisms for human rights violations by CSDP missions: Available and sufficient, in International & Comparative Law Quarterly, 66 (1), 2017, pp. 184ss.

[512]O. SPIJKERS, The evolution of United Nations peacekeeping in the Congo: From ONUC, to MONUC, to MONUSCO and its force intervention brigade, in Journal of International Peacekeeping, 19 (1), 2015, pp. 90ss. M.W. DOYLE, N. SAMBANIS, Making war and building peace: United nations peace operations, ed. Princeton, New Jersey, 2011.

route could be to consider, in cases of violations of international obligations committed during a CSDP mission, two distinct international offenses and two different types of consequences, for example in terms of reparation (parallel attribution and responsibility).

This approach clashes with the one adopted (we repeat) by the German courts in the Rheinland-Pfalz case, in which the first and second instance judges have identified Germany as the only entity responsible for the violations of human rights committed against Somali pirates. In our opinion, the case could be an excellent opportunity to consolidate a line of jurisprudential prone to the recognition of a dual attribution and responsibility. To this end, the judges should have given less weight to the criterion of the final operational control, in the wake of the criticized Behrami and Saramati cases,[513] and to admit that Germany had (a part of) responsibility, since it had concretely implemented the illegal transfer, but the EU should also respond to a certain extent internationally, since it was the legal entity that had authorized it.[514]

We believe that national and international jurisprudence should move more decisively towards a "shared" responsibility in relation to military operations conducted under the aegis of IOs and, more specifically, those of CSDP, gradually moving away from the road of exclusive responsibility, so dear to classical international law, but perhaps inadequate in the current international scenario. A final consideration is opportune: If on the one hand the works of the ILC have allowed, albeit in a not yet definitive way, to codify the legal regime regarding the international responsibility of the organizations, on the other hand pronounced on the attribution of the committed offenses in the course of operations carried out by the UN, as well as the German one on the issue of pirate transfer in the context of operation Atalanta, it seems to move more and more towards the recognition of a state responsibility rather than the ego. This situation, in our humble opinion, in addition to constituting a paradox, represents a dangerous tendency that could prejudice the development of international law in matters of responsibility.

My suggestion is to conduct an attribution of analysis in each of these cases applying the principle of effective control understood in its traditional meaning, i.e., the Nicaragua formula[515] and not the doctrine of

---

[513]L. DOSWALD-BECK, Human rights in times of conflict and terrorism, op. cit., pp. 159ss.

[514] M. DIXON, M. MCCORQUODALE, S. WILLIAMS, Cases and materials on international law, op. cit.

[515]Military and Paramilitary Activities in and against Nicaragua (Nicaragua v. United States of America), Judgement, ICJ Reports, 27 June 1986 ("Nicaragua case"). A.

ultimate control as developed in ECtHR jurisprudence. As to the tension between the interests of the injurer organization and party, international law fails to provide a satisfactory solution. The system fails at the procedural level of enforcement of responsibility. The international law provides for instruments safeguarding the autonomy of IOs. The natural course of action would be that they could be held responsible for their acts violating international law. However, the deficiencies of the enforcement mechanisms of international law often render this impossible. Immunity of IOs, lack of standing before international courts and tribunals, and absence of arbitration arrangements allowing for settlement of disputes involving IOs create a situation in which a victim of a violation of international law is deprived of remedies under international and as consequence EU law, too. This also has its consequence in the application of substantial law on responsibility, as the injured parties will be likely to argue that the actions of the organizations are to be attributed to Member States, hoping to obtain a remedy in the more effective mechanisms of enforcement of state responsibility. Thus, the degree of control that the state must have over an entity, formally not having a "state organ" status, is the same as the State has over its de jure organs, namely complete dependence. The only difference between a de jure and de facto state organ is the recognition of the former in State's internal law, which per se does not affect the state responsibility under international law.

At the national level, restricting of the immunity of IOs should be recommended. In my view, the limitations should be based not on the restrictive doctrine of immunity of State implying the acta iure imprerii and acta iure gestionis division, i.e. the inappropriateness of this distinction to IOs. The restrictions should go back to the very justification of their immunity under international law. The "functional necessity" analysis would constitute a useful tool for proving whether the acts in question in fact fall within the scope of activities requiring jurisdictional immunity.

4.9. Concluding remarks

CSDP has great potential, especially following the changes introduced by the Lisbon Treaty and the new configuration of article 43 TEU. The EU can conduct a very wide range of operations outside its borders, many of which involve military intervention, and is, at least on

---

ZIMMERMANN, C.J. TAMS, K. OELLERS-FRAHAM, The statute of the International Court of Justice. A commentary, op. cit.

paper, a "new" actor for international security. The provision concerning the progressive definition of a "common European defense" further emphasizes the role and type of functions that the Organization intends to take on the international scene, no longer limited only to the economic and trade sectors. On the other hand, the great potential of CSDP has, to date, remained largely unexpressed. The missions conducted were, with the exception of sporadic cases, of reduced scale and involved a small number of units in the field. The "common defense"[516] has not yet been achieved and nevertheless seems destined to do so in the short term.[517] CSDP is currently in a sort of "limbo" between a real security policy and a mere civil action. The reasons for a modest development and the "lack of enthusiasm" towards CSDP we believe are primarily due to its markedly intergovernmental character and its sui generis nature. Regarding the first aspect, it is clear that the Member States are the real "protagonists" of the CSDP[518] and those who can influence their development and progressive definition. The CSDP still appears, in fact, as the set of decisions taken at the level of individual national governments, rather than a real "common policy." On the other hand, the relationship between EU, Member States and third parties in this sector still appears to be obscure and, in some respects, controversial. In particular, it is not clear what kind of competence the Organization has and which room for maneuver have the Member States. The military missions (EUNAVFOR Somalia and EUNAVFOR MED on all)[519] seem to have, in some way, marked the passage of the CSDP to a more advanced phase and a more incisive type of military intervention, but this development must in our opinion necessarily also be accompanied a general change in the intergovernmental nature of this sector, which must become more supranational. To this end, a viable hypothesis could be that of modifying

---

[516]M.K. CROSS, The military dimension of European security: An epistemic community approach, in Millennium, 42 (10), 2013, pp., 47ss. H. DIJKSTRA, Policy-making in EU security and defense: An institutional perspective, ed. Palgrave Macmillan, Basingstoke, 2013.

[517]J. BLACK, A. HALl, K. COX, M. KEPE, E. SILVERSEN, Defense and security after Brexit: Understanding the possible implications of the UK's decision to leave the EU, Santa Monica: RAND Corporation, 2017. P.J. CARDWELL, Values in the European Union's foreign policy: An analysis and assessment of CFSP declarations, in European Foreign Affairs Review, 21 (4), 2016, pp. 602ss.

[518]F. NAERT, International law aspects of the EU's security and defense policy with a particular focus on the law of armed conflict and human rights, op. cit.

[519] J. HOWORTH, Security and Defense Policy in the European Union, Palgrave Macmillan, Basingstoke, 2014.

the norm foreseen by art. 42 (4) TEU,[520] replacing the unanimity rule currently in force for the adoption of decisions by the Council in this area, with that of the qualified majority. Furthermore, in our opinion, it is appropriate to clarify what kind of competence the EU possesses, possibly by introducing a new type that better fits the specifics of this sector. To conclude on this point, it seems to us that, at the present time, the CSDP is still in a phase of development and adjustment and does not enjoy a sufficient level of credibility, first of all by EU Member States. For the realization of a complete CSDP to become just a matter of time, it is necessary to move more decisively towards a real common supranational policy.

Secondly, despite the problems and uncertainties that characterize the CSDP, the legal implications of its implementation are significant and complex. In order to analyze the question of the international EU responsibility in CSDP conduct, we first discussed the objective element of the international crime. In this regard, the explicit conferment of legal personality to the Organization confirms its international subjectivity. As a consequence, EU is subject to the rules deriving from international law, which are imposed during the conduct of operations in non-Member States. These obligations can be derived, first of all, from some provisions contained in the Treaties, such as those that provide for the respect of human rights and the principles contained in the UN Charter. However, these provisions are formulated in a generic manner and appear to represent "standards of behaviour" rather than actual legal obligations. As far as the obligations of a conventional nature are concerned, these are also contained in the decisions issued by the Council for the launching of a mission, but also in this case they are indications expressed in fairly vague terms.[521] Other obligations derive from the agreements on the status of forces concluded by EU with the hosting States the various missions (SOFA) and status of mission agreements (SOMAs),[522] as well as the agreements on the participation of non-Member States to the operations

---

[520]D. THYM, The intergovernmental constitution of the EU's foreign security & defense executive, in European Constitutional Law Review, 11 (3), 2011, pp. 453ss.

[521]A change, which may hopefully signal an inversion of the trend, is represented in this sense by the Council Decision (CFSP) 2015/778 on the military operation EUNAVFOR Med, which enumerates the various international conventions and protocols that apply there. Council Decision (CFSP) 2015/778 of 18 May 2015 on a European Union military operation in the Southern Central Mediterranean (EUNAVFOR MED), OJ L 122, 19.5.2015, recital 6.

[522]N. ZIPPERLE, European Union international agreements: An analysis of direct effect and judicial review pre and post-Lisbon, ed. Springer, Berlin, 2017, pp. 69ss.

and resolutions of the Security Council authorizing the initiation of these and the use of force. A large part of the binding obligations of the Organization in conducting the CSDP derives from general international law, in particular the customary law and the general principles of law.[523] In this regard, the most relevant sectors are the law concerning the use of force, human rights and, finally, international humanitarian law.[524] The role of unwritten international law in the field of CSDP is extremely important, since EU, like all IOs, cannot adhere to the main international conventions on issues such as human rights or international humanitarian law. Also in this case, however, the problem of the vagueness of the content of these obligations is presented. In this spirit we note the Council Joint Action 2008/749/CFSP of 19 September 2008 on EU military coordination action in support of UN Security Council resolution 1816 (2008) (EU NAVCO).[525] The unilateral acts of EU can also be a source of obligation as they are in international humanitarian law. By way of an example, Council Joint Action 2088/749/CFSP, Council Joint Action 2008/851/CFSP and Council Decision 2008/918/CFSP [526] contain references to respect for the relevant International Law and the UN Security Council Resolutions 1816 (2008) of 2 June 2008 in which there are express demands for the respect of human rights. The EU is bound by international human rights rules of jus cogens, and it must respect them in the deployment of EU military operations, in which special circumstances and conflict require particular attention to be paid to these kinds of norms, and also according to ICJ case law, which in the Advisory Opinion on the Legal Consequences of the Construction of a Wall in the Occupied Palestinian Territory stated that "the Court considers that the protection offered by human rights conventions does not cease in case of armed conflict, save through the effect of provisions for derogation of the kind to be found in article 4 of the International Covenant on Civil and Political

---

[523]N. HACHEZ, J. WOUTERS, Promoting the rule of law: A benchmarks approach, KU Leuven Working paper No. 105, April 2013.

[524] M. ZWANENBURG, The duty to respect international humanitarian law during European Union-led operations, in CLEER Working paper, 2012/6. pp.24ss.

[525]OJ 2008 L 252/389.

[526]Council Joint Action 2008/851/CFSP of 10 November 2008 on a EU military operation to contribute to the deterrence, prevention and repression of acts of piracy and armed robbery of the Somali coast. OJ 2008 L 301/33. 59 Council Decision 2008/918/CFSP of 8 December 2008 on the launch of a EU military operation to contribute to the deterrence, prevention and repression of acts of piracy and armed robbery of the Somali coast (Atalanta), OJ 2008 L 330/19. C. FAHRON-HUSSEY, Military crisis management operations by NATO and the European Union. The decision making process, ed. Spinger, Berlin, 2018.

Rights."[527] In speciem, Zwanenburg makes reference to the Advisory Opinion on the Legal Consequences of the Construction of a Wall in the Occupied Palestinian Territory of 9 July 2004[528] in which the CIJ "suggest that at least certain norms of international humanitarian law may have a peremptory character," but it does not establish which of them should be classed as such. The norms that can be considered to be peremptory are the basic rules of humanitarian law, derived from the Vienna Conventions on the Law of Treaties, and can be identified by taking into account the prohibition of derogatory agreements.[529]

As we can see in the same spirit in the Kasumaj v. Greece case of 5 July 2007[530] and Gajić v. Germany of 28 August 2008[531] the ECtHR reiterated its view on the attribution of the action of national contingents allocated for KFOR to UN. In Berić and others v. Bosnia and Herzegovina of 16 October 2007[532] the ECtHR furthermore restated its decision in Behrami and Saramati when concluding that the conduct of the High Representative in Bosnia and Herzegovina was to be attributed to UN.[533] And we must take into consideration that the responsibility of the IO in relation to the protection of human rights has started from the IACtHR

---

[527]G. DAHLHOFF, International Court of Justice. Digest of judgments and advisory opinions, canon and case law 1946-2012, Martinus Nijhoff Publishers, 2012, pp. 1657ss. S. VILLALPANDO, On the International Court of Justice and the determination of rules of law, in Leiden Journal of International Law, 26, 2013, pp. 248ss.

[528]ICJ, Advisory opinion, 2004, ICJ, 136. G. DAHLHOFF, International Court of Justice. Digest of judgments and advisory opinions, canon and case law 1946-2012, op. cit., pp. 1657ss. A. ZIMMERMANN, C.J. TAMS, K. OELLERS-FRAHAM, The Statute of the International Court of Justice. A commentary, op. cit.

[529]M. ZWANENBURG, Toward a more mature ESDP: Responsibility for violations of international humanitarian law by EU crisis management operations, in S. BLOCKMANSI (ed.), The European Union and crisis management. Policy and legal aspects, op. cit., pp. 396ss.

[530]K. MUJEZINOVIĆ LARSEN, The human rights treaty obligations of peacekeeping, Cambridge University Press, Cambridge, 2012.

[531]S. WILLS, Protecting civilians: The obligations of peacekeeping, Oxford University Press, Oxford 2009. C. RYNGAERT, I.F. DEKKER, R.A. WESSEL, Judicial missions on the law of international organizations, Oxford University Press, Oxford, 2016, pp. 325ss.

[532]C. STAHN, J.S. EASTERDAY, I. IVERSON, Jus post bellum, Oxford University Press, Oxford, 2014, pp. 121ss. C. FOLEY, UN peacekeeping operations and the protection of civilians saving succeeding generations, Cambridge University Press, Cambridge, 2017. C. CINKIN, M. KALDOR, International law and new wars, Cambridge University Press, Cambridge, 2017, pp. 367ss. C. TOMUSCHAT, Human rights. Between idealism and realism, Oxford University Press, Oxford, 2014.

[533]A. KIHARA HUNT, Holding UNPOL to account: Individual criminal accountability of United Nations police personnel, ed. Brill/Martinus Nijhoff Publishers, Leiden, Boston, 2017. M. EVANS, International law, Oxford University Press, Oxford, 2014.

structured its decision around the rules of state responsibility. It found that whenever a "state organ, official or public entity violates one of those rights, this constitutes a failure of the duty to respect the rights and freedoms set forth in the Convention (...)."[534] In so doing, the IACtHR established that international responsibility may arise from an action of any authority, official, agent or person who is a member of the state machine. The IACtHR noted it is "a tenet of international law that the State is responsible for the acts and omissions of its agents acting in their official capacity, even when those agents act outside the scope of their authority (...)."[535] The linkage between acts by agents of the State with the state apparatus expands avenues available to human rights courts to prosecute wrongful acts by States. The judgment in Velàsquez of 29 July 1988 places a "duty to guarantee" on States, requiring them to take active steps towards monitoring, regulating and policing their agents, ensuring that a violation of international rights will not go unpunished, and upholding the right to life by all of their citizens.[536]

In this regard, we believe that the establishment of a more precise regulatory framework regarding international law applicable under CSDP and a clearer indication of the division of competences between EU, Member States and third parties participating in the missions is necessary, whereas the latter have different international obligations and only partly coincide with those binding EU.

Equally important the attribution of conduct within the framework of the CSDP is a complex and difficult to resolve issue, both because of the incorrect definition of the relationship between EU and the States participating in the missions, and above all because of a state of law, we can say, still uncertain in the matter. The main normative reference in this case is article 7 of the ILC Project on the responsibility of IOs, since the

---

[534]M. EVANS, International law, op. cit.

[535]E.K. BOON, The law of responsibility: A response to fragmentation, in Global Business & Development Law Journal, 25, 2012, pp. 398ss.

[536] See in argument: Velàsquez Rodriguez Case, Judgment of July 29, 1988, Inter-Am.Ct.H.R. (Ser. C) No. 4 (1988).; Anzualdo Castro v. Peru, Inter-Am.Ct.H.R. (ser. C) No. 202, paras. 37-38 (Sept. 22, 2009) and Kawas-Ferndndez, Inter-Am.Ct.H.R. (ser.C) No. 196. From ECtHR: Bevacqua v. Bulgaria of 9 December 2008; Opuz v. Turkey of 9 June 2009. See also: U.N. Human Rights Commission, General Comment No. 31, The Nature of the General Legal Obligation Imposed on States Parties to the Covenant, IN 8, 13, 16, U.N. Doc. CCPR/C/2 1/Rev. 1/Add. 13 (May 26, 2004); Hajrizi Dzemajil v. Yugoslavia, Case No. 161/1999, U.N. Human Rights Comm., In 8, 10, U.N. Doc. CAT/C/29/D/161/2000 (2002); Jegatheeswara Sarma v. Sri Lanka, case No. 950/2000, U.N. Human Rights Comm., 1 8.5 U.N. Doc. CCPR/C/78/D/950/2000 (2003). For details in argument see: E.K. BOON, The law of responsibility: A response to fragmentation, op. cit.

quotas that carry out CSDP operations are state bodies made available to EU. The first problem that has emerged is the determination of the exact scope of the "effective control" criterion contained in this provision. We believe that it does not correspond to a simple operational and general command and control over the troops, which are normally carried out by the EU, whose institutions are at the top of the chain of command, but are exercised by the entity that issued the order to carry out the conduct that caused the occurrence of the unlawful event and which had the power to prevent the completion of such action. This necessarily requires an analysis of the specific circumstances of the case, while it cannot be determined ex ante, that is before the start of an operation and only on the basis of its command structure, which entity has exercised this "effective control" on the unlawful conduct. Another problem posed by article 7 is whether it admits a double attribution of conduct, a solution that we consider acceptable with reference to EU missions and, more generally, to operations conducted under the auspices of an IO which provide for participation of state bodies. In this regard, article 7, as well as the other provisions of the Project concerning the attribution of conduct, does not rule the case of a dual attribution, configuring itself as a "one-off" rule, whose purpose is solely to attribute a conduct to IO. Although the UN Secretariat confirms the existence of practice of applicability of "effective control" test to the allocation of responsibility for the conduct of PSOs, it disagrees with the ILC Drafting Committee on the content of this control. It stated that in the UN practice the "effective command and control" test is applied "horizontally" to distinguish between the UN authorized operations under national command, whereas the ILC suggested the application of "effective control" test "vertically" to condition the responsibility on the possession of factual control by either of the entities. Therefore although both articles (of ARSIWA and ARIO) seem to be similar from the first view, they appear to be qualitatively different in their essence. While ASR understands "placed at the disposal of" requirement as an existence of "exclusive direction and control" of receiving entity, DARIO excludes from its cover "fully seconded" organs, and by contrast includes those on which the control is joint or shared by entities (which are in turn excluded by ARSIWA article 6).[537]

The jurisprudence, for its part, has tried and tries to move towards a dual attribution of conduct in the context of illicit conduct during UN peace missions, but this attempt was based on an incorrect reading of the

---

[537]R. KOLB, The international law or State responsibility. An introduction, Edward Elgar Publishers, Cheltenham, 2017.

Project of ILC. In this regard, we believe that the attribution of the same conduct to more than one legal entity is one of the most important developments that the right of international responsibility can do in the future, especially in light of the ever-increasing complexity of practice and uncertainty application of the "effective control" criterion. However, this development cannot really be said as long as there is not a suitable legal framework, which foreshadows which are the extremes for configuring this dual attribution, on what kind of criteria to evaluate its presence, etc. Once this case has been better defined, international law can move from the traditional concept of exclusive responsibility to that, so to speak "evolved," of shared responsibility or, according to the phrase introduced by some scholars, shared. This development will contribute to strengthening the rule of law and will provide more chances for an adequate reparation to the victims of an international offense. At the time of writing, both the criterion of the "effective control" provided for in article 7 of Project,[538] and, to a greater extent, the hypothesis of a dual attribution of conduct, still seem far from a clear and uniform definition (and application) in law.

---

[538] R. KOLB, The international law or State responsibility. An introduction, op. cit.

Bibliography

A.A.V.V., Commentary on the second Geneva Convention, Cambridge University Press, Cambridge, 2017.

ABASS, A., Complete international law: Text, cases and materials, Oxford University Press, 2014.

ABASS, A., Consent precluding state responsibility. A critical analysis, in International and Comparative Law Quarterly, 53 (2), 2004, pp. 212ss.

ABELLO GALVIS, R., CAVELIER, G., Derecho internacional contemporaneo, Editorial Universidad del Rosario, Bogotà, 2013.

ABI-SAAB, G., The Appellate Body and treaty interpretation, in M. FITZMAURICE, O. ELIAS, P. MERKOURIS, Treaty interpretation and the Vienna Convention on the Law of Treaties: 30 Years on, Martinus Nijhoff Publishers, Leiden/Boston, 2010, pp. 100ss.

ABI-SAB, G., The uses of article 19, in European Journal of International Law, 10 (2), 1999, pp. 340ss.

ACCIOLY, H., Principles gènèraux de la responsabilitè internationale d'après la docrine et la jurisprudence, Recueil des cours, ed. Brill, Bruxelles, vol. 96, 1959, pp. 354ss.

ACHTEN, N., Compensation claims of individuals for violations of rules on conduct of hostilities. Comment on a judgment of the District Court of Bonn, Germany-LG Bonn 1 0 460/11, 11 December 2013, in Humanitares Volkerrecht, 28, 2015, pp. 35ss.

ACOSTA ESTÉVEZ, J.B., Normas de ius cogens, efecto erga omnes, crimen internacional y la teoria de los circulo concèntricos, in Anuario de Derecho Internacional, 11, 1995, pp. 4ss.

ADAM, H.T., Les organismes internationaux spècialisès, LGDJ, Paris, 1965, pp. 130ss.

ADAM, H.T., Les organismes internationaux spècialisès. Contribution à la thèorie gènèrale des ètablissements publics internationaux, LGDJ, Paris, 1992.

ADAMS, M., MEUWESE, A., HIRSCH BALLIN, E., Constitutionalism and the rule of law. Bridging realism and realism, Cambridge University Press, Cambridge, 2017, pp. 423ss.

AEBERHARD, P., CHAUMET, P.O., Droit et stratègies de l'action humanitaire, ed. Mare & Martin, Paris, 2018.

AGO, R., Le dèlit international, in Recueil des cours, ed. Brill, Bruxelles, vol. 68, 1939, pp. 416ss.

AGO, R., Premier sur la responsabilitè des États-Historique de l'oeuvre accomplie jusqu'ici en ce qui concerne la codification du sujet de la responsabilitè internationale des États, Doc. A/CN.4/217 and Corr. 1 and Add.1, in Annuaire de la Commission du Droit International, 1969, vol. II, pp. 128ss.

AGO, R., Quatrième rapport sur la responsabilitè des États-le fait internationalement illicite de l'État, source de responsabilitè internationale (suite), UN Doc. A/CN.4/264 and Add. 1, in Annuaire de la Commission du Droit International, 1972, vol. II, pp. 27ss.

AGO, R., Troisième rapport sur la responsabilitè des États. Le fait internationalement illicite de l'État, source de responsabilitè internationale, UN Doc. A/CN.4/246 and Add. 1-3, in Annuaire de la Commission du Droit International, 1971, vol. II, p. 209-215, par. 29.

AGUILAR NAVARRO, M., La responsabilidad internacional y la organizacon de la sociedad internacional, in Escuela de funcionarios internacionales, cursos y conferencias, 9 (3), 1955-1956, Madrid, 1957, pp. 157ss.

AHLBORN, C., Remedies against International Organizations. A relational account of international responsibility, in K. WALLENS, Remedies and responsibility for the actions of international organizations, ed. Brill, Hague, 2014, pp. 545ss.

AHLBORN, C., The rules of international organizations and the law of international responsibility and the law of international responsibility, in SHARES Research Paper 02 (2011), ACIL 2011-03, pp. 29ss.

AHLBORN, C., The use of analogies drafting the articles on the responsibility of international organizations: An appraisal of the "copy-paste approach," in International Organizations Law Review, 9, 2012, pp. 54ss.

AHLBORN, C., To share or not to share? The allocation of responsibility between international organizations and their member states, in Die Friedens-Warte, 88, 2013, pp. 46ss.

AHLSTRÖM, C., The status of multilateral export control regimes: An examination of legal and non-legal agreements in international cooperation, Iustus Forlag, Uppsala, 1999.

AJIBOLA, B., Dispute resolution by the International Court of Justice, in Leiden Journal of International Law, 21, 1998, pp. 124ss.

AKANDJI-KOMBE, J., Positive obligations under the European Convention on Human Rights. A guide to the implementation of the European Convention on Human Rights, Human Rights Handbook No. 7, Council of Europe Publishing, 2007.

AKEHURST, A., Reprisals by third states, in British Yearbook of International Law, 44, 1970, pp. 4ss.

AKEHURST, M., The hierarchy of the sources of international law, in British Yearbook of International Law, 47, 1975, pp. 274ss.

AKSENOVA, M., Complicity in international criminal law, Oxford University Press, Oxford, 2016.

ALAMUDDIN, A., NABIL JURDI, N., TOLBERT, D., The special tribunal for Lebanon law and practice, Oxford University Press, Oxford, 2014, pp. 64ss.

ALBORN, C., The rules of international organizations and the law of international responsibility, in international organizations Law Review, 8, 2011, pp. 398ss.

ALCAIDE FERNÁNDEZ, J., Contre-mesures et règlement des diffèrends, in Revue Gènèrale de Droit Intenational Public, 108 (2), 2004, pp. 348ss.

ALEXY, H., Völkerrechtliche Praxis der Bundesrepublick Deutschland im jahre 1958, in Zeitschrift für ausländisches Recht und Völkerrecht, 20, 1960, pp. 663ss.

ALLAN, C., Attribution issues in cyberspace, in Chicago-Kent Journal of International and Comparative Law, 14, 2013.

ALLAND, D., Countermeasures of general interest, in European Journal of International Law, 13, 2002, pp. 1232ss.

ALLAND, D., Justice privèe et ordre juridique international. Etude thèorique des contre-mesures en droit international public, ed. Pedone, Paris, 1994.

ALLAND, D., L'interprétation du droit international public, in Recueil des Cours, ed. Brill, Bruxelles, vol. 362, 2012, pp. 216ss.

ALLAND, D., The definition of countermeasures, in J. CRAWFORD, A. PELLET, S. OLLESON, The law of international responsibility, Oxford University Press, Oxford, 2010, pp. 1135ss.

ALLEN, S., COSTELLOE, D., FITZMAURICE, M., The oxford handbook of jurisdiction in international law, Oxford University Press, Oxford, 2019.

ALLIN, D.H., Unintended consequences. Managing Kosovo independence, in What status for Kosovo?, Chaillot paper, Institute for Security Studies of WEU, October 2001

ALLOTT, P., Eunomia. New order a new world, Oxford, New York, 1990, pp. 325ss.

ALMQVIST, J., ESPOSITO, C., The role of courts in transitional justice. Voices from Latin America and Spain, ed. Routledge, London & New York, 2013, pp. 177ss.

ALONSO, H., Current trends on modes of liability for genocide, crimes against humanity and war crimes, in C. STAHN, L. VAN DEN HERIK (eds.), Future perspectives on international criminal justice, T.M.C. Asser press, The Hague, 2010, pp. 522-524.

ALSTON, P., Non-State actors and human rights, Oxford University Press, Oxford, 2005, pp. 80, and 113ss.

ALVAREZ-JIMENEZ, A., Methods for the identification of customary international law in the International Court of Justice's jurisprudence: 2000-2009, in International and Comparative Law Quarterly, 60, 2011, pp. 681-711.

ALVAREZ, J., The United Nations in the Time of Cholera, in AJIL Unbound, 108, 2014-2015.

ALVAREZ, J.E., International organizations as law-makers, Oxford University Press, Oxford, 2005, pp. 85ss.

ALVAREZ, J.E., Limits of change by way of subsequent agreements and practice, in G. NOLTE, Treaties and subsequent practice, Oxford University Press, Oxford, 2013, pp. 124ss.

AMBOS, K., Der Allgemeine Teil des Völkerstrafrechts: Ansätze einer Dogmatisierung, Duncker and Humblot, Berlin, 2002.

AMERASINGHE, C., Principles of the institutional law of international organizations, Cambridge University Press, Cambridge, 2005, pp. 244ss.

AMERASINGHE, C.F., An assessment of the ILC's articles on the responsibility of international organizations, in M. RAGAZZI (ed.), Responsibility of International Organizations. Essays in Memory of Sir Ian Brownlie, ed. Brill, Bruxelles, 2013.

AMERASINGHE, C.F., Principles of the Institutional Law of International Organizations, Cambridge University Press, Cambridge, 2005, pp. 486ss,

AMERASINGHE, C.F., State responsibility for injuries to aliens, Clarendon Press, Oxford, 1963.

AMERASINGHE, F., Local remedies in international law, Cambridge University Press, Cambridge 2004, pp. 64ss.

AMERASNIGHE, C., Liability to third parties of member states of international organizations: Practice, principle and judicial precedence, in American Journal of International Law, 85, 1991, pp. 273ss.

AMOROSO, D., Moving towards complicity as a criterion of attribution of private conducts. Imputation to states of corporate abuses in the US case law, in Leiden Journal of International Law, 24, 2011, pp. 990ss.

AMRALLAH, B., The international responsibility of the United Nations for activities carried out by U.N. peace-keeping forces, in Revue Egyptienne de Droit International, 17, 1976, pp. 57-82.

ANDENAS, M., BJORGE, E., A farewell to fragmentation. Reassertion and convergence in international law, Cambridge University Press, Cambridge, 2015.

ANDENAS, M.T., Jurisdiction procedure and the transformation of international law. From Nottebohm to Diallo in the International Court of Justice, in European Business Law Review, 23 (1), 2012, pp. 130ss.

ANGELET, N., Droit du pouvoir, pouvoir du droit: Mélanges offerts à Jean Salmon, ed. Bruylant, Brussels, 2007, pp. 94ss.

ANNACKER, C., The legal règime of erga omnes obligation, in Austrian Journal of Public International Law, 46, 1994, pp. 158ss.

ANNACKER, E., Die Durchsetzung von erga omnes Verpflichtungen vor dem

Internationalen Gericthshof, D. Kovac Verlag, Hamburg, 1994.

ANZILOTTI, D., Cours de droit international, LGDJ, Paris, 1999, pp. 529ss.

ANZILOTTI, D., La responsabilitè internationale des Etats à raion des dommages soufferts par des ètrangers, in Revue Gènèrale de Droit International Public, 1, 1906, pp. 152ss.

ANZOLA-RORDRÍGUEZ, S.I., Governing through customary international law?, in International Law, Revista Colombiana de Derecho Internacional, 20, 2012, pp. 168ss.

APOLLIS, G., Le règlement de l'affaire du "Rainbow Warrior," in Revue Gènèrale de Droit International Public, 32, 1987, pp. 14ss.

ARABIAN, M.J., KUCH NEGAD, A., BABAE, M., RAMIN NIA, M., Disputes on sovereignty over the islands in the light of international judicial decisions, in International Journal of Humanities and Cultural Studies, 3 (1), 2016, pp. 893ss.

ARAI-TAKAHASHI, Y., Excessive collateral civilian casualties and military necessity, in C. CHINKIN, F. BAETENS, Sovereignty, statehood and state responsibility, Cambridge University Press, Cambridge, 2015, pp. 326ss.

ARAJÄRV, M., The changing nature of customary international law: Methods of interpreting the concept of custom in international criminal tribunals, ed. Routledge, London & New York, 2013.

ARANGIO-RUIZ, G., Customary law: A few more thoughts about the theory of "spontaneous" international custom, in N. ANGELET, Droit du pouvoir, pouvoir du droit: Mélanges offerts à Jean Salmon, ed. Bruylant, Brussels, 2007, pp. 93-10.

ARANGIO-RUIZ, G., The federal analogy and UN Charter, in the European Journal of International Law, 1, 1997, pp. 16ss.

ARANZIO-RUIZ, G., Dualism revisited. International law and interindividual law, in Rivista di Diritto Internazionale, 2004, pp. 985ss.

ARANZIO-RUIZ, G., Fourth report on state responsibility, Doc. A/CN.4/444 and Add.1-3, in Yearbook of International Law Commission, 1992, pp. 35ss.

ARANZIO-RUIZ, G., The normative role of the General Assembly of the United Nations and the Declaration of principles of friendly relations with an appendix on the concept of international law and the theory of international organization, in Recueil des cours, ed. Brill, The Hague, vol. 136, 1972, pp. 42ss.

ARATO, J., Subsequent practice and evolutionary interpretation: Techniques of treaty interpretation over time and their different consequences, in The Law and Practice of the International Courts and Tribunals, 9, 2010, pp. 444ss.

ARATO, J., Treaty interpretation and transformation: informal change in international organizations, in Yale Journal of International Law, 38, 2013, pp. 290ss.

ARCHER, C., International organizations, ed. Routledge, London & New York, 2014.

ARGÉS, J.R., Jus cogens: La actualidad de un tòpico juridico clàsico, Editorial Reus, Madrid, 2019.

ARMSTRONG, D., Routledge handbook of international law, ed. Routledge, London & New York, 2009

ASCENSIO, H., La responsabilitè selon la cour internationale de justice dans l'affaire du gènocide bosniaque, in Revue Gènèrale de Droit International Public, 111, 2007, pp. 298ss.

ASHIAGBOR, D., COUNTOURIS, N., LIANOS, I., The European Union after the Treaty of Lisbon, Cambridge University Press, Cambridge, 2012, pp. 109-135.

ASHLEY DEEKS, S., "Unwilling or unable:" Toward a normative framework for extraterritorial self-defence, in Virginia Journal of International Law, 53 (3), 2012, pp. 484ss.

ASHWORTH, A., HORDER, J., Principles of criminal law, Oxford University Press, Oxford, 2013, pp. 426ss.

AUST, A., Handbook of international law, Cambridge University Press, Cambridge, 2010, pp. 230ss.

AUST, A., Modern treaty law and practice, Cambridge University Press, Cambridge, 2007.

AUST, H.P., Article 2 (5), in B. SIMMA, D.E. KHAN, G. NOLTE, A. PAULUS, The charter of the United Nations. A commentary, Oxford University Press, Oxford, 2012, pp. 244ss.

AUST, H.P., Complicity and the law of state responsibility, Cambridge University Press, Cambridge, 2011.

AUST, H.P., Complicity in international law, Oxford University Press, Oxford, 2015.

AUST, H.P., NOLTE, G., The interpretation of international law by domestic courts: Uniformity, diversity, convergence, Oxford University Press, Oxford, 2016.

AUST, H.P., Through the prism of diversity-the articles on state responsibility in the light of the ILC fragmentation report, in German Yearbook of International Law, 2006, pp. 277ss.

AVBELJ, M., KOMÁREK, J., Constitutional pluralism in the EU and beyond, Hart Publishing, Oxford & Oregon, Portland, 2012.

AZNAR GÓMEZ, M.J., Responsabilidad internacional del Estado y accion del Consejo de Seguridad de las Naciones Unidas, ed. Ministerio de Asuntos Exteriores, Madrid, 2000.

AZNAR, M.J., FOOTER, M.E., Select proceedings of the European Society of International Law, Hart Publishing, Oxford & Oregon, Portland, 2016.

BAARDE, B., MÜHREL, L., PETROV, A.O., International humanitarian law in areas of limited state hood: Adaptable and legitimate or rigid and unreasonable?, Nomos Verlag, Baden-Baden, 2018, pp. 222ss.

BADAR, M.E., The mental element in the Rome Statute of the International Criminal Court: A commentary from a comparative criminal law perspective, in Criminal Law Forum, 19 (3), 2008, pp. 477ss.

BADAR, M.W., The concept of mens rea in international criminal law. The case for a unified approach, Hart Publishing, Oxford & Oregon, Portland, 2013.

BAGIŃSKA, E., Damages for violations of human rights: A comparative study of domestic legal systems, ed. Springer, Berlin, 2015.

BAILLIET, C., MUJEZINOVIĆ LARSEN, K., Promoting peace through international law, Oxford University Press, Oxford, 2015.

BAIMU, E., PANOV, A., Responsibility of international organizations and the World Bank inspection panel: Parallel tracks unlikely to converge?, in The World Bank Legal Review, 2011, vol. 3, pp. 149ss.

BAKER, R.B., Customary International Law: A reconceptualization, in Brooklyn Journal of International Law, 41, 2016, pp. 442ss.

BAKIRCIOGLOU, O., Self-defense in international and criminal law: The doctrine of imminence, ed. Routledge, London & New York, 2011, pp. 204ss.

BAKKER, C., Dual attribution of acts committed by a UN peacekeeping force: An emerging norm of customary international law? The Dutch Supreme Court's judgments in Nuhanoviç and Mustafić, in Italian Yearbook of International Law, 23, 2013, pp. 288ss.

BANNER, C., THOMSON, A., Human rights review of state acts performed in compliance with EC law-Bosphorus Airways v Ireland, in European Human Rights Law Review, 6, 2005, pp. 650ss.

BANTEKAS, I., OETE, L., International human rights law and practice, Cambridge University Press, Cambridge, 2013, pp. 686ss.

BARBER, N.W., CAHILL, M., EKINS, R., The rise and face of the European constitution, Hart Publishing, Oxford & Oregon, Portland, 2019.

BARBERIS, J.A., Nouvelles questiones concernant la personalitè juridique internationale, in Recueil des cours, ed. Brill, Bruxelles, vol. 180, 1983, pp. 216ss.

BARBIER, S., Assurances and guarantees of non-repetition, in J. CRAWFORD, A. PELLET, S. OLLESON, The law of international responsibility, Oxford University Press, Oxford, 2010, pp. 554ss.

BARBOZA, J., State crimes: A decaffeinated coffee?, in L. BOISSON DE CHAZOURNES, V. GOWLLAND-DEBBAS, The international legal system in quest of equity and universality. Liber amicorum Georges Abi-Saab, Kluwer Law International, The Hague, 1998, pp. 164ss.

BARNES, S.H., The contribution of democracy to rebuilding post-conflict societies, in American Journal of International Law, 95 (1), 2000, pp. 1ss.

BARNICE, R.P., The due diligence principle under international law, in International Community Law Review, 8, 2006, pp. 81ss.

BARRAS, A.S., RYNGAERT, C., WOUTERS, J., International organizations and member state responsibility. Critical perspectives, ed. Brill, Bruxelles, 2016, pp. 130ss.

BARRETTE, B., Croyances et cooperation: Analyse du résau des acteurs de la Politique de sécurité et de défense commune de l'UE, in Swiss Political Science Review, 20 (1), 2014, pp. 118ss.

BARROS, A.S., Member states and the international legal (dis)order, in International Organizations of Law Review, 12, 2015, pp. 334ss.

BARROS, A.S., RYNGAERT, C., WOUTERS, J., International organizations and member State responsibility: Critical perspectives, ed. Brill, The Hague, 2016, pp. 154ss.

BARTHE-GRAY, C., Rèflexions sur la satisfaction en droit international, in Annuaire Français de Droit International, 49, 2003, pp. 54ss.

BASTID-BURDEAU, G., Le commerce international des armes: de la sécurité à la défense de l'éthique et des droits de l'homme?, in Journal du Droit International, 2 (4), 2007, par. 7.

BAUER, E.F., Die Völkerrechtswidrige Entführung, Duncker & Humblot, Berlin, 1968, pp. 92ss.

BAXTER, R.R., Multilateral treaties as evidence of customary international law, in British Yearbook of International Law, 41, 1965-1966, pp. 285ss.

BAXTER, R.R., Treaties and custom, in Recueil des cours, ed. Brill, The Hague, vol. 129, 1970, pp. 64ss.

BECKER, T., Terrorism and the state: Rethinking the rules of state responsibility, Bloomsbury Publishing, New York, 2006.

BECKER, Y., LANGE, F., Linien der Rechtsprechung des Bundesverfassungsgerichts: erörtert von den wissenschaftlichen Mitarbeiterinnen und Mitarbeitern, De Gruyter, Berlin, 2014.

BEDERMAN, D.J., Acquiescence, objection and the death of customary international law, in Duke Journal of Comparative and International Law, 21, 2010, pp. 32ss.

BEHAM, M.P., State interest and the sources of international law: Doctrine, morality and non-treaty law, ed. Routledge, London & New York, 2018.

BEHRENS, P., Diplomatic interference and the law, Hart Publishing, Oxford & Oregon, Portland, 2016.

BEHRENS, R., HENNAM, J., Elements of genocide, ed. Routledge, Taylor & Francis, Glass House Book, New York, 2013, pp. 194ss.

BEIGBEDER, Y., International Criminal Tribunals, ed. Palgrave, London, 2011.

BEKKER, P.H.F., Land and maritime boundary between Cameroon and Nigeria, in American Journal of International Law, 97 (2), 2003, pp. 388ss.

BELL, C.A., Reassessing multiple attribution: The International Law Commission and the Behrami and Saramati decision, in International Law and Politics, 42, 2010, pp. 352ss.

BELLAL, A., CASEY-MASLEN, S., GIACCA, G., Implications of international law for a future arms trade treaty, UNIDIR Resources, 2012, pp. 13ss.

BELLAMY, A.J., Libya and the responsibility to protect: The exception and the norm, in Ethics & International Affairs, 25 (3), 2011, pp. 263ss.

BELLAMY, A.J., Responsibility to protect, polity, Cambridge University Press, Cambridge, 2009.

BELLIER, S., Le recours à l'arbitrage par les organizations internationales, Harmattan, Paris, 2011, pp. 25ss.

BELLINGER III, J.B., VIJAY PADMANABHAN, M., Detention operations in contemporary conflicts. For challenges for the Geneva Convention and other existing law, in American Journal of International Law, 105, 2011, pp. 248ss.

BENADAVA, S., Derecho internacional pùblico, ed. Universitaria, Santiago, 2005.

BENDIECK, A., Due diligence in cyberspace, in Stiftung Wissenschaft und Politik German Institute for International and Security Affairs, ed. Palgrave Macmillan, London, 2016, pp. 12ss.

BENNOUNA, M., Le droit international entre la lettre et l'esprit. Cour gènèral de droit international public, in Recueil des cours, ed. Brill, Bruxelles, vol. 383, 2016, pp. 12ss.

BENVENISTI, E., NOLTE, G., Community interests across international law, Oxford University Press, Oxford, 2018.

BENVENISTI, E., The law of global governance, ed. Brill, The Hague, 2014, pag. 99,

BENVENUTI, P., Ensuring observance of the international humanitarian law: Function, extent and limits of the obligation to ensure respect for IHL, in Yearbook of the International Institute of Humanitarian Law, 1989-1990, pp. 27ss.

BENVENUTI, P., Le respect du droit international humanitaire par les forces des Nations Unies: La circulaire de Secrètaire gènèral, in Revue Gènèrale de Droit International Public, 105, 2001, pp. 373ss.

BERBER, F., Lehrbuch des Völkerrechts, C.H. Beck, München, 1960, pp. 8ss.

BERGMANN, A., Zur Souveränitatskonzeption des Europäischen Gerichtshofs: Die Autonomie des Unionsrechts und des Völkerrecht, Mohr Siebeck, Tübingen, 2018.

BERKES, A., The Nagorno-Karabakh cases before the European Court of Human Rights: Pending cases and certain forecasts on jurisdiction and State responsibility, in The Military Law and Law of War Review, 52, 2013, pp. 415ss.

BERNER, K., Authentic interpretation in public international law, in Zeitschrift für äuslandisches öffentliches Recht, 76 (4), 2016, 848ss.

BERNHARDT, R., Art. 103, in B. SIMMA (ed.), The Charter of the United Nations: A Commentary, Oxford University Press, New York-Oxford, 2002, pp. 1293ss.

BERNHARDT, R., Decision of international courts and tribunals and international arbitrations, ed. Elsevier, Amsterdam, New York, Oxford, 2014.

BERNHARDT, R., International organizations in general universal international organization and cooperation, in Encyclopedia of Public International Law, 2014, pp. 147ss.

BERNHARDT, R., Interpretation and implied (tacit) modification of treaties-Comments on Arts. 27, 28, 29 and 38 of the ILC's 1966 Draft Articles on the Law of Treaties, in Heidelberg Journal of International Law, 27, 1967, pp. 492ss.

BERNHARDT, R., The Charter of the United Nations, a commentary. Article 103, vol. II, Oxford University Press, Oxford, 2002, pp. 1293ss.

BERRY, E., HOMEWOOD, M.Y., BOGUSZ, B., Complete European Union law. Texts, cases and materials, Oxford University Press, Oxford, 2013.

BESNÉ MAŇERO, R., El crimen internacional. Nuevos aspectos de la responsabilidad internacional de los Estados, Universidad de Deusto, Bilbao, 1999.

BESSELINK, L., CLAES, M., REESTMAN, J.H., A Constitutional moment: Acceding to the ECHR (or not), in European Constitutional Law Review, 11, 2015, pp. 2ss.

BESSON, S., La pluralitè d'États responsable. Vers une solidaritè international?, in Revue Suisse de Droit International et de Droit Europèen, 17, 2007, pp. 14ss.

BETTS, W.S., CARLSON, N., GISVOLD, G., The post-conflict transitional administration of Kosovo and the lessons-learned in efforts to establish a judiciary and rule of law, in Michigan Journal of International Law, 22, 2001.

BETTWY, D.S., The genocide Convention and unprotected groups: Is the scope of protection expanding under customary international law?, in Notre Dame Journal of International and Comparative Law, 1 (1), 2011, pp. 102ss.

BIANCHI, A., PEAT, D., WINDSOR, M., Interpretation in international law, Oxford University Press, Oxford, 2015.

BIEHL, H., GIEGERICH, B., JONAS, A., Strategic cultures in Europe. Security and Defense Policies across the continent, ed. Springer, Wiesbaden, 2013.

BILLING, F.M.W., The right to silence in transnational criminal proceedings. Comparative law perspectives, ed. Springer, Berlin, 2016, pp. 323ss.

BILLON-GALLAND, A., QUENCEZ, M., Can France and Germany make PESCO work as a process toward EU defense?, in Policy Brief, n. 33, Washington, DC: German Marshall Fund of the United States, 2017.

BINDER, C., Die Grenzen der Vertragstreue im Völkerrecht: am Beispiel der nachträglichten Änderung der Umstände, ed. Springer, Berlin, 2013.

BINDSCHEDLER, R., International organizations, general aspects, in Encyclopdia of Public International Law, 1992, pp. 1299ss.

BINGHAM, T., The rule of law, Penguin Books, London, 2011, pp. 48ss, f Justice and the concept of state practice, in The University of Pennsylvania Journal of International Law, 31, 2009, pp. 295ss.

BISCOP, S., All or nothing? The EU global strategy and defense policy after Brexit, in Contemporary Security Policy, 37 (3), 2016, pp. 432ss.

BISSONNETTE, P.A., La satisfaction comme mode de rèparation en droit international, Imprimerie Granchamp, Genève, 1952.

BJORGE, E., MILES, C., Landmark cases in public international law, Hart Publishing, Oxford & Oregon, Portland, 2017.

BJORGE, E., The evolutionary interpretation of treaties, Oxford University Press, Oxford, 2014, pp. 83ss.

BLACK, J., HALl, A., COX, K., KEPE, M., SILVERSEN, E., Defense and security after Brexit: Understanding the possible implications of the UK's decision to leave the EU, Santa Monica: RAND Corporation, 2017.

BLAISE NGAMENI, H., La diffusion du droit international pènal dans les ordres juridiques africaines, ed. L'Harmattan, Paris, 2017.

BLECKMANN, A., Zur Festellung und Auslegung von Völkergewohnheitsrecht, in Zeitschrift für ausländisches Recht und Völkerrecht, 37, 1977, pp. 504ss.

BLOKKER, N.M., Preparing articles on responsibility of international organizations: Does the International Law Commission take international organizations seriously? A midterm view, in J. KLABBERS, A. WALLENDAHL (eds), Research handbook on the law of international organizations, Edward Elgar Publishers, Cheltenham 2011, pp. 313ss.

BLOKKER, N.M., SCHRIJNER, N.J., Immunity of international organizations, ed. Brill, The Hague, 2015.

BLUM, Y.Z., Eroding the United Nations Charter, Martinus Nijhoff Publishers, Leiden, 1993, pp. 252ss.

BOAS, G., Public international law. Contemporary principles and perspectives, Edward Elgar Publishers, Cheltenham, 2012.

BOBBIO, N., Nouvelles rèflexions sur les normes primaires et secondaries, in C. PERELMAN, La règle de droit, ed. Bruylant, Brussels, 1971, pp. 111ss.

BODANSKY, D., Customary (and not so customary) international environmental law, in Indiana Journal of Global Legal Studies, 3, 1995, pp. 106ss.

BODEAU-LIVINEC, P., Les faux-semblants de la lex specialis: l'exemple de la résolution 52/247 de l'assemblée générale des Nations unies sur les limitations temporelles et financières de la responsabilité de l'ONU, in Revue Belge de Droit International, 117, 2013, pp. 118ss.

BOGGERO, G., The legal implications of sentence no. 238/2014 by Italy's Constitutional Court for italian municipal judges: Is overcoming the "triepelian approach" possible?, in Zeitschrift für ausländisches öffentliches Recht und Völkerrecht, 76, 2016, pp. 204ss.

BOHOSLAVSKY, J.P., CERNIC, J.L., Making sovereign financing and human rights work, Bloomsbury Publishing, New York, 2014, pp. 125ss.

BOISON DE CHAZOURNES, L., ROMANO, C., MACKENZIE, R., International organizations and international dispute settlement: Trends and prospects, Martinus Nijhoff Publishers, New York, 2002, pp. 73-88.

BOISSON DE CHAZOURNES, L., FROMAGEAU, E., Le mècanisme de sanction de la Banque mondiale contre la fraude et la corruption. Le droit administratif global comme outil d'èlaboration et de consolidation d'une procèdure, in C. BORIES, Un droit administratif global?, A global administrative law? ed. Pedone, Paris, 2012, pp. 262ss.

BOISSON DE CHAZOURNES, L., KOHEN, M., International law and the quest for Its implementation. Liber Amicorum Vera Gowlland-Debbas, Martinus Nijhoff Publishers, Leiden, 2010, 73-84.

BOISSON DE CHAZOURNES, L., SANDS, P., International law, the International Court of Justice and nuclear weapons, Cambridge University Press. Cambridge, 1999, pp. 38ss.

BOISSON DE CHAZOURNES, L., Subsequent practice, practices, and "family-resemblance:" Towards embedding subsequent practice in its operative milieu, in G. NOLTE, Treaties and subsequent practice, Oxford University Press, Oxford, 2013, pp. 54ss.

BOIVIN, A., Complicity and beyond. International law and the transfer of small arms and light weapons, in International Review of the Red Cross, 94, 2012, pp. 255ss.

BOLLECKER-STERN, B., Le prèjudice dans la thèorie de la responsabilitè internationale, ed. Pedone, Paris, 1973, pp. 192ss.

BONAFÉ, B.I., The relationship between state and individual responsibility for international crimes, Martinus Nijhoff Publishers, The Hague, 2009.

BONN, K.E., New directions in responsibility: Assessing the International Law Commission's Draft Articles on the Responsibility of international organizations, in The Yale Journal of International Law, 37, 2011, pp. 4ss.

BONN, K.E., The role of lex specialis in the Articles on the responsibility of international organizations, in M. RAGAZZI, Responsibility of international organizations. Essays in memory of Sir Ian Brownlie, Martinus Nijhoff Publishers, Leiden, Boston, 2013, pp. 129ss.

BOON, E.K., The law of responsibility: A response to fragmentation, in Global Business & Development Law Journal, 25, 2012, pp. 398ss.

BOON, K.E., The United Nations as good samaritan: Immunity and responsibility, in Chicago Journal of International Law, 17, 2016, pp. 361-362.

BOOTHBY, W.H., The law of targeting, Oxford University Press, Oxford, 2012, pp. 88ss.

BORCHARD, E.M., The diplomatic protection of citizens abroad. The law of international claim, Tha Banks Law Publishing Company, New York, 1914, pp. 217ss.

BORDIN, F.L., Reflections of customary international law. The authority of codification Conventions and ILC draft articles in international law, in International & Comparative Law Quarterly, 63 (3), 2014, pp. 537ss.

BORDIN, F.L., The analogy between and international organizations, Cambridge University Press, Cambridge, 2018, pp. 154ss.

BOS, A., The identification of custom in international law, in German Yearbook of International Law, 25, 1982, pp. 10ss.

BOSCHIERO, N., Jurisdictional immunities of the state and exequatur of foreign judgements: A private international law evaluation of the recent ICJ judgement in Germany v. Italy, in N. BOSHIERO, T. SCOVAZZI, C. RAGNI, C. PITEA, International courts and the development of international law. Essays in Honour of Tullio Treves, ed. Springer, The Hague, 2013, pp. 781ss.

BOSCHIERO, N., SCOVAZZI, T., PITEA, T., RAGNI, C., International courts and the development of international law. Essays in honour of Tullio Treves, Asser Press, The Hague, 2013, pp. 782ss.

BOSSUYT, M., VERRIJDT, W., The full effect of EU law and of constitutional review in Belgium and France after the Melki judgment, in European Constitutional Law Review, 7, 2011, pp. 356ss.

BOSTER, V., An introduction to transnational criminal law, Oxford University Press, Oxford, 2012, pp. 24ss.

BOTHE, M., Der Irak-Krieg und das völkerrechtliche Gewaltverbot, in Archiv des Völkerechts, 41, 2003, pp. 46ss.

BOTHE, M., Le droit de la guerre et le Nations Unies à propos des incidents armès au Congo, in Etudes et travauz de l'Institut Univeritaire des Haute Etudes Internationales, 5, 1967, pp. 208ss.

BOTHE, M., Peace-keeping, in B. SIMMA, The charter of the United Nations. A commentary, Oxford University Press, Oxford, 2002, pp. 648ss.

BOTHE, M., Peacekeeping forces, in Max Planck Encyclopedia of Public International Law, 2016, par. 51.

BOTTIGLIERO, L., Redress for victims of crimes under international law, ed.

Springer, Leiden, 2004.

BOUTIN, B., Atttribution of conduct in international military operations. A causal analysis of effective law, in Melbourne Journal of International Law, 18, 2017, pp. 158ss.

BOUTIN, B., Responsibility of the Netherlands for the acts of Dutchbat in Nuhanović and Mustafić: The continuous quest for a tangible meaning for "effective control" in the context of peacekeeping, in Leiden Journal of International Law, 25, 2012, pp. 522ss.

BOUVERESSE, A., RITLENG, D., L'effectivitè du droit de l'Union europèenne, ed. Larcier, Bruxelles, 2018.

BOVIN, A., Complicity and beyond. International law and the transfer of small arms and light weapons, in International Review of Red Cross, 87, 2005, pp. 468ss.

BOWETT, B.W., A legal study of United Nations practice, The Lawbook Exchange, London, 1964, pp. 484ss.

BOWETT, D., Reprisals involving recourse to armed force, in American Journal of International Law, 66 (1), 1972.

BOWETT, D., The court's role in relation to international organizations, in Fifty years of the International Court of Justice. Essays in honour of Sir Robert Jennings, Cambridge University Press, Cambridge, 1996, pp. 190ss.

BOWETT, D., The impact of Security Council Decisions on dispute settlement procedures, in European Journal of international law, 5, 1994, pp. 89-101.

BOWETT, D.W., Crimes of state and the 1996 report of the International Law Commission on state responsibility, in European Journal of International Law, 9, 1998, pp. 164ss.

BOWMAN, M.J., KRITSIOTIS, D., Conceptual and contextual perspectives on the modern law of treaties, Cambridge University Press, Cambridge, 2018, pp. 41, 165, 779ss.

BOYLE, A.E., State responsibility and international liability for injurious consequences of acts not prohibited by international law. A necessary distinction?, in International and Comparative Law Quarterly, 39 (1), 1990. pp. 5ss.

BOYLE, F.A., The entebbe hostages crisis, in Indian Journal of International law, 29 (1), 1982, pp. 20ss.

BRAIBANT, G., Le principe de proportionnalitè, in Mèlanges offerts à M. Waline. Le juge et le droit public, LGDJ, Paris, 1974, pp. 298ss.

BRAND, M.G., Institution-building and human rights protection in Kosovo in the light of UNMIK legislation, in Nordic Journal of International Law, 70, 2001.

BRANDES, M., "All's well that ends well" or "much ado about nothing?" A commentary on the arms trade treaty, in Goettingen Journal of International Law, 5 (2), 2013, pp. 399-429.

BRATSPIES, R., Transboundary harm in international law, Cambridge University Press, Cambridge, 2006.

BREAU, C., The constitutionalization of the international legal order, in Leiden Journal of International Law, 21, 2008, pp. 546ss.

BREGALDA, G., Direito internacional pùblico & direito internacional privado, ed. saràiva, São Paulo, 2014.

BRESLIN, A., Ensuring respect: The European Union's guidelines on promoting compliance with international humanitarian law, in Israel Law Review, 43 (2), 2010, pp. 382ss.

BRIERLY, J.L., The theory of implied state solicity in international claims, in The British Yearbook of International Law, 9, 1928, pp. 42ss.

BRIGGS, H.W., Nicaragua v. United States: Jurisdiction and admissibility, in American Journal of International Law, 79, 1985, pp. 374ss.

BRIGGS, H.W., The travaux prèparatoires of the Vienna Convention on the Law of Treaties, in The American Journal of International Law, 65, 1971, pp. 705-712.

BROCKMAN-HAWE, B.E., Questioning the UN's immunity in the Dutch Courts: Unresolved issues in the Mothers of Srebrenica litigation, in Washington University Global Studies Law Review, 10, 2011, pp. 727ss.

BRÖLLMANN, C., The 1986 Vienna Convention on the law of treaties: The history of draft article 26 bis, in J. KLABBERS, R. LEFEBER, Essays on the law of treaties. A collection of essays in honour of Bert Vierdag, ed. Brill, The Hague, 1998, pp. 122ss.

BROLMANN, C., Member states and international legal responsibility. Developments of the institutional veil, in International Organizations Law Review, 12, 2015, pp. 358-381.

BRÖLMANN, C., The institutional veil in public international law. International organizations and the law of treaties, Hart Publishing, Oxford & Oregon, Portland, 2007, pp. 20ss

BRÖLMANN, C.M., Specialized rules of treaty interpretation: International Organizations, in D.B. HOLLIS, The Oxford guide to treaties, Oxford University Press, Oxford, 2012, pp. 508ss.

BROWER, H., Why the FTC notes of interpretation constitute a partial amendment of NAFTA article 1105, in Virginia Journal of International Law, 46, 2006, pp. 348ss.

BROWN WEISS, E., Invoking state responsibility in the twenty-first century, in American Journal of International Law, 96, 2002, pp. 798ss.

BROWNLIE, I., Brownlie's principles of public international law, Oxford University Press, Oxford, 2012, pp. 24ss.

BROWNLIE, I., International law and the use of force, Oxford University Press, Oxford, 1963, pp. 349ss.

BROWNLIE, I., Principles of public international law, Oxford University Press, Oxford, 2003, pp. 650ss.

BROWNLIE, I., Some problems in the evaluation of the practice of states as an element of custom, in International Law Studies in Honor of Gaetano Arangio Ruiz, vol. I, Editoriale Scientifica, Napoli, 2004, pp. 313-318.

BROWNLIE, I., State responsibility, Oxford University Press, Oxford, 1983.

BROWNLIE, I., System of the law of nations. State responsibility, Oxford University Press, Oxford, 1983, pp. 200ss.

BROWNLIE, I., The responsibility of states of the acts of international organizations, in M. RAGAZZI, International responsibility today. Essays in memory of Oscar Schachter, ed. Brill, Leiden, 2005, pp. 335ss.

BUCHAM, R., Cyber attacks: Unlawful uses of force or prohibited interventions?, in Journal of Conflict and Security Law, 17, 2012, pp. 214ss.

BUCHAN, R., Cyberspace, non-state actors and the obligation to prevent transboundary harm, in Journal of Conflict & Security Law, 21, 2016, pp. 430ss.

BUCHAN, R., UN peacekeeping operations: When can unlawful acts committed by peacekeeping forces be attributed to the UN?, in Legal Studies, 32 (2), 2012, pp. 284ss.

BUERGENTHAL, T., MURPHY, S.D., Public international law, West Group, Saint Paul, Minnesota, 2007.

BUGA, I., Modification of treaties by subsequent practice, Oxford University Press, Oxford, 2018.

BUIRETTE, P., Le droit international humanitaire, ed. La Dècouverte, Paris, 2019.

BURBER, M.D., HÖRNLE, T., The Oxford handbook of criminal law, Oxford University Press, 2014.

BURCKARDT, V., Die völkerrechtLiche Verantwortlichkeit der Staaten, ed. P. Hart, Bern, 1924, pp. 6ss.

BURKE, N., A change in perspective: Looking at occupation through the lens of the law of treaties, in International Law and Politics, 41 (1), 2008, pp. 104.

BUTKIEWITCZ, E., The premises of international responsibility of intergovenrnmental organization, in Polish Yearbook of International Law, 11, 1981-1982, pp. 132ss.

BUXBAUM, M., A legal history of international reparations, in Berkeley Journal of International Law, 23, 2005, pp. 315ss.

BUYSE, A., Lost and regained? Restitution as a remedy for human rights violations, in Heidelberg Journal of International Law, 68, 2008, pp. 132ss.

BÜYÜKBAY, C., ERTIN, D., EU-Skeptizismus am Bosporus?, in Zeitschrift für Internationale Beziehungen, 2017, n. 2.

BYERS, M., Conceptualizing the relationship between jus cogens and erga omnes rules, in Nordic Journal of International Law, 62 (2-3), 1997, pp. 4ss.

CAHIN, G., La variètè des fonctions imparties aux organizations internationales, in E. LAGRANGE, J.M. SOREL, Droit des organizations internationales, LGDJ, Paris, 2013, pp. 678ss.

CAHIN, G., Le coutume internationale et les organizations internationales: L'incidence institutionnelle sur le proessus coutumier, ed. Pedone, Paris, 2001.

CALVO-GOLLER, K., La procèdure et la jurisprudence de la Cour pènale internationale, ed. Lextenso, Paris, 2012.

CAMARGOS, L.A., A responsabilidade penal internacional dos individuos: Estudo do caso Darfur, in Revista de Direito Brasileira, 2013, pp. 199ss.

CAMERON, L., CHETAIL, V., Privatizing war: Private military and security companies under public international law, Cambridge University Press, Cambridge, 2013, pp. 162Ss, 205-208.

CAMMAERT, P.C., KLAPPE, B., Authority, command and control in United Nations-led peace operations, in T. GILL, D. FLECK (eds.), Oxford University Press's handbook of the international law of military operations, Oxford University Press, Oxford, 2010, pp. 262ss.

CANAL-FORGUES, É., RAMBAUD, P., Droit international public, LGDJ, Paris, 2007.

CANAL-FORGUES, É., RAMBAUD, P., Droit international public, LGDJ, Paris, 2016.

CANÇADO TRINDADE, A., The application of the rule of exhaustion of local remedies in international law, Cambridge University Press, Cambridge 1983, pp. 46ss.

CANNIZZARO, E., A machiavallian moment? The UN Security Council and the rule of law, in International Organizations Law Review, 3, 2006, pp. 190ss.

CANNIZZARO, E., Is there an individual right to reparation? Some thoughts on the ICJ judgment in the jurisdictional immunities case, in D. ALLAND, V. CHETAIL, OP. DE FROUVILLE, J.E. VIÑUALES, Unity and diversity of international law. Essays in Honour of Professor Pierre-Marie Dupuy, Oxford University Press, Oxford, 2014, pp. 498.

CANNIZZARO, E., The European Union as an actor in international relations, The Hague-London-New York, 2002, pp. 219-230.

CANNIZZARO, E., The law of treaties beyond the Vienna Convention, Oxford University Press, Oxford, 2011.

CAPOTORTI, F., Cours gènèral de droit international public, in Recueil des cours, ed. Brill, Bruxelles, vol. 218, 1994, pp. 256ss.

CARDONA LLORENS, J., PUEYO LOSA, J., RODRIGUEZ-VILLASANTE PRIETO, J.L., (eds.) Estudios de Derecho Internacional y de Derecho

Europeo en Homenaje al Profesor Manuel Pérez González, ed. Tirant lo Blanch, Valencia, 2012, pp. 168ss.

CARDWELL, P.J., Values in the European Union's foreign policy: An analysis and assessment of CFSP declarations, in European Foreign Affairs Review, 21 (4), 2016, pp. 602ss.

CARLEBACH, A., Le problème de la faute et sa place dans la norme du droit international, LGDJ, Paris, 1962, pp. 4ss.

CARTER, B.E., TRIMBLE, P.R., WEINER, A.S., International law, Aspen publishers, New York, 2007.

CARTER, B.E., WEINER, A.S., HOLLIS, D.B., International law, Wolters Kluwer, New York, 2018, pp. 706ss

CARTY, A., Doctrine versus State practice, in B. FASSBENDER, A. PETERS, The Oxford Handbook of the history of international law, Oxford University Press, Oxford, 2012, pp. 972.

CASSELLA, S., La nècessite en droit international: De l'ètat de nècessite aux situations de nècessitè, ed. Brill, Bruxelles, 2011, pp. 488ss.

CASSESE, A., A follow-up forcible humanitarian countermeasures and opinion necessitatis, in European Journal of International Law, 10 (4), 1999, pp. 792ss.

CASSESE, A., Ex iniuria ius oritur: Are we moving towards international legitimation of forcible humanitarian countermeasures in the world community?, in European Journal of international Law, 10 (2), 1999, pp. 23ss.

CASSESE, A., International law, 2nd edition, Oxford University Press, 2005, pp. 164ss.

CASSESE, A., Remarks on Scelle's theory of "role splitting" (dédoublement fonctionnel in international law), in European Journal of International Law, 1, 1990, pp. 210ss

CASSESE, A., The Geneva Protocols of 1977 on the humanitarian law of armed conflict and customary international law, in UCLA Pacific Basin Law Journal, 3, 1984, pp. 55ss.

CASSESE, A., The nexus requirement for war crimes, in Journal of International Criminal Justice, 10, 2012.

CASSESE, A., The Nicaragua and Tadić test revisited in light of the ICJ judgment on genocide in Bosnia, in European Journal of International Law, 18 (4), 2007, pp. 649-668.

CASSESE, Q., On the use of criminal law notions in determining state responsibility for genocide, in Journal of International Criminal Justice, 5, 2007, pp. 888ss.

CASTILLO DE LA TORRE, F., Tribunal constitucional (Spanish Constitutional Court), Opinion 1/2004 of 13 December 2004, in Common Market Law Review, 42, 2005, pp. 1170s

CASTILLO DE LA TORRE, V.F., Article 340 TFEU on contractual and non-contractual liability of the Union, in P.E. HERZOG, C. CAMPBELL, G. ZAGEL, Smit & Herzog on the law of the European Union, LexisNexis, New York, 2010, pp. 340-347.

CENGIC, A., Commentary, in A. KLIP, G. SLUITER (eds), Annotated leading cases of International Criminal Tribunals, Vol. XXIII, ed. Intersentia, Antwerp/Oxford, 2010, pp. 182-184.

CEPELKA, C., Les consèquences juridiques du dèlit en droit international contemporain, Prague, 1965.

CHAINOGLOU, K., Re-conceptualising self-defense in international law, Oxford University Press, Oxford, 2007.

CHARNEY, J.J., Universal international law, in American Journal of International Law, 87, 1993, pp. 532ss.

CHAUMONT, C., Cours gènèral de droit international public, in Recueil des cours, ed. Brill, Bruxelles, vol. 129, 1970-1971, pp. 495ss.

CHECHI, A., Judgment n. 238-2014 (IT. Const. Ct.), in International Legal Materials, 54 (3), 2015, pp. 472ss.

CHEN, Y., Structural limitations and possible future of the work of the ILC, in Chinese Journal of International Law, 9, 2010, pp. 478ss.

CHENG, B., United Nations Resolutions on outer space: "Instant" international customary law?, in The Indian Journal of International Law, 5, 1965, pp. 4ss.

CHERIF BASSIOUNI, M., Crimes against humanity: Historical evolution and contemporary application, Cambridge University Press, Cambridge, 2011, pp. 206ss.

CHERIF BASSIOUNI, M., Legal control of international terrorism, in Harvard International Law Journal, 43, 2002, pp. 84ss.

CHESTERMAN, S., Leading from behind: The responsibility to protect, the Obama doctrine, and humanitarian intervention after Libya, in Ethics & International Affairs, 25 (3), 2011, pp. 282ss.

CHESTERMAN, S., Rule of law, in Max Planck Encylcopedia of Public International Law, 2015, parr. 42ss.

CHETAIL, V., Permanence et mutation du droit des conflits armès, ed. Bruylant, Bruxelles, 2013

CHINKIN, C., Third parties in international law, Oxford University Press, Oxford, 1993, pp. 4ss.

CHINKIN, C.C., Crisis and the performance of international agreements: The outbreak of war in perspective, in Yale Journal of Public Order, 7, 1981-1982, pp. 177ss.

CHODOSH, H.E., Neither treaty not custom: The emergence of declarative international law, in Texas International Law Journal, 26, 1991, pp. 88ss.

CHUKWUEMEKE OKEKE, E., Jurisdictional immunities of states and international organizations, Oxford University Press, Oxford, 2018.

CIAMPI, A., Security Council targeted sanctions and human rights, in B. FASSBENDER, Securing human rights?: Achievements and challenges of the UN, Oxford University Press, Oxford, 2011, pp. 123ss.

CINKIN, C., KALDOR, M., International law and new wars, Cambridge University Press, Cambridge, 2017, pp. 367ss.

CIORCIARI, J.D., Request for interpretation of the judgment of 15 June 1962 in the Temple of Preah Vihear case (Cambodia v. Thailand), in American Journal of International Law, 108 (2), 2014, pp. 290ss.

CLARK, R.S., The mental element in international criminal law: The Rome Statute of the International Criminal Court and the elements of offences, in Criminal Law Forum, 12, 2001, pp. 296ss.

CLASS, W., Die Kausalität der Beihilfe, in G. SPENDE, Festschrift für Ulrich Stock. Studium zur Strafrechtswissenschaft, Holzner, Würzburg, 1966, pp. 116ss.

CLÊMENT-WILZ, L., Le rôle politique de la Cour de justice de l'Union européenne, ed. Larcier, Bruxelles, 2019.

CLOSA, C., KOCHENOV, D., Reinforcing rule of law oversight in the EU, Cambridge University Press, Cambridge, 2016.

COHN, M.G., La thèorie de la responsabilitè internationale, in Recueil des cours, ed. Brill, Bruxelles, vol. 68, 1939, pp. 2010ss.

COLLINS, P.T., Civil-military "legal" relations: Where to from here? The civilian courts and the military in the United Kingdom, United States and Australia, ed. Brill, The Hague, 2018.

COLLINS, R., The institutional problem in modern international law, Bloomsbury Publishing, New York, 2016.

COLLINS, R., WHITE, N., (eds.) international organizations and the idea of autonomy. Institutional independence in the international legal order, ed. Routledge, London & New York, 2011, pp. 10ss.

COMAN-KUND, F., European Union agencies as global actors. A legal study of the European aviation safety agency, frontex and europol, ed. Routledge, London & New York, 2018.

COMBACAU, J., ALLAND, D., "Primary" and "secondary" rules in the law of state responsibility: Categorizing international obligations, in Netherlands Yearbook of International Law, 16, 1985, pp. 82ss.

COMBACAU, J., Obligations de résultat et obligations de comportement. Quelques questions et pas de rèponse, in Mélanges offerts à Paul Reuter: Le droit international: Unitè et diversitè, ed. Pedone, Paris, 1981, pp. 189ss.

CONDORELLI, L., BOISSON DE CHAZOURNES, C., Common article 1 of the Geneva conventions revisited: Protecting collective interests, in International

Review of Red Cross, 82, 2000.

CONDORELLI, L., BOISSON DE CHAZOURNES, L., Quelques remarques à propos de l'obligation des Etats de "respecter et faire respecter" le droit international humanitaire "en toute circonstances," in C. SWINIARSKI, Études et essais sur le droit international humanitaire et sur le principes de la Croix-Rouge en l'honneur de Jean Pictet, Martinus Nijhoff Publishers, Genève, The Hague, 1984, pp. 18ss.

CONDORELLI, L., Conclusions Generales, in La soumission des organizations internationales aux normes internationales relatives aux droits de l'homme. Journée d'études de Strasbourg/Societe Francaise pour le Droit International. Institut International des Droits de l'Homme, ed. Pedone, Paris, 2009.

CONDORELLI, L., Customary international law: The yesterday, today, and tomorrow of general international law, in A. CASSESE, Realizing utopia: The future of international Law, Oxford University Press, Oxford, 2012, pp. 147, 150.

CONDORELLI, L., De la responsabilité internationale de l'ONU et/ou de l'État d'envoi lors d'actions de Forces de Maintien de la Paix: l'écheveau de l'attribution (double?) devant le juge néerlandais, in QIL-Questions of International Law, Zoom-in 1 (2014), pp. 3-15.

CONDORELLI, L., DE SENA, P., Les droits de l'homme à Guantanamo: en attendent la Cour suprême des Etats-Unis, in P. AMSELEK, Liberté, Justice, Tolérance. Mélanges en hommage au Doyen Gérard Cohen- Jonathan, ed. Brill, Bruxelles, 2001, pp. 450ss.

CONDORELLI, L., DIPLA, H., Solutions traditionnelles et nouvelles tendances en matière d'atttributon à l'État d'un fait internationalement illicite dans la convention de 1982 sur le droit de la mer, in A.A.V.V., Le droit international à l'heure de sa codificaton. Études à l'honneur de R. Ago, vol. III, ed. Giuffrè, Milano, 1987, pp. 66ss.

CONDORELLI, L., Imputation à l'Etat of an internationalement illicite: class solutions and nouvelles tendances, in Recueil des cours, ed. Brill, Brussels, vol. 189, 1984, pp. 186ss.

CONDORELLI, L., KRESS, C., The rule of attribution. General considerations, in J. CRAWFORD, A. PELLET, S. OLLESON, The law of international responsibility, Oxford University Press, Oxford, 2010, pp. 222ss.

CONDORELLI, L., L'imputation à l'Etat d'un fait internationalement illicite: Solutions classiques et nouvelles tendances, in Recueil des cours, ed. Brill, Bruxelles, vol. 189, 1984, pp. 10ss.

CONDORELLI, L., L'évolution du Champ d'Application de la Protection Diplomatique, in La protection diplomatique: Mutations contemporaines et pratiques nationales: Actes de la journée d'études du 30 mars 2001 organisée à la mémoire de Georges Perrin, ed. Bruylant, Bruxelles, 2003, pp. 20ss.

CONDORELLI, L., La Cour pènale internationale. Un pas de gèant (pourvu qu'il soit accompli), in Revue Gènèrale de Droit International Public, 111, 1999, pp. 12ss.

CONDORELLI, L., La protection diplomatique et l'évolution de son domaine d'application, in Rivista di Diritto Internazionale, 2003, pp. 5ss.

CONDORELLI, L., Le Conseil de sécurité, les sanctions ciblées et le respect des droits de l'homme, ed. Brill, Bruxelles, 2010, pp. 78ss.

CONDORELLI, L., Le statut des forces de l'Onu et le droit international humanitaire, in Rivista di Diritto Internazionale, 1995, pp. 881ss.

CONDORELLI, L., MÉRIBOUTE, Z., Some remarks on the state of international law concerning military activities in outer space, in Indian Yearbook of International Law, 6, 1975, pp. 17ss.

CONWAY, G., European Union law, ed. Routledge, London & New York, 2015.

CONWAY, G., The limits of legal reasoning and the European Court of Justice, Cambridge University Press, Cambridge, 2012, pp. 156ss.

CONZE, A., Die völkerrechtliche Haftung der Europäischen Gemeinschaft, ed. Nomos, Baden-Baden, 1987, pp. 68ss.

CORREALE, F., Les origines de la "question du Sahara occidental:" enjeux historiques, défis politiques, in M. BALBONI, G. LASCHI (eds), The European Union approach towards Western Sahara, ed. Peter Lang, Bruxelles, 2017, pp. 34ss.

CORTEN, O., KLEIN, P., The limits of complicity as a ground for responsibility. Lessons learned from the Corfu channel case, in K. BANNELIER, T. CHRISTAKIS, S. HEATHCOTE, The ICJ and the evolution of international law. The enduring impact of the Corfu channel case, ed. Routledge, London & New York, 2012, pp. 315ss.

CORTEN, O., KLEIN, P., The Vienna Conventions on the law of treaties. A commentary, Oxford University Press, Oxford, 2011.

CORTEN, O., La "complicitè" dans le droit de la responsabilitè international. Un concept inutile?, in Annuaire Français de Droit International, 57, 2011, pp. 58ss.

CORTEN, O., The "unwilling or unable" test: Has it been and could it be, accepted?, in Leiden Journal of International Law, 29, 2016, pp. 794ss.

CORTEN, O., The law against war: The prohibition in the use of force in contemporary international law, Bloomsbury Publishing, 2010, pp. 250ss.

CORTEN, O., The obligation of termination, in J. CRAWFORD, A. PELLET, S. OLLESON, The law of international responsibility, Oxford University Press, Oxford, 2010, pp. 545ss.

CORTÉS MARTÍN, J.M., Las organizaciones internacionales: Codificación y desarrollo progresivo de su responsabilidad internacional, ed. Instituto Andaluz de Administración Pública, Sevilla, 2008, pp. 30ss.

COSTA, J.P., La Cour europèenne des droits de l'homme. Des juges pour la libertè, ed. Dalloz, Paris, 2017.

COSTELLO, C., The Bosphorus ruling of the European Court of Human Rights: Fundamental rights and blurred boundaries in Europe, in Human Rights Law Review, 6 (1), 2006, pp. 88ss.

COT, J.P., La conduite subséquente des parties à un traité, in Revue Générale de Droit International Public, 70, 1966, pp. 634ss.

COT, P., PELLET, M., FORTEAU, A., La Charte des Nations Unies. Commentaire article par article, vol. II, ed. Economica, Paris, 2006, pp. 2134-2147.

COUVEINHES MATSUMOTO, F., L'effectivitè en droit international, ed. Bruylant, Bruxelles, 2014.

COUVREUR, P., Reflexions sur la portèe et les effets de l'engagement conentionnel externe de la CEE, in Melanges Tryol Serra, Madrid, 1986, pp. 330ss.

CRAIG BARKER, J., International law and international relations, Bloomsburry Publishing, New York, 2000, pp. 127ss.

CRAWFORD, J., (ed. by), State responsibility. The general part, Cambridge University Press, Cambridge, 2014, pp. 487ss.

CRAWFORD, J., Brownlie's principles of public international law, Oxford University Press, Oxford, 2012, pp. 24ss.

CRAWFORD, J., Chance, order, change. The course of international law, ed. Brill, Bruxelles, 2014.

CRAWFORD, J., KOROMA, A., MAHMOUD, S., PELLET, A., The international legal order: Current needs and possible responses. Essays in honour of Djamchrd Momtaz, ed. Brill, Bruxelles, 2017.

CRAWFORD, J., Multilateral rights and obligations in international law, in Recueils des cours, ed. Brill, Bruxelles, vol. 327, 2007, pp. 325ss.

CRAWFORD, J., PELLET, A., OLLESON, S., PARLETT, K., The law of international responsibility, Oxford University Press, Oxford, 2010.

CRAWFORD, J., Responsibility to the international community as a whole, in Indian Journal of Global Legal Studies, 9, 2001-2002, pp. 304ss.

CRAWFORD, J., Revising the draft articles on state responsibility, in European Journal of International Law, 10 (2), 1999, pp. 444ss.

CRAWFORD, J., The identification and development of customary international law, Keynote Speech, Spring Conference of the ILA British Branch-Foundations and Future of International Law, 23 May 2014, a p. 13.

CRAWFORD, J., The international law introduction. Text and commentaries, Cambridge University Press, Cambridge, 2002, pp. 14ss.

CRAWFORD, J.R., Military and paramilitary activities in and against Nicaragua case (Nicaragua v. United States of America), in Max Planck Encyclopedia of Public International Law, 2011.

CREMONA, M., DE WITTE, B., EU foreign relations law-Constitutional fundamentals, Oxford University Press, Oxford, 2008, pp. 65ss.

CREMONA, M., Implementation of the Lisbon treaty. Improving functioning of the EU: Foreign Affairs (Brussels: Policy Department C: Citizens' Rights and Constitutional Affairs, European Parliament, 2016.

CREMONA, M., SCOTT, J., European Union law beyond EU borders: The extraterritorial reach of European Union law, Oxford University Press, Oxford, 2019, pp. 79ss.

CROOK, J.R., The fiftieth session of the UN Commission on human rights, in American Journal of International Law, 90 (1), 1994.

CROQUET, N., The import of international customary law into the EU legal order: The adequacy of a direct effect analysis, in Cambridge Yearbook of European Legal Studies, 15, 2012-2013, pp. 48ss.

CROSS, M.K., The military dimension of European security: An epistemic community approach, in Millennium, 42 (10), 2013, pp., 47ss.

CROWE, J., WESTON-SCHEUBEL, K., Principles of international humanitarian law, Edward Elgar Publishers, Cheltenham, 2013, pp. 8, 149ss.

CRYER, R., FRIMAN, H., ROBINSON, D., WILMSHURST, E., An introduction to international criminal law and procedure, Cambridge University Press, Cambridge, 2010.

CURRIE, J.H., FORCESE, C., OOSTERVELD, V.L., International law, Irwin law, Toronto, 2007.

CZAPLIŃSKI, W., HLECZKOWSKA, A., Unrecognized subjects in international law, Scholar Publishing, Warsaw, 2019.

CZAPLINSKI, W., Sources of international law in the Nicaragua case, in The International and Comparative Law Quarterly, 38 (1), 1989, pp. 152ss.

D'AMATO, A., The concept of custom in international law, Cornell University Press, Ithaca, 1971, pp. 89-90.

D'AMATO, A., Trashing customary international law, in American Journal of International Law, 81, 1987, pp. 102ss.

D'ARGENT, P., La personnalitè juridique internationale de l'organization internationale, in E. LAGRANGE, J.M. SOREL, Droit des organizations internationales, LGDJ, Paris, 2013, pp. 439ss.

D'ARGENT, P., Les rèparations de guerre en droit international public. La responsabilitè internaitonale des États à l'èpreuve de la guerre, ed. Bruylant, Bruxelles, 2002.

D'ARGENT, P., Reparation, cessation, assurances and guarantees of non repetition, in A. NOLLKAEMPER, I. PLAKOKEFALOS, Principles of shared responsibility in international law. An appraisal of the state of the art, Cambridge University Press, Cambridge, 2015, pp. 228ss.

D'ASPREMONT, D., BESSON, S., KNUCHEL, S., The oxford handbook of the sources of international law, Oxford University Press, Oxford, 2017.

D'ASPREMONT, J., Epistemic forces in international law, Edward Elgar Publishers, Cheltenham, 2015, pp. 118ss.

D'ASPREMONT, J., The idea of "rules" in the sources of international law, in British Yearbook of International Law, 84, 2014, pp. 106ss.

D'ASPREMONT, D., A European law of international responsibility? The Articles on the responsibility of international organizations and the European Union, in ACIL Research Paper (SHARES Series) n. 22, 2013, pp. 7-8.

D'ASPREMONT, J., The law of international responsibility and multilayered institutional veils: The case of authorized regional peace-enforcement operations, in SHARES Research Paper n. 24, 2013, pp. 9ss.

DAHLHOFF, D., International Court of Justice. Digest of judgments and advisory opinions, canon and case law 1946-2012, Martinus Nijhoff Publishers, The Hague, 2012, pp. 1657ss.

DAHM, C.G., DELBRÜCK, J., WOLFRUM, R., Völkerrecht, De Gruyter, Berlin, 2019.

DAHM, F., Völkerrecht, De Gruyter, Stuttgart, 1961, pp. 204ss.

DAHM, G., Völkerrecht, De Gruyter, Stuttgart, 1941, pp. 88ss.

DAHM, G., Völkerrecht, De Gruyter, Stuttgart, 1958, pp. 13ss.

DAILLER, P., Article 74 (Convention de Vienne de 1986), in O. CORTEN, P. KLEIN, Les Conventions de Vienne sur le droit des traitès. Commentaire article par article, ed. Bruylant, Bruxelles, 2006, pp. 2634ss.

DAILLER, P., FORTEAU, M., PELLET, A., Droit international public, LGDG, Paris, 2009, pp. 680ss.

DAILLER, P., PELLET, A., QUOC DINH, N., Droit international public, ed. LGDJ, Paris, 1999, pp. 715ss.

DALACOURA, K., Islamist movements as non-state actors and their relevance to international relations, in D. JOSELLIN, W. WALLACE, Non-state actors in world politics, ed. Palgrave, London, New York, 2001, pp. 236ss.

DAMNJANOVIC, V., Die Beteilingunsformen im deutschen und serbischen Stafrecht sowie in der ICTY-Rechtsprechung, BWN Berliner Wissenschafts Verlag, Berlin, 2013, pp. 246ss.

DAMROSCH, L., Multilateral disputes in the International Court of Justice, in L. DAMROSCH, The International Court of Justice as a crossroads, Transnational publications Inc., Dobs Ferry, New York, 1987, pp. 376ss.

DANIEL, D.C.F., HAYES, B.C., Beyond traditional peacekeeping, ed. Springer, Berlin, 2016, pp. 17ss.

DANILENKO, G.M., The theory of international customary law, in the German Yearbook of International Law, 31, 1988, pp. 12ss.

DANNENBAUM, T., Killings at Srebrenica, effective control, and the power to prevent unlawful conduct, in International and Comparative Law Quarterly, 62 (3), 2012, pp. 713-728.

DANNENBAUM, T., Translating the standard of effective control into a system of effective accountability: How liability should be apportioned for violations of human rights by member state troop contingents serving as United Nations peacekeepers, in Harvard Journal of International Law, 51, 2010, pp. 113ss.

DARCY, S., Collective responsibility and accountability under international law, ed. Brill, Bruxelles, 2007.

DASTOOR, N.F., The responsibility to refine: The need for a Security Council Committee on the responsibility to protect, in Harvard Human Rights Journal, 22, 2009, pp. 25ss.

DAUGIRDAS, K., How and why international law binds international organizations, Harvard International Law Journal, 57 (2), 2016, pp. 330ss.

DAUGIRDAS, K., Reputation and the responsibility of international organizations, in European Journal of International Law, 25 (4), 2014, pp. 994ss.

DAVID, E., Primary and secondary rules, in J. CRAWFORD, A. PELLET, S. OLLESON, The law of international responsibility, Oxford University Press, Oxford, 2010, pp. 29ss.

DAVID, E., Principles de droit des conflits armès, ed. Bruylant, Bruxelles, 2019.

DAVID, E., Principes de droit des conflicts armés, ed. ULB, Bruxelles, 2002, pp. 109ss.

DAWIDOWICZ, M., The obligation of non recognition of an unlawful situation, in J. CRAWFORD, A. PELLET, S. OLLESON, The law of international responsibility, Oxford University Press, Oxford, 2010, pp. 683ss.

DAWIDOWICZ, M., Third party countermeasures in international law, Cambridge University Press, Cambridge, 2017.

DE BAAERE, G., WOUTERS, J., The contribution of international and supranational courts to the rule of law, Edward Elgar Publishers, Cheltenham, 2015, pp. 268ss.

DE BRABANDERE, E., Immunity of international organizations in post-conflict international administrations, in International Organizations Law Review, 7, 2010, pp. 79ss.

DE FROUVILLE, O., Attribution of conduct to the State: Private individuals, in J. CRAWFORD, The law of international responsibility, Oxford University Press, Oxford, 2010.

DE HERT, P.J.A., KORENICA, F., The doctrine of the equivalent protection: Its life and legitimacy before and after the European Union's Accession to the European Convention on Human Rights, in German Law Journal, 13, 2012, pp. 884ss.

DE HOOGH, A., Australia and East Timor-rights erga omnes, complicity and non recognition, in American Journal of International Law, 93, 1999, pp. 79ss.

DE HOOGH, A., Obligations erga omnes and international crimes: A theoretical inquity into the implementation and enforcement of the international responsibility of states, Martinus Nijhoff Publishers, Brill, The Hague, Boston, London, 1996.

DE HOOGH, A.J.J., Articles 4 and 8 of the 2001 ILC articles on State responsibility, in British Yearbook of International Law, 72, 2001, pp. 278ss.

DE LA RASILLA DEL MORAL, I., Nihil novum sub soli since the South West Africa cases? On ius standi, the ICJ and community interests, in International Community Law Review, 10, 2008, pp. 172ss.

DE OLIVERIA MAZZUOLI, B., Direito internacional pùblico, ed. RT, São Paulo, 2005.

DE PAUW, M., The inter-American Court of human rights and the imperative method of external referencing regional consensus v. universality, in Y. HAECK, O. RUIZ-CHIRIBOGA, V. CHERRERA, The inter-American Court of human rights: Theory and practice, present and future, ed. Intersentia, Antwerp, Oxford, 2016, pp. 4ss.156.

DE SENA, P., The notion of "contracting parties' jurisdiction" under Article 1 of the ECHR: Some marginal remarks on Nigro's paper, in Italian Yearbook of International Law, 20, 2010, pp. 75ss.

DE SENA, P., VITUCCI, M.C., The European Courts and the Security Council: Between dédoublement fonctionnel and balancing of values, in The European Journal of International Law, 20, 2009, pp. 193-228.

DE VATTEL, E., The law of nations or the principles of natural law applied to the conduct and to the affairs of nations and sovereigns, 1758, pag. 136.

DE VISSCHER, C., La responsabilitè des Etats, in Bibliotheca Visseriana, vol. II, ed. Brill, Leiden, 1924.

DE VISSCHER, C., Thèories et rèalitès en droit international public, ed. Pedone, Paris, 1970, pp. 312ss.

DE VRIES, S., BERNITZ, U., WEATHERILL, S., The EU Charter of fundamental rights as a binding instrument: Five years old and grooming, Hart Publishing, Oxford & Oregon, Portland, 2015, pp. 32ss.

DE WECK, D., Non refoulement under the European Convention of Human Rights and the UN Convention against torture, ed. Brill, The Hague, 2016, pp. 98ss.

DE WET, E., From Kadi to Nada: Judicial techniques favouring human rights over United Nations Security Council sanctions, in Chinese Journal of International Law, 12, 2013, pp. 787-808.

DE WET, E., The role of human rights in limiting the enforcement power of the Security Council: A principled view, in E. DE WET, A. NOLLAKAEMPER,

Review of the Security Council by member states, Oxford University Press, Oxford, 2003, pp. 7ss.

DE WET, E., The governance of Kosovo: Security Council Resolution 1244 and the establishment and functioning of EULEX, in American Journal of International Law, 103 (1), 2009, pp. 85ss.

DE WITTE, B., Article 53, in S. PEERS et al. (eds.), The EU Charter of Fundamental Rights, A Commentary, Hart Publishing, Oxford & Oregon, Portland, 2014, pp. 1523-1538.

DECAUX, E., La rèciprocitè en droit international, LGDJ, Paris, 1980.

DEKKER, I.F., WERNER, W.G., Governance and international legal theory, ed. Springer, Berlin, 2014.

DEL MAR, K., The International Court of Justice and standards of proof, in K. BANNELIER, T. CHRISTAKIS, S. HEATHCOTE, The ICJ and the evolution of international law. The enduring impact of the Corfu channel case, ed. Routledge, London & New York, 2012, pp. 108ss.

DELBRÜCK, J., Proportionality, Encyclopedia of Public International Law, 1984, pp. 396ss.

DELBRÜCK, J., War, effect on treaties, in R. BERNHARDT, Encyclopedia of Public International Law, Amsterdam, 2000, pp. 1371ss.

DELGADO CASTELEIRO, A., The international responsibility of the European Union-The EU perspective: Between pragmatism and proceduralization, in Cambridge Yearbook of European Legal Studies, 15, 2012-2013, pp. 564ss.

DEMAN, C., La cessarion de l'acte illicite, in Revue Belge de Droit International, 94, 1990, pp. 88ss.

DEN DEKKER, G., The law of arms control. International supervision and enforcement, Martinus Nijhoff Publishers, Dordrecht, 2001, pp. 50ss.

DENZA, E., Diplomatic law. A Commentary on the Vienna Convention on Diplomatic Relations, Oxford University Press, Oxford, 2008, pp. 189ss.

DENZA, E., Nationality and diplomatic protection, in Netherlands International Law Review, 65 (3), 2018, pp. 465ss.

DEPLANO, R., Assessing the role of resolutions in the ILC Draft conclusions on identification of customary law. Substantive and methodological issues, in International Organizations Law Review, 14 (2), 2017, pp. 224ss.

DERLÉN, M., LINDHOLM, J., The Court of Justice of the European Union. Multidiciplinary perspectives, Hart Publishing, Oxford & Oregon, Portland, 2018

DEUITCH, S.T., Putting the spotlight on "the terminator:" How the ICC prosecution of Bosco Ntaganda could reduce sexual violence during conflict, in William & Mary Journal of Women & Law, 23, 2016, pp. 656ss.

DEVISSER, M., Constitutional review in Europe: A comparative analysis, Hart Publishing, Oxford & Oregon, Portland, 2013.

DEYRA, M., Droit international public, LGDJ, Paris, 2007.

DEYRA, M., Droit international public, LGDJ, Paris, 2018.

DI STEFANO, F., Fait continu, fait composè et fait complexe dans le droit de la responsabilitè internationale, in Annuaire Français de Droit Internationl. 52, 2006, pp. 4ss.

DIACONU, I., La responsabilitè internationale des Etats. Quelques aspects rècents, in Revue Roumaine d'Études Internationales, 3, 1978, pp. 360ss.

DÍAZ BARRADO, C.M., El consentimiento, causa de exclusion de la ilicitud del uso de la forza, and derecho internacional, ed. Universidad de Zaragoza, Zaragoza, 1989, pp. 24ss.

DÍAZ-GONZÁLEZ, L., Fourth report on relations between states and international organizations (second part of the topic), UN Doc. A/CN/424/Corr.1., in Yearbook of International Law Commission, vol. II. pp. 153ss, par. 36.

DIEZ DE VELASCO, D., Instituciones de derecho internacional publico, ed. Tecno, Madrid, 2013, pp. 538ss.

DIJKSTRA, H., Policy-making in EU security and defense: An institutional perspective, ed. Palgrave Macmillan, Basingstoke, 2013.

DINSTEIN, Y., The interaction between customary international law and treaties, in Recueil des cours, ed. Brill, Bruxelles, vol. 322, 2006, pp. 244ss.

DINSTEIN, Y., The interaction between customary law and treaties, in Recueil des Cours, ed. Brill, The Hague, vol. 322, 2006, pp. 242ss.

DINSTEIN, Y., War, aggression and self-defence, Cambridge University Press, Cambridge, 1988.

DINSTEIN, Y., War, aggression and self-defence, Cambridge University Press, Cambridge, 2017, pp. 184ss.

DIPLA, H., La responsabilitè de l'Etat pour violation des droits de l'homme: problèmes d'imputation, ed. Pedone, Paris, 1994.

DIREK, Ö.F. Responsibility in peace support operations: Revisiting the proper test for attribution conduct and the meaning of the "effective control" standard, in Netherlands International Law Review, 61, 2014, pp. 7ss.

DISTEFANO, G., Fundamentals of public international law: A sketch of the international legal order, ed. Brill, The Hague, 2019, pp. 621ss.

DISTEFANO, G., La pratique subséquente des États parties à un traité, in Annuaire Français de Droit International, 40, 1994, pp. 42ss.

DIXON, M., MCCORQODALE, R., WILLIAMS, S., Cases and materials on international law, Oxford University Press, Oxford, 2011, pp. 41ss.

DJEFFAL, C., Static and evolutive treaty interpretation-a functional reconstruction, Cambridge University Press, Cambridge, 2016, pp. 165ss.

DJEFFAL, C., Static and evolutive treaty interpretation. A functional reconstruction, Cambridge University Press, Cambridge, 2015.

DODGE, W.S., Customary international law and the question of legitimacy, in Harvard Law Review Forum, 120 2007, pp. 19ss.

DOEHRING, K., Unlawful resolution of the Security Council and their legal consequence, in Max Planck Yearbook of United Nations Law, 2, 1997, pp. 92ss, C. GRAY, Application of the convention on the prevention and punishment of the crime of genocide (Bosnia and Herzeovina v. Yugoslavia (Serbia and Montenegro)), orders of provisional measures of 8 April 1993 and 13 September 1993, in International and Comprative Law Quarterly, 43, 1994, pp. 704ss.

DOMINICÉ, C., Attribution of conduct to multiples states and the implication of a state in the act of another state, in J. CRAWFORD, A. PELLET, S. OLLESON, The law of international responsibility, Oxford University Press, Oxford, 2010, pp. 282ss.

DOMINICÉ, C., La responsabilitè internationale des Nations Unies, in J.P. COT, A. PELLET, M. FORTEAU, La Charte des Nations Uines-commentaire aricle par article, Economica, Paris, 2005, pp. 142ss.

DOMINICÉ, C., La satisfaction en droit des gens, in B. DUTOIT, E. GRISEL, L'ordre juridique international entre tradition et innovation. Mèlanges Perrin: Recueil de travaux offerts à Georges Perrin, ed. PUF, Paris, 1997, pp. 350ss.

DOMINICÉ, C., Observations sur le contentieux des organizations internationales avec les personnes privées, in Annuaire Français de Droit International, 45, 1999, pp. 623ss.

DOMINICÉ, C., The international responsibility of states for breach of multilateral obligations, in The European Journal of International Law, 10, 1999, pp. 360ss.

DOMINICÉ, C., The international responsibility of the United Nations for injuries resulting from non-military enforcement measures, in M. RAGAZZI, Responsibility of international organizations. Essays in memory of Sir Ian Brownlie, Martinus Nijhoff Publishers, Leiden, Boston, 2013, pp. 367ss.

DON TAYLOR III, B,, Crimes against humanity in the Former Yugoslavia, in R. BELLELLI (ed. by), International criminal justice. Law and practice from the Rome Statute to its review, ed. Ashgate Publishing, Farnham, 2010, pp. 285-294.

DOPAGNE, F., La responsabilitè de l'Etat du fait des particuliers: les causes d'imputation par les articles sur la responsabilitè de l'Etat pour fait internationalement illicite, in Revue Belge de Droit International, 34, 2001, pp. 522ss.

ĐORĐESKA, M., The process of international law. Making: The relationship between the International Court of Justice and the International Law Commission, in International Comparative Law Review, 15 (1), 2015, pp. 14ss

DORMOY, D., Sanction ciblèes et respect des droits de l'homme: Quelques rèflections sur la responsabilitè des organizations internationales et de leurs ètats membres, in Revue Quebècoise de Droit International, 28 (2), 2015, pp. 8ss.

DÖRR, O., Article 31. General rule of interpretation, in O. DÖRR, K. SCHMALENBACH (a cura di), Vienna Convention on the Law of Treaties. A commentary, Springer, Heidelberg-New York 2012, pp. 536ss.

DOSWALD-BECK, L., Human rights in times of conflict and terrorism, Oxford University Press, Oxford, 2011, pp. 159ss.

DOSWALD-BECK, L., The legal validity of military intervention by invitation of the government, in British Yearbook of International Law, 56 (1), 1985, pp. 190ss.

DOWHERING, K., Unlawful resolutions of the Security Council and their legal consequences, in Max Planck Yearbook of United Nations Law, 1, 1997, pp. 92ss.

DOYLE, M., International ethics and the responsibility to protect, in International Studies Review, 13, 2011.

DOYLE, M.W., Dialectics of a global constitution. The struggle over the UN Charter, in European Journal of International Relations, 18 (4), 2011, pp. 602ss.

DOYLE, M.W., SAMBANIS, N., Making war and building peace: United nations peace operations, ed. Princeton, New Jersey, 2011.

DRAHOZAL, C.R., GIBSON, C.S., The Iran-US claims tribunal at 25, Oxford University Press, Oxford, 2007.

DRUMBL, M.A., Rule of law amid lawlessness: Counseling the accused in Rwanda's domestic genocide trials, in Columbia Human Rights Law Review, 29, 1998.

DUBOUT, E., Les règles ou principles inhèrented à l'identitè constitutionelle de la France: une supra-constituionnalitè, in Revue Française de Droit Constitionnel, 108, 2010, pp. 452ss.

DUDLEY, L., Until we achieve universal peace: Implications of the International Law Commission's Draft Articles on the "effects of armed conflict on treaties, in American University National Security Law Brief, 2016 (1), pp. 32ss.

DUFFY, H., Strategic human rights litigation: Understanding and maximizing impact, Bloomsbury Publishing, New York, 2018, pp. 154ss.

DUFFY, H., The war on terror and the framework of international law, Cambridge University Press, Cambridge, 2015.

DUGARD, J., Diplomatic protection, in Max Planck Encyclopedia of Public International Law, 2009.

DUMBERRY, P., The function and identification of rules of customary international law in international investment law, Cambridge University Press, Cambridge, 2018.

DUNBAR, N.H., The myth of customary international law, in the Australian Yearbook of International Law, 8, 1978-1980, pp. 4ss.

DUPUY, P.M., Action publique et crime international de l'Etat, in Annuaire Français de Droit International, 25, 1979, pp. 540ss.

DUPUY, P.M., A general stocktaing of the connections between the multilateral dimension of obligations and codification of the law of responsibility, in European Journal of International Law, 13, 2002, pp. 108ss.

DUPUY, P.M., Action publique et crime international de l'État. A propos de l'article 19 du projet de la commission du droit international sur la responsabilitè des États, in Annuaire Français de Droit International, 25, 1979, pp. 540ss.

DUPUY, P.M., Crime sans châtiment ou mission accomplie?, in Revue Gènèrale de Droit International Public, 111, 2007, pp. 247s

DUPUY, P.M., Droit des traitès, codification et responsabilitè internationale, in Annuaire Français de Droit International, 43, 1997, pp. 7ss.

DUPUY, P.M., FASSBENDER, B., SHAW, M.N., SOMMERMANN, K.P., Völkerrecht als Weltordnung. Festschrift für Christian Tomuschat, Engel Verlag, Kehl, 2006, pp. 308ss.

DUPUY, P.M., L'unitè de l'ordre juridique international. Cours général de droit international public, in Recueil des cours de l'Académie de Droit International de La Haye, ed. Brill, Brussels, vol. 296, 2002, pp. 413-427.

DUPUY, P.M., Le fait gènèrateur de la responsabilitè internationale des Etats, in Recueil des cours, ed. Brill, Bruxelles, 1984, pp. 12ss.

DUPUY, P.M., Obligations multilatèrales, droit impèratif et responsabilitè international de l'État, Paris, 2003, pp. 26ss.

DUPUY, P.M., Quarante ans de codification du droit de la responsabilitè intrnationale des Etats. Un bilan, in Revue Gènèrale de Droit International Public, 107, 2003, pp. 336ss.

DÜSTERHERF, I.K., GERLACH, A.I., The successes and failures of the interventions of the European Union, the African Union and neighbouring powers in Somalia, in Sicherheit und Frieden, 31 (1), 2013, pp. 19ss.

EAGLETON, C., International oganization and the law of responsability, in Recueil des cours, ed. Brill, Bruxelles, vol. 77, 1950, pp. 324ss.

EAGLETON, C., The responsibility of states in international law, New York University Press, New York, 1928, pp. 206ss.

ECKES, C., EU Counter-terrorist policies and fundamental rights, Oxford University Press, Oxford 2009, pp. 32ss.

ECKES, C., HOLLENBERG, S., Reconciling different legal spheres in theory and practice: Pluralism and constitutionalism in the cases of Al Jedda, Ahmed and Nada, in Maastricht Journal of European and Comparative Law, 20, 2013, pp. 218ss.

ECKHOUT, P.E., Opinion 2/13 on European union accession to the ECHR and judicial dialogue. Autonomy or autarchy, in Fordham International Law Journal, 38 (4), 2015, pp. 964ss.

EDWARDS, S.S.M., The European Court of Human Rights. Universalist aspirations of protection in the middle of the edge of occupation, in Denning Law Journal, 22, 2010, pp. 146ss.

EECKHOUT, P., The EU and its Member States in the WTO-Issues of responsibility, in L. BARTELS, F. ORTINO (eds.), Regional trade agreements and the WTO legal system, Oxford University Press, Oxford, 2006, pp. 450ss.

EECKHOUT, P., The EU's Common Foreign and Security Policy after Lisbon: From pillar talk to constitutionalism, in A. BIONDI, P. EECKHOUT, S. RIPLEY, (eds.), EU Law after Lisbon, Oxford University Press, Oxford, New York, 2012, pp. 265-291.

EGEDE, E., Politics of international law and international justice, Edinburgh University Press, Edinburgh, 2013, pp. 372ss.

ELAGAB, O.Y., The legality of non-forcible counter-measures in international law, Clarendon Press, Oxford, 1988.

ELGEBEILY, S., The rule of law in the UN security Council decision-making process. Turning the focus inwards, ed. Routledge, London & New York, 2017.

ELIAS, O., The relationship between general and particular customary international law, in African Journal of International & Comparative Law, 8, 1996, pp. 68ss.

ELLIS, M.S., DOUTRIAUX, Y., RYBACK, T.W., Justice and diplomacy resolving contradictions in diplomatic practice and international humanitarian law, Cambridge University Press, Cambridge, 2018.

ELLIS, M.S., The consequence of the Kosovo conflict on Southeastern Europe, in The International Lawyer, 34, 2000.

ELSDTRÖM, H., GYLLENSPORRE, D., Minding the gap between words and needs: Towards a new European Union strategy on security in, in European Foreign Affairs Review, 25, 2015, pp. 6ss.

EMANUELLI, C., Les conflits armès et le droit, ed. Wilson et Laflaeur, Montrèal, 2017.

ENGBERG, K., The European Union and military operations: A comparative analysis, ed. Routledge, London & New York, 2013, pp. 53ss.

ENGDAHL, O., Multinational peace operations forces involved in armed conflict: Who are the parties?, in K.M. LARSEN, C. GULDAHL COOPER, G. NYSTUEN, Searching for a "principle of humanity" in international humanitarian law, Cambridge University Press, Cambridge, 2013, pp. 256ss.

ENGEL, S., "Living" international constitutions and the world Court (the subsequent practice of international organs under their constituent instruments), in International and Comparative Law Quarterly, 16, 1967, pp. 867ss.

ENGEL, S., Procedures for the de facto revision of the Charter, in American Society International Law Proceedings, 59, 1965, pp. 110ss.

ENGEL, S., The changing Charter of the United Nations, in G.W. KEETON, G. SCHWARZENBERGER, The Yearbook of World Affairs, ed. Stevens, London, 1953, pp. 72ss.

EPINEY, A., Nachbarrechtliche Pflichten im internationalen Wasserecht und Implikationen von "Drittstaaten," in Archiv des Völkerrechts, 39, 2001, pp. 49ss.

EPPS, V., GRAHAM, L., Examples and explanations for international law, Wolters Kluwer Law, Alphen aan den Rijn, 2014.

ESER, A., Mental elements-Mistake of fact and mistake of law, in A. CASSESE, P. GAETA, G.R.W.D JONES (eds.), The Rome Statute of the International Criminal Court: A Commentary, Oxford University Press, Oxford, 2002, pp. 890ss.

ESTREICHER, S., Rethinking the binding effect of customary international law, in Virginia Journal of International Law, 44, 2003, pp. 6ss.

EUSTATHIADES, C.T., Les sujets du droit international et la responsabilitè internationale. Nouvelles tendences, in Recueil des cours, ed. Brill, Bruxelles, vol. 84, 1953, pp. 460ss.

EVANS, M., International law, Oxford University Press, Oxford, 2014

EVANS, M., KOUTRAKOS, P., (eds.), The international responsibility of the European Union. European and international perspectives, Hart Publishing, Oxford & Oregon, Portland, 2013, pp. 6ss.

EVANS, M.D., International law, Oxford University Press, Oxford, 2018, pp. 103ss.

EVERILL, B., KAPLAN, J., The history and practice of humanitarian intervention and aid in Africa, ed. Springer, Berlin, 2013.

FAHRON-HUSSEY, C., Military crisis management operations by NATO and the European Union. The decision making process, ed. Spinger, Berlin, 2018.

FALK, R., The Iran hostage crisis: Easy answers and hard questions, in American Journal of International Law, 74 (2), 1980, pp. 411ss.

FARALL, J., Strengthening the rule of law through the UN Security Council, ed. Routledge, London & New York, 2016.

FARRAL, J.M., United Nations sanctions and the rule of law, Cambridge University Press, Cambridge, 2009, pp. 6ss.

FASOLI, E., Declaratory jurisdiction and official apologies as forms of reparation for the non-material damage suffered by the state. The Djibouti-France case, in The Law and Practice of International Courts and Tribunals, 7, 2008, pp. 178ss.

FAUCHALD, O.K., The legal reasoning of ICSID Tribunals-An empirical analysis, in European Journal of International Law, 2, 2008, pp. 302ss.

FEICHTER, L., Waiver, in Max Planck Encyclopedia of Public International Law, 2008.

FELDER, A., Die Beihilfe im Rect der völkerrechtlichen Staatenverantwortlichkeit, Shultheness, Zurich, 2007.

FELDMAN, A.M., Evolving treaty obligations: A proposal for analyzing subsequent practice derived from WTO Dispute Settlement, in New York University Journal of International Law & Politics, 41, 2009, pp. 656ss

FENWICK, G., International law, Apleton Century Crofts inc., New York, 1965, pp. 328ss.

FERNÁNDEZ ARRIBAS, G., International responsibility of the European Union for the activities of its military operations. The issue of effective control, in Spanish Yearbook of International Law, 18, 2013-2014, pp. 58ss.

FERRARI BRAVO, L., Mèthods de recherche de la coutume internationale dans la pratique des États, in Recueil des cours, ed. Brill, Bruxelles, vol. 192, 1985, pp. 247ss.

FERRER MAC-GREGOR, A.E., Conventionality control and the new doctrine of the inter-American Court of Human Rights, in AJIL Unbound, 109, 2015, pp. 95ss.

FERSTMAN, C., International organizations and the fight for accountability. The remedies and reparations gap, Oxford University Press, Oxford, 2017, pp. 207ss

FIDELL, E.R., HILLMAN, E.L., SULLIVAN, D.H., Military justice: Cases and materials, Lexis Nexis, New York, 2012.

FIDLER, D.P., Challenging the classical concept of custom: Perspectives on the future of customary international law, in German Yearbook of International Law, 39, 1996, pp. 198ss.

FITSCHEN, T., Inventing the rule of law for the United Nations, in Max Planck United Nations Yearbook, 12, 2008, pp. 348ss.

FITZMAURICE, G., Environmental protection and the International Court of Justice, in LOWE, G. FITMAURICE, Fifty years of the International Court of Justice. Essays in Honour of Sir Robert Jennings, Cambridge University Press, Cambridge, 1996, pp. 294ss.

FITZMAURICE, G.G., The juridical clauses of peace treaties, in Recueil des cours, ed. Brill, Bruxelles, vol. 73, 1948, pp. 308ss

FITZMAURICE, G.G., The law and procedure of the International Court of

Justice, in British Yearbook of International Law, 23, 1952, pp. 28ss.

FITZMAURICE, M., ELIAS, O., MERKOURIS, P., Treaty interpretation and the Vienna Convention on the Law of Treaties: 30 Years on, Martinus Nijhoff Publishers, Leiden/Boston, 2010.

FITZMAURICE, M., International liability for injurious consequences of acts not prohibited by international law, in Polish Yearbook of International Law, 24, 1999-2000, pp. 48ss.

FITZMAURICE, M., SAROOSHI, D., Issues of state responsibility before international judicial institutions, Oxford University Press, Oxford, 2004.

FITZMAURISCE, M., Third parties and the law of treaties, in Max Planck Yearbook of United Nations Law, 2002, pp. 40ss.

FLAUSS, J., (a cura di), La protection diplomatique. Mutations contemporaines et pratiques nationales, ed. Bruylant, Bruxelles, 2003.

FLECK, D., The handbook of humanitarian law in armed conflicts, Oxford University Press, Oxford, 1995, pp. 40ss.

FLECK, D., The law of non-international armed conflict, in D. FLECK (ed. by), The Handbook of International humanitarian law, Oxford University Press, Oxford, 2013, pp. 581-610.

FLETCHER, G., Rethinking criminal law, Oxford University Press, Oxford, 2000, pp. 635ss.

FOCARELLI, C., Ahead to the past? Responsibility to protect and the global system, in Groningen Journal of International Law, 1, 2012, pp. 4ss.

FOCARELLI, C., Common article 1 of the 1949 Geneva Conventions: A soap bubble?, in European Journal of International Law, 21, 2010, pp. 126ss.

FOCARELLI, C., International law as social construct. The truggle for global justice, Oxford University Press, Oxford, 2012, pp. 178ss.

FOLEY, C., UN peacekeeping operations and the protection of civilians saving succeeding generations, Cambridge University Press, Cambridge, 2017.

FOLK, R.A., Toward authoritativeness: The ICJ ruling on Israel's security wall, in American Journal of International Law, 99 (1), 2005, pp. 44ss.

FORD, C.M., WILLIAMS, W., Complex battlespaces: The law of armed conflict and the dynamics of modern warfare, Oxford University Press, Oxford, 2019.

FORLATI, S., The International Court of Justice. An arbitral tribunal or a judicial body?, ed. Springer, Berlin, 2014, pp. 148ss.

FORLIN, K., The accountability of armed groups under human rights law, Oxford University Press, Oxford, 2017.

FORREST, C., International law and the protection of cultural heritage, ed. Routledge, London & New York, 2012, pp. 51ss.

FORTEAU, M., Le droit applicable en matiere de droits de l'homme aux administrations territoriales gerees par des organizations internationales, in

S.F.D.I., La soumission des organizations internationales aux normes internationales relatives aux droits de l'homme. Journée d'études de Strasbourg, ed. Pedone, Paris, 2009, pp. 14ss.

FORTEAU, M., Régime général de responsabilité ou lex specialis?, in Revue Belge de Droit International, 117 (1), 2013, pp. 147-160.

FORTIN, K., The accountability of armed groups under human rights law, Oxford University Press, Oxford, 2017.

FRANCIONI, F., Multilateralism à la carte: The limits to unilateral withholdings of assessed contributions to the UN budget, in European Journal of International Law, 11 (1), 2000, pp. 43ss.

FRANCK, T.M., Preemption, prevention and anticipatory self-defence: New law regarding recourse to force?, in Hastings International and Comprative Law Review, 27, 2004, pp. 426ss.

FRANK, D., Verantwortlichkeit für die Verletzung der Europäischen Menshenrechtkonvention durch internationale Organizationen, Helbing & Lichtenhahn, Basel, 1999.

FREEDMAN, R., UN Immunity or Impunity: A human rights based challenge, in European Journal of International Law, 29 (4), 2014, pp. 4ss.

FREEMAN, A.V., The international responsibility of states, ed. Longman, London, 1970.

FRIEDE, W., Das Estoppel-Prinzip im Völkerrecht, in Zeitschrift für ausländisches Recht und Völkerrecht, 5, 1935, pp. 545ss.

FRIEDMAN, W., The changing structure of international law, Columbia University Press, Columbia, Princeton, 1973, pp. 198ss.

FRIEDMANN, W., The changing structure of international law, Stevens & Sons, London, 1964, pp. 10ss.

FRÖHLICH, M., WILLIAMS, A., The UN Secretary General and the Security Council. A dynamic relationship, Oxford University Press, Oxford, 2018.

FROWEIN, J.A., Recognition, in Max Planck Encyclopedia of Public International Law, 2010, par. 1

FRY, J.D., Coercion, causation and the fictional elements of indirect state responsibility, in Vanderbilt Journal of Transnational Law, 40, 2007, pp. 631ss.

FUENTES, I., Normative plurality in international law. A theory of the determination of applicable rules, ed. Springer, Berlin, 2016, pp. 234ss.

FURGLER, K., Grundprobleme der völkerrechtlichen Verantwortlichkeit der Staaten, Mohr Siebeck, Zürich, 1948, pp. 13ss.

GAETA, P., Gènocide d'Etat et responsabilitè penale individuale, in Revue Gènèrale de Droit International Public, 111, 2007, pp. 278ss.

GAETA, P., The UN genocide convention. A commentary, Oxford University

Press, Oxford, 2009, pp. 283ss.

GAJA, G., A "new" Vienna Convention on treaties between states and international organizations: A critical commentary, in British Yearbook of International Law, 58, 1987, pp. 264ss.

GAJA, G., I have been specially affected when its nationals' human rights are infringed, in L.C. VORAH, Man's inhumanity to man. Essays in international law in honor of Antonio Cassese, Kluwer Law International, The Hague, 2003, pp. 394ss.

GAJA, G., Is a State specially affected when its nationals' human rights are infringed?, L.C. VORAH, Man's inhumanity to man. Essays in international law in honour of Antonio Cassese, Kluwer Law International, The Hague, 2003, pp. 376ss.

GAJA, G., Primary and secondary rules in the international law of state responsibility, in Rivista di Diritto Internazionale, 2014, pp. 982ss.

GAJA, G., Should all references to international disappear from the ILC draft articles on state responsibility?, in European Journal of International Law, 10 (2), 1999, pp. 366ss.

GAJA, G., Some reflections on the European Community international responsibility, in H.G. SCHERMERS, T. HEUCKLES, P. MEAD, Non-contractual liability of the European Communities, ed. Brill, Dordrecht, 1988, pp. 168ss.

GAJA, G., The concept of an injured state, in J. CRAWFORD, A. PELLET, S. OLLESON, The law of international responsibility, Oxford University Press, Oxford, 2010, pp. 942ss.

GAJA, G., The protection of general interest in the international community. General course on public international law, in Recueil des cours, ed. Brill, Bruxelles, vol. 364, 2012, pp. 10ss.

GAJA, R., Sould all references to international crimes disappear form the ILC draft articles on state responsibility?, in European Journal of International Law, 12, 1999, pp. 366ss.

GALBRAITH, J., What should the restatement (fourth) say about treaty interpretation?, in Brigham Young University Law Review, 2016, pp. 1467ss.

GALLAS, W., Strafbares Unterlassen im Fall einer Selbsttötung, in Juristen Zeitung, 15, 1960, pp. 686ss.

GANGALE, T., How high the sky? The definition and territorial airspace in international law, ed. Brill/Nijhoff, Leiden/Boston, 2018.

GARBEN, S., GOVAERE, I., The division of competences between the European Union and the member states. Reflection on the past, the present and the future, Hart Publishing, Oxford & Oregon, Portland, 2017.

GARCIA AMADOR, F.V., State responsibility in the light of the new trends of international law, in American Journal of International Law, 49, 1955, pp.

347ss.

GARCIA AMADOR, F.V., State responsibility. Some new problems, in Recueil des cours, ed. Brill, Bruxelles, vol. 94, 1958, pp. 370ss.

GARCIA, T., La reconnaissance du statut d'Etats à des entitès constestèes: Approches de droit international, règional et interne, ed. Pedone, Paris, 2018, pp. 64ss.

GARCIN, M., The haitian cholera victims complaints against the United Nations, in Zeitschrift für ausländisches öffentliches Recht und Völkerrecht, 75, 2015, pp. 680ss.

GARDAM, J., The contribution of the International Court of Justice to international humanitarian law, in Leiden Journal of International Law, 14, 2001, pp. 350ss.

GARDINER, R., The Vienna Convention rules on treaty interpretation, in D.B. HOLLIS, The Oxford guide to treaties, Oxford University Press, Oxford, 2012, pp. 475-48.

GARDINER, R., Treaty interpretation, Oxford University Press, Oxford, 2008, pp. 211ss.

GARVEY, J., Nuclear weapons counter proliferation. A new grand bargain, Oxford University Press, Oxford, 2013, pp. 58ss.

GASSER, H.P., International humanitarian law: An introduction, in H. HAUG (ed. by), Humanity for all. The International Red Cross and red crescent movement, Paul Haupt, Berne, 1993, pp. 510ss.

GATTINI, A., A return ticket to communitarisme, please, in European Journal of International Law, 13, 2002, pp. 1182ss.

GATTINI, A., Breach of the obligation to prevent and reparation thereof in the ICJ's genocide judgment, in European Journal of International Law, 18, 2007, pp. 696ss.

GATTINI, A., La notion de faute à la lumière du projet de convention de la commission du droit international sur la responsabiloitè internationale, in European Journal of International Law, 3, 1992, pp. 254ss.

GATTINI, A., Les obligations des États en droit d'invoquer la responsabilitè d'un autre État pour violations graves d'obligations dècoulant de normes impèratives du droit international gènèral, in P.M. DUPUY, Obligations multilatèrales. Droit impèratif et responsabilitè internationale, ed. Pedone, Paris, 2003.

GATTINI, A., Smoking/no smoking: Some remarks on the current place of fault in the ILC Draft articles on state responsibility, in European Journal of International Law, 10, 1999, pp. 398ss.

GATTINI, A., Zufall und force majeure im System der Staatenvernatwortlichket anhand der ILC-Kodifikationsarbeit, Duncker & Humblot, Berlin, 1991.

GAZZINI, T., Personality of international oganizations, in J. KLABBERS, Å.

WALLENDAHL, Research handbook on the law of international oganizations, Edward Elgar Publishers, Cheltenham, 2001, pp. 34ss.

GEERT, J., KNOOPS, J., Defenses in contemporary international law, The Martinus Nijhoff, The Hague, 2008, pp. 7ss.

GEISER, H.J., Les effets des accords conclus par les organizations internationales, ed. PeterLang, Berne, Las Vegas, 1977, pp. 140ss

GENONI, M.M., Die Notwehr im Völkerrecht, Schulthess, Zürich, 1987.

GENSER, J., STAGNO UGARTE, B., The UN security Council in the age of human rights, Cambridge University Press, Cambridge, 2014.

GÉRARD, P., VERRIJDT, W., Belgian Constitutional Court adopts national identity discourse: Belgian Constitutional Court n. 62/2016, 28 April 2016, in European Constitutional Law Review, 13, 2017, pp. 182ss.

GERSON, A., Peace building: The private sector's role, in American Journal of International Law, 95, 2001.

GESLIN, A., Rèflexions sur la repartition de la responsabilitè entre l'organization internationale et ses États membres, in Revue Gènèrale de Droit International Public, 109, 2005, pp. 570ss.

GIEGERICH, T., Retorsion, in Max Planck Encycopedia of Public International Law, 2011, par. 4.

GIEGERICH, T., Wege zu einer vertieften Gemeinsamen Außen-und Sicherheits-politik: Reparatur von Defiziten als "kleine Lösung," in S. KADEBACH, Die Europäische Union am Scheideweg: mehr oder weniger Europa?, ed. Nomos, Baden-Baden, 2015, pp. 138ss.

GIL, A.G., Mens rea in co-perpetration and indirect perpetration according to article 30 of the Rome Statute. Arguments against punishment for excesses committed by the agent or the co-perpetrator, in International Criminal Law Review, 14, 2014, pp. 87ss.

GILL, T., FLECK, D., (eds.), Oxford University Press's handbook of the international law of military operations, Oxford, 2010.

GILL, T.D., FLECK, D., The handbook of the international law of military operations, Oxford University Press, Oxford, 2011, pp. 523ss.

GINIFER, j., Beyond the emergency: Development within UN peace missions, Frank Cass, London, Portland, OR, 1997, pp. 85ss.

GINTHER, C., ZEMANEK, K., Völkerrecht zwischen normativen Anspruch und politischer Realität. Festschrift für Karl Zemanek zum 65. Geburtstag, Duncker & Humblot, Berlin, 1994, pp. 320ss.

GINTHER, K., international organizations, responsibility, in Ecyclopedia of Public International Law, 1983, pp. 162ss.

GLAD, B., DOLAN, V., Striking first. The pre-emption and preventive war doctrines and the reshaping of US foreign policy, ed. Springer, Berlin, 2016.

GLANVILLE, L., The responsibility to protect beyond borders, in Human Rights Law Review, 12, 2012, pp. 4ss.

GLASER, J., Abhandlungen aus dem Österreichischen Strafrecht, Verlag von Tendler & Comp., Wien, 1958, pp. 298ss.

GOLDIE, L.F.E., Liability for damage and the progressive development of international law, in International and Comparative Law Quarterly, 14, 1965, pp. 1190ss.

GOLDSMITH, J.L., POSNER, E.A., A theory of customary international law, University of Chicago Law School, John M. Olin Law & Economics Working Paper No. 63, 2000, pp. 1114ss.

GOLDSTONE, R.J., HAMILTON, R.J., Bosnia v. Serbia: Lessons from the encounter of the International Court of Justice with the International Criminal Tribunal for the Former Yugoslavia, in Leiden Journal of International Law, 21, 2008, pp. 96ss.

GOMEZ-ROBLEDO VERDUZCO, A., Concepto de responsabilidad internacional del Estado segùn Hans Kelsen, in Boletin Mexicano de Derecho Comparado, 62, 1985, pp. 66ss.

GONZÁLEZ-SALZBERG, D., The effectiveness of the inter-American human rights system. A study of the American States compliance with the judgments of the inter-American Court of human rights, in Revista Colombiana de Derecho Internacional, 15, 2015, pp. 116ss.

GOODRICH, L.M., HAMBRO, E.I., Charter of the United Nations, Columbia University Press, Boston, 1949, pp. 153ss.

GORDILLO, L.I., Interlocking constitutions: towards an interordinal theory of national European and UN law, Hart Publishing, Oxford & Oregon, Portland, 2012.

GORDON, G., The oil platforms opinion: An elephant in the eye of a needle, in Amsterdam Law Forum, 1 (2), 2009.

GORDON, G.S., Hate speech and persecution. A contextual approach, in Vanderbilt Journal of Transnational Law, 46, 2013, pp. 332ss.

GOULD, W.L., An introduction to international law, ed. Harper, New York, 1957, pp. 508ss.

GOUNELLE, M., Quelques remarques sur la notion de crime international et sur l'èvolution de la responsabilitè internationale de l'Etat, in Mèlanges Reuter: Le droit international: Unitè ed diversitè, ed. Pedone, Paris, 1980.

GOURGOURINIS, A., General/particular international law and primary/secondary rules: Unitary terminology of a fragmented system, in European Journal of International Law, 21, 2011, pp. 994ss.

GOUVEINHES, F., Retour sur un clasique: Le plaidioiries de Paul Reuter dans l'affaire du Temple de Prèah Vichear (Cambodge v. Thailand), in Revue Gènèrale de Droit International Public, 116 (2), 2012, pp. 468ss.

GOW, J., KERR, R., PAJIC, Z., Prosecuting war crimes, lessons and legacies of the International Criminal Tribunal for the Former Yugoslavia, ed. Routledge, Abington & New York, 2014.

GOWLLAND-DEBBAS, V., Collective responses to illegal acts in international law. United Nations action in the question of Southern Rhodesia, Martinus Nijhoff Publishers, Dordrecht, 1990, pp. 290ss.

GRABENWARTER C., European Convention on human rights: ECHR, C.H. Beck, München, 2014.

GRABITZ, E., Der Grundsatz der Verhältnismäßigkeit in der Rechtsprechung des Bundesverfassungsgerichts, in Archiv des öffentliches Recht, 98 (4), 1973, pp. 568ss.

GRAEFRATH, B., Complicity in the law of state responsibility, in Revue Belge de Droit International, 29, 1996, pp. 370ss.

GRAEFRATH, B., Die völkerrechtliche Verantwortlichkeit der Staaten-ein wichtiges Instrument zur Durchsetzung des Völkerrechts, in Neue Justiz, 1980, pp. 252ss.

GRAEFRATH, B., OESER, E., STEINIGER, P.A., Völkerrechtliche Verantwortlichkeit der Staaten, Duncker & Humblot, Berlin, 1977, pp. 310ss.

GRAEFRATH, B., OESER, E., Teilnahmeformen bei der völkerrechtlichen Verantwortlichkeit, in Staat und Recht, 1980, pp. 445ss.

GRAEFRATH, B., Responsibility and damage caused. Relationship between responsibility and damage, in Recueil des cours, ed. Brill, Bruxelles, vol. 185, 1984, pp. 62ss.

GRAMLICH, L., Diplomatic protection against acts of intergovernmental organs, in German Yearbook of International Law, 27, 1984, pp. 396ss.

GRAY, C., Is there an international law of remedies?, in British Yearbook of International Law, 56, 1985, pp. 27ss.

GRAY, C., International law and the use of force, Oxford University Press, Oxford, 2000, pp. 144ss.

GRAY, C., Judicial remedies in international law, Oxford University Press, Oxford, 1987, pp. 6ss.

GREEN, J.A., WATERS, C.P.M., Adjudicating international human rights. Essays in honour of Sandy Ghandi, Martinus Nijhoff Publishers, The Hague, 2014.

GREEN, L., The raw materials of international law, in International & Comparative Law Quarterly, 29, 1980, pp. 188ss.

GREEN, N.A., International law. Law of peace, Macdonald & Evans, London, 1973, pp. 22ss.

GREENWOOD, C., Customary law status of the 1997 Additional Protocols, in A.J.M. DELISSEN, G.J. TANJA (ed. by), Humanitarian law of armed conflict, Martinus Nijhoff Publishers, The Hague, 1991, pp. 93ss.

GREENWOOD, C., International humanitarian law and United Nations military operations, in Yearbook of International Humanitarian Law, 1, 1998, pp. 18ss.

GREENWOOD, C., Scope of application of humanitarian law, in D. FLECK (ed), The Handbook of international humanitarian law, Oxford University Press, Oxford, 2008, pp. 45ss.

GRENFELL, K., Partnerships in UN Peacekeeping, in International Organizations Law Review, 13, 2016, pp. 55-73.

GREY, C.D., Remedies in international law, Oxford University Press, Oxford, 1990.

GREY, R., SHEPHERD, L.J., Stop rape now?: Masculinity, responsibility, and conflict-related sexual violence, in Men & Masculinities, 15, 2012, pp. 117ss.

GRILLER, S., The Court of Justice and the common foreign and security policy, in CJEU, The Court of Justice and the construction of Europe, T.M.C. Asser Press, Bruxelles, 2013, pp. 675ss.

GROUSSOT, X., LOCK, T., PECH, L., Adhésion de l'Union européenne à la Convention européenne des droit de l'homme: Analyse juridique du projet d'accord d'adhésion du 14 octobre 2001, in Fondation Robert Schuman/Question d'Europe, n. 218 (7 November 2011), pp. 5ss.

GROVER, L., Interpreting crimes in the Rome statute of the International Criminal Court, Cambridge University Press, Cambridge, 2014, pp. 426ss.

GROVER, L., UN human rights treaty bodies law and legitimacy, Cambridge University Press, Cambridge, 2012.

GROVER, S., The responsibility to protect: Perspectives on the concepts meaning, property application and value, ed. Routledge, London & New York, 2018.

GUILD, E., BIGO, D., GIBNEY, M., Extraordinary rendition: Addressing the challenges of accountability, ed. Routledge, London & New York, 2018.

GUTIÉRREZ ESPADA, C., La contramedidas de Estados "terceros" for the violation of the international laws, in Anuario Argentino de Derecho Internacional, 11, 2001-2002, pp. 30ss.

GUTIERREZ ESPADA, C., La responsabilidad internacional de las organizaciones internacionales a la luz del proyecto definitive de artículos de la Comisión de Derecho Internacional (2011), ed. Comares, Granada, 2012.

GUZMAN, A.T., MEYER, T.L., Customary international law in the 21st century, in R. A. MILLER, R. M. BRATSPIES, Progress in international law, Martinus Nijhoff Publishers, Leiden/Boston, 2008, pp. 199ss.

HACHEZ, N., WOUTERS, J., Promoting the rule of law: A benchmarks approach, KU Leuven Working paper No. 105, April 2013.

HAECK, Y., RUIZ CHIRIBOGA, O., HERRERA, C., The inter-American Court of human rights: Theory and practice, present and future, ed. Intersentia, Antwerp, Oxford, 2016, 46ss.

HAFNER, G., Is the topic of responsibility of international organizations ripe for codification? Some critical remarks, in U. FASTENRATH et al. (ed. by), From bilateralism to community interest: Essays in honour of Judge Bruno Simma, Oxford University Press, Oxford University Press, Oxford, 2011, pp. 697ss.

HAFNER, G., Liability and compensation: "civil liability" and other forms of transnational accountability, in Yearbook of International Environment Law, 12, 1991, pp. 92ss.

HAFNER, G., Subsequent agreements and practice: Between interpretation, informal modification, and formal amendment, in G. NOLTE, Treaties and subsequent practice, Oxford University Press, Oxford, 2013, pp. 106ss.

HAHN, M.J., SCHUSTER, G., Le droit des Etats membres de se prèvaloir en justice d'un accord liant la Communqutè: l'invocabilitè du GATT dans l'affaire Rèpublique fèdèrale d'Allemagne contre Conseil de l'Unione europèenne, in Revue Gènèrale de Droit International Public, 99, 1995, pp. 378ss.

HAJJAMI, N., Que signifie l'expression "prendre toutes les mesures nécessaires" dans la pratique du Conseil de Sécurité des Nations Unies?, in Revue Belge de Droit International, 46, 2013, pp. 232ss.

HALBERSTRAM, D., "It's the autonomy, stupid!. A modest defense of opinion 2/13 on EU accession to the ECHR, and the way forward, in German Law Journal, 16, 2015, pp. 114ss

HALDEMANN, F., UNGER, T., The United Nations principles to combat impunity: A commentary, Oxford University Press, Oxford, 2018, pp. 32ss.

HALLESKOV STORGAARD, L.H., EU law autonomy versus European fundamental rights protection-On Opinion 2/13 on EU accession to the ECHR, in Human Rights Law Review, 15, 2015, pp. 485.

HALLESLOV STORGAARD, L., European Union law autonomy versus European fundamental rights protection. On opinion 2/13 on EU accession to the ECHR, in Human Rights Law Review, 15 (3), 2015, pp. 487ss.

HALMAI, G., The hungarian national(ist) constitutional identity, in Quaderni Costituzionali, 2017, pp. 152ss.

HAMONIC, A., Les relations entre l'Union europèenne et l'ONU dans le domaine de la gestion des crises, ed. Bruylant, Bruxelles, 2018.

HANDL, G., Liability as an obligation established by a primary rule of international law, in Netherlands Yearbook of International Law, 16, 1985, pp. 62ss.

HAPPOLD, M., EDEN, P., Economic sanctions and international law, Bloomsbury Publishing, New York, 2016.

HARAMOTO, S., SAKAI, H., SHIBATA, A., L'être situè. Effectiveness and purposes of international law. Essays in honour of Professor Ryuichi Ida, ed.

Brill, Bruxelles, 2015, pp. 223ss.

HARLOW, C., LEINO, P., DELLA CANNANEA, G., Research handbook on EU administrative law, Edward Elgar Publishers, 2017. pp. 453ss.

HARRIS, C., Extraterritorial application of human rights treaties, Oxford University Press, Oxford, 2012.

HARRIS, D., O'BOYLE, M., WARBRICK, C., Law of the European Convention on Human rights, Oxford University Press, Oxford, 2014, pp. 372ss.

HART, H.L.A., HONORÉ, T., Causation on the law, Oxford University Press, Oxford, 1985, pp. 438ss.

HART, H.L.A., RAZ, J., The concept of law, Clarendon Press, London, 1961, pp. 95ss.

HARTKAMP, A., SIBURGH, C., DEVROE, W., Cases, materials and text on European Union law and private law, Hart Publishing, Oxford & Oregon, Portland, 2017, pp. 282ss.

HARTWIG, M., Die Haftung der Mitgliedstaaten für internationale Organizationen, ed. Springer, Berlin, 1993, pp. 290ss.

HARTWIG, M., International organizations or institutions. Responsibility and liability, in Max Planck Encyclopedia of Public International Law, 2013, pp. 4, par. 18.

HARTWIG, M., International Organizations or institutions. Responsibility and liability, in Max Planck Encyclopedia of Public International Law, 2011.

HATJE, A., TERHECHTE, J.P., MÜLLER-GRAFF, P.C., Europarechtswissenschaft, ed. Nomos, Baden-Baden, 2018.

HEATHCOTE, G., OTTO, D., Rethinking peacekeeping gender equality and collective security, ed. Springer, Berlin, 2014.

HEHIR, A., The responsibility to protect: Rhetoric, reality and the future of humanitarian intervention, Palgrave MacMillian, London, 2012.

HELFER, L.R., WUERTH, I.B., Customary international law: An instrument choice respective, in Michigan Journal of International Law, 37, 2016, pp. 564ss.

HELGESON, E., LAUTERPACHT, E., Iran-US claim tribunal, Cambridge University Press, Cambridge, 2000.

HELLER, K.J., Specially-affected States and the formation of custom, in American Journal of International Law, 112 (2), 2018, pp. 194ss.

HELLER, K.J., The Rome Statute of the International Criminal Court, in K.J. HELLER, D. DUBBER (eds.), The handbook of comparative criminal law, Stanford Law Books, Stanford, 2011, pp. 597ss.

HELMKE, B., Under attack: Challenges to the rules governing the international use of law, ed. Routledge, London & New York, 2016.

HENCKAERTS, J.M., DOSWALD-BECK, L., Customary international

humanitarian law, Cambridge University Press, Cambridge, 2005, pp. 510ss.

HENCKAERTS, J.M., DOSWALD-BECK, L., Customary international humanitarian law. Vol. I: Rules, Cambridge University Press, Cambridge, 2009.

HENDERSON, C., Commissions of inquiry. Problems and prospects, Bloomsbury Publishing, New York, 2017.

HENNEBEL, L., The inter-American Court of human rights: The Ambassador of universalism, in Quebec Journal of International Law, 57, 2011, pp. 58ss.

HENQUET, T., international organizations in the Netherlands: Immunity from the jurisdiction of the Dutch courts, in Netherlands International Law Review, 49, 2010, pp. 267ss.

HENRY, E., Alleged acquiescence of the international community to revisionist claims of international customary law (with special reference to the jus contra bellum regime), in Melbourne Journal of International Law, 18, 2017, pp. 264ss.

HERDEGEN, M., Interpretation in international law, in Max Planck Encyclopedia of International Law, 2010.

HERDEGEN, M., Principles of international economic law, Oxford University Press, Oxford, 2016, pp. 458ss.

HERDEGEN, M., The insolvency of international organizations and the legal position of creditors. Some observations in the light of the international Tin Council crisis, in Netherlands International Law Review, 37, 1988, pp. 142ss.

HERDEGEN, M., Völkerecht, C.H. Beck, München, 2019.

HERNANDEZ, G.I., Beyond the control paradigm? International responsibility and the European Union, in The Cambridge Yearbook of European Legal Studies, 15, 2012-2013, pp. 644ss.

HERZBERG, R.D., Die Unterlassung im Strafrecht und das Garantenprinzip, De Gruyter, Berlin, New York, 1972, pp. 2.

HERZOG, P.E., WESER, M., Civil procedure in France, ed. Springer, Berlin, 2014, pp. 162ss.

HERZOG, S., Revisiting the estonian cyber attacks: Digital threats and multinational responses, in Journal of Strategic Security, 4, 2011, pp. 52ss.

HESSBRUEGGE, J.A., The European Court of Human Rights: Catan and others v. Moldova and Russia, in International Legal Materials, 52 (1), 2013, pp. 219ss.

HEUSA VINAIXA, R., Algunas consideraciones sobre el Convenio de Viena de 1986 sobre Tratados celebrados entre Estados y organizaciones internaconales o entre organizaciones internacionales, in Revista Española de Derecho Internacional, 41, 1989, pp. 65ss.

HEXNER, E., Teleological interpretation of basic instruments of public international organizations, in S. ENGEL, R.A. MÉTALL, Law, State, and international legal order: Essays in honor of Hans Kelsen, University of Tennessee Press, Knoxville, 1964, pp. 120ss.

HIGGINS, R., Problems and process. International law and how we use it, in Oxford University Press, Oxford, 1994, pp. 47ss.

HIGGINS, R., WEBB, P., AKANDE, D., SLOAN, J., SIVAKUMARAN, S., Oppenheim's international law: United Nations, Oxford University Press, Oxford, 2017.

HILPOLD, P., (ed.), Responsibility to protect (R2P): A new paradigm of international law?, ed. Brill Martinus Nijhoff Publishers, Leiden-Boston, 2015.

HIRSCH, M., The responsibility of international organizations toward third parties. Some basic principles, Martinus Nijhoff Publishers, Dordrecht, Boston, London, 1995, pp. 102ss.

HLAVAC, M., Less than a State, more than an international organizations: The sui generis nature of the European Union, in MPRA paper, 2010.

HOFFMANN, A., Zur Unterscheidung Verbrechen und Delikt im Bereich der Staatenvernatworlichkeit, in Zeitschrift für ausländisches Recht und Völkerrecht, 45, 1985, pp. 196ss.

HOFFMANN, J., NOLLKAEMPER, A., (eds.), Responsibility to protect: From principle to practice, Pallas, Amsterdam, 2012.

HOFFMEISTER, F., Bosphorus Hava Yollari Turizm ve Ticaret Anonim Sirket v. Ireland. App. No. 45036/98, in American Journal of international law, 100, 2006, pp. 447ss.

HOFFMEISTER, F., Litigating against the European Union and its Member States-Who responds under the ILC's Draft Articles on international responsibility of international organizations?, in European Journal of International Law, 21 (3), 2010, pp. 724ss.

HOFFMEISTER, L., Bosphorus Hava Yollari Turizm ve Ticaret Anonim Sirket v. Ireland. App. No. 45036/98, in American Journal of international law, 100, 2006, pp. 447ss.

HOIJER, O., La responsabilitè internationale des États, Les Éditions Internationales, Paris, 1930, pp. 31ss.

HOLDER, W.E., International organizations: Accountability and responsibility, in ASIL Proceedings, 97, 2003, pp. 232ss.

HOLLENBERG, S., The diverging approaches of the European Court of Human Rights in the cases of Nada and Al-Dulimi, in International and Comparative Law Quarterly, 64, 2015, pp. 454ss.

HOLLIS, D.B., The Oxford guide to treaties, Oxford University Press, Oxford, 2012, pp. 437ss.

HONG, M., Human dignity, identity review of the European Arrest Warrant and the Court of justice as a listener in the dialogue of Courts: Solange-II and

Aranyosi: Bverfg 13 December 2015, 2 BvR 2735/154 Solange III and ECJ (Grand Chamber) 5 April 2006, joined cases C-404715 and C-659/15 PPU, Aranyosi and Căldăraru, in European Constitutional Law Review, 12, 2016, pp. 550ss.

HOOGH, A.J.J., Articles 4 and 8 of the 2001 ILC articles on state responsibility, the Tadić case and attribution of acts of Bosnian Serb authorities to the Federal Republic of Yugoslavia, in British Yearbook of International Law, 72 (1), 2001, pp. 256ss.

HORBACH, N.L., BEKKER, P.H., State responsibility for injurious transboundary activity in retrospect, in Nordic International Law Review, 72, 2003, pp. 328ss.

HOSS, C., Satisfaction, in Max Planck Encyclopedia of Public International Law, 2011, par. 10.

HOVELL, D., The power of process. The value of due process in Security Council of sanctions decision-making, Oxford University Press, Oxford, 2016.

HOWARD, J., Invoking state responsibility or aiding the Commission of international crimes-Australia, the United States and the question of East Timor, in Melbourne Journal of International Law, 2, 2001.

HOWORTH, J., Security and Defense Policy in the European Union, Palgrave Macmillan, Basingstoke, 2014.

HUMMELBRUNNER, S., PRICKARTZ, A.C., It's not the fish that stinks! EU trade relations with Morocco under the scrutiny of the General Court of the European Union, in Utrecht Journal of International and European Law, 84, 2016, 19ss.

HUNEEUS, A., Courts resisting courts: Lessons from the Inter-American Court's struggle to enforce human rights, in Cornell International law Journal, 44, 2011, pp. 520ss.

HUTCHINSON, D.N., Solidarity and breaches of multilateral treaties, in British Yearbook of International Law, 59 (1), 1988, pp. 152ss.

ILIOPOULOS STRANGAS, J., La responsabilitè de l'Etat en tant que lègislateur, in Revue Hellènique de Droit International, 51 (1), 1998, pp. 48ss.

IMSEIS, A., Critical reflections on the international humanitarian law aspects of the ICJ wall opnion in American Journal of International Law, 99, 2005, pp. 102ss. D. TURNS, Implementation and compliance, in E. WILMSHURST, S. BREAU, Pespectives on the ICRC study on customary international humanitarian law, Cambridge University Press, Cambridge, 2007, pp. 354ss.

IWASAWA, Y., IWATSUKI, N., Procedural conditions, in J. CRAWFORD, A. PELLET, S. OLLESON, The law of international responsibility, Oxford University Press, Oxford, 2010, pp. 1149ss.

JACKSON, M., Complicity in international law, Oxford University Press, Oxford, 2015.

JACOB, P., Les définitions des notions "d'organe et d'agent" retenues par la ILC sont-elles opérationnelles?, in Revue Belge de Droit International, 117, 2013, pp. 18ss.

JACOVIDES, A., International law and diplomacy. Selected writings by Ambassador Andrew Jacovides, ed. Brill, Bruxelles, 2011, pp. 49ss.

JACQUÉ, J.P., CJUE-CEDH: 2-0, in Revue Trimestrielle de Droit Européen, 40 (4), 2014 pp. 823ss.

JACQUÉ, J.P., La Cour de Justice de!'Union et!'application de la Charte dans les Etats membres: "Mehr Licht," in European Yearbook on Human Rights, 14, 2014 pp. 125-147.

JACQUÉ, J.P., The accession of the European Union to the European Convention on Human Rights and Fundamental Freedoms, in Common Market Law Review, 48 (4), 2011, pp. 995, 1005.

JAIN, N., Perpetrators and accessories in international criminal law: Individual modes of responsibility for collective crimes, Bloomsbury Publishing, New York, 2014, pp. 156ss.

JAKUBOWSKI, A., WIECZYŃSKA, K., Fragmentation vs the constitutionalization of international law: A practical inquiry, ed. Routledge, London & New York, 2016.

JALLOH CHEVROR, C., MARONG A., Promoting accountability under international law for gross human rights violations in Africa. Essays in honour of prosecutor Hasan Bubacar Jallow, ed. Brill, The Hague, 2015.

JANIS, M.V., An introduction to international law, Aspen Law & Business, New York, 2008.

JANSEN, N., The making of legal authority. Non-legislative codifications in historical and corporating perspective, Oxford University Press, Oxford, 2010, pp. 8ss.

JANSSENS, C., The principle of mutual recognition in European Union law, Oxford University Press, Oxford, 2013, pp. 208ss.

JEFFREY, A., The American hostages in Tehran: the ICJ and the legality of rescue missions, in International and Comparative Law Quarterly, 30, 1981, pp. 718ss.

JENNINGS, R., The identification of international law, in B. CHENG, International law: Teaching and practice, ed. Stevens, London, 1982, pp. 4ss.

JENNINGS, R.Y., What is international law and how do we tell it when we see it?, in The Cambridge Tilburg Lectures, Kluwer, 1983, pp. 2ss.

JENSEN, D., LONERGAN, S., Assessing and restoring natural resources in post-conflict peacebuilding, ed. Routledge, London & New York, 2015.

JENSEN, E., State obligations in cyber operations, in Baltic Yearbook of International Law, 14, 2014, pp. 29ss.

JENSEN, E., TALBOT, E., Cyber sovereignty: The way ahead, in Texas

International Law Journal, 50, 2015, pp. 276ss.

JESCHECK, H., WEIGEND, T., Lehrbuch des Strafrechts. Allgemeiner Teil, Duncker & Humblot, Berlin, 1996, pp. 686ss.

JESSUP, P.C., A modern law of Nations, Macmillan, New York, 1948, pp. 153ss.

JESSUP, P., A modern law of nations. An introduction, Macmillan, New York, 1958, pp. 94ss.

JEUTNER, V., Irresolvable norm conflicts in international legal dilemma, Oxford University Press, Oxford, 2017.

JIA, B.B., The relations between treaties and custom, in Chinese Journal of International Law, 9, 2010, pp. 82ss.

JIMENEZ DE ARECHAGA, E., International responsibility, in M. SØRENSEN, Manual of public international law, Macmillan & Co, London, New York, 1968, pp. 532ss.

JIMÉNEZ DE ARÉCHAGA, E., TANZI, A., La responsabilitè des Etats in M. BEDJAOUI, Droit international. Bilan et perspectives, ed. Pedone, Paris, 1991, pp. 368ss.

JOHANSEN, S.Ø., Accountability mechanisms for human rights violations by CSDP missions: Available and sufficient, in International & Comparative Law Quarterly, 66 (1), 2017, pp. 184ss.

JOHNSTONE, I., Law making through the operational activities of international organizations, in The George Washington International Law Review, 40, 2008, pp. 88ss.

JØRGENSEN, M.H.B., The obligation of cooperation, in J. CRAWFORD, A. PELLET, S. OLLESON, The law of international responsibility, Oxford University Press, Oxford, 2010, pp. 696ss.

JØRGENSEN, N.H.B., The responsibility of states for international crimes, Oxford University Press, Oxford, 2000.

JOUANNET, E., Emer de Vattel et l'èmergence du droit international classique, ed. Pedone, Paris, 1998, pp. 407ss.

JOYNER, C.C., International law in the 21st century: Rules for global governance, Rowmann & Littlefield Publishers, Lanham, 2005.

JUNCOS, A.E., European Union foreign and security policy in Bosnia. The politics of coherence and effectiveness, Manchester University Press, Manchester & New York, 2015, pp. 145ss.

JUSS, S., SUNKIN, M., Landmark cases in public law, Hart Publishing, Oxford & Oregon, Portland, 2017, pp. 258ss.

KACZOROWSKA-IRELAND, I., Public international law, ed. Routledge, London & New York, 2015.

KADELBACH, S., Al-Dulimi and Montana management Inc v. Switzerland (ECtHR), in International Legal Materials, 55 (6), 2016, pp. 1023ss.

KADENS, E., YOUNG, E.A., How customary is customary international law?, in William & Mary Law Review, 54, 2013, pp. 886ss.

KADISH, H., Acts and omission, mens rea and complicity. Approaches to codification, in Criminal Law Forum, 1, 1989, pp. 65ss.

KADISH, S.H., Complicity, cause and blame. A study in the international of doctrine, in California Law Review, 73, 1985, pp. 323ss.

KALIMO, H., STAAL, T., "Softness" in international instruments-The case of transnational corporations, in Syracuse Journal of International Law & Commerce, 41, 2014, pp. 258ss.

KALSHOVEN, F., The year at the international humanitarian law, ed. Brill, Bruxelles, 1997, pp. 48ss.

KAMBER, K., Prosecuting human rights offences: Rethinking the sword function of human rights, ed. Brill, The Hague, 2017.

KAMMERHOFER, J., Orthodox generalists and political activists in international legal scholarship, in M. HAPPOLD, International law in a multipolar world, ed. Routledge, London & New York, 2012.

KAMMERHOFER, J., Uncertainty in the formal sources of international law, in European Journal of International Law, 15, 2004, pp. 524ss.

KANETAKE, M., The UN security Council and domestic actors: Distance in international law, ed. Routledge, London & New York, 2017.

KAPLAN, J., WEIBERG, R., BINDER, G., Criminal law. Cases and materials, Wolters Kluwer Law & Business, Aspen, 2012.

KARMS, M.P., MINGST, K.A., International organizations. The politics and processes of global governance, ed. Lynne Rienner, New York, 2009.

KATZ COGAN, J., HURD, I., JOHNSTONE, I., (eds), The Oxford handbook of international organizations, Oxford University Press, Oxford, 2016.

KAUFMANN-KOHLER, G., Interpretive powers of the Free Trade Commission and the rule of law, in E. GAILLARD, F. BACHAND, Fifteen years of NAFTA Chapter 11 arbitration, ed. Juris Net, New York, 2011, pp. 181.

KAWASAKI, K., Draft articles on state responsibility adopted by the International Law Commission in 2001: A brief overview, in Hitotsubashi Journal of International Law, 29, 2002, pp. 49ss.

KEEFE, O., TAMS, C.J., TZANAKOPOLOS, A., The United Nations Convention on jurisdictional immunities of States and their property, Oxford University Press, Oxford, 2013, pp. 241ss.

KEINLEIN, T., Konstituutionalisierung im Völkerrecht: Konstruktion und Elemente einer idealischen Völkerrechtslehre, ed. Springer, Berlin, 2011, pp. 400ss.

KEITH, K., The processes of law-making: The law relating to international organization as an example, in M. RAGAZZI, Responsibility of International Organizations. Essays in memory of Sir Ian Brownlie, ed. Brill, Bruxelles,

2013, pp. 15ss.

KEITH, K.M.F., The mens rea of superior responsibility as developed by ICTY Jurisprudence, in Leiden Journal of International Law, 14, 2001, pp. 618ss.

KELIN, E., Beihilfe zum Völkerrechttsdelikt, in I. VON MÜNCH, Staatsrecht-Völkerrecht-Europarecht für Hans-Jurgen Schlochauer, De Gruyter, Berlin, 1981, pp. 434ss.

KELLERBAUER, M., KLAMERT, M., TOMKIN, J., Commentary on the European Union treaties and the Charter of fundamental rights, Oxford University Press, Oxford, 2019.

KELLY, M.G., The debate or genocide in Darfur, Sudan, in University of California, in Davis Journal of International Law & Policy, 19, 2012, pp. 208ss.

KELLY, M.J., The parameters of vicarious corporate criminal liability for genocide under international law, in A. BYRNES, C. HAYASHI-MICHAELSEN, International law in the age of globalization, ed. Brill, The Hague, 2013.

KELSEN, H., The draft declaration on rights and duties of states. Critical remarks, in American Journal of International Law, 44, 1950, pp. 272ss.

KELSEN, H., Unrecht und Unrechtsfolge im Völkerrecht, in Zeitscrhift für öffentliches Recht, 1932, pp. 482ss.

KENT, A., SKOUTARIS, N., TRINIDAD, J., The future of international courts. Regional, institutional and procedural challenges, ed. Routledge, London & New York, 2019.

KEPPLER, E., Preventing human rights abuses by regulating arms brokers: The US. Brokering amendment to the arms export control act, in Berkeley Journal of International Law, 19 (2), 2001, pp. 381-411, 386ss.

KERBAT, Y., Sanctions et contre-mesures: risques de confusion dans les articles de la ILC sur la responsabilité des organizations internationales, in Revue Belge de Droit International, 117, 2013, pp. 105ss.

KERBRAT, Y., The interaction between the forms of reparation, in J. CRAWFORD, A. PELLET, S. OLLESON, The law of international responsibility, Oxford University Press, Oxford, 2010, pp. 573ss.

KESSLER, B., Die Durchsetzung der genfer Abkommen von 1949 in nicht-internationalen bewaffneten Konflikten auf Grundlage ihres gemeinsamen Art. 1, Duncker & Humblot, Berlin, 2001, pp. 108ss.

KESSLER, B., The duty to "ensure respect" under the common article 1 of the Geneva conventions: Its implications on international and non-international armed conflicts, in The German Yearbook of International Law, 44, 2001, pp. 507ss.

KEWENIG, W.A., Der Internationale Zinrat. Ein Lehrstück des Wirtschaftsvölkerrechts, in Recht der internationalen Wirtshaft, 16, 1990, pp.

782ss.

KIHARA HUNT, A., Holding UNPOL to account: Individual criminal accountability of United Nations police personnel, ed. Brill/Martinus Nijhoff Publishers, Leiden, Boston, 2017.

KINCHIN, N., Administrative justice in the UN: Procedural protections, gaps and proposals for reform, Edward Elgar Publishers, Cheltenahm, 2018.

KINGSBURY, B., En guise d'ouverture-Views on the development of a global administrative law, in C. BORIES, Un droit administratif global?/A global administrative law?, ed. Pedone, Paris, 2012, pp. 16-17.

KIRBY, P., How is rape a weapon of war?, Feminist international relations, modes of critical explanation and the study of wartime sexual violence, in European Journal of International Relations, 18, 2012.

KIRGIS, F.L., Custom on a sliding scale, in American Journal of International Law, 81, 1987, pp. 148ss.

KIRGIS, F.L., Security Council Resolution 1483 on the rebuilding of Iraq, in American Journal of International Law, 97, 2003.

KIRKMAN, C.C., Fair and equitable treatment: Methanex v. United States and the narrowing scope of NAFTA Article 1105, in Law & Policy International Business, 34, 2002, pp. 344ss.

KISS, A., State responsibility and liability for nuclear damage, in Denver Journal of International Law and Policy, 35 (1), 2006, pp. 68ss.

KISS, A.C., La notion de patrimoine commun de l'humanitè, in Recueil des cours, ed. Brill, Bruxelles, vol. 175, 1982, pp. 243ss.

KITHARIDIS, S., The power of article 103 of the UN Charter on Treaty obligations. Can the Security Council authorize non-compliance of human right treaty obligations in UN peacekeeping operations?, in Journal of International Peacekeeping, 20 (1-2), 2016.

KJELDGAARD-PEDERSEN, A., The international legal personality of the individual, Oxford University Press, Oxford, 2018.

KLABBERS, J., Advanced introduction of the law of international organizations, Edward Elgar Publishers, Cheltenham, 2015, pp. 92ss.

KLABBERS, J., An introduction to international institutional law, Cambridge University Press, Cambridge, 2009, pp. 89ss.

KLABBERS, J., International Courts and Informal International Law, J. PAUWELYN, R. WESSEL, J. WOUTERS, Informal international lawmaking, Oxford University Press, Oxford, 2012, pp. 220ss.

KLABBERS, J., International organizations in the formation of customary international law, in E. CANNIZARO, P. PALCHETTI, Customary international law on the use of force, Martinus Nijhoff Publishers, The Hague, 2005, pp. 179-182.

KLABBERS, J., LEFEBER, R., Essays on the law of treaties: A collection of essays in honour of Bert Vierdag, Martinus Nijhoff Publishers, The Hague, 1998, pp. 31ss.

KLABBERS, J., Reflections on role responsibility. The responsibility of international organizations for failing to act, in European Journal of International Law, 28 (4), 2017, pp. 1138ss.

KLABBERS, J., The changing image of international organizations, in J.M. COICAUD, V. HEISKANEN, The legitimacy of international organizations, United Nations University Press, Tokyo, 2001, pp. 221-255.

KLABBERS, J., The transformation of international organizations law, in European Journal of International Law, 26, 2015, pp. 10ss.

KLABBERS, J., WALLENDAHL, A., (eds.) Research handbook on the law of international organizations, Edward Elgar Publishers, Cheltenham, 2011, pp. 314ss.

KLEIN, E., Beihilfe zum Völkerrechtsdelikt, in I. VON MÜNCH, Staasrecht, Völkerrecht, Europarecht Festschrift für Hans-Jurgen Schlochauer, De Gruyter, Berlin, 1981, pp. 425ss.

KLEIN, F., Die mittelbare Haftung im Völkerrecht, Klosrtermann, Frankurt, 1941.

KLEIN, K., Les articles sur la responsabilité des organizations internationales: quel bilan tirer des travaux de la CDI?, in Annuaire Français de Droit International, 58, 2012, pp. 15.

KLEIN, N., KLEIN, N.S., Litigation international law disputes: Weighting the options, Cambridge University Press, Cambridge, 2014, pp. 169ss.

KLEIN, P., La responsabilitè des organizations internationales dans le ordres juridiques internes et en droit des gens, ed. Bruylant, Bruxelles, 1998.

KLEIN, P., Le panel consultatif des droits de l'homme (human rights advisory panel) de la MINUK: une étape dans le processus de responsabilization des Nations Unies?, in M. KOHEN, R. KOLB, D.L. TEHINDRAZENARIVELO, Perspectives du droit international au 21e siècle-Liber Amicorum Christian Dominicé, ed. Brill, Leiden/Boston, 2012, pp. 226ss.

KLEIN, P., Les compètences et pouvois de l'organization internationale, in E. LAGRANGE, J.M. SOREL, Droit des organizations internationales, LGDJ, Paris, 2013, pp. 721ss.

KLEIN, P., Panels, médiateurs et mécanismes informels de controle des activités des organizations internationales: entre accountability et responsibility, in Select Proceedings of the European Society of International Law, vol. 3, Oxford University Press, Oxford, 2010, pp. 228ss.

KLEIN, P., Responsabilitè pour les faits commis dans le cadre d'opèrations de paix et ètendue du pouvoir de contrôle de la cour europèenne des droits de l'homme: quelques considèrations critiques sur l'arrêt Behrami et Saramati, in Annuaire Français de Droit International, 53 (1), 2007, pp. 44ss.

KLEIN, P., The attribution of acts to international organizations, in J.

CRAWFORD, A. PELLET, S. OLLESON, The law of international responsibility, Oxford University Press, Oxford, 2010, pp. 310ss.

KNOLL, B., Rights without remedies: The European Court's failure to close the human rights gap in Kosovo, in Zeitschrift für äuslandisches öffentliches Recht, 68, 2008, pp. 432ss.

KNOOPS, G.J., Defences in contemporary international criminal law, Transnational Publishers, New York, 2001, pp. 97ss.

KOCHENOV, D., PECH, L., Monitoring and enforcement of the rule of law in the EU rhetoric and reality, in European Constitutional Law Review, 12, 2015, pp. 514ss.

KOHEN, M.C., Individual reparation claims in instances of grave human rights violations: The position under general international law, in A. RANDELZHOEFER, C. TOMUSCHAT, State responsibility and the individual. Reparation in instances of grave violations of human rights, ed. Brill, The Hague, 1999.

KOHEN, M.G., Keeping subsequent agreements and practices in their right limits, in G. NOLTE, Treaties and subsequent practice, Oxford University Press, Oxford, 2013, pp. 34.

KOHEN, M.G., La pratique et la théorie des sources du droit international, in La pratique et le droit international, colloque de Genève de la Societe française pour le droit international, ed. Pedone, Paris, 2004, pp. 9, 81ss.

KOIVUROVA, T., Due diligence, in Max Planck Encyclopedia of Public International Law, 2010, par. 8.

KOK, E., The principle of complicity under international law. Its application to states and individuals in cases involving genocide, crimes against humanity and war crimes, in C. STAHN, L. VAN DEN HERIK, The diversification and fragmentation of international criminal law, Martinus Nijhoff Publishers, Leiden/Boston, 2012, pp. 558ss.

KOLB, A.S., The UN Security Council member's responsibility to protect a legal analysis, ed. Springer, Berlin, 2017.

KOLB, R., Does Article 103 of the Charter of the United Nations apply only to decisions or also to authorizations adopted by the Security Council?, in Zeitschrift fur äuslandisches öffentliches Recht und Völkerrecht, 64, 2004, pp. 21ss.

KOLB, R., Droit international et opèrations de paix internationales, Helbing & Lichtenhahn, Genève, 2002, pp. 20ss.

KOLB, R., GAGGIOLI, G., (ed. by), Research handbook on human rights and humanitarian law, Edward Elgar Publishers, Cheltenham, 2013, pp. 560ss.

KOLB, R., Ius in bello. Le droit internationale des conflits armès, Helbing & Lichtenhahn, Basel, 2003, pp. 244ss.

KOLB, R., La bonne foi en droit international public. Contribution à l'ètude des principes gènèraux de droit, ed. PUF, Paris, 2000, pp. 18ss.

KOLB, R., Peremptory international law: Ius cogens. A general inventory, Bloomsbury Publishing, New York, 2015, pp. 91ss.

KOLB, R., Reflections on due diligence duties and cyberspace, in German Yearbook of International Law, 58, 2015, 114ss.

KOLB, R., Selected problems in the theory of customary international law, in Netherlands International Law Review, 50, 2003, pp. 120ss.

KOLB, R., The International Court of Justice, Hart Publishing, Oxford & Oregon, Portland, 2013, pp. 762ss.

KOLB, R., The international law or State responsibility. An introduction, Edward Elgar Publishers, Cheltenham, 2017.

KOLB, R., Theory of international law, Hart Publishing, Oxford & Oregon, Portland, 2016, pp. 442ss.

KOMORI, T., Public international rules of international law: Towards effective implementation, ed. Routledge, London & New York, 2016, pp. 202ss.

KOMORI, T., WELLENS, J., Public interest rules of international law: Towards effective implementation, ed. Routledge, London & New York, 2016, pp. 203ss.

KONDOCH, B., The responsibility of peacekeepers, their sending States, and International Organizations, in T.D. GILL, D. FLECK, The handbook of the international law of military operations, Oxford University Press, Oxford, 2010, pp. 524ss.

KONSTADINIDES, T., The rule of law in the EU: The internal dimension, Hart Publishing, Oxford & Oregon, Portland, 2017.

KORENICA, F., The EU accession to the ECHR: Between Luxembourg's search for autonomy and Strasbourg's credibility on human rights protection, ed. Springer, Berlin, 2015, pp. 282ss.

KORHONEN, O., International governance in post-conflict situations, in Leiden Journal of International Law, 14 (3), 2001, pp. 3ss.

KORKEAKIVI, A., Consequences of "higher" international law: Evaluating crimes of state and erga omnes, in Journal of International Legal Studies, 2, 1996, pp. 82ss.

KOSKENNIEMI, M., From apology to utopia. The structure of international legal argument. Reissue with a new epilogue, Cambridge University Press, Cambridge, 2005, pp. 258ss.

KOSKENNIEMI, M., From the apology to utopia: The structure of the international legal argument, Cambridge University Press, Cambridge, 2006.

KOSKENNIEMI, M., Solidarity measures: state responsibility as a new international order?, in The British Yearbook of International Law, 72, 2001, pp. 338ss.

KOSKENNIEMI, M., Sources of international law, ed. Routledge, London & New York, 2017, pp. 222ss.

KOTZUR, M., Intertemporal law, in Max Planck Encyclopedia of International Law, 24, 2008, par. 6.

KOUTRAKOS, P., EU international relations law, Hart Publishing, Oxford & Oregon, Portland, 2015.

KOUTRAKOS, P., Judicial review in EU's common foreign and security policy, Cambridge University Press, Cambridge, 2018.

KOUTRAKOS, P., The EU Common Security and Defense Policy, Oxford University Press, Oxford, 2013.

KRAHMANN, E., FRIESENDORF, C., The role of private security companies (PSCs) in CSDP missions and operation, European Parliament Directorate-General for External Policies, Policy Department, 2011, pp. 6-7.

KRENC, F., La Belgique "condamnée" pour la première fois par le Comité des droits de l'homme sur fond de lutte contre le terrorisme: cap sur Genève!, in Journal des Tribunaux, 2009, n. 6367 (24 oct. 2009), pp. 621 ss.

KRENN, C., Autonomy and effectiveness as common concerns: A path to ECHR accession after Opinion 2/13, in German Law Journal, 16 (1), 2015, pp. 147ss.

KRESS, C., Universal jurisdiction over international crimes and the Institut de Droit International, in Journal of International Criminal Justice, 4, 2006, pp. 561-585.

KRETZMER, D., Rethinking the application of international humanitarian law in non-international armed conflicts, in Israel Law Review, 42, 2009.

KRETZMER, S., The advisory opinion. The light treatment of international humanitarian law, in American Journal of International Law, 99, 2005, pp. 89ss.

KRIEG, A., Motivations for humanitarian intervention: Theoretical and empirical considerations, ed. Springer, Dordrecht, 2013.

KRIEGER, H., Addressing the accountability gap in peacekeeping. Law-making by domestic courts as a way to avoid UN reform?, in Netherlands International Law Review, 62, 2015, pp. 262ss.

KRIEGER, H., Common European Defence: Competition or compatibility with Nato?, in M. TRYBUS, N.D. WHITE (eds.), European security law, Oxford University Press, Oxford 2007, pp. 174-197.

KRÜCK, H., Völkerrechtliche Verträge im Recht der Europäischen Gemeinschaften, ed. Springer, Berlin, 1977, pp. 126ss.

KRUGER, H., WALTER, V., Self-determination and secession in international law, Oxford University Press, Oxford, 2014, pp. 214-220.

KRUMREY, J., Die Immunität der Vereinten Nationen: Verantwortlichkeit für Friedenswissenshaft, Mohr Siebeck, Tübingen, 2018, pp. 312ss.

KUHN, M., Verschuldens-oder Verursachungshaftung der Staaten im allgemeinen Völkerrecht, Frankfurt am Main, 1961, pp. 116ss.

KUIJER, M., The accession of the European Union to the ECHR: A gift for ECHR's 60th anniversary or an unwelcome intruder at the party?, in Amsterdam Law Forum, 4 (3), 2011, pp. 17-32.

KUIJPER, P.J., Introduction to the symposium on responsibility of international organizations and of (member) states: Attribute or direct responsibility or both?, in International Organizations Law Review, 7, 2010, pp. 22ss.

KUIJPER, P.J., The Court and Tribunal of the EC and the Vienna Convention on the Law of Treaties 1969, in Legal Issues of European Integration, 25, 1998, pp. 4ss.

KUNZ, J.L., The nature of customary international law, in American Journal of International Law, 47, 1953, pp. 664ss.

KÜNZLI, A., Exercising diplomatic protection the fine line between litigation, demarches and consular assistance, in Heidelberg Journal of International Law, 66, 2006, pp. 329ss.

KUWALI, D., VILJOEN, F., By all means necessary: Protecting civilians and preventing mass atrocities in Africa, Pretoria University Law Press, Pretoria, 2017.

KWAKWA, E., Globalization and international organizations, ed. Routledge, London & New York, 2017.

LACCHI, C., The ECtHR's interference in the dialogue between National Courts and the Court of Justice of the EU: Implications for the preliminary reference procedure, in Review of European Administrative Law, 9 (1), 2015, pp. 96ss.

LACHENMANN, F., WOLFRUM, K., The law of armed conflict and the use of force. The Max Planck Encyclopedia of public international law, Oxford University Press, Oxford, 2017.

LACHMANN, P., The international legal personality of the European Communities: Capacity and competence, in Leiden Journal of International Law, 3, 1984, pp. 12ss.

LADENBURGER, C., Vers l'adhésion de l'Union européenne à la Convention européenne des droits de l'homme, in Revue Trimestrielle de Droit Européen, 47 (1), 2011, pp. 20-26.

LAGRANGE, P., Responsabilitè des Etats pour actes accomplis en application du Chapitre VII de la Charte des Nations Unies, in Revue Gènèrale de Droit International Public, 112, 2008, pp. 86ss.

LAIS, R., Die Rechtsfolgen völkerrechtlicher Delikte, Dunker & Humblot, Berlin, 1932.

LAMBRECHT, S., The sting is in the Tail: CJEU Opinion 2/13 objects to draft agreement on accession of the EU to the European Convention on Human Rights, in European Human Rights Law Review, 15 (1), 2015, pp. 185ss.

LAMMERS, G., New developments concerning international responsibility and liability for damage caused by environmental interferences, in The Hague Yearbook of International Law, 20, 2007, pp. 88ss.

LANDAU, J.L., Living law: Modern constitutionalism and its effect on emerging and dynamic democracies: Bridging governments: The role of international law in State government, in Willamette Journal of International Law and Dispute Resolution, 20 (1-2), 2012, pp. 50ss.

LANG, A.F., WIENER, A., Handbook on global constitutionalism, Edward Elgar Publishers, Cheltenham, 2017, pp. 362ss.

LANGFORD, M., VANDENHOLE, W., SCHEININ, M., VAN GENUGTEN, W., (ed. by), Global justice, State duties: The extraterritorial scope of economic, social and cultural rights in international law, Cambridge University Press, Cambridge 2013.

LANOVOY, V., Complicity and its limits in the law of international responsibility, Hart Publishing, Oxford & Oregon, Portland, 2016.

LANSING, R., The North Atlantic coast fisheries arbitration, in University of Pennsylvania Law Review and American Law Register, 59 (3), 1910, pp. 122ss.

LARENZ, K., Methodenlehre der Rechtswissenschaft, ed. Springer, Berlin, 1975, pp. 251ss.

LARIVÉ, M.H.A., Debating European security and defense policy understanding the complexity, ed. Routledge, London & New York, 2016, pp. 197ss.

LARSEN, K.M., Attribution of conduct in peace operations: the "ultimate control and authority test," in European Journal of International Law, 19, 2008, pp. 522ss.

LARSEN, K.M., COOPER, C.G., NYSTUEN, G., Searching for a principle of humanity in international humanitarian law, Cambridge University Press, Cambridge, 2013.

LAUTERPACHT, E., The contemporary practice of the United Kingdom in the field of international law. Survey and comment, Cambridge University Press, Cambridge, 2008.

LAUTERPACHT, H., General rules of the law of peace, in E. LAUTERPACH, International law being the collected papers of Hersch Lauterpacht, vol. 1. The general works, Cambridge University Press, Cambridge, 1970, pp. 384ss.

LAUTERPACHT, H., The grotian tradition in international law, in British Yearbook of International Law, 17, 1946, pp. 4ss.

LAVAL, P.F., Les activitès opèrationnelles, du conseil à l'administration international du territoire, in E. LAGRANGE, J.M. SOREL, Droit des organizations internationales, LGDJ, Paris, 2013, pp. 767ss.

LAVIOLETTE, N., Commanding rape: Sexual violence, command responsibility and the prosecution of superiors by the international criminal Tribunals for the Former Yugoslavia and Rwanda, in The Canadian Yearbook of International Law, 36, 1998, pp. 94ss.

LAWSON, R.A., Life after Bankovic: On the extraterritorial application of the European Convention of Human Rights, in Extraterritorial application of the Human Rights Treaties, ed. Intersentia, Antwerp, 2004, pp. 83-123.

LEACH, P., Taking a case to the European Court of Human Rights, Oxford University Press, Oxford, 2011, pp. 55ss.

LEANDRO, A., Arms transfer and complicity in war crimes, in F. POCAR, M. PEDRAZZI, M. FRULLI (eds.), War crimes and the conduct of hostilities, Edward Elgar Publishers, Cheltenham, Northampton, 2013, pp. 225ss.

LEB, C., Cooperation, the law of transboundary water resources, Cambridge University Press, Cambridge, 2013.

LEBEN, C., Les contre-mesures inter-ètatiques et les rèactions à l'illicite dans la sociètè internationale, in Annuaire Français de Droit International, 28, 1982, pp. 10ss.

LEBEN, CH., Les sanctions privatives de droit ou de qualitè dans les organizations internationales spècialisèes, ed. Bruylant, Bruxelles, 1979, pp. 41ss.

LECK, C., International responsibility in United Nations peacekeeping operations. Command and control arrangements and the attribution of conduct, in Melbourne Journal of International Law, 10, 2009, pp. 346ss.

LECKOW, R., PLITH, E., Codification, progressive development or innovation? Some reflections on the ILC Articles on responsibility of international organizations, in M. RAGAZZI, Responsibility of International Organizations. Essays in memory of Sir Ian Brownlie, ed. Brill, Bruxelles, 2013, pp. 228ss.

LEE, L.T., Consular law, Oxford University Press, Oxford, 1991, pp. 112ss.

LEFEBER, R., Transboundary environmental interference and the origin of state liability, ed. Brill, The Hague, 1996.

LEISTENSCHNEIDER, N.A.A., La responsabilidad internacional de los estados por actos ilicitos, crimines internacionales y daños transfronterizos, in Anuario Mexicano de Derecho Internacional, 12, 2012.

LENAERTS, K., Federalism and the rule of law: Perspectives from the European Court of Justice, in Fordham International Law Journal, 33, 2011, pp. 1338ss.

LENAERTS, K., MASELIS, I., GUTMAN, K., European Union procedural law, Oxford University Press, Oxford, 2014, pp. 133ss.

LENNARD, M., Navigating by the Stars: Interpreting the WTO agreements, in Journal of International Economic Law, 5, 2002, pp. 19ss.

LEONARD, E., RAMSAY, G., Globalizing Somalia: Multilateral international and transnational recpercussions of conflict, Bloomsbury Publishing, New

York, 2013.

LESTER, S., MERCURIO, B., BARTELS, L., Bilateral and regional trade agreements. Commentary and analysis, Cambridge University Press, Cambridge, 2016.

LÉVY, J.P., De quelques “modifications” et’interprètations” de la Convention sur le droit de la mer, in Revue Générale de Droit International Public, 111, 2007, pp. 408ss.

LIAKOPOULOS, D., Art. 275 TFUE, in P.E. HERZOG, C. CAMPBELL, G. ZAGEL, Smit & Herzog on the law of the European Union, ed. LexisNexis, New York, 2018.

LIAKOPOULOS, D., Conflits de normes à la Cour internationale de Justice: rôle du Conseil de sécurité des Nations Unies, in Juris Gradibus, 2017.

LIAKOPOULOS, D., Cooperation and coordination of arbitral proceedings in merger and acquisition transactions, in International and European Union Legal Matters, 2011.

LIAKOPOULOS, D., Die Hybridität des Verfahrens der Internationalen ad hoc Strafgerichtshöfe und die Bezugnahme auf innerstaatliches Recht in der Rechtsprechun, in International and European Union legal Matters, 2012.

LIAKOPOULOS, D., Equo processo nella Convenzione europea dei diritti dell’uomo e nel diritto comunitario, ed. Cedam, 2007.

LIAKOPOULOS, D., European integration and its relation with the jurisprudence of European Court of Human Rights and private international law of European Union, in Homa Publica. Revista Internacional de Direitos Humanos e Impresa, 2 (2), 2018.

LIAKOPOULOS, D., Evolutionary, dynamic or contemporary interpretation in WTO system?, in The Chinese Journal of Global Governance, 5, 2019, pp. 28ss.

LIAKOPOULOS, D., International Law Commission and protection of environment in times of armed conflict: The case of protection of international cultural heritage, in ArtPaths, 2012.

LIAKOPOULOS, D., Kritik an friedenserhaltenden/Peacekeeping Operationen und die Entwicklung des Konzepts der Souveränität im Völkerrecht, in International and European Union Legal Matters, 2011.

LIAKOPOULOS, D., L’ingerenza umanitaria nel diritto internazionale e comunitario, ed. Cedam, Padova, 2007, pp. 69ss.

LIAKOPOULOS, D., La tutela cautelare nella Corte internazionale di giustizia. Aspetti processuali e comparati, ed. AMON, Firenze, 2012.

LIAKOPOULOS, D., Parità di armi nella giustizia penale internazionale, vol. 1, ed. Libellula, Puglia, 2018.

LIAKOPOULOS, D., Protection of human rights between European Court of Human Rights and Court of European Union, in International and European

Union Legal Matters, 2015.

LIAKOPOULOS, D., The function of accusation in International Criminal Court. Structure of crimes and the role of Prosecutor according to the international criminal jurisprudence, ed. Maklu, The Hague, Antwerp, New York, 2019.

LIAKOPOULOS, D., The legal system of climate change and the mechanism of control in the European Union, in International Journal of Environment and Health, 6, (1), 2011.

LIANG, J., Modifying the UN Charter through subsequent practice: Prospects for the charter's revitalization, in Nordic Journal of International Law, 81, 2012, pp. 4ss.

LIEFLÁNDER, T.R., The Lubanga judgment of the ICC: More than just the First Step?, in Cambridge Journal of International and Comparative Law, 2012, pp. 191–212.

LIIVOJA, R., The scope of the supremacy clause of the United Nations Charter, in International and Comparative Law Quarterly, 57, 2008, pp. 583ss.

LINDAHL, H., Fault lines of globalization. Legal order an the politics of a-legality, Oxford University Press, Oxford, 2013.

LINDERFALK, U., On the interpretation of treaties. The modern international law as expressed in the 1969 Vienna Convention on the Law of Treaties, ed. Springer, Dordrecht, 2007.

LINDERFALK, U., State responsibility and the primary-secondary rules terminology. The role of language for an understanding of the international legal system, in Nordic Journal of International Law, 78 (1), 2009, pp. 54ss.

LINDROOS, A., Addressing norm conflicts in a fragmented legal system. The doctrine of lex specialis, in Nordic Journal of International Law, 74, 2005, pp. 45ss.

LINGAAS, C., Imagined identities: Defining the racial group in the crime of genocide, in Genocide Studies and Prevention: An International Journal, 9 (1), 2016, pp. 80ss.

LINNAN, D.K., Legitimacy, legal development and change: Law and modernization reconsidered, ed. Routledge, London & New York, 2016.

LIVOJA, R., The scope of the supremacy clause of the United Nations, in International and Comparative Law Quarterly, 57 (3), 2008, pp. 583-612.

LOCK, T., Beyond Bosphorus: The European Court of Human Rights case law in the responsibility of Member States of international organizations under the European Convention on Human Rights, in Human Rights Law Review, 10 (4), 2010, pp. 530ss.

LOCK, T., The ECJ and the ECtHR: The future relationship between the two European courts, in The Law and Practice of International Courts and Tribunals, 8, 2010, pp. 375-398

LOCK, T., The European Court of Justice and international courts, Oxford

University Press, Oxford, 2015.

LOCK, T., The future of EU accession to the ECHR after Opinion 2/13: Is it still possible and is it still desirable?, in Edinburgh School of Law Research Paper Series, 2015.

LOOMER, K., Australia v. Japan: Is it possible for Japanese compliance?, in North Carolina Journal of International Law, 36, 2016, pp. 4, 9ss.

LORENZ, N.L.A., GROUSSOT, Z., PETURSSON, G.T., The European human rights culture. A paradox of human rights protection in Europe?, Martinus Nijhoff Publishers, Leiden, 2013.

LOVE, B., The International Court of Justice: Jurisdictional immunities of the state (Germany v. Italy: Greece intervening. Jurisdictional immunities of the state (Ger. v. IT. Greece intervening (ICJ), in International Legal Materials, 51 (3), 2012, pp. 564ss.

LOWE, V., International law, Oxford University Press, Oxford, 2015.

LOWE, V., Precluding wrongfulness or responsibility. A plea for excuses, in European Journal of International Law, 10 (2), 1999, pp. 408ss.

LOWE, V., Responsibility for the conduct of other states, in Japanese Journal of International Law and Diplomacy, 101, 2002, pp. 4ss.

LUERS, W.H., Choosing engagement. Uniting the U.N with U.S interests, in Foreign Affairs, 79, 2000.

LUSA BORDIN, F., The analogy between States and international organizations, Cambridge University Press, Cambridge, 2018.

LYONS, T., European Union customs law, Oxford University Press, Oxford, 2018.

LYSÉN, J., State responsibility and internationaliability of states for lawful acts, ed. Justus, Uppsala, 1997.

MACAK, K., Decoding article 8 of the International Law Commission's articles on state responsibility: Attribution of cyber operations by non state actors, in Journal of Conflict & Security Law, 16, 2016, pp. 406.

MACAK, K., International law and practice, from cyber norms to cyber rules: Re-engaging states as law-makers, in Leiden Journal of International Law, 30, 2017, pp. 883ss.

MACGIBBON, IC., Customary international law and acquiescence, in British Yearbook of International Law, 33, 1957, pp. 116ss.

MACGIBBON, IC., Means for the identification of the international law: General Assembly Resolutions: Custom, practice and mixed identity, in B. CHENG, International law: Teaching and practice, ed. Stevens, London, 1982, pp. 12, 21ss.

MADDOCK DILLON, E., DEXTER, M., The Haitian revolution and the early United States: Histories, textualities, geography, University of Pennsylvania Press, Pennsylvania, 2016.

MAGGIO, A.R., Environmental policy, non product related process and production methods and the law of the World Trade Organization, ed. Springer, Berlin, 2017.

MAISSON, R., Justice pènale internationale, ed. PUF, Paris, 2017.

MAJOR, C., Towards an EU peacebuilding strategy: The effects of the Lisbon Treaty on the comprehensive approach of the EU in the area of civilian crisis management, in European Foreign Affairs Review, 18, 2014, pp. 46ss.

MALANCZUK, P., Zur Repressalie im Entwurf der International Law Commission zur Staatenverantwortlichkeit, in Zeitschrift für ausländisches Recht und Völkerrecht, 45, 1985, pp. 294ss.

MALINTOPPI, A., La fonction normative de l'OACI, in Revue Gènerale de l'Air, 10, 1950, pp. 1050ss.

MANACORDA, S., MELONI, C., Indirect perpetration versus Joint Criminal Enterprise: Concurring approaches in the practice of international criminal law?, in Journal of International Criminal Justice, 9 (1), 2011, pp. 165ss.

MANIN, F., Droit international public, ed. Masson, Paris, 1979, pp. 182ss.

MANIN, P.H., La Convention de Vienne entre Etats et organizations internationales ou entre organizations internationales, in Annuaire Français de Droit International, 32 (1), 1986, pp. 454ss.

MANN, F.A., The consequences of an international wrong in international and national law, in British Yearbook of International Law, 48 (1), 1975-1976, pp. 4ss.

MARAHAUN, G., MARAHAUN, T., ZIMMERMANN, A., (ed. by), Making treaties work. Human rights, environment, arms control, Oxford University Press, Oxford, 2007, pp. 267ss.

MARAHAUN, T., Dispute resolution, compliance control and enforcement of international arms control law, in G. ULFSTEIN T. MARAHAUN, A. ZIMMERMANN (ed. by), Making treaties work. Human rights, environment, arms control, Oxford University Press, Oxford, 2007, pp. 243ss.

MARCHADIER, F., Convention européenne des droit de l'homme et des libertès fondamentales, in Revue Critique de Droit International Privè, 193 (4), 2014, pp. 679-694.

MARHIC, G., Le règime de responsabilitè des opèrations de paix de l'unione europèenne. Quelles règles applicables?, in Revue Belge de Droit International, 46, 2013, pp. 137ss.

MARÍN-LÓPEZ, A., La responsabilidad internacional objetiva y la responsabilidad internacional por riesgo, ed. Beramar B.L. Madrid, 1995.

MAROSSI, A.Z., BASSETT, M.R., Economic sanctions under international law. Unilateralism, multilateralism, legitimacy and consequences, ed. Springer, Berlin, 2015.

MÁRQUEZ CARRASCO, C., The applicability of human rights instruments to European Union's CSDP operations: Framing the challenges, in Cuadernos Europeos de Deusto, 53, 2015, pp. 60ss.

MARTHA, R.S.J., The financial obligation in international law, Oxford University Press, Oxford, 2015.

MARXSEN, C., Violation and confirmation of the law: The intricate effects of the invocation of the law in armed conflict, in Journal on the Use of Force and International Law, 5 (1), 2018, pp. 12ss.

MARXSEN, C., What do different theories of customary international law have to say about the individual right to reparation under international humanitarian law?, in Zeitschrift für äuslandisches öffentliches Recht, 78 (3), 2018.

MATHESON, M.J., United Nations governance of postconflict societies, in American Journal of International Law, 95, 2001.

MATHIAS, S., The work of the International Law Commission on identification of customary international law: A view from the perspective of the office of legal affairs, in Chinese Journal of International Law, 15, 2016, pp. 20ss.

MATSUCHITA, M., SCHOENBAUM, T.J., MAVROIDIS, P., The World Trade Organization: Law, practice and policy, Oxford University Press, Oxford, 2015, pp. 849ss.

MATZ-LÜCK, N., Treaties, conflict clauses, in Max Planck Encyclopedia of Public International Law, 2006, pp. 6ss.

MAZIAU, N., PECH, L., L'administration internationale de la Bosnie-Herzègovine: Un modale pour le Kosovo?, in Civitas Europa, 2000.

MAZZOCCHI, S., Humanitarian intervention in a post-Iraq, post-Darfur world: Is there now a duty to prevent genocide even without Security Council approval?, in Annual Survey of International Law & Comparative Law, 17, 2011, pp. 112ss.

MCCONNELL, F., MOREAU, T., DITTMER, J., Mimicking state diplomacy: The legitimizing strategies of unofficial diplomacies, in Geoforum, 43 (4), 2012, pp. 806ss.

MCCORQUODALE, R., Defining the international rule of law. Defying gravity?, in International and Comparative Law Quarterly, 65 (2), 2016, pp. 278ss.

MCCOUBREY, H., MORRIS, J., Regional peacekeeping in the post-colf war era, Kluwer Law International, The Hague, London, Boston, 2000, pp. 228ss.

MCDOUGAL, M.S., The hydrogen bomb tests and the international law of the sea, in American Journal of International Law, 49, 1955, pp. 358ss.

MCDOUGAL, M.S., The International Law Commission's Draft Articles upon interpretation: Textuality redivivus, in American Journal of International Law, 61, 1967, pp. 994ss.

MCGINLEY, G.P., Practice as a guide to treaty interpretation, in Fletcher Forum of World Affairs, 9, 1985, pp. 211ss

MCGINNIS, J.O., The comparative advantage of customary international law, in Harvard Journal of Law and Public Policy, 30, 2006, pp. 7-12.

MCHENRY, J.R., The prosecution of rape under international law: Justice that is long overdue, in Vanderbilt Journal of Transnational Law, 35, 2002, pp. 1310ss.

MCINTRYE, J., The role of the dispute requirement in assessing jurisdiction and admissibility before the international court, in Melbourne Journal of International Law, 19 (2), 2018.

MCINTRYRE, S.H., Legal effect of world war II on treaties of the United States, ed. Springer, Berlin, 2012, pp. 160ss.

MCINTYRE, J., The declaratory judgment in recent jurisprudence of the International Court of Justice. Conflicting approaches to state responsibility, in Leiden Journal of International Law, 29 (1), 2016, pp. 180ss.

MCLACHLAN, C., The evolution of treaty obligations in international law, in G. NOLTE, Treaties and subsequent practice, Oxford University Press, Oxford, 2013, pp. 70ss.

MCNAIR, A.D., The law of treaties, Oxford University Press, Oxford, 1961, pp. 486, 697ss.

MCRAE, D., The work of the International Law Commission 2007-2011: Progress and prospect, Cambridge University Press, Cambridge, 2012, pp. 325ss.

MCWHINNEY, E., The illegal diversion of aircraft and international law, Sijthoff, Leiden, 1975, pp. 10.

MEDELLÍN URQUIAGA, X., The normative impact of the inter-American Court of Human Rights on Latin-america national prosecution of mass atrocities, in Israel Law Review, 46 (3), 2013, pp. 410ss.

MEDLONG, J., All other breaches: State practice and the Geneva Conventions' nebulous class of less discussed prohibitions, in Michigan Journal International Law, 34, 2013, pp. 830ss.

MELISCHEK, A., The relevant market in international economic law: A comparative antitrust and GATT analysis, Cambridge University Press, Cambridge, 2013, pp. 70ss.

MENDELSON, M., The definition of international organization in the International Law Commission's current project on the reponsibility of international organizations, in M. RAGAZZI, Responsibility of international organizations. Essays in memory of Sir Ian Brownlie, Martinus Nijhoff Publishers, Leiden, Boston, 2013, pp. 384ss.

MENDELSON, M.H., The formation of customary international law, Recueil des Cours, ed Brill, The Hague, vol. 271, 1998, pp. 156, 272ss.

MENDELSON, M.H., The International Court of Justice and the sources of international law, in V. LOWE, M FITZMAURICE, Fifty years of the International Court of Justice: Essays in Honour of Sir Robert Jennings, Cambridge University Press, Cambridge, 1996, pp. 86s.

MENDELSON, M.H., The subjective element in customary international law, in The British Yearbook of International Law, 66, 1995, pp. 184ss.

MENG, W., Internationale Organizationen im Völkerrechtichen Deliktsrecht, in Zeitschrift für ausländisches Recht und Völkerrecht, 45, 1985, pp. 324ss.

MERIBOUTE, Z., Le facteur temps et la violation des obligations internationales, in Revue de Droit et des Sciences Diplomatiques, 62, 1984, pp. 186ss.

MERKET, H., The European Union and the seurity-development nexus briding the legal divide, ed. Brill, Leiden, Boston, 2016, pp. 130ss.

MERON, T., Revival of customary humanitarian law, in American Journal of International Law, 99, 2005, pp. 817ss.

MERON, T., The continuing role of custom in the formation of international humanitarian law, in American Journal of International Law, 90, 1996, pp. 238ss

MERON, T., The Geneva Conventions as customary law, in American Journal of International Law, 81, 1987, pp. 348ss.

MERON, T., The humanization of humanitarian law, in American Journal of International Law, 94, 2000, pp. 239ss.

MERRILLS, J.G., Interim measures of protection in the recent jurisprudence of the International Court of Justice, in International and Comparative Law Quarterly, 44, 1995, pp. 128ss.

MERRILLS, J.G., International dispute settlement, Cambridge University Press, Cambridge, 1999.

MERRILS, J.G., International dispute settlement, Cambridge University Press, Cambridge, V° ed., 2011, pp. 4ss

MESSINEO, F., Attribution of conduct, in A. NOLLKAEMPER, I. PLAKOKEFALOS, Principles of shared responsibility in international law. An appraisal of the state of the art, Cambridge University Press, Cambridge, 2015, pp. 71ss.

MEYER, D., Les contrats de fourniture de biens et services dans le cadre des opèrations de maintien de la paix, in Annuaire Français de Droit International, 42, 1996, pp. 79ss.

MEYER, F.C., From "Solange II to Forever I." The German Federal Constitutional Court and the European Arrest Warrant (and how the CJEU responded), in New Journal of European Criminal Law, 7, 2016, pp. 278ss.

MEYER, J., (ed.), Charta der Grundrechte der Europäischen Union, ed. Nomos, Baden-Baden, 2014, pp. 813-826.

MEZGER, E., Strafrecht. Ein Lehrbuch, Duncker & Humblot, Leipzig, 1933, pp. 413ss.

MICHIE, A., The law of arms control. International supervision and enforcement, in Journal of Conflict and Security Law, 10 (3), 2005, pp. 345-377.

MILANO, E., The Security Council and territorial sovereignty: The Case of Kosovo, in International Community Law Review, 12, 2010, pp. 172ss.

MILANOVIC, M., Extraterritorial application of human rights treaties, Oxford University Press, Oxford, 2011, pp. 136-142.

MILANOVIC, M., PAPIC, T., As bad as it gets: The European Court of Human Rights' Behrami and Saramati decision and general international law, in International and Comparative Law Quarterly, 58 (2), 2009, pp. 268ss.

MILANOVIC, M., State responsibility for genocide: A follow-up, in European Journal of International Law, 18, 2007, pp. 670ss.

MILANOVIC, M., The Human Rights Committee's views in Sayadi v. Belgium: A missed opportunity, in Goettingen Journal of International Law, 3, 2009, pp. 520ss.

MILLER, R.A., BRATSPIES, R.M., Progress in international law, ed. Brill, Bruxelles, 2008.

MINOW, M., TRUE-FROST, C., WHITTING, A., The first global prosecutor: Promise and constraints, University of Michigan Press, Michigan, 2015.

MOECKLI, D., SHAH, S., SIVAKUMARAN, S., International human rights law, Oxford University Press, Oxford, 2010, pp. 598ss.

MOELLE, M.P., The international responsibility of international organizations. Cooperation in peacekeeping operations, Cambridge University Press, Cambridge, 2017, pp. 168ss.

MÖLDNER, M., Responsibility of international organizations-Introducing the ILC's DARIO, in Max Planck Yearbook of United Nations Law, 16, 2012, pp. 282ss.

MÖLER, B., European security. The roles of regional organizations, ed. Routledge, London & New York, 2016.

MOLOO, R., Changing times, changing obligations: The interpretation of treaties over time, in American Society International Law Proceedings, 106, 2012, pp. 262ss.

MOLOO, R., When actions speak louder than words, in Berkeley Journal of International Law, 31, 2013, p. 40ss.

MOMIROV, A., Dutch courts and Srebrenica: Ascribing responsibilities and defending legally relevant relationships, in Netherlands Yearbook of International Law, 43, 2012, pp. 233ss.

MOORMAN, W., Humanitarian intervention and international law in the case of Kosovo, in New England Law Review, 37, 2002-2003, pp. 776ss.

MORANO-FOADI, S., VICKERS, L., (eds.), Fundamental Rights in the EU-A matter for two Courts, Oxford University Press, Oxford, 2015.

MORISSE-SCHILBACH, M., HALFMANN J., (eds), Wissen, Wissenschaft und Global Commons: Forschungen zu Wissenschaft und Politik jenseits des Staates am Beispiel von Regulierung und Konstruktion globaler Gemeinschaftsgüter, ed. Nomos, Baden-Baden, 2012, pp. 134ss.

MORTENSON, J.D., The travaux of travaux. Is the Vienna Convention hostile to drafting history, in American Journal of International Law, 107 (4), 2013, pp. 782ss.

MOUTHAAN, S., Sexual violence against men and international law. Criminalising the unmentionable, in International Criminal Law Review, 13, 2013, pp. 668ss.

MOUTON, J.D., KOVÁCS, P., La concept de citoyennetè en droit international, ed. Brill, The Hague, 2019.

MRAZEK, Y., Prohibition of the use and threat of force: Self-defense and elf-help in international law, in Canadian Yearbook of International Law, 2, 1989, pp. 82ss.

MUJEZINOVI Ć LARSEN, K., Attribution of conduct in peace operations: The "ultimate authority and control" test, in European Journal of International law, 19 (3), 2008, pp. 512ss.

MUJEZINOVIĆ LARSEN, K., The human rights treaty obligations of peacekeeping, Cambridge University Press, Cambridge, 2012.

MÜLLER, W., WTO agreement on subsidies and countervailing measures. A commentary, Cambridge University Press, Cambridge, 2017

MÜLLERSON, R., The Interplay in K. WELLENS, International Law: Theory and practice-Essays in Honor of Eric Suy, Martinus Nijhoff Publishers, The Hague, 1998, pp. 162ss.

MURPHY, C.C., EU counter terrorism law: Pre-emption and the rule of law, Hart Publishing, Oxford & Oregon, Portland, 2012.

MURPHY, S.D., Codification, progressive development, or scholarly analysis? The art of packaging the ILC's work product, in M. RAGAZZI (ed.), Responsibility of international organizations-Essays in Memory of Sir Ian Brownlie, Martinus Nijhoff Publishers, Leiden, Boston, 2013, pp. 29-40.

MURPHY, S.D., Humanitarian intervention. The United Nations in an evolving world order, University of Pennsylvania Press, Pennsylvania, 1966, pp. 106ss.

MURPHY, S.D., The relevance of subsequent agreement and subsequent practice for the interpretation of treaties, in G. NOLTE, Treaties and subsequent practice, Oxford University Press, Oxford, 2013, pp. 84ss.

MUSA, S., Victim reparation under the ius post bellum. An historical and normative perspective, Cambridge University Press, Cambridge, 2019.

NADYA SADAT, L., Seeking accountability for the unlawful use of force, Cambridge University Press, 2018, pp. 50ss.

NAERT, F., International law aspects of the EU's security and defense policy with a particular focus on the law of armed conflict and human rights, ed. Intersentia, Antwerp, Oxford, Portland, 2010.

NAGY, K., Le problème de la lègitime dèfense en droit international, in Acta juridica et Politica, Szeged, 42, 1992.

NAHAPETIAN, K., Confronting state complicity in international law, in UCLA Journal of International Law and Foreign Affairs, 7, 2002-2003, pp. 100ss.

NASU, H., The UN Security Council's responsibility and the "responsibility to protect," in Max Planck Yearbook of United Nations, 15, 2011, pp. 379ss.

NEBESAR, D.A., Gender-based violence as a weapon of war, in U.C. Davis Journal of International Law and Policy, 4, 1998, pp. 148ss.

NEDESKI, A., NOLLKAEMPER, N., Responsibility of international organizations "in connection with the acts of States," in International law Review, 9 (1), 2012

NEFRAMI, E., Les accords mixtes de la Communautè Europèenne aspects communautaires et internationaux, ed. Bruylant, Bruxelles, 2007, pp. 562ss.

NEGRELIUS, J., KRISTOFFERSSON, E., Human rights in contemporary European law, Hart Publishing, Oxford & Oregon, Portland,2015, pp. 17ss.

NEUHOLD, H., Die Pflicht zur Zusammenarbeit zwischen den Staaten: Moralisches Postulat oder völkerrechtliche Norm?, in H. MIEHSLER, E. MOCK, B. SIMMA, I. TAMMELLO, Ius Humanitas. Festschrift zum 90. Geburtstag von Alfred Verdross, Duncker & Humblot, Berlin, 1980, pp. 578ss.

NEUMANN, G.L., Inter-American Court of Human Rights (IACtHR), in R. WOLFRUM, The Max Planck Encyclopedia of Public International Law, Oxford University Press, Oxford, 2012.

NEWCOMBE, A.P., PARADELL, L., Law and practice of investment treaties. Standards of treatment, Kluwer Law International, The Hague, 2009, pp. 527ss.

NICOLA, F., DAVIES, B., European Union law stories, Cambridge University Press, Cambridge, 2017.

NIETONAVIA, R., Responsabilidad internacional del Estado por genocidio. La sentencia de la Corte Internacional de Justicia en el caso de Srebrenica, International Law, in Revista Colombiana de Derecho Internacional, 22, 2010, pp. 18ss.

NOLLAEMPER, A., PLAKOKEFALOS, I., The practice of shared responsibility in international law, Cambridge University Press, Cambridge, 2017.

NOLLAKAEMPER, A., Dual attribution: Liability of the Netherlands for conduct of Dutchbat in Srebrenica, in Journal of International Criminal Justice, 9, 2011, pp. 1144ss.

NOLLKAEMPER, A., Dual distribution, in Journal of International Criminal

Justice, 9, 2011, pp. 1144ss.

NOLLKAEMPER, A., Issues of shared responsibility before the International Court of Justice, in E. RIETER, H. DE WAELE, Evolving principles of international law. Studies in honor of Karel v. Wellens, ed. Brill, Leiden, Boston, 2011, pp. 219ss.

NOLLKAEMPER, A., JACOBS, D., SCHECHINGER, J.N.M., Distribution of responsibilities in international law, Cambridge University Press, Cambridge, 2015, pp. 283ss.

NOLLKAEMPER, A., JACOBS, D., Shared responsibility in international law. A conceptual framework, in Michigan Journal of International Law, 34, 2013, pp. 36.

NOLLKAEMPER, A., PLAKEFALOS, I., Principles of shared responsibility in international law, Cambridge University Press, Cambridge, 2014.

NOLLKAEMPER, A., PLAKOKEFALOS, I., Principles of shared responsibility in international law. An appraisal of the state of the art, Cambridge University Press, Cambridge, 2015.

NOLLKAEMPER, A., REINISCH, A., JANIK, R., International law in domestic courts. A case book, Oxford University Press, Oxford, 2019.

NOLLKAEMPER, A., The duality of shared responsibility, in Contemporary Politics, 24 (5), 2018, pp. 528ss.

NOLLKAEMPER, A., The internationalized rule of law, in Hague Journal on the Rule of Law, 1, 2009, pp. 76ss.

NOLLKAEMPER, A., The power of secondary rules to connect the international and national legal orders, in T. BROUDE, Y. SHANY, Multisourced equivalent norms in international law, Hart Publishing, Oxford & Oregon, Portland, 2011, pp. 45ss.

NOLTE, G., AUST, H.P., Equivocal helpers. Complicity states, mixed messages and international law, in International and Comparative Law Quarterly, 58, 2009, pp. 14ss.

NOLTE, G., The International Law Commission facing the second decade of the twenty first century, in U. FASTENRATH et al., From bilateralism to community interests, Oxford University Press, Oxford 2011, pp. 782ss.

NOLTE, G., Third Report for the ILC Study Group on Treaties over time: Subsequent agreements and subsequent practice outside of judicial or quasi-judicial proceedings, in G. NOLTE, Treaties and subsequent practice, Oxford University Press, 2013, pp. 310ss.

NOLTE, G., Treaties and subsequent practice, Oxford University Press, Oxford, 2013.

NOORTMANN, M., Enforcing international law: From self-help to self-contained regimes, ed. Routledge, London & New York, 2016.

NORTMANN, M., REINISCH, A., RYNGAERT, C., Non state actors in international law, Bloomsbury Publishing, New York, 2015, pp. 172ss.

NOUTE, G., Treaties and subsequent practice, Oxford University Press, Oxford, 2013, pp. 224ss.

NOVÁKY, N.I.M., European Union military operations: A collective action perspective, ed. Routledge, London & New York, 2018.

NOVOSSELOFF, A., United Nations-European Union. Cooperation in the field of peacekeeping. Challenges and prospects, in Global Governance Institute, Analysis Paper, June 2012.

NOYES, J.E., SMITH, B.D., State responsibility and the principle of joint and national liability, in Yale Journal of International Law, 13, 1988, pp. 234ss.

NTUBE NGANG, S., The position of witnesses before the International Criminal Court, ed. Brill, The Hague, 2015.

NYSTEN, C., CASEY-MASLEN, S., GOLDEN BERSAGEL, A., Nuclear weapons under international law, Cambridge University Press, Cambridge, 2014.

O'KEEFE, R., World cultural heritage: Obligations to the international community as a whole?, in International and Comparative Law Quarterly, 53, 2004, pp. 190ss.

O'MEARA, N., A more secure Europe of rights? The European Court of Human Rights, the Court of Justice of the European Union and EU Accession to the ECHR, in German Law Journal, 12, 2011, pp. 1813-1832.

O'KEEFE, R., Universal jurisdiction: Clarifying the basic concept, in Journal of International Criminal Justice, 2, 2004, pp. 735-760.

OBERMATT, J., The development of customary international law by international organizations, in International & Comparative Law Quarterly, 66 (2), 2017, pp. 494ss.

OCHOA RUIZ, N., Las cláusulas compromisorias de las convenciones de derechos humanos de las Naciones Unidas a la jurisdicción de la ICJ Internacional de Justicia: ¿un mecanismo jurisdiccional de protección de los derechos humanos?, in Anuario Español de Derecho International, 19, 2003, pp. 263ss.

OCHOA-RUIZ, N., SALAMANCA-AGUADO, E., Exploring the limits of international law on the use of force, in European Journal of International Law, 16 (3), 2005, pp. 500ss.

ODELLO, M., PIOTROWIC, R., International military missions and international law, ed. Brill, Bruxelles, 2011, pp. 136ss.

ODENDAHL, K., Article 30, in K. SCHMALENBACH, O. DÖRR, Vienna convention on the law of treaties. A commentary, ed. Springer, Berlin, Berlin, Heidelberg, 2012, pp. 512ss.

ODRIOZOLA GURRUTZAGA, M., Responsabilidad penal por crìmenes internacionales y coautoria medita, in Revista Electrònica de Ciencia Penal y

Criminologia, 17, 2015, pp. 7ss.

OHLIN, J.D., GOVERN, K., FINKELSTEIN, C., (eds.), Cyber war, law and ethics for virtual conflicts, Oxford University Press, Oxford, 2015, pp. 130ss.

OHLIN, J.D., Targeting and the concept of intent, in Cornell Law Faculty Publications, paper 774, 2013, pp. 84ss.

OLALEKAN YUSSUF, E., A critical evaluation of the UN Security Council's power in form of article 39 of the United Nations Charter: Interpretation, invocation and the morder threat to international peace and security, in Independent Student Journal Law, 2018 (1), pp. 7-9.

OLIVECRONA, K., Law as fact, Oxford University Press, Oxford, 1939, pp. 130ss.

OLSON, P.M., A NATO perspective on applicability and application of international humanitarian law to multinational forces, in International Review of Red Cross, 95, 2013, pp. 654ss.

OOSTHUIZEN, G.H., Playring the devil's advocate: The United Nations Security Council is unbound by law, in Leiden Journal of International Law, 12, 1999, pp. 562ss.

OPPENHEIM, L., International law. A treatise, Longmann Green & Co., London, 1955, pp. 354ss.

ORAKHELASHVILI, A., Division of reparation between responsible entities, in J. CRAWFORD, A. PELLET, S. OLLESON, The law of international responsibility, Oxford University Press, Oxford, 2010, pp. 648ss.

ORAKHELASHVILI, A., International public order and the international court's adivosry opinion on the construction of a wall in the occupied Palestinian territory, in Archiv des Völkerrechts, 43, 2005, pp. 248.

ORAKHELASHVILI, A., Peremptory norms in international law, Oxford University Press, Oxford, 2006.

ORAKHELASHVILI, Q., Division of reparation between responsible entities, in J. CRAWFORD, A. PELLET, S. OLLESON, The law of international responsibility, Oxford University Press, Oxford, 2010, pp. 658ss.

ORAKHELASHVILL, A., Jurisdictional immunities of the state (Germany v. Italy; Greece intervening), in American Journal of International Law, 106 (3), 2012, pp. 610ss.

ORENTLICHER, D., Some kind of justice. The ICTY's impact in Bosnia and Serbia, Oxford University Press, Oxford, 2018, pp. 376ss.

ORFORD, A., Jurisdiction without territory: From the holy roman empire to the responsibility to protect, in Michigan Journal of International Law, 30 (3), 2009, pp. 982ss.

ORREGO VICUÑA, F., Le règime d'exploration et d'exploitation, in R.J. DUPUY, D. VIGNES, Traitè du nouveau de la mer, ed. Economica, PaResolution Bruxelles, 1985, pp. 552ss.

ORTIZ, P.J.C., EU treaties and the judicial politics of national courts: A law and politics approach, ed. Routledge, London New York, 2015.

OSSENBÜHL, F., Rechtliche grundfragen der Erteilung von Schulzeugnbissen, Duncker & Humblot, Berlin, 2019, pp. 51ss.

OSTOJIC, M., Between justice and stability: The politics of war crimes prosecutions, Ashgate Publishing, Farnham, 2014.

OSWALD, B., DURHAM, H., BATES, A., Documents on the law of UN peace operations, Oxford University Press, Oxford, 2010, pp. 52ss.

OUDE ELFERINIC, A.G., HENRIKSEN, T., VEIERUD BUSCH, S., Maritime boundary delimitation: The case law: Is it consistent and predictable?, Cambridge University Press, Cambridge, 2018.

OUDE ELFERINK, A.G., The delimitation of the continental shelf between Denmark, Germany and the Netherlands, Cambridge University Press, Cambridge, 2014.

PAASIVIRTA, E., KUIJPER, P.J., Does one size fit all? The European Community and the responsibility of international organizations, in Netherlands Yearbook of International Law, 36, 2005, pp. 169-226.

PADDEU, F., Justification and excuse in international law. Concept and theory of general defences, Cambridge University Press, Cambridge, 2018.

PADDEU, F.I., Countermeasures, in Max Planck Encyclopedia of International Law, 2015.

PAJUSTE, T., The evolution of the concept of immunity of international organizations, in East West Studies, 8, 2017.

PALCHETTI, P., Attributing the conduct of dutchbat in Srebrenica: The 2014 Judgment of the District Court in the Mothers of Srebrenica Case, in The Netherlands International Law Review, 62, 2015, pp. 279-294, 283-285.

PALCHETTI, P., Can State action on behalf of victims be an alternative to individual access to justice in case of grave breaches of human rights?, in Italian Yearbook of International Law, 24, 2014, pp. 53ss.

PALCHETTI, P., Exploring alternative routes: The obligation of members to enable the organization to make reparation, in M. RAGAZZI, Responsibility of international organizations. Essays in memory of Sir Ian Brownlie, Martinus Nijhoff Publishers, Leiden, Boston, 2013, pp. 303ss.

PALCHETTI, P., Litigating member state responsibility. The Monetary Gold principle and the protection of absent organizations, in International Organization Law Review, 12, 2015, pp. 468ss.

PALCHETTI, P., The allocation of responsibility for internationally, committed in the course of multinational operations, in International Review of the Red Cross, 95, 2013, pp. 727-742.

PALM, T., The changing character of EUFOR Althea: Power politics or learning?, in Cambridge Review of International Affairs, 30 (1), 2017, pp. 68ss.

PALMISANO, G., Les causes d'aggravation de la responsabilitè des États et la distinction entre "crimes" et "dèlits" internationaux, in Revue Gènèrale de Droit International Public, 98, 1994, pp. 629ss.

PALWANKAR, U., Applicability of international humanitarian law to United Nations peacekeeping forces, in International Review of Red Cross, 81, 1993, pp. 228.

PANARA, C., The sub-national dimension of the EU: A legal study of multilevel governance, ed. Springer, Berlin, 2015.

PAPARINSKIS, M., Procedural aspects of shared responsibility in the International Court of Justice, in Journal of International Dispute Settlements, 4 (2), 2013, pp. 310ss.

PAPASTAVRIDIS, E., Interpretation of Security Council Resolutions under Chapter VII in the aftermath of the Iraqi crisis, in International and Comparative Law Quarterly, 56 (1), 2007, pp. 84ss.

PARRY, J., (Review): Ways and means of making the evidence of customary international law more readily available: Preparatory work within the purview of article 24 of the statute of the International Law Commission (Memorandum submitted by the Secretary-General), in International Law Quarterly, 3, 1950, pp. 462ss.

PARRY, J., The political theory of treaties in the restatements of foreign relations law, Brigham Young University Law Review, 2016, pp. 1618ss.

PATTERSON, D., SÖDERSTEN, A., European Union law and international law, ed. Wiley Blackwell, New York, 2016.

PAUST, J.J., The U.N. is bound by human rights: Understanding the full reach of human rights, remedies, and non immunity, in Harvard International Law Journal, 51, 2010, pp. 4-9.

PAVONI, R., Human rights and the immunities of foreign states and international organizations, in E. DE WET, J. VIDMAR, Hierarchy in International law: The place of human rights, Oxford University Press, Oxford, 2012, pp. 71ss.

PAYÁ MARTÍNEZ, I., Derecho internacional pùblico: teorìa y casos pràcticos, Murcia, Madrid, 2008.

PAYNE, T., Teaching old law new tricks: Applying and adapting state responsibility to cyber operations, in Lewis & Clark Law Review, 20, 2016, pp. 686ss.

PEAY, J., Mental incapacity and criminal liability: Redrawing the fault lines?, in International Journal of Law and Psychiatry, 42, 2015, pp. 4ss.

PECK, C., The United Nations as a dispute settlement system. Improving mechanisms for the prevention and resolution of conflict, Kluwer Law International, The Hague, London, Boston, 1996.

PEEL, J., Notice of claim by an injured state, in J. CRAWFORD, A. PELLET, S. OLLESON, The law of international responsibility, Oxford University Press,

Oxford, 2010, pp. 1032.

PEERS, S., The EU's Accession to the ECHR: The dream becomes a nightmare, in German Law Journal, 16, 2015, pp. 213, 222.

PEGORIER, C., Ethnic cleansing: A legal qualification, ed. Routledge, London, New York, 2013.

PEJIC, J., The protective scope of common article 3: More than meets the eye, in International Review of the Red Cross, 93, 2011, pp. 5-7.

PELLET, A., International Organizations are definitely not States, in M. RAGAZZI, Responsibility of International Organizations. Essays in memory of Sir Ian Brownlie, ed. Brill, Bruxelles, 2013, pp. 41ss.

PELLET, A., L'imputabilitè d'èventuels actes illicites. Responsabilitè de l'OTAN ou des États membres, in C. TOMUSCHAT, Kosovo and the international community: A legal assessment, ed. Brill, The Hague, 2002, pp. 194ss.

PELLET, A., Les articles de la CDI rur la responsabilité de l'État pour faits internationalement illicite suite-et fin ?, in Annuaire Français de Droit International, 48, 2002, pp. 17.

PELLET, A., Shaping the future of international law: The role of the world court in law-making, in M. H. ARSANJANI, Looking to the future: Essays on International Law in Honor of W. Michael Reisman, Martinus Nijhoff Publishers, The Hague, 2011, pp. 1066ss.

PELLET, A., Vive le crime! Remarques sur les degrès de l'illicite en droit international, in International law on the eve of the twentieth century, views from the international law commission, United Nations Publications, New York, 1997, pp. 288ss.

PERELMAN, C., Le raisonnable et le dèraisonnable en droit, in Archives de Philosphie du Droit, 29, 1978, pp. 35ss.

PEREZ GONZALEZ, M., Les organizations internationale et le droit de la responsabilitè, in Revue Gènèrale de Droit International Public, 92, 1988, pp. 67ss.

PERNICE, I., Die Haftung internationaler Organizationen und ihrer Mitarbeiter-dargetellt am "Fall" des internationalen Zinnrates, in Archiv des Völkerrechts, 26, 1988, pp. 419ss.

PEROVA, N., Disentangling "effective control" test for the purpose of attribution of the conduct of UN peacekeepers to the State and the UN, in Nordic Journal of International Law, 86 (1), 2017, pp. 32ss.

PERRET, R.L., De la faute et du devoir en droit international, Polygraphischer Verlag, Zürich, 1962, pp. 1506ss.

PERRIN, G., L'agression contre la lègation de Roumanie à à Berne et les fondements de la responsibilitè internationale dans les dèlits d'omission, in Revue Gènèrale de Droit International Public, 61, 1957, pp. 410ss.

PERSONNAZ, J., La rèparation du prèjuice en droit international public, ed.

Sirey, Paris, 1939.

PERUGINI, N., GORDON, N., The human right to dominate, Oxford University Press, Oxford, 2015.

PESCATORE, P., Les relations extèrieurs des Communautès europèennes, in Recueil des cours, ed. Brill, Bruxelles, 1961, pp. 134ss.

PETCULESCU, I., Droit international de la responsabilitè et droits de l'homme, in Revue Gènèrale de Droit International Public, 109, 2005, pp. 590ss.

PETERS, A., International organizations: Effectiveness and accountability, in Max Planck International Law Research Paper Series, No. 2016-01, p. 10.

PETERS, A., Subsequent practice and established practice of International Organizations: in Göttingen Journal of International Law, 3/2, 2011, pp. 618ss.

PETERS, A., The responsibility to protect and the permanetnt five-the obligation to give reasons for a veto, in J. HOFFMANN, A. NOLLAEMPER, Responsibility to protect. From principle to practice, Palas Publication, Amsterdam, 2012, pp. 205ss.

PETERS, A., The Security Council's responsibility to protect, in International Organizations Law Review, 8, 2011, pp. 4ss.

PETERSEN, N., Customary law without custom? Rules, principles, and the role of State practice in international law creation, in American University International Law Review, 23, 2008, pp. 276ss.

PETITE, M., The battle over Strasbourg: The protection of human rights across Europe has suffered a setback, thanks to the Court of Justice of the European Union, in Competition Law Insight, 2015, pp. 10ss.

PETROV, P., Early institutionalization of the ESDP governance arrangements: Insights from the operations Concordia and Artemis, in S.VANHOONACKER, D. HYLKE, M. HEIDI (eds). Understanding the role of bureaucracy in the European Security and Defense Policy, in European Integration online Papers, 14 (1), 2010.

PETSCHE, M., Jus cogens as a vision of the international legal order, in Penn State International Law Review, 29 (2), 2010, pp. 242ss.

PFANNER, T., Various mechanisms and approaches for implementing international humanitarian law and protecting and assisting war victims, in International Law Red Cross, 91, 2009, pp. 280ss.

PHELAN, W., What is sui generis about the European Union? Costly international cooperation in a self-contained regime, in International Studies Review, 14 (3), 2012, pp. 368ss.

PICCOLO, I., The crime of rape in international criminal law, International Courts Association, 2013.

PICHON, J., The principle of complementarity in the cases of the sudanese nationals Ahmad Harun and Ali Kushayb before the ICC, in International

Criminal Law Review, 8 (1-2), 2008.

PICOD, F., La Cour de justice a dit non à l'adhésion de l'Union européenne à la Convention EDH, in La Semaine Juridique, Édition Générale, 2015, pp. 230, 234.

PINGEL-LENUZZA, I., Remarques sur le procèdure dans l'affaire de la dèlimitation maritime et des questions teritoriales entre Quatar et Bahrèn. Cour Internationale de Justice, arrêts du 1er juillet 1994 et du 15 fèvrier 1995, in Revue Gènèrale de Droit International Public, 101, 1996, pp. 180ss.

PISILLO MAZZESCHI, R., Access to justice in constitutional and international law: The recent judgment of the Italian Constitutional Court, in Italian Yearbook of International Law, 24, 2014, pp. 9-23.

PISILLO MAZZESCHI, R., Impact on the law of diplomatic protection, in M.T. KAMMINGA, M. SCHEININ, The impact of human rights law on general international law, Oxford University Press, Oxford, 2009, pp. 219ss.

PISILLO MAZZESCHI, R., International obligations to provide for reparation claims?, in A. RANDELZHOFER, C. TOMUSCHAT, State responsibility and the individual. Reparation in instances of grave violations of human rights, ed. Brill, The Hague, 1999, pp. 159ss.

PISILLO MAZZESCHI, R., Reparation claims by individuals for state breaches of humanitarian law and human rights: An overview, in Journal of International Criminal Justice, 1 (3), 2003, pp. 339-347.

PISILLO MAZZESCHI, R., The marginal role of the individual in the ILC's articles on State responsibility, in Italian Yearbook of International law, 14 (1), 2004, pp. 44ss.

PITSCHAS, C., Die volkerrechtliche Verantwortlichkeit der Europaischen Gemeinschaft und ihrer Mitgliedstaaten, Duncker & Humblot, Berlin, 2001.

PLAKOKEFALOS, I., Causation in the law of state responsibility and the problem of overdetermination. In search of clarity, in European Journal of International Law, 26, 2015, pp. 472ss.

PLENGE, A., The special tribunal for Lebanon. Decision on the disclosure of materials from the criminal file of Mr El Sayed, in International Legal Materials, 50 (6), 2011, pp. 1099ss.

PODESTÁ COSTA, L.A., Derecho internacional publico, Editora Argentina, Buenos Aires, 1955, pp. 414ss.

POELLE, M.P., The international responsibility of international organizations in peacekeeping operations, Cambridge University Press, Cambridge, 2017, pp. 168ss.

POHLREICH, E., Das rechtliche Gehör im Strafverfahren, Mohr Siebeck, Tübingen, 2016, pp. 148ss.

POLAKIEWICZ, J., EU law and the ECHR: Will the European Union's accession square the circle?, in European Human Rights Law Review, 6, 2013, pp. 592-

605.

POLITIS, N.S., The problème des limitations de la souverainetè and the théorie de la abus de droits dans les rapports internationaux, in Recueil des cours, ed. Brill, Brussels, vol. 6, 1925, pp. 10ss.

POMERANCE, M., The ICJ's advisory jurisdiction and the crumbling wall between the political and the judicial, in American Journal of International Law, 99, 2005, pp. 28ss.

POMMIER, B., The use of force to protect civilians and humanitarian action: The case of Lybia and beyond, in International Review of the Red Cross, 93, 2011, pp. 1063ss.

PORRO, S., Risk and mental element: An analysis of national and international law on core crimes, ed. Nomos, Baden-Baden, 2014.

PORTMANN, R., Legal personality in international law, Cambridge University Press, Cambridge, 2010, pp. 233ss.

POSTEMA, G.L., Custom in international law: A normative practice account, in A. PERREAU-SAUSSINE, J. B. MURPHY, The nature of customary law: Legal, historical and philosophical perspectives, Cambridge University Press, Cambridge, 2007, pp. 280ss.

POTTEAU, A., Quelle adhésion de l'Union Européenne à la CEDH pour quel niveau de protection des droits et de l'autonomie de l'ordre juridique de l'UE?, in Revue Générale Droit International Public, 115, 2011, pp. 77-111.

POWELL, C., You have no God: An analysis of the prosecution of genocidal rape in international criminal law, in Richmond Public Interest Law Review, 20, 2017, pp. 26ss.

PROELLS, A., Article 34, K. SCHMALENBACH, O. DÖRR, Vienna convention on the law of treaties. A commentary, ed. Springer, Berlin, 2012, pp. 622-642.

PROELSS, A., United Nations Convention on the law of the sea. A commentary, H. Beck/Hart Publishing, München/Oxford & Oregon, Portland, 2017, pp. 970ss.

PROST, M., The concept of unity in public international law, Hart Publishing, Oxford & Oregon, Portland, 2012.

PROULX, V.J., An uneasy transition?, in M. RAGAZZI, Responsibility of International Organizations. Essays in memory of Sir Ian Brownlie, ed. Brill, Bruxelles, 2013, pp. 112ss.

PROULX, V.J., Institutionalizing state responsibility, Oxford University Press, Oxford, 2016.

PROVOST, R., State responsibility in international law, ed. Routledge, Aldershot, 2002.

PROVOST, R., State responsibility in international law, ed. Routledge, London & New York, 2017.

PRZETACZNIK, F., La responsabilitè internationale de l'Etat à raison des prèjudices de caractère moral et politique causès à un autre Etat, in Revue Gènèrale de Droit International Public, 78, 1974, pp. 943ss.

QUENEUDEC, J.D., La responsabilitè internationale de l'Etat pour les fautes personnelles de ses agents, LGDJ, Paris, 1966, pp. 252ss.

QUIGLEY, J., Complicity in international law. A new direction in the law of state responsibility, in British Yearbook of International Law, 57, 1986, pp. 78ss.

QUIGLEY, J., Responsabilitè internationale, ed. Pedone, Paris, 1987.

QUIGLEY, J., State responsibility for ethnic cleansing, in University of California Davis Law Review, 32, 1999, pp. 342ss.

QUIGLEY, J., The International Law Commission's crime-delict distinction: A toothless tiger?, in Revue de Droit International de Sciences Diplomatiques et Politiques, 65, 1987, pp 118ss.

QUIRILO, O., The international responsibility of the European Union. A basic interpretive pattern, in Hungarian Yearbook of International and European Law, 63, 2013.

QUISPE-REMÓN, D.J.L., El debido proceso en el derecho internacional y en el sistema interamericano, ed. Tirant lo Blanc, Valencia, 2010.

RABI, U., International intervention in local conflicts. Crisis management and conflict resolution in the cold war, I.B. Tauris Publishers, London & New York, 2010.

RAGAZZI, M., International responsibility today, Martinus Nijhoff Publishers, Leiden, 2005.

RAGAZZI, M., Responsibility of International Organizations. Essays in memory of Sir Ian Brownlie, Martinus Nijhoff Publishers, Leiden, 2013.

RAGAZZI, M., The concept of international obligations erga omnes, Clarendon Press, Oxford, 1997, pp. 43-72.

RAGNI, C., The contribution of Special Tribunal for Lebanon to the notion of terrorism: Judicial creativity or progressive development of international law, in N. BOSCHIERO, T. SCOVAZZI, C. PITEA, C. RAGNI, International courts and the development of international law. Essays in Honour of Tullio Treves, T.M.C. Asser Press-Springer, The Hague, 2013, pp. 671ss.

RAINEY, B., WICKS, W., OVEY, C., Jacobs, White and Ovey: The European Convention on Human Rights, Oxford University Press, Oxford, 2017.

RAMA MONTALDO, M., International legal personality and implied powers of international organizations, in The British Yearbook of International Law, 44, 1970, pp. 112ss.

RANJEVA, R., L'environnement, la Cour Internationale de Justice et la chambre spèciale pour les questions de l'environnement, in Annuaire Français de Droit International, 40, 1994, pp. 434ss.

RANK, R., Modern war and the validity of treaties: A comparative study, in Cornell Law Quarterly, 38 (1), 1952-1953, pp. 321ss.

RAO, P.S., Comments on article 19 of the draft articles on state responsibility adopted by the International Law Commission, in Indian Journal of International Law, 37, 1997, pp. 694ss.

RASHKOW, B., Remedies for harm caused by UN peacekeepers, in AJIL Unbound, 108, 2014, pp. 125ss.

RAUBER, J., Struktur Wandel als Prinzipien Wandel: Theoretische, dogmatische und methodische Bausteine eines Prinzipien modelles des Völkerrechts und seiner Dynamik, ed. Springer, Berlin, 2017, pp. 22ss.

RAVASI, E., Doctrine of equivalent protection in human rights protection by the ECtHR and the ECJ, ed. Brill, The Hague, 2017, pp. 24ss.

RAYFUSE, R., War and the environment. New approaches to protecting the environment in relation to armed conflict, Martinus Nijhoff Publishers, The Hague, 2014, pp. 180ss.

RAZ, J., ALEXY, R., BULYGIN, E., Un discusiòn sobre la teorìa del derecho, Marcial Pons, Madrid, 2007, pp. 100ss.

REIBSTEIN, E., Völkerrecht-Eine Geschichte seiner Ideen und Praxis, Alber Verlag, Freiburg-München, 1958, pp. 338ss.

REICHARD, M., The European Union-NATO relationship: A legal and political perspective, ed. Routledge, London & New York, 2016, pp. 247ss.

REICHEL, P., ALBANESE, J., Handbook of transnational crime and justice, Sage Publications, New York, 2013.

REICHLER, P., The impact of the Nicaragua case on matters of evidence and fact-finding, in Leiden Journal of International Law, 25 (1), 2012, pp. 152ss.

REINALDA, B., BERBEEK, B., Autonomous policy making by international organizations, ed. Routledge, London & New York, 1998, pp. 4ss.

REINISCH, A., Aid or assistance and direction and control between states and international organizations in the commission of internationally wrongful acts, in International Organization Law Review, 7, 2010, pp. 64ss.

REINISCH, A., Developing human rights and humanitarian law accountability of the Security Council for the imposition of economic actions, in American Journal of International Law, 95, 2001, pp. 852ss.

REINISCH, A., international organizations before national courts, Cambridge University Press, Cambridge, 2000.

REINISCH, A., KNAHR, C., From United Nations administrative tribunal to the United Nations appeals tribunal-Reform of administration of justice system within the United Nations, in Max Planck Yearbook of United Nations Law, 12, 2008, pp. 447ss.

REINISCH, A., The privilege and immunities of international organizations in domestic courts, Oxford University Press, Oxford, 2013, pp. 324ss.

REINISCH, A., Veerfahrensrechtliche Aspekte der Rechtskontrolle von Organen der Staatengemeinschfat in R. HOFMANN, A. REINISCH, T. PFEIFFER, S.

OETER, A. STADLER, Berichte der Deutschen Gesellschaft für Völkerrecht: Die Rechtskontrolle von Organen der Staatengemeischaft; Vielfalt der Fericht-Einheit des Prozessrecht?, C.F. Müller, Heidelberg, 2007, pp. 44ss.

REINOLD, T., The responsibility to protect-much ado about nothing?, in Review of International Studies, 36, 2010.

REISMAN, W.M., Kosovo's antinomies, in American Journal of International Law, 93 (4), 1999.

REISMAN, W.M., Nullity and revision, Yale University Press, New Haven, 1970, pp. 329ss.

REISMAN, W.M., The cult of custom in the late 20th century, in California Western International Law Journal, 17, 1987, pp. 134ss.

REISMAN, W.M., The democratization of contemporary international law-making processes and the differentiation of their application, in R. WOLFRUM, V. RÖBEN, Developments of international law in treaty making, ed. Springer, Berlin, 2005, pp. 16.

REITZER, L., La rèparation comme consèquence de l'acte illicite en droit international, ed. Sirey, Paris, 1938, pp. 134ss.

RENSMANN, T., Die Humansierung des Völkerrects durch das ius in bello. Von der Marten'schen Klausel zur Responsibility to protect, in Zeitschrift für ausländisches Recht und Völkerrecht, 68, 2008, pp. 120ss.

RENZIKOWSKI, J., Teilnahme, in R. MAURACH, K.H. GÖSSEL, H. ZIPF, Strafrecht, allegemeiner teils. Teilband 2: Erscheinungsformen des Verbrechens und Rechtsfolgen der Tat, ed. Springer, Heidelberg, 2014, pp. 531ss.

REUTER, P., Droit international public, ed. Brill, Bruxelles, 1983, pp. 224ss.

REUTER, P., La responsabilitè internationale. Droit international public, ed. Thèmis, Paris, 1956, pp. 56ss.

REUTER, P., Sixième rapport sur la question des traitès conclus entre États et organizations internationales ou entre deux ou plusiers organizations internationales, UN Doc. A/CN. 4/298, in Anuaire de la Commission du Droit International, 1977, vol. II, p. 127ss, par. 25.

REUTER, P., Trois observations sur la codification de la responsabilitè internationale des Etats pour fit illicite, in Mèlanges Virally, ed. Pedone, Paris, 1991.

REYNOLDS, R., Human rights in the line of fire: Al-Skeini v. United Kingdom, in Judicial Review, 16, 2011, pp. 340ss.

RID, T., BUCHANAN, R., Attributing cyber attacks, in The Journal of Strategic Studies, 38, 2015, pp. 7ss.

RIDDERVOLD, M., ROSÉN, G., Trick and treat: How the Commission and the European Parliament exert influence in EU Foreign and Security Policies, in

Journal of European Integration 38 (6), 2016, pp. 688ss.

RIDEAU, J., GREWE, C., BALMOND, L. ARCARI, A., Sanctions ciblèes et protection juridictionnelle des droit fondamentaux dans l'Union europèenne. Équilibre et dèsèquilibre de la balance, ed. Anthemis, Bruxelles, 2010.

RIGAUX, F., International responsibility and the principle of causality, in M. RAGAZZI, International responsibility today. Essays in memory of Oscar Schachter, Martinus Nijhoff Publishers, Leiden, Boston, 2005, pp. 88ss.

RIPHAGEN, W., Cinquième rapport siur le contenu, les formes et les degrès de la responsabilitè internatonale (deuxième partie du projet d'articles), Annuaire de la Commissione de Droit International, 1984, II, p. 1ss, p. 4.

RIPHAGEN, W., Quatrème rapport sur le contenu, les formes et le degrès de la responsabilitè internationale (deuxième partie du projet d'articles), in Annuaire de la Commission de Droit International, 1983, II, 1, p. 4ss.

RIPHAGEN, W., Sixth report on the content, forms and degrees of international responsibility (part two of the draft articles) and "implementation" (mise en oeuvre) of international responsibility and the settlement of disputes (part three of the draft articles), Doc. A/CN.4/389 and Corr. 1&2, in Yearbook of International Law Commission, 1985, vol. II, p. 3ss.

RIPHAGEN, W., The international concern for the environment as expressed in the concepts of the "common heritage of mankind" and of "shared natural resources," in M. BOTHE, Trends in environmental policy and law, Gland, Switzerland, 1980, pp. 343ss.

RITTER, J.P., La protective diplomatique à l'egard d'une organization internationale, in Annuaire Français de Droit International, 8, 1962, pp. 445ss.

ROBERT, E., The jurisdictional immunities of International Organizations: The balance between the protection of the organizations interest and individual rights, in Mélanges en l'honneur de Jean Salmon, ed. Bruylant, Bruxelles, 2007, pp. 1115ss.

ROBERTS, A.E., Traditional and modern approaches to customary international law: A reconciliation, in American Journal of International Law, 95, 2001, pp. 758ss.

ROBERTS, F.R.J., ARAUJO, S.J., Implementation of the ICJ advisory opinion. Legal consequences of the construction of a wall in the occupied Palestinian territory. Hences (do not) make good neighbors?, in Boston University of International Law Journal, 23, 2004, pp. 358ss.

ROBERTS, I., Satow's diplomatic practice, Oxford University Press, Oxford, 2017, pp. 314ss.

ROBINSON, P.H., GRALL, J.A., Element analysis in defining criminal liability: The model penal code and beyond, in Stanford Law Review, 35, 1983, pp. 685ss.

RODENHÄUSER, T., Organizing rebellion: Non-state armed groups under international humanitarian law, human rights and international criminal law, Oxford University Press, Oxford, 2018.

RONZITTI, N., NATO's intervention in Libya: A genuine action to protect a civil population in mortal danger or an intervention aimed at regime change?, in Italian Yearbook of International Law, 21, 2011, pp. 4ss.

ROONEY, J.M., The relationship between attribution and jurisdiction after Jaloud v. Netherlands, in Netherlands International Law Review, 62, (3), 2015, pp. 407.

ROSAS, A., Balancing fundamental rights in EU law, in Cambridge Yearbook of European Legal Studies, 16, 2014, pp. 348ss.

ROSCINI, M., Cyber operations and use of force, Oxford University Press, Oxford, 2014, pp. 34ss.

ROSCINI, M., Evidentiary issues in international disputes related to state responsibility for cyber operations, in Texas International Law Journal, 50, 2015.

ROSENBERG, S.P., Responsibility to protect: A framework for prevention, in Global Responsibility to Protect, 1, 2009, pp. 442ss.

ROSENNE, S., State responsibility and international crimes further reflections on article 19 of the draft articles on state responsibility, New York Journal of Law & Policy, 30, 1998, pp. 146ss.

ROSENNE, S., The law and practice of the international Court, ed. Brill, Dordrecht, Boston, 1985, pp. 324ss.

ROSENSTOCK, R., The ILC and state responsibility, in American Journal of International Law, 96, 2002, pp. 794ss.

ROSS, A., A textbook of international law, general part, The Lawbook Exchange Ltd., London, 1947 and reprinted edition of 2013.

ROSENTRETER, D., Article 31 (3) c) of the Vienna convention on the law of treaties and the principle of systemic integration in international investment law and arbitration, ed. Nomos, Baden-Baden, 2015, pp. 217ss.

ROTH, A., Das völkerrechtiche Delikt vor und in den Verhandlungen auf der Haager Kodificationskonferenz 1930, Robert Noske, Leipzig, 1932, pp. 54ss.

ROUSSEAU, C., La responsabilitè internationale, in Cours de droit international public, ed. Pedone, Paris, 1959-1960, pp. 8ss.

ROXBURGH, R.F., International conventions and third states, Longmans Green, London, 1917.

ROXSTRUM, E., GIBSON, M., EINARSEN, T., The NATO bombing case (Banković et al. v. Belgium et al.) and the limits of western human rights protection, in Boston University International Law Journal, 23, 2005, pp. 58ss.

RUSSO, D., The Injured individual's right to compensation in the law on diplomatic protection, in Rivista di Diritto Internazionale, 2016, pp. 725ss.

RUYS, T., CORTEN, O., HOFER, A., The use of force in international law. A case based approach, Oxford University Press, Oxford, 2018, pp. 538ss.

RUZIÉ, D., Droit international public, Dalloz, Paris, 2015.

RYNGAERT, C., Apportioning responsibility between the UN and member states in UN peace-support operations: An inquiry into the application of the effective control standard after Behrami, in Israel Law Review, 45, 2012, pp. 152ss.

RYNGAERT, C., BUCHANAN, H., Member state responsibility for the acts of international organizations, in Utrecht Law Review, 7, 2011, pp. 132ss.

RYNGAERT, C., The European Court of Human Rights approach to Member States responsibility in connection with acts of International Organizations, in International and Comparative Law Quarterly, 60 (4), 2011, pp. 1000ss.

RYNGAERT, C., The responsibility of Member States of International Organizations. Concluding observations, in International Organization Law Review, 12, 2015, pp. 516ss.

RYNGAERT, C., WOUTERS, J., Impact on the process of the formation of customary international law, in M.T. KAMMINGA, M. SCHEININ, The impact of human rights law on general international law, Oxford University Press, Oxford, 2009, pp. 112ss.

RYNGAERT, S., DEKKER, I.F., WESSEL, R.A., Judicial missions on the law of international organizations, Oxford University Press, Oxford, 2016, pp. 325ss.

RYNIKER, A., L'application du droit international humanitaire et les opèrations militaires organisèes en vertu de la Charte des Nations Unies, in International Review of Red Cross, 86, 1999, pp. 796ss.

SADURSKA, R., CHINKIN, C.M., The collapse of the international tin council: A case of state responsibility?, in Virginia Journal of International Law, 30, 1989-1990, pp. 845ss.

SALINAS DE FRÍAS, A.M., SAMUEL, K., WHITE, N., Counter terrorism. International law and practice, Oxford University Press, Oxford, 2012.

SALMON, J., Dictionnaire du droit international public, ed. Bruylant, Bruxelles, 2001, pp. 587.

SALMON, J., La fait ètatique complexe: une notion contestable, in Annuaire Français de Droit International, 28, 1982, pp. 710ss.

SALMON, J., Les accords Spaak-U Thant du 20 fevrier 1965, in Annuaire Français de Droit International, 11, 1965, pp. 479ss.

SALMON, J., Les circonstances excluant l'illiceitè, in J. SALMON, K. ZEMANEK, La responsabilitè internationale, ed. Pedone, Paris, 1987, pp. 90ss.

SALVIOLI, G., La responsabilitè des États et la fixation des dommages-intèrêts par les tribunaux internationaux, in Recueil des cours, ed. Brill, Bruxelles, vol. 28, 1929, pp. 238ss.

SAMSO, M., High hopes, scant resources: A word of skepticism about the anti-fragmentation function of article 31(3)(c) of the Vienna Convention on the Law of Treaties, in Leiden Journal of International Law, 24, 2011, pp. 5ss.

SAMUEL, K.L.H., WHITE, N.D., Counter-terrorism and international law, ed. Routledge, London & New York, 2017.

SÁNCHEZ REVERTE, R.S., Referencia al crimen de genocidio aprocimation genocide crime, in Revista de Estudios Juridicos, 16, 2016.

SANDHOLTZ, W., WHYTOCK, C.A., Research handbook on the politics of international law, Edward Elgar Publishers, Cheltenham, 2017, pp. 379ss.

SANDS, P., KLEIN, P., Bowett's law of international institutions, Sweet & Maxwell, London, 2009.

SARI, A., Jurisdiction and international peace support operations. The Behrami and Saramati cases, in Human Rights Law Review, 8 (1), 2008, pp. 154ss.

SARI, A., UN peacekeeping operations and article 7 ARIO: The missing link, in international organizations Law Review, 9 (1), 2012, pp. 77-85.

SARI, A., WESSEL, R.A., International responsibility for EU military operations: Finding the EU's place in the global accountability regime, in B. VAN VOOREN, S. BLOCKMANS, J. WOUTERS (eds.), The EU's role in global governance: The legal dimension, Oxford University Press, Oxford 2013, pp. 128ss.

SARKIN, J., Is the responsibility to protect an accepted norm of international law in the post-Libya era? How its third pillar ought to be applied, in Groningen Journal of International Law, 3, 2012, pp. 12ss.

SARKIN, J., The responsibility to protect and humanitarian intervention in Africa, in Global Responsibility to Protect, 2, 2010, pp. 371ss.

SAROOSHI, D., (ed.), Remedies and responsibility for the actions of international organizations, Martinus Nijhoff Publishers, The Hague, 2014, pp. 444ss.

SAROOSHI, D., International organizations and state responsibility, in M. RAGAZZI, Responsibility of international organizations. Essays in memory of Sir Ian Brownlie, Martinus Nijhoff Publishers, Leiden, Boston, 2013, pp. 86ss.

SAROOSHI, D., La responsabilité des organizations internationales: un état des lieux à l'issue des travaux de la Commission du droit international des Nations Unies, in Revue Belge de Droit International, 217, 2013.

SAROOSHI, D., Remedies and responsibility for actions of international organizations, ed. Brill, The Hague, 2014.

SASSÓLI, M., State responsibility for violations of international humanitarian law, in International Review of Red Cross, 84, 2002, pp. 414ss.

SAUER, F., System des Völkerrecht, V & R Unipress, Bonn, 1952, pp. 432ss.

SAUL, B., KINLEY, D., MOWBRAY, J.,The International Covenant on Economic, Social and Cultural Rights: Commentary, cases and materials, Oxford University Press, Oxford, 2014.

SAVARESE, E., Complicitè de l'État dans la perpètration d'actes de gènocide: les notions contiguës et la nature de la norme. En marge de la dècision application de la convention sur la prèvention et la rèpression du crime de gènocide (Bosnie-Herzègovine v. Serbie-et-Montenegro), in Annuaire Français de Droit International, 53, 2007, pp. 286ss.

SCHABAS, A.W., The European Convention on Human Rights: A commentary, Oxford University Press, Oxford, 2015, pp. 1755ss.

SCHABAS, W.A., Genocide and the International Court of Justice: Finally, a duty to prevent the crime of crimes, in Genocide Studies and Preventions, 2, 2007, pp. 101ss.

SCHABAS, W.A., Genocide law in a time of transition: Recent developments in the law of genocide, in Rutgers Law Review, 40, 2008-2009, pp. 162ss.

SCHABAS, W.A., The European Convention on Human Rights: A commentary, Oxford University Press, Oxford, 2015, pp. 1755ss.

SCHACHTER, O., Entangled treaty and custom, in Y. DINSTEIN, International law in a time of perplexity: Essays in Honor of Shabtai Rosenne, Martinus Nijhoff Publishers, Leiden/Boston, 1989, pp. 718ss.

SCHACHTER, O., Interpretation of the charter in the political organs of the United Nations, in S. ENGEL, Law, state and international legal order. Essays in Honor of Hans Kelsen, University of Tennesse Press, US, 1964, pp. 274ss.

SCHACHTER, O., New custom: Power, opinio juris and contrary practice, in J. MAKARCZYK, Theory of international law at the threshold of the 21st Century, Kluwer Law International, The Hague, 1996, pp. 532ss.

SCHACHTER, O., Self-defense and the rule of law, in American Journal of International Law, 83, 1989, pp. 26.

SCHACKELFORD, S., Holding States accountable for the ultimate human rights abuses: A review of the ICJ's Bosnian genocide case, in Human Rights Brief, 2007.

SCHARF, M.P., Accelerated formation of customary international law, in ILSA Journal of International & Comparative Law, 20 (2), 2014, pp. 310ss.

SCHARF, M.P., How the Tadić appeals chamber decision fundamentally altered customary international law, in M. STERIO, M. SCHARF, The legacy of ad hoc tribunals in international criminal law. Assessing the ICTY's and the ICTR's most significant legal accomplishments, Cambridge University Press, Cambridge, 2019.

SCHEININ, M., The Italian Constitutional Court's judgment 238 of 2014 is not another Kadi case, in Journal of International Criminal Justice, 13 (3), 2016, pp. 616ss.

SCHERMERS, H.G., BLOKKER, N.M., International institutional law. Unity within diversity, ed. Brill, Dordrecht, Bruxelles, 2011, par. 1579.

SCHERMERS, H.G., International institutional law, ed. Brill, Leiden, 1980, pp. 780ss.

SCHERMERS, H.G., Liability of international organizations in Leiden Journal of International law, 1 (1), 1988, pp. 4ss.

SCHERMES, H.G., BLOKKER, N.M., International institutional law. Unity within diversity, ed. Springer, Leiden, Boston, 2003, pp. 26ss.

SCHIELE, S., Evolution of international, environmental regimes. The case of climate change, Cambridge University Press, Cambrdige, 2014, pp. 83ss.

SCHINDLER, D., Die erga-omnes Wirkung des humanitären Völkerrecths, in U. BEYERLIN, M. BOTHE, R. HOFMANN, Recht zwischen Umbruch und Bewährung. Festschrift für Rudolf Bernhardt, ed. Springer, Berlin, 1995, pp. 200ss.

SCHINDLER, D., The different types of armed conflicts according to the Geneva Conventions and Protocols, in Recueil des Cours de l'Académie de Droit International, vol. 163, 1979, pp. 131ss.

SCHLÜTTER, B., Developments in customary international law, ed. Brill, Bruxelles, 2010, pp. 113ss.

SCHMALENBACH, K., Article 2, in K. SCHMALENBACH, O. DÖRR, Vienna convention on the law of treaties. A commentary, ed. Springer, Berlin, Heidelberg, 2012, pp. 45ss.

SCHMALENBACH, K., Die Haftung Internationaler Organizationen im Rahmen von Militäreinsätzen und Territorialverwaltungen, ed. Peter Lang, Frankfurt am Main, 2004, pp. 249.

SCHMALENBACH, K., DÖRR, O., Vienna convention on the law of treaties. A commentary, ed. Springer, Berlin, 2012, pp. 622-642.

SCHMALENBACH, K., Preserving the gordian knot: UN legal accountability in the aftermath of Srebrenica, in Netherlands International Law Review, 62, 2015, pp. 313ss.

SCHMITT, M.N., In defense of due diligence in cyber space, in Yale Journal Law Forum, 24, 2015, pp. 79ss.

SCHMITT, M.N., The development and principles of international humanitarian law, ed. Routledge, New York, 2017.

SCHNABEL, A., Kosovo and the challenge of humanitarian intervention: Selective indignation, collective action and international citizenship, United Nations University Press, Tokyo, 2000.

SCHÖN, P., Die völkerrechtliche Haftung der Staaten aus unerlaubten Handlugen, Breslau, Kern, 1917, pp. 34ss.

SCHRIJVER, N.J., The use of economic sanction by the UN Security Council: An international law perspective, in H.G. POST, International Economic Law and Armed Conflict, ed. Brill, Bruxelles, 1994, pp. 125ss.

SCHRÖDER, E., Die Grenzen der staatlichen Verantwortlichkeit für Handlungen von Staats-Organen im völkerrectkichen Verkehr, Zürich, 1939, pp. 22ss.

SCHÜTZE, R., TRIDIMAS, T., Oxford principles of European Union law, Oxford University Press, Oxford, 2018.

SCHWABACH, A., Yugoslavia v. NATO, Security Council Resolution 1244 and the law of humanitarian intervention, in Syracuse Journal of International Law and Commerce, 27 (1), 2000, pp. 92ss.

SCHWARTZBERG, J.E., Transforming the UN system designs for a workable world, Brookings Institution Press, Tokyo, New York, Paris, 2016.

SCHWARZE, J., BECKER, V., HATJE, A., SCHOO, J., EU-Kommentar, ed. Nomos, Baden-Baden, 2019.

SCHWARZENBERGER, G., A manual of international law, Cambridge University Press, Cambridge, 1967, pp. 192ss.

SCHWARZENBERGER, G., Myths and realities of treaty interpretation: Articles 27-29 of the Vienna Draft Convention on the Law of Treaties, in Virginia Journal of International Law, 9, 1968, pp. 2ss.

SCHWARZENBERGER, J., International law, Stevens & Sons, London, 1957, pp. 348ss.

SCOBBIE, I., The invocation of responsibility for the breach of "obligations under peremptory norms of general international law," in European Journal of International Law, 13, 2002, pp. 1210.

SCOTT, G.L., CARR, L., Multilateral treaties and the formation of customary international law, in Denver Journal of International Law and Policy, 25, 1996, pp. 72ss.

SCOTT, J., The new EU extraterritoriality, in Common Market Law Review, 52, 2015, pp. 1343ss.

SCOVAZZI, T., Within and beyond mutatis mutandis, in M. RAGAZZI, The responsibility of international organizations. Essays in memory of Sir Ian Brownlie, Martinus Nijhoff Publishers, Leiden, Boston, 2013, pp. 122ss.

SEAMAN, P.J., International bounty hunting. A question of state responsibility, in California Western International Law Journal, 15, 1985, pp. 408ss.

SEAMAN, K., UN-tied Nations: The United Nations, peacekeeping and global governance, ed. Routledge, London & New York, 2016.

SEIBERT-FOHR, A., VILLIGER, M.E., Judgments of the European Convention of Human Rights. Effects and implementation, ed. Nomos, Baden-Baden, 2017.

SEIDL HOHENVELDERN, I., Responsibility of members states of an international organization for acts of that organization, in Studi in onore di R. Ago, III, ed. Giuffrè, Milano, 1987, pp. 415ss.

SEIDL-HOHENVELDER, I., Die völkerrectiche Haftung für Handlungen internationaler organizationen im Verhältnis zu Nichtmitgliedstaaten, in Österreichische Zeitschrift für öffentliches Recht, 11, 1961, pp. 498ss.

SEIDL-HOHENVELDERN, I., L'ordre public international et la fraude à la loi-Luer importance en droit international public, in Mèlanges offerts à Jacques Maury, ed. Sirey, Paris, 1960, pp. 475ss.

SEIDL-HOHENVELDERN, I., Liability of member states for acts or omissions of an international oganization, in S. SCHLEMMER-SCHULTE, K.U. TUNG, Liber amicorum F.I. Shihata. International finance and development law, ed. Springer, The Hague, Boston, New York, 2001, pp. 732ss.

SEIDL-HOHENVELDERN, I., LOIBL, G., Das Recht der Internationalen Organizationen entischliesslich der Supranationalen Gemeinschaften, Heymanns Verlag, Köln, 2000, pp. 4ss.

SEIDL-HOHENVELDERN, I., Responsible of member states of an international organization for acts of that organization, in A.A.V.V., Le droit international à l'heure de sa codification. Études à l'honneur de R. Ago, ed. Giuffrè, Milan, 1987, pp. 416ss.

SEIDL-HOHENVELDERN, I., Völkerrecht, C. Heymanns, Berlin, Bonn, 1986, pp. 366ss.

SENDER, O., WOOD, M., A mystery no longer! Opinio juris and other theoretical controversies associated with customary international law, in Israel Law Review, 50 (3), 2017, pp. 300ss.

SEYERSTED, F., United Nations forces in the law of peace and war, A.E. Sijthoff, Leyden, 1966, pp. 194ss.

SHACKELFORD, S., State responsibility for cyber attacks: Competing standards for a growing problem, in Conference on Cyber Conflict Proceedings, 2010.

SHACKLEFORD, S., RUSSELL, S., KUEHN, A., Unpacking the international law on cybersecurity due diligence: Lessons from the public and private sectors, in Chicago Journal of International Law, 16, 2016, pp. 8ss.

SHAHABUDDEEN, M., Does the principle of legality stand in the way of progressive development of law?, in Journal of International Criminal Justice, 2, 2004, pp. 1007ss.

SHARP, D.N., Rethinking transitional justice for the twenty-first century: Beyond the end of history, Cambridge University Press, Cambridge, 2018.

SHAW, M.N., International law, Cambridge University Press, Cambridge, 2008, pp. 120ss.

SHAW, M.N., International law, Cambridge University Press, Cambridge, 2014.

SHAW, M.N., International law, Cambridge University Press, Cambridge, 2017, pp. 81ss.

SHELTON, D., International law and domestic legal systems: Incorporation, transformation and persuasion, Oxford University Press, Oxford, 2011, pp.

330ss.

SHELTON, D., Reparation, in Max Planck Encyclopedia of Public International Law, 2015.

SHEPSON, S., Jurisdiction in complicity cases. Rendition and refoulement in domestic and international courts, in Columbia Journal of Transnational Law, 54, 2015-2016, pp. 713ss.

SIBERT, M., Traitè de droit international public, ed. Dalloz, Paris, 1951, pp. 316ss.

SICILIANOS, A.L., Les rèactions dècentralisèes à l'illicite. Des contremesures à la lègitime dèfense, LGDJ, Paris, 1990.

SICILIANOS, A.L., Sanctions institutionnelles et contre-mesures: tendances rècentes, in L. PICCHIO FORLATI, A.L., SICILIANOS, Les sanctions èconomiques en droit internatonal-economic sanctions in international law, Leiden, Boston, 2004, pp. 58ss.

SICILIANOS, A.L., The classification of obligations and the multilateral dimension of the relations of international responsibility, in European Journal of International Law, 13, 2002, pp. 1137ss.

SICILIANOS, L.A., L'innovation de la lègitime dèfense face aux activitès d'entitès non-ètatiques, in Hague Yearbook of International Law, 2, 1989, pp. 150ss.

SICURELLI, D., The European Union's Africa policies: Norms, interests and impact, ed. Routledge, London & New York, 2016.

SIEKMANN, R.C.R., National contingents in United Nations peace-keeping forces, ed. Springer, Dordrecht, 1991, pp. 112ss.

SILANDER, D., WALLACE, D., International organizations and the implementation of the responsibility to protect, ed. Routledge, London & New York, 2015.

SILVERBURG, S., International law. Contemporary issues and future developments, ed. Routledge, London & New York, 2018.

SIMMA, B., ALSTON, P., The sources of human rights law: Custom, human rights and general principles, in Australian Yearbook of International Law, 5, 1988 pp. 88ss.

SIMMA, B., Das Reziprozitätelement im Zustandekommen Völkerrecht Verträge, Ducker & Humblot, Berlin, 1972.

SIMMA, B., From bilateralism to community interest in international law, in Recueil des cours, ed. Brill, Bruxelles, vol. 189, 1994, pp. 302ss.

SIMMA, B., GEIGER, R., KHAN, D.E., VON SCHORLEMER, S., From bilaterism to community interest: Essays in honour of judge Bruno Simma, Oxford University Press, Oxford, 2011.

SIMMA, B., Genocide and International Court of Justice, in C. SAFFERLING, W. CONZE (eds.), The genocide convention sixty years after its adoption,

T.M.C. Asser Press, The Hague, 2010, pp. 259-264.

SIMMA, B., Grundfragen der Staatenverantwortlichkeit in der Arbeit der International Law Commission, in Archiv des Völkerrechts, 53, 1985, pp. 358ss.

SIMMA, B., KHAN, D.E., NOLTE, G., PAULUS, A., WESSENDORF, N., The Charter of the United Nations, a commentary. Oxford University Press, Oxford, 2012, pp. 1293-1301.

SIMMA, B., Miscellaneous thoughts on subsequent agreements and practice, in G. NOLTE, Treaties and subsequent practice, Oxford University Press, Oxford, 2013, pp. 46ss.

SIMMA, B., PULKOWSKI, D., Leges speciales and self-contained regimes, in J. CRAWFORD, A. PELLET, S. OLLESON, The law of international responsibility, Oxford University Press, Oxford, 2010, pp. 141ss.

SIMMA, B., Reciprocity, in Encyclopedia of Public International Law, 1984, pp. 29ss.

SIMMA, B., Reciprocity, in Max Planck Encyclopedia of Public International Law, 2008, par. 91.

SIMMA, B., Reflections on article 60 of the Vienna Convention on the law of treaties, in Österreichische Zeitschrift für öffentliches Recht, 20, 1970, pp. 11ss.

SIMMA, B., Universality of international law from the perspective of a practitioner, in European Journal of International Law, 20, 2009, pp. 280ss.

SIMMA, D., PULKOWSKI, D., Of planets and the universe: Self-contained regimes in international law, in European Journal of International Law, 17, 2006, pp. 494ss.

SIMMONDS, R., Legal problems arising from the United Nations military operations in the Congo, ed. Springer, Berlin, 1968, pp. 238ss.

SIMMS, B., TRIMM, D., (ed.), Humanitarian intervention: A history, Cambridge University Press, Cambridge, 2011.

SIMÓN, L., No mighty, no right: Europeans must rediscover military power, in Real Instituto Elcano, European Global Strategy Project, EGS 2/2013, 19 March 2013.

SIMONDS, S., Conventional warfare and environmental protection: A proposal for international legal reform, in Stanford Journal of International Law, 29, 1992, pp. 190ss.

SINCLAIR, I., The impact of the unratified codification Convention, in A. BOS, H. SIBLESZ, Realism in law-making: Essays on International Law In Honour of Willem Riphagen, Martinus Nijhoff Publishers, Leiden, 1986, pp. 211.

SLOSS, D.L., The death of treaty supremacy. An invisible constitutional change, Oxford University Press, Oxford, 2016, pp. 357ss.

SLUITER, G., FRIMAN, H., LINTON, S., VASILIEV, S., ZAPPALÁ, S., International criminal procedural principles and rules, Oxford University Press, Oxford, 2013, pp. 373ss.

SMITH, L.V., Sovereignty at the Paris peace conference of 1919, Oxford University Press, Oxford, 2018, pp. 67ss.

SMITH, M.E., Europe's common security and defense policy: Capacity-building, experimental learning and institutional change, Cambridge University Press, Cambridge, 2017.

SOBENES OBREGON, E., SAMSON, B., Nicaragua before the International Court of Justice: Impacts on international law, ed. Springer, Berlin, 2017.

SÖFKER, C., Durch die Besatzungsmacht geprägte Neuordnungen besetzter Staaten: Welche Auswirkungen haben Völkerrechtlich verbotene Angriffsriege und die Reichweite der Kompetenzen von Besatzungsmächten Untersucht am Beispiel des Irak-krieges, H. Utz Verlag, München, 2014.

SOHN, L.B., "Generally accepted" international rules, in Washington Law Review, 61, 1986, pp. 1073ss.

SOHN, L.B., Sources of international law, in Georgia Journal of International and Comparative Law, 25, 1995-1996, pp. 399ss.

SOHN, L.B., Unratified treaties as a source of customary international law, in A. BOS, H. SIBLESZ (eds.), Realism in law-making: Essays in international law in Honour of Willem Riphagen, Martinus Nijhoff Publishers, The Hague, 1986, pp. 232s.

SOLIS, G.D., The law of armed conflict: International humanitarian law in war, Cambridge University Press, Cambridge, 2010.

SOMMARIO, E., Responsibility under international law for human rights violations committed by UN peacekeepers: Reconsidering issues of attribution, in A. DE GUTTRY, E. SOMMARIO, L. ZHU (eds.), China's and Italy's participation in peacekeeping operations: Existing models, emerging challenges, Lexington Books, London, 2014, pp. 369-397.

SOREL, J.M., BORÉ EVENO, V., Article 31. General rule of interpretation, in O. CORTEN, P. KLEIN, The Vienna Convention on the law of treaties. A commentary, Oxford University Press, Oxford, 2011, pp. 806ss.

SOREL, J.M., L'avenir du "crime" en droit international à la lumière de l'expèrience du jus congens, in Polish Yearbook of International Law, 23, 1997-1998, pp. 70ss.

SPAVENTA, E., A very fearful Court? The protection of fundamental rights in the European Union after Opinion 2/13, in Maastricht Journal of European and Comparative Law, 22, 2015, pp. 51ss.

SPERDUTI, G., Responsibility of states for activities of private law persons, in Encyclopedia of Public International Law, vol. IV, 2000, pp. 216ss.

SPIELMANN, D., L'adhésion de l'Union européenne à la Convention européenne des droits de l'homme, (Réunion conjointe de la Cour de justice de l'Union européenne et de la Cour européenne des droits de l'homme-Réseau des présidents des Cours suprêmes judiciaires de l'Union européenne, Helsinki 6 septembre 2013.

SPIJKERS, O., The evolution of United Nations peacekeeping in the Congo: From ONUC, to MONUC, to MONUSCO and its force intervention brigade, in Journal of International Peacekeeping, 19 (1), 2015, pp. 90ss.

SPIJKERS, O., The immunity of the United Nations in relation to the genocide in Srebrenica in the eyes of a Dutch District Court, in Journal of International Peacekeeping, 9, 2009, pp. 197ss.

SPIROPOULOS, J., Die Haftung der Staaten für "indirekten Schaden" aus völkerrechtlichen Delikten, in Niemeyers Zeitschrift für Völkerrecht, 35, 1925-1926, pp. 60ss.

SPRIK, L., Protection of civilian and individual accountability: Obligations and responsibilities of military commanders in UN peacekeeping operations, ed. Routledge, London & New York, 2019.

STAHN, C., EASTERDAY, J.S., IVERSON, I., Jus post bellum, Oxford University Press, Oxford, 2014, pp. 121ss.

STAHN, C., International territorial administration in the former Yugoslavia: Origins, development and challenges ahead, in Zeitschrift für ausländisches öffentliches Rechts und Völkerrecht, 61, 2001.

STAHN, C., VAN DEN HERIK, L., The diversification and fragmentation of international criminal law, Martinus Nijhoff Publishers, Leiden/Boston, 2012, pp. 34ss.

STARKE, J.G., An introduction to international law, Butterworth & Co., London, 1963, pp. 409ss.L. CAFLISCH, The effect of armed conflict on treaties, in BOSCHIERO N., PITEA C., RAGNI C., SCOVAZZI T., International Courts and the development of international law, ed. Springer, The Hague, 2013, pp.

STARSKI, P., Right to self-defence, attribution and the non-State actor. Birth of the "unable" of "unwilling" standard?, ion Zeitscrhift für ausländisches und öffentliches Recht und Völkerrecht, 75, 2015, pp. 456ss.

STARSKI, P., Silence within the process of normative change and evolution use of force: Normative volatility and legislative responsibility, in Journal of Use of Force & International Law, 14, 2017, pp. 248ss.

STEIN, T., BUTTLAR, C., KOTZUR, M., Völkerrecht, F. Vahlen Verlag, München, 2017.

STEIN, T., Kosovo and international community. The attribution of possible internationally wrongful acts: Responsibility of NATO or of its member states?, in C. TOMUSCHAT, Kosovo and the international community: A legal assessment, ed. Brill, The Hague, 2002, pp. 182ss.

STEIN, T., The approach of the different drummer: The principle of the persistent objector in international law, in Harvard International Law Journal, 26, 1985, pp. 458ss.

STERN, B., A plea for "reconstruction" of international responsibility based on the notion of legal injury, in M. RAGAZZI, International responsibility today. Essays in memory of Oscar Schachter, Martinus Nijhoff Publishers, Leiden, Boston, 2005, pp. 104ss.

SCHMITT, M.N., PEJIC, J., International law and armed conflict exploring the facultlines. Essays in honour of Yoram Dinstein, Martinus Nijhoff Publishers, 2007, The Hague, 2007, pp. 67ss.

STERN, B., Custom at the heart of international law, in Duke Journal of Comparative & International Law, 11, 2001, pp. 89ss.

STERN, B., The elements of an internationally wrongfull acts, in J. CRAWFORD, A. PELLET, S. OLLESON, The law of international responsibility, Oxford University Press, Oxford, 2010.

STEWART, J.G., The end of "modes of liability" for international crimes, in Leiden Journal of International Law, 25 (1), 2012, pp. 168ss.

STILLMUNKES, P., Le "forum prorogatum" devant la court permanente de justice internationale e la court internationale de justice, in Revue Gènèrale de Droit International Public, 35, 1964, pp. 676ss.

STRUPP, K., Das völkerrechtliche Delikt, Mohr Siebeck, Stuttgart, 1920.

STRUPP, K., Grundzüge des positiven Völkerrechts, L. Rohrscheid, Bonn, 1972, pp. 120ss.

SUBOTIĆ, J., Legitimacy, scope, and conflicting claims on the ICTY: In the aftermath of Gotovina, Haradinaj and Perišić, in Journal of Human Rights, 13(2), 2014, pp. 172ss.

SUR, S., Interpretation en droit international public, LGDJ, Paris, 1974, pp. 164ss.

SUR, S., Les organizations internationales. Dynamiques et dèsenchantement, in Revue Gènèrale de Droit International Public, 116, 2012, pp. 668ss.

SUZUKI, E., Responsibility of international organizations, in Michigan Journal of International Law, 27, 2005, pp. 178ss.

SZABÓ, M., International legal responsibility of the European Union according to the Draft Articles of the International Law Commission, in M. SZABÓ (ed.), State responsibility and the law of treaties, Eleven International, The Hague, 2009, pp. 186ss.

SZASZ, P.C., The law and practices of the International Agency for Atomic Energy, Wien, 1970, pp. 989ss.

TALMON, S., A plurality of responsible actors. International responsibility for acts of the coalition provisional authority in Iraq, in P. SHINER, A. WILLIAMS, The Iraq war and international law, Bloomsbury Publishing, New York, 2008, pp. 186ss.

TALMON, S., Determining customary international law. The ICJ's methodology between induction, deduction and assertion, in European Journal of International Law, 26 (2), 2015, pp. 422ss.

TALMON, S., Jus cogens after Germany v. Italy: Substantive and procedural rules distinguished, in Leiden Journal of International Law, 25 (4), 2012, pp. 979.

TALMON, S., Kollektive Nichtanerkennung illegaler Staaten: Grundlagen und Rechtsfolgen einer internationaler koordinierten Sanktion dargestellt am Beispiel der Türkischen Republik Nord-Zypern, Mohr Siebeck, Tübingen, 2006, pp. 334ss.

TALMON, S., The responsibility of outside powers for acts of secessionist entities, in International and Comparative Law Quarterly, 58, 2009, pp. 498ss.

TAMS, C.J., All's well that ends well. Comments on the ILC's articles on state responsibility, in Zeitschrift für ausländisches Recht und Völkerrecht, 62, 2002, pp. 759ss.

TAMS, C.J., Countermeasures against multiple responsible actors, in A. NOLLKAEMPER, I. PLAKOKEFALOS, Principles of shared responsibility in international law. An appraisal of the state of the art. An appraisal of the state of the art, Cambridge University Press, Cambridge, 2015, pp. 312ss.

TAMS, C.J., SLOAN, J., The development of international law by the International Court of Justice, Oxford University Press, Oxford, 2013, pp. 118ss.

TAMS, C.J., ZIMMERMANN, A., The federating shall occur to agreements providing for general, comprehensive and compulsory international arbitration. The German optional clause declaration of 1 May 2008, in German Yearbook of International Law, 51, 2008, pp. 392ss.

TAMS, J., The continued relevance of compromissory clauses as a source of ICJ jurisdiction, in T. GIEGERICH, A wiser century? Judicial dispute settlement, disarmament and the laws of war 100 years after the second Hague peace conference, Duncker & Humblot, Berlin, 2009, pp. 461ss.

TANAKA, Y., The peaceful settlement of international disputes, Cambridge University press, Cambridge, 2018, pp. 55ss.

TANCREDI, A., Enforcing WTO law, in A. JAKAB, D. KOCHENOV, The enforcement of EU law and values. Ensuring member states' compliance, Oxford University Press, Oxford, 2017, pp. 342ss.

TANZI, A., Is damage a distinct condition for the existence of an international wrongful act?, in M. SPINEDI, B. SIMMA, United Nations codification of state responsibility, Oceana Publications, Dobbs Ferry, New York, Rome, 1987, pp. 4ss.

TASIOULAS, J., In defense of relative normativity: Communitarian values and the Nicaragua case, in Oxford Journal of Legal Studies, 16, 1996, pp. 88ss.

TASIOULAS, J., Opinio juris and the genesis of custom: A solution to the "paradox," in Australian Yearbook of International Law, 26, 2007, pp. 200ss.

TAVERNIER, J., La responsabilité des Etats au regard de la Convention européenne des droits de l'homme pour la mise en oeuvre de résolutions adoptées dans la cadre du chapitre VII de la Charte des Nations Unies, in Revue Générale de Droit International Public, 117, 2013, pp. 102ss.

TEHINDRAZANARIVELO, D.L., Targeted sanctions and obligations of states on listing and de-listing procedures, in L. BOISSON DE CHAZOURNES, M. KOHEN, International law and the quest for its implementation. Liber Amicorum Vera Gowlland-Debbas, ed. Brill/Martinus Nijhoff Publishers, Leiden, 2010, pp. 127-171.

TEITGEN COLLY, C., La Convention européenne des droits de l'homme: 60 ans et après?, ed. LGDJ, Paris, 2013.

THAKUR, R., MALEY, W., (ed.)., Theorising the responsibility to protect, Cambridge University Press, Cambridge, 2015.

THALLINGER, G., The rule of exhaustion of local remedies in the context of the responsibility of international organizations, in Noridc Journal of International Law, 77, 2008, pp. 414ss.

THIRLWAY, H., Human rights in customary law, in Leiden Journal of International Law, 28, 2015, pp. 496ss.

THIRLWAY, H., Responsibility of international organizations. What role for the International Court of Justice?, in M. RAGAZZI, Responsibility of international organizations. Essays in memory of Sir Ian Brownlie, Martinus Nijhoff Publishers, Leiden, Boston, 2013, pp. 354ss.

THIRLWAY, H., The International Court of Justice, Oxford University Press, Oxford, 2016, pp. 578ss.

THIRLWAY, H., The law and procedure of the International Court of Justice 1960-1989 (part eleven), in The British Yearbook of International Law, 72, 2001, pp. 72ss.

THIRLWAY, H., The law and procedure of the International Court of Justice, in British Yearbook of International Law, 60, 1989, pp. 143ss.

THIRLWAY, H., The sources of international law, in M. D. EVANS, International law, Oxford University Press, Oxford, 2018, pp. 95ss.

THOUVENIN, J.M., Responsibility in the context of the European legal order, in J. CRAWFORD, A. PELLET, S. OLLESON (eds.), The law of international responsibility, Oxford University Press, Oxford, 2010, pp. 861ss.

THYM, D., The intergovernmental constitution of the EU's foreign security & defense executive, in European Constitutional Law Review, 11 (3), 2011, pp. 453ss.

TIMMERMANS, F., Fundamental rights protection in Europe before and after accession of the European Union to the European Convention on Human Rights, in Liber amicorum Pieter Van Dijk, M. Van Roosmalen and others (eds.), Intersentia, Antwerp, Oxford, 2013, pp. 225ss.

TITTEMORE, B.D., Belligerents in blue helmets: Applying international humanitarian law to United Nations peace operations, in Stanford Journal of International Law, 33, 1997, pp. 80ss.

TIZZANO, A., Les Cours européennes et l'adhésion de l'Union à la CEDH, in Il Diritto dell'Unione Europea, 2011, pp. 12ss.

TOMKA, P., Custom and the International Court of Justice, in The Judge and International Custom, CAHDI, Council of Europe, 19-20 September 2012, The Law and Practice of International Courts and Tribunals, 12, 2013, pp. 28ss.

TOMUSCHAT, C., Article 36, in A. ZIMMERMANN, C. TOMUSCHAT, K. OELLRS-FRAHM, The statute of the International Court of Justice. A commentary, Oxford University Press, Oxford, 2006, pp. 602ss.

TOMUSCHAT, C., Die internationale Gemeinschaft, in Archiv des Völkerrechts, 33, 1995, pp. 25ss.

TOMUSCHAT, C., Human rights between idealism and realism, Oxford University Press, Oxford, 2011.

TOMUSCHAT, C., Human rights between idealism and realism, Oxford University Press, Oxford, 2014.

TOMUSCHAT, C., Individual reparation claims in instances of grave human rights violations: The position under general international law, in A. RANDELZHOFER, C. TOMUSCHAT, State responsibility and the individual. Reparation in instances of grave violations of human rights, ed. Brill, The Hague, 1999.

TOMUSCHAT, C., International crimes by states: An endangered species?, in E. SUY, K. WELLENS, International law: Theory and practice. Essays in honour of Eric Suy, Martinus Nijhoff Publishers, The Hague, 1998.

TOMUSCHAT, C., Reparation in favour of individual victims of gross violations of human rights and international humanitarian law, in M.C. KOHEN, Promoting justice, human rights and conflict resolution through international law. Liber Amicorum Lucius Caflisch, ed- Brill, Leiden, 2007, pp. 569-590.

TOMUSCHAT, C., Specificities of human rights law and international humanitarian law regarding state responsibility, in R. KOLB, G. GAGGIOLI, Research handbook on human rights and humanitarian law, Edward Elgar Publishers, Cheltenham, 2013, pp. 198ss.

TOMUSCHAT, C., The European Court of Human Rights and the United Nations, in A. FØLLESDAL, B. PETERS, G. ULFSTEIN, Constituting Europe: The European Court of Human Rights in a national, european and global context, Cambridge University Press, Cambridge, 2013, pp. 334ss.

TOMUSCHAT, C., The international responsibility of the European Union, in E. CANNIZZARO, The European Union as an actor in international relation, Wolters Kluwer, Deventer, 2002, p. 178ss.

TÖRBER, G., The contractual nature of the optional clause, Bloomsbury Publishing, New York, 2015.

TORRES PEREZ, A., Too many voices? The prior involvement of the Court of Justice of the European Union? in European Journal of Human Rights, 40, 2013, pp. 565-583.

TOURNIER, A., De Brunsbüttel a Kinshasa. Le droit de la rèparation dans la jurisprudence des cours mondiales à l'aune de l'arrêt Diallo, in Annuaire Français de Droit International, 58, 2012, pp. 210ss.

TOWNSEND, G., State responsibility for acts of de facto agents, in Arizona Journal of International and Comparative Law, 14, 1997, pp. 662ss.

TRAPP, K.N., MILLS, A., Smooth runs the water where the brook is deep: The obscured complexities of Germany v. Italy, in Cambridge Journal of International and Comparative Law, 1, 2012, pp. 154ss.

TRAVISS, A., Temple of Preah Vihear. Lessons on provisional measures, in Chicago Journal of International Law, 13, 2012, pp. 327ss.

TREBILCOCK, J., Waiver, in Encyclopedia of Public International Law, 2000, pp. 1327ss.

TRIEPEL, H., Völkerrecht und Landesrecht, Verlag Von G.L. Hirscefeld, Leipzig, 1899, pp. 333ss.

TRIMBLE, P., Beyond verification: The next step in arms control, in Harvard Law Review, 102, 1989, pp. 885-912.

TSAGOURIAS, N., BUCHAN, R., International law and cyber space, ed. Edward Elgar Publishers, Cheltenham, 2015, pp. 66ss.

TSAGOURIAS, N., The responsibility of international organizations for military missions, in M. ODELLO, R. PIOTROWICZ (eds.) International military missions and international law, Martinus Nijhoff Publishers, The Hague, 2011, pp. 246ss.

TSAGOURIAS, N., MORRISON, A., International humanitarian law: Cases, materials and commentary, Cambridge University Press, Cambridge, 2018.

TUCKER, R.W., Principles of international law, Holt, Rinehart and Winston, New York, 1966, pp. 16ss.

TUNKIN, G.I., Remarks on the juridical nature of customary norms of international law, in California Law Review, 49, 1961, pp. 422ss.

TURAN, G., Responsibility to prosecute in an age of global governmentality: The International Criminal Court, in Cooperation and Conflict, 50, 2015.

TÜRK, A.H., Judicial review in European Union law, Edward Elgar Publishers, Cheltenham, 2010.

TZANAKOPOULOS, A., Disobeying the Security Council, Oxford University Press, Oxford, 2011.

TZENG, P., Jurisdiction and applicable law under UNCLOS, in Yale Law Journal,

126, 2016-2017.

TZEVELEKOS, V.P., Reconstructing the effective control criterion in extraterritorial human rights breaches. Direct attribution of wrongfulness, due diligence and concurrent responsibility, in Michigan Journal of International Law, 35, 2014, pp. 129ss.

ULESTEIN, G., Les activitès normatives de l'organization internationale, in E. LAGRANDE, J.M. SOREL, Droit des organizations intrnationales, LGDJ, Paris, 2013, pp. 746ss.

ULFSTEIN, G., MARAHAUN, T., ZIMMERMANN, A., (ed. by), Making treaties work. Human rights, environment, arms control, Oxford University Press, Oxford, 2007, pp. 3ss.

USHAKOV, N., Statement at the 1518th meeting of the International Law Commission, in Yearbook of International Law Commission, 1999, pp. 398ss.

USHERWOOD, J., PINDER, S., The European Union. A very short introduction, Oxford University Press, Oxford, 2018.

VADI, V., Cultural heritage in international investment law and arbitration, Cambridge University Press, Cambridge, 2014, pp. 100ss.

VALLEJO FRANCO, B.E., La responsabilidad de proteger. Una nueva dimensión de la soberanía, in Oasis, 15, 2011, pp. 8ss.

VAN AAKEN, A., MOTOC, I., The ECHR and general international law, Oxford University Press, Oxford, 2018, pp. 194ss.

VAN CALSTER, G., VANDENBERGHE, W., REINS, L., Research handbook on climate change mitigation law, Edward Elgar Publishers, Cheltenham, 2015.

VAN DAMME, I., Treaty interpretation by the WTO Appellate Body, in European Journal of International Law, 21, 2010, pp. 606ss.

VAN DEN BOSSCHE, P., ZDOUC, W., Law and policy of the World Trade Organization, Cambridge University Press, Cambridge, 2013, pp. 140ss.

VAN DEN HERIK, L., Research handbook on UN sanctions and international law, Edward Elgar Publishers, Cheltenham, 2017, pp. 218ss.

VAN DER HAVE, N., The prevention of gross human rights violations under international human rights law, ed. Springer, Berlin, 2018.

VAN HOUTTE, H., International law and community treaty-making, in Northwestern Journal of International Law & Business, 3, 1981, pp. 633ss.

VAN RAEPENBUSCH, S., La convergence entre les régimes de responsabilité extracontractuelle de l'Union Européenne et des États Membres, in ERA Forum, 12 (4), 2012, pp. 672ss.

VAN SLIEDREGT, E., Pluralism in international criminal law, in Leiden Journal of International Law, 25 (4), 2012, pp. 849ss.

VANDENBROUKE, F., BARNARD, V., DE BAERT, G., A European social union after the crisis, Cambridge University Press, Cambridge, 2017.

VARGAS CARREÑO, E., Derecho internacional pùblico, Editorial Jurìdica, Santiago de Chile, 2007.

VENTURA, M.J., The duty to investigate Zimbabwe crimes against humanity (torture) allegations: The Constitutional Court of South Africa speaks on universal jurisdiction and the ICC act, in Journal of International Criminal Justice, 13, 2015, pp. 861-889.

VENZKE, I., How interpretation makes international law. On semantic change and normative twists, Oxford University Press, Oxford, 2012, pp. 38ss.

VENZKE, I., The role of International Courts as interpreters and developers of the law: Working out the juris generative practice of interpretation, in Loyola of Los Angeles International & Comparative Law Review, 34, 2011, pp. 100ss.

VERDIRAME, G., Breaches of the European Convention on Human Rights resulting from the conduct of international organizations, in European Human Rights Law Review, 8, 2008, pp. 220ss.

VERDIRAME, G., The UN and human rights: Who guards the guardians? Cambridge University Press, Cambridge, 2011, pp. 225ss.

VERDROSS, A., Règles gènèrales de droit de la paix, in Recueil des cours, ed. Brill, Bruxelles, vol. 30, 1929, pp. 272ss.

VERDROSS, A., SIMMA, B., Universelles Völkerrecht. Theorie und praxis, Duncker & Humblot, Berlin, 1984, pp. 413ss.

VERDROSS, A., Theorie der mittelbaren Staatenhaftung, in Österreichische Zeitschrift für öffentliches Recht, 2, 1948, pp. 410ss.

VERDROSS, A., Völkerrecht, ed. Springer, Wien, 1964.

VERHOEVEN, J., The law of responsibility of the law of treaties, in J. CRAWFORD, A. PELLET, S. OLLESON, The law of international responsibility, Oxford University Press, Oxford, 2010, pp. 106ss.

VERLAGE, V., Responsibility to protect: ein neur Ansatz im Völkerrecht zur Verhindernung von Völkerrechtmord, Kriegsverbrechen und Verbrechen gegen die Menschlkichkeit, ed. Mohr Siebeck, Tübingen, 2009.

VEZZANI, S., Countermeasures by member states against international organizations, in M. RAGAZZI, Responsibility of international organizations. Essays in memory of Sir Ian Brownlie, Martinus Nijhoff Publishers, Leiden, Boston, 2013.

VEZZANI, S., Prior exhaustion of internal remedies in cases involving the international responsibility of the European Union, in Italian Yearbook of International Law, 22, 2012, pp. 61-89.

VILLALPANDO, S., Codification light. A new trend in the codification of international law at the United Nations, in Brazilian Yearbook of International Law, 10, 2013, pp. 118ss.

VILLALPANDO, S., L'èmergence de la communautè internationale dans la responsabilitè des États, ed. PUF, Paris, 2005.

VILLALPANDO, S., On the International Court of Justice and the determination of rules of law, in Leiden Journal of International Law, 26, 2013, pp. 248ss.

VILLIGER, M.E., Commentary on the 1969 Vienna Convention on the Law of Treaties, Martinus Nijhoff Publishers, The Hague, Boston, 2009, pp. 432ss.

VILLIGER, M.E., Customary international law and treaties, Kluwer Law International, The Hague, 1997, pp. 39ss.

VILLIGER, M.E., The rules on interpretation: Misgivings, misunderstandings, miscarriage? The "crucible" intended by the International Law Commission, in E. CANNIZZARO, The law of Treaties beyond the Vienna Convention, Oxford University Press, Oxford, 2011, pp. 106s.

VIOLINI, L., BARAGGIA, A., The fragmented landscape of fundamental rights protection in Europe, Edward Elgar Publishers, Cheltenahm, 2018, pp. 95ss.

VIRALLY, M., Definition and classification of international organizations, in G. ABI-SAAB, The concept of international organization, UNESCO, Paris, 1981, pp. 50ss.

VIRALLY, M., La notion de fonction dans la thèorie de l'organization internationale, in G. ABI-SAAB, La communautè internationale. Mèlanges offerts à Charles Rousseau, ed. Pedone, Paris, 1974, pp. 278ss.

VIRALLY, M., Le principle de rèciprocitè dans le droit internatonal contemporain, in Recueil des cours, ed. Brill, Bruxelles, vol. 122, 1967, pp. 54ss.

VIRALY, M., La valeur juridique des recommanations des organizations internationales, in Annuaire Français de Droit International, 2, 1956, pp. 66ss.

VIRZO, R., INGRAVALLO, I., (eds.), Evolutions in the law of International Organizations, ed. Brill, Leiden-Boston, 2015.

VISSER, L., May the force be with you: The legal classification of intervention by invitation, in Netherlands International Law Review, 66 (1), 2019, pp. 22ss.

VOENEKY, S., NEUMAN, G.L., Human rights democracy and legitimacy in a world of disorder, Cambridge University Press, Cambridge, 2018, pp. 216ss

VOGLER, J., The global commons: Environmental and technological governance, Wiley, New York, 2000.

VOJDIK, V.K., Sexual violence against men and women in war: A masculinities approach, in Nevada Law Journal, 15, 2014-2015, pp. 925ss.

VON ARNAULD, A., Völkerrecht, C.F. Müller, Heidelberg, 2016.

VON ARNAULD, A., Völkerrecht, C.F. Müller, Tübingen, 2014.

VON BOGDANDY, A., DANN, P., GOLDMANN, M., Developing the publicness of public international law. Towards a legal framework for global governance, in German Law Journal, 9, 2008, pp. 1381ss.

VON BOGDANDY, A., General principles of international public authority: Sketching a research field, in A. VON BOGDANDY, R. WOLFRUM, J. VON BERNSTORFF, M B. DANN, M. GOLDMANN, The exercise of public authority by international institutions, ed. Springer, Berlin. pp. 733ss.

VON BOGDANDY, A., IOANNIDIS, M., Systemic deficiency in the rule of law: What it is, that has been done, what can be done, in Common Market Law Review, 51, 2014, pp. 60ss.

VON BOGDANDY, A., KOTTMANN, M., ANTPÖHLER, C., DICKSCHEN, J., HENTREI, S., SMRKOLJ, M., Reverse Solange-protecting the essence of fundamental rights against the Member States, in Common Market Law Review, 49, 2012, pp. 490ss.

VON BOGDANDY, A., VENZKE, I., International judicial law making, ed. Springer, New York, London, 2012.

VON BURI, M., Über Kausalität und deren Verantwortung, J.M. Gebhardt's Verlag, Leipzig, 1873.

VON HIPPEL, R., Lehrbuch des Strafrechts, ed. Springer, Berlin, 1932, pp. 99ss.

VON LUDEN, FH., Abhandlungen aus dem gemeinen deutschen Strafrecht, vol. II, Göttingen, 1840.

VON MÜNCH, I., Das Völkerrechtliche Delikt in der Modernen Entwicklung der Völkerrechtsgemeinschaft, P. Keppler Verlag, Frankfurt, 1963, pp. 170ss.

VON MÜNCH, I., Völkerrecht, De Gruyter, Berlin, New York, 2019.

VÖNEKY, S., HÖFELMEIER, A., Article 139, in A. PROELS, United Nations Convention on the law of the sea. A commentary, C.H. Beck, Hart Publishing, München/Oxford, Oregon & Portland, 2017, pp. 968ss.

VÖNEKY, S., A new shield for the environment: Peacetime treaties as legal restraints of wartime damage, in Review of European Community and International Environmental Law, 9 (1), 2000, pp. 20ss.

VÖNEKY, S., Analogy in International Law, in Max Planck Encyclopedia of Public International Law, 2008.

VÖNEKY, S., Implementation and enforcement of international humanitarian law, in D. FLECK, The handbook of international humanitarian law, Oxford University Press, Oxford, 2013, pp. 648ss.

VOULGARIS, N., Allocating international responsibility between member states and international organizations, Bloomsbury Publishing, New York, 2019.

VOULGARIS, N., Rethinking indirect responsibility: A study of article 17 of the Draft Articles on the Responsibility of International Organizations, in International Organizations Law Review, 11, 2014, pp. 8ss.

WAGNER, E., The rule of law and its application to the United Nations: Conference report, in Max Planck United Nations Yearbook, 18, 2014, pp. 347ss.

WÄHLISCH, M., Peace making power-sharing and international law. Imperfect peace, Hart Publishing, Oxford, Oregon, Portland, 2019.

WAIBEL, M., Demystifying the art of interpretation, in The European Journal of International Law, 22 (2), 2011, pp. 572ss.

WALKER N., Intimations of global law, Cambridge University Press, Cambridge, 2014, pp. 66ss.

WALKER, H., Modern treaties of friendship, commerce and navigation, in Minnesota Law Review, 42, 1957-1958, pp. 805ss.

WALLACE, R., International law, Sweet & Maxwell, London, 1986, pp. 160ss.

WALTER, C., VON UNGERN-STERNBERG, A., ABUSHOV, K., (eds), Self-determination and secession in international law, Oxford University Press, Oxford, 2014, pp. 262ss.

WALTER, C., VON UNGERN-STERNBERG, A., ABUSHOV, K., Self-determination and secession in international law, Oxford University Press, Oxford, 2014.

WARNER, D., Human rights and humanitarian law. The quest for universality, Martinus Nijhoff Publishers, The Hague, Boston, London, 1997.

WATSON, K.W., Behrami v. France: Constructive blue helmets protect KFOR nations from accountability, in Tulane Journal of International and Comparative Law, 16, 2007-2008, pp. 576ss.

WATSON, R., The “wall” decisions in legal and political context, in American Journal of International Law, 99, 2005, pp. 27ss.

WATTS, A., The international rule of law, in German Yearbook of International Law, 36, 1993, pp. 15ss.

WEBB, P., International judicial interpretation and fragmentation, Oxford University Press, Oxford, 2013, pp. 140ss.

WECKEL, P., Convergence du droit des traitès et du droit de la responsabilitè internationale, in Revue Gènèrale de Droit International Public, 102 (3), 1998, pp. 648ss.

WEIBUST, I., MEADOWCROFT, J., Multilevel environmental governance. Managing water and climate change in Europe and North America, Edward Elgar Publishers, Cheltenham, 2014.

WEIGEND, T., Intent, mistake of law, and co-perpetration in the Lubanga Decision on the confirmation of charges, in Journal of International Criminal Justice, 8, 2008, pp. 476ss.

WEIL, P., Droit international en quête de son identitè, Recueil des cours, ed. Brill, Bruxelles, vol. 237, 1996.

WEIL, P., Towards relative normativity in international law?, in American Journal of International Law, 77, 1983, pp. 41ss.

WEILER, J.H.H., The geology of international law. Governance, democracy and legitimacy, in Zeitschrift für ausländisches Recht und Völkerrecht, 64, 2004, pp. 548ss.

WEINER, P., The evolving jurisprudence of the crime of rape in international criminal law, in Boston College Law Review, 54, 2013, pp. 1210ss.

WEISBURD, A.M., Customary international law: The problem of treaties, in Vanderbilt Journal of Transnational Law, 21, 1988, pp. 2ss.

WEISBURD, A.M., International crimes of states. The decay of an idea, in Polish Yearbook of International Law, 23, 1997-1998, pp. 52ss.

WEISS, N., THOUVENIN, J.M., The influence of human rights on international law, ed. Springer, Berlin, 2015, pp. 61ss.

WELER, T., NAFTA investment arbitration and the growth of international economic law, in Business Law International, 158, 2002, pp. 180ss.

WELLENS, K., International Law: Theory and Practice Essays in the Honor of Eric Suy, Martinus Nijhoff Publishers, The Hague, 1998, pp. 161ss.

WELLENS, K., Remedies against international organizations, Cambridge University Press, Cambridge, 2002, pp. 14

WELLENS, W., Remedies against international organizations, Cambridge University Press, Cambridge, 2004, pp. 30ss

WELLER, M., SOLOMOU, A., RYLATT, J.W., The oxford handbook of the use of force in international law, Oxford University Press, Oxford, 2015, pp. 645ss.

WELLER, M., The oxford handbook of the use of force in international law, Oxford University Press, Oxford, 2015, pp. 724ss.

WENDEL, M., Exceeding judicial competence in the name of democracy. The German Federal Constitutional Court's OMT reference, in European Constitutional Law Review, 10, 2014, pp. 264ss.

WENGLER, W., Recours judiciaire à instituer contre le dècisions d'organes internationaux: Rapport et projet de résolution, in Annuaire de l'Institut du Droit International, 1952, pp. 224ss.

WENGLER, W., Völlkerecht, ed. Springer, Berlin, Heidelberg, 1964, pp. 178ss.

WENZEL, N., Das Spannungsverhältnis zwischen Gruppenschutz und Individualschutz im Völkerrecht, ed. Springer, Berlin, 2007.

WERLE, G., JESSBERGER, F., Principles of international criminal law, Oxford University Press, Oxford, 2014.

WERLE, G., JESSBERGER, F., Unless otherwise provided: Article 30 of the ICC Statute and the mental element of crimes under international criminal law, in Journal of International Criminal Justice, 3, 2005, pp. 37ss.

WESSEL, R.A., BLOCKMANS, S., (eds.) Between autonomy and dependence. The EU legal order under the influence of international organizations, T.M.C. Asser Press, The Hague, 2013, pp. 14ss.

WESSEL, R.A., Division of international responsibility between the EU and its member States in the area of foreign policy, security and defense policy, in Amsterdam Law Forum, 3 (3), 2011, pp. 44.

WESSEL, R.A., ŁAZOWSKI, A., When Caveats Turn into Locks: Opinion 2/13 on Accession of the European Union to the ECHR, in German Law Journal, 16, 2015, pp. 179ss.

WESTON, B.H., FALK, R.A., CHARLESWORTH, H., International law and world order. A problem-oriented course-book, West Academic, Saint Paul, Minnesota, 2006.

WHEELER, C.H., The right to be present at trial in international criminal law, ed. Brill, Bruxelles, 2018.

WHITE, N., The law of international organization, Manchester University Press, Manchester, 2005.

WHITE, N.D., The law of international organizations, Oxford University Press, Oxford, 2016.

WHITEMAN, M.M., Digest of international law, Washington, 1970, pp. 509ss.

WHITTLE, D., The intervention brigade, Monusco, and the application of international humanitarian law to UN forces, in Georgetown Journal of International Law, 6, 2014-2015, pp. 838ss.

WIERZBOWSKI, M., GUBRYNOWICZ, A., International investment law for the 21st century, Oxford University Press, Oxford, 2015.

WILDE, R., The legal space or espace juridique of the European Convention on Human Rights: Is it relevant to extraterritorial State action?, in European Human Rights Law Review, 2, 2005, pp. 116ss.

WILLIAMSON, J.A., Some consideration on command responsibility and criminal liability, in International Review of the Red Cross, 90, 2008, pp. 306ss.

WILLIAMSON, R.L., Jr., Is international law relevant to arms control? Hard law, soft law and non-law in multilateral arms control: Some compliance hypotheses, in Chicago Journal of International Law, 4, 2003, pp. 59ss.

WILLMOT, H., WELLER, M., MAMIYA, R., SHEERAN, S., The protection of civilians, Oxford University Press, Oxford, 2016, pp. 238ss.

WILLS, S., Protecting civilians: The obligations of peacekeeping, Oxford University Press, Oxford, 2009.

WILMSHURST, E., BREAU, S., Perspectives on the ICRC study on customary international humanitarian law, Cambridge University Press, Cambridge, 2008, pp. 43ss.

WILMSHURTS, E., (ed. by), International law and the classification of conflicts, Oxford University Press, Oxford, 2012.

WITTBERGER, V., ZANGL, B., KRUCK, A., International organization, ed. Palgrave Macmillan, London & New York, 2012.

WITTICH, S., Joint tortfeasors in investment law, in C. BINDER, U. KRIEBAUM, A. REINISCH, S. WITTICH, International investment law for the 21st century, Oxford University Press, Oxford, 2009, pp. 708ss.

WOLF, J., Gibt es im Völkerrecht einen einheitlichen Schadensbegriff?, in Zeitschrift für ausländisches Recht und Völkerrecht, 49, 1989, pp. 444ss.

WOLF, J., Zurechnungsfragen beim Handlungen privatpersonen, in Zeitschrift für ausländisches Recht und Völkerrecht, 45, 1985, pp. 232ss.

WOLFKE, K., Custom in international law, Martinus Nijhoff Publishers, Leiden/Boston, 1993, pp. 162ss.

WOLFKE, K., Some persistent controversies regarding customary international law, in Netherlands Yearbook of International Law, 24, 1993, pp. 4ss.

WOLFKE, K., Treaties and custom: Aspects of interrelation, in J. KLABBERS, R. LEFEBER, Essays on the Law of Treaties: A collection of Essays in Honour of Bert Vierdag, Martinus Nijhoff Publishers, The Hague, 1998, pp. 32ss.

WOLFRUM, J., Reparation of internationally wrongful acts, in Encyclopedia of Public International Law, 2000, pp. 178ss.

WOLFRUM, R., RÖBEN, E., Developments of international law in treaty making, ed. Springer, Berlin, 2005, pp. 16ss.

WOLFRUM, R., The principle of the common heritage of mankind, Zeitschrift für ausländisches Recht und Völkerrecht, 53, 1983, pp. 314ss.

WOLTAG, J.C., Military cyber warfare: Cross-border computer network operations under international law, ed. Intersentia, London/Antwerp, 2014, pp. 274ss

WOOD, B., International initiatives to prevent illicit brokering of arms and related materials, in Disarmament Forum, 2009, n. 3, pp. 5-16.

WOOD, M., "Weighing" the articles on responsibility of international organizations, in M. RAGAZZI, Responsibility of international organizations. Essays in memory of Sir Ian Brownlie, Martinus Nijhoff Publishers, Leiden, Boston, 2013, pp. 55ss.

WOOD, M., SENDER, O., State practice, in Max Planck Encyclopedia of International Law, 2014, par. 16.

WOOD, M., The General Assembly and the International Law Commission: What happens to the Commission's work and why?, in I. BUFFARD et al., International law between universalism and fragmentation, Martinus Nijhoff Publishers, The Hague, 2008, pp. 373ss.

WOOD, M., The present position within the ILC on the topic: Identification of customary international law, in The Chinese Journal of International Law, 15, 2016, pp. 3-14.

WOODS, L., WATSON, P., Steiner & Woods European Union law, Oxford University Press, Oxford, 2017, pp. 37ss.

WOUTERS, J., BREMS, E., SMIS, S., SCHMITT, P., Accountability for human rights violations by international organizations, Oxford University Press, Oxford, 2010.

WOUTERS, J., RYNGAERT, C., RUYS, T., DE BAERE, G., International law. A European perspective, Bloomsbury, New York, 2018.

WOUTERS, J., VERHOEVEN, S., "Desuetudo," in Max Planck Encyclopedia of International Law, 2011.

WOUTERS, J., VERHOEVEN, S., The prohibition of genocide as a norm of ius cogens and its implications for the enforcement of the law of genocide, in International Criminal Law Review, 5, 2005, pp. 401ss.

WUERTH, I., Treaty interpretation, subsequent agreements and practice, and domestic constitutions, in G. NOLTE, Treaties and subsequent practice, Oxford University Press, Oxford, 2013, pp. 154ss.

WYLER, W., PAPAUX, A., The different forms of reparation. Satisfaction, in J. CRAWFORD, A. PELLET, S. OLLESON, The law of international responsibility, Oxford University Press, Oxford, 2010, pp. 625ss.

XIONG, P., An international law perspective on the protection of human rights in the TRIPS agreement: An interpretation of the TRIPS agreement in relation to the right of health, Martinus Nijhoff Publishers, The Hague, 2012.

YASSEEN, M.K., L'interprétation des traités d'après la Convention de Vienne sur le Droit des Traités, ed. Brill, Recueil des Cours, ed. Brill, Bruxelles, vol. 151, 1976, pp. 48ss.

YEE, S., A reply to Sir Michael Wood's Response to AALCOIEG's Work and I report on the ILC project on the identification of customary international law, in Chinese Journal of the International Law, 15, 2016, pp. 34ss.

YEE, S., Report on the ILC Project on "identification of customary international law," in Chinese Journal of International Law, 14, 2015, pp. 385ss.

YEE, S., Towards an international law of co-progressiveness, Martinus Nijhoff Publishers, The Hague, 2014.

ZABALZA, G.O., The principle of systemic integration. Towards a coherent international legal order, LIT Verlag, Münster, 2017.

ZACKLIN, R., Beyond Kosovo: The United Nations and the humanitarian intervention, in Virginia Journal of International Law, 41, 2001.

ZACKLIN, R., The amendment of the constitutive instruments of the United Nations and Specialized Agencies, A.W. Sijthoff, Leiden, 1968, pp. 172ss.

ZAGEL, G., Responsibility of international organizations for international law, in Sudebnik, 11, 2006, pp. 652ss

ZARKA, J.C., Droit international public, Dalloz, Paris, 2013.

ZARKA, J.C., Droit international public, ed. Ellipses, Paris, 2015.

ZEEGERS, K., International criminal tribunals and human rights law. Adherence and contextualization, ed. Springer, Berlin, 2016, pp. 17ss.

ZEMANEK, K., General course on public international law, in Recueil des Cours de l'Académie de Droit International, ed. Brill, Bruxelles, vol. 158, 1977, pp. 230ss.

ZEMANEK, K., The legal foundations of the international legal system, in Recueil des cours, ed. Brill, Bruxelles, vol. 270, 1997, pp. 272ss.

ZEMANEK, K., What is "state practice" and who makes it ?, in U. BEYERLIN and others, Festschrift für Rudolf Bernhardt, ed. Springer, Berlin, 1995, pp. 289ss.

ZHUANG, W., Intellectual property rights and climate change. Interpreting the TRIPS agreement for environmentally sound technologies, Cambridge University Press, Cambridge, 2017.

ZICCARDI CAPALDO, G., International Court of Justice, legal maxims: Summaries and extracts from selected case law, in The Global Community Yearbook of International Law Journal, 1, 2001, pp. 159, 182ss.

ZICCARDI CAPALDO, G., The pillars of global law, Ashgate Publishing, London, 2013, pp. 295ss.

ZIMMERMANN, A., TAMS, J., OELLERS-FRAHAM, K., The statute of the International Court of Justice. A commentary, Oxford University Press, Oxford, 2019.

ZIMMERMANN, A., The obligation to prevent genocide: Towards a general responsibility to protect?, in U. FASTENRATH et al. (eds.), From bilateralism to community interest. Essays in honour of judge Bruno Simma, Oxford University Press, Oxford, 2011, pp. 629ss.

ZIPPERLE, N., European Union internatonal agreements: An analysis of direct effect and judicial review pre and post-Lisbon, ed. Springer, Berlin, 2017, pp. 69ss.

ZOLLER, E., Peacetime unilateral remedies, Martinus Nijhoff Publishers, Dobbs Ferry, New York, 1984.

ZOLLER, E., Quelques rèflexions sur les contre-mesures en droit international public, in Etudes offèrts à C.A. Colliard, ed. Pedone, Paris, 1984, pp. 362ss.

ZRILIC, J., The protection of foreign investment in times of armed conflict, Oxford University Press, Oxford, 2019, pp. 216ss.

ZWANENBURG, M., Accountability of peace support operations, Martinus Nijhoff Publishers, Leiden, Boston, 2005.

ZWANENBURG, M., The duty to respect international humanitarian law during European Union-led operations, in CLEER Working paper, 2012/6. pp.24ss.

ZWANENBURG, M., The duty to respect international humanitarian law during European union-led operations, in A. SARI, R.A. WESSEL, Human rights in EU crisis management operations. A duty to respect and to protect?, T.M.C. Asser Institute, The Hague, 2012.

ZWANENBURG, M., Toward a more mature ESDP: Responsibility for violations of international Humanitarian Law by EU crisis management operations, in S. BLOCKMANS (ed.), The European Union and crisis management. Policy and legal aspects, T.M.C. Asser Institute, The Hague, 2008, pp. 395ss.

ZWOLSKI, K., The European Union and international security: Developing a comprehensive approach, in C. KAUNERT, S. LÉONARD (eds) European security, terrorism and intelligence, ed. Palgrave Macmillan, London, 2013.

ZYBERI, G., The development and interpretation of international human rights and humanitarian law rules and principles through the case-law of the International Court of Justice, in Netherlands Quarterly of Human Rights, 25, 2007, pp. 118ss.

ZYBERI, G., Enforcemenet of international humanitarian law, in G. OBERLKEITNER, International human rights institutions, tribunals and courts. International human rights, ed. Springer, Berlin, 2018.